THE POLICE IN AMERICA

AN INTRODUCTION

McGraw-Hill Series in Criminology and Criminal Justice

Binder and Geis: Methods of Research in Criminology and Criminal Justice
Callison: Introduction to Community-Based Corrections
De Forest, Gaensslen, and Lee: Forensic Science: An Introduction to Criminalistics
Klockars: Thinking about Police: Contemporary Readings
Walker: The Police in America: An Introduction

THE POLICE IN AMERICA

AN INTRODUCTION

Samuel Walker

University of Nebraska at Omaha

McGRAW-HILL BOOK COMPANY
New York   St. Louis   San Francisco   Auckland   Bogotá
Hamburg   London   Madrid   Mexico   Montreal   New Delhi
Panama   Paris   São Paulo   Singapore   Sydney   Tokyo   Toronto

This book was set in Times Roman by University Graphics, Inc. (ECU).
The editors were Eric M. Munson and Stephen Wagley;
the production supervisor was Diane Renda.
The photo editor was Inge King.
The drawings were done by Fine Line Illustrations, Inc.
The cover was designed by Mark Wieboldt.
Halliday Lithograph Corporation was printer and binder.

THE POLICE IN AMERICA
An Introduction

9 0 HALHAL 8 9

ISBN 0-07-067854-5

Library of Congress Cataloging in Publication Data

Walker, Samuel, date
   The police in America, an introduction.

   (McGraw-Hill series in criminology and criminal
justice)
   Includes bibliographical references and index.
   1. Police—United States. I. Title. II. Series.
HV8138.W3418 1983   363.2′0973   82-14013
ISBN 0-07-067854-5

CHAPTER-OPENING PHOTO CREDITS
 1 The Bettmann Archive, Inc.
 2 James H. Karales/Peter Arnold, Inc.
 3 Costa Manos/Magnum
 4 Martin J. Dain/Magnum
 5 David Margolin/Black Star
 6 Ken Heyman
 7 Gerhard E. Gscheidle/Peter Arnold, Inc.
 8 Photo by Tony O'Brien/© Corrections Magazine 1981
 9 Martin J. Dain/Magnum
10 Sybil Shelton/Peter Arnold, Inc.
11 Alex Webb/Magnum
12 Leonard Freed/Magnum
13 Cary Wolinsky/Stock, Boston, Inc.

CONTENTS

PREFACE

The Police in America: An Introduction is written to provide a comprehensive introduction to the basic elements of policing in the United States. It is essentially descriptive, designed to acquaint the reader with the most current knowledge about police organizations, police officers, police work, and the most critical police problems. It is not prescriptive in that it does not recommend particular styles or tactics of policing. Where it does comment on the apparent effectiveness of various concepts or tactics, it does so by citing the relevant social science literature.

This is not to say that the book is without perspective. A consistent bias informs the presentation of the material. *The Police in America* reflects the commitment to the ideal of a professional police in a free society. That means the police should be responsive to the needs of the public, as indicated through an open political process, and responsive to the rule of law. Much of this book deals with the difficulties in achieving this ideal.

The primary audience for *The Police in America* is the undergraduate college student. The book is designed to be used in a student's first course on law enforcement. Because it provides a comprehensive overview of police and policing, many instructors may find it useful in courses on law enforcement organization and management or police-community relations.

The book will also be useful to others. Police officials, whether patrol officer or top executive, will find it a useful overview. It will guide them to the most recent and most relevant literature on particular topics. The footnote references will guide them to specific items and allow them to pursue topics in greater depth. Finally, the concerned citizen will find this book a helpful guide in sorting out the controversies and complex issues surrounding the police in America.

ACKNOWLEDGMENTS

This book is the product of my own education about the police and I would like to thank the many people who have contributed to that process. Policing in my own community is a volatile political issue as it is in other cities. I have attempted to maintain lines of communication with all sides and have learned much in the process of reconciling very different points of view. From many people in the community I have gained insight into the impact of policing on the lives of ordinary citizens and the intensity of feelings about the police and police operations. At the same time, individual police officers I have come to know, initially as students, have taught me much about the gritty reality of police work in an urban community. From them I have gained insight into the human reality of policing: what it means to carry out unpleasant tasks and to work in an organizational environment that is ill-equipped to recognize and reward good performance.

A number of individuals have contributed to the production of this manuscript. Egon Bittner, Lawrence Sherman, John Angell and Carl Klockars read the manuscript twice and made extremely helpful comments. The arrangement of the chapters, the focus of particular chapters, and the discussion of certain topics has been greatly improved as a result of their efforts. Whatever mistakes remain, of course, are my own responsibility. Finally, my editor, Eric Munson, has provided encouragement and support throughout the past two and a half years.

Samuel Walker

THE POLICE IN AMERICA

AN INTRODUCTION

CHAPTER 1

THE DEVELOPMENT OF THE AMERICAN POLICE

THE RELEVANCE OF HISTORY

To understand the police in America today it is necessary to examine the history of American policing. To a great extent, the police are the prisoners of the past. Day-to-day practices are influenced by deeply ingrained traditions, citizen attitudes toward the police, and relations between police and community.

The study of police history can serve as a guide to the present and heighten our awareness of the complex interaction between past problems, reforms, and change.

The Legacy of Past Problems Corruption and inefficiency have dominated American policing through much of its history. These ancient problems linger on, although some departments have succeeded in raising personnel standards and improving the quality of police work. More important, these past problems affect the *public image* of American policing. Bad reputations die hard, and police-community relations are deeply affected by this legacy.

The Impact of Reform The quality of police personnel, the nature of police organizations, and the state of police-community relations are products of the long struggle to professionalize the police, which began roughly in 1900.[1]

Many current police problems are the result of solutions to yesterday's problems. In the 1960s, experts awoke to discover that the special form of American police professionalism was itself a problem. Many of the proposed changes of the 1960s and 1970s were designed to undo the work of earlier reformers.

The Direction of Change Change is constant. Contrary to popular belief, the nature of American policing is continually changing. To understand the contemporary police it is important to recognize the direction of change, to know, for example, how some police departments have substantially reduced the use of firearms, or why police unions emerged and how they have affected policing. It is useful to understand the nature of change, or the lack of it, in the area of police-community relations.

Once we can see the direction of change, it is possible to isolate the factors that brought it about. In this respect, the study of history can contribute directly to contemporary police planning and policy making.

THE ENGLISH HERITAGE

American policing is a product of its English heritage. The colonists brought to this country the institutions and practices of their criminal justice system, including their established patterns of law enforcement.[2]

Three dominant features of American policing can be attributed to this heritage. The first is a tradition of *limited authority* for police officers. The powers and responsibilities of law enforcement agents are closely circumscribed by law. The Anglo-American tradition places a premium on individual liberty at the expense of social control. Continental European countries give their law enforcement personnel much broader powers. German citizens, for example, are required to carry identity cards and report changes of address to police authorities.[3]

Other countries, including those in continental Europe, have a tradition of centralized responsibility for law enforcement. The Anglo-American tradition is characterized by *local control*. As a result, American policing today is highly decentralized and fragmented. There are an estimated 20,000 different law enforcement agencies, with only minimal coordination between them (see Chapter 3). This is related to the third feature, a system of *fragmented law enforcement authority*. Responsibility for law enforcement is divided among several different local agencies, including the constable, the sheriff, the justice of the peace, and finally, the metropolitan police.

Formal law enforcement agencies emerged in England in the thirteenth century. The office of the constable acquired responsibility for keeping the peace. The constable was also the elected official of the manor or county parish and functioned as the executive of this local unit of government. The Statute of Winchester in 1285 added important elements to the emerging system of law enforcement. It introduced the "watch and ward," which required all men in a given town to serve on the night watch to guard against fires, crimes, and suspicious persons. It also revived the ancient "hue and cry," making all citizens responsible for pursuing fugitives from justice. Finally, the statute required all males to maintain weapons in their homes for use in protecting the public peace.[4]

The Statute of Winchester set the pattern for English law enforcement until the nineteenth century. English institutions, however, were a jungle of overlapping offices inherited from the past. Alongside the constable was the sheriff (originally "shire reeve") from whom the American sheriff is descended. The English sheriff was more a tax collector than a law enforcement agent. The justice of the peace emerged in the fourteenth century as an important element of the local system of justice.

The London Metropolitan Police

By the nineteenth century, London had developed into a vast industrial city, and existing law enforcement agencies were completely inadequate. The Gordon riots of 1780 were only the most serious example of a pervasive level of disorder. For nearly fifty years, Parliament debated the question of police protection. The issue was finally settled in 1829 with the creation of the London Metropolitan Police, an agency that set the model for subsequent British and American police forces.[5]

The "new" police, as they were called, represented a radically different approach to the problem of maintaining order. The London Metropolitan Police embodied a new mission, strategy, and organizational structure. The *mission* of the new police was crime prevention. It represented the utilitarian philosophy that it was better to prevent crime from occurring than to merely respond after the fact. This mission was to be accomplished through the *strategy* of preventive patrol. Officers would conduct continuous patrol over fixed "beats." The continuous presence of police would effectively deter crime.

While others, including Patrick Colquhoun, contributed to the theoretical concept, the true founder of the London Metropolitan Police was Robert Peel. Peel led the legislative fight from the introduction of his first bill in 1785 until his final success in 1829. The London police owe their popular name "bobbies" to Sir Robert.

The *organizational structure* of the London Metropolitan Police was also unique. Peel borrowed, with some modification, the structure and terminology of the military. The 3000-officer force was divided into seventeen divisions, each commanded by a superintendent, who in turn commanded four inspectors and sixteen sergeants. The entire force was directed by two commissioners who were responsible to the Home Office, a cabinet-level position in British government. In addition to rank designations, officers wore distinctive uniforms and were commanded through a military-style discipline. The London Metropolitan Police were the source of the military model in American policing.

In practice, the new police were a radical innovation. Allan Silver argues that the police "represented the penetration and continual presence of central political authority throughout daily life."[6] The control and regulation of daily life is one of the major features of modern society. Initially, the London Metropolitan Police aroused the hostility of the public. Eventually, however, the police—who were unarmed and commanded to treat citizens with civility—won their respect and support.

LAW ENFORCEMENT IN COLONIAL AMERICA

English settlers in America brought with them the institutions they had known in the old world. These institutions, however, were gradually transformed to suit the conditions of the new environment. Eventually, American law enforcement acquired its own unique character and traditions.[7]

Institutions

The principal institutions of law enforcement in colonial America were the sheriff, the constable, and the watch. The *sheriff* soon emerged as the most important law enforcement agent. Appointed by the governor of the colony, the sheriff became the principal government official in the county. Because the population was dispersed throughout rural areas in most colonies, the county became the major unit of local government. In addition to law enforcement, the sheriff was responsible for collecting taxes, conducting elections, and maintaining public facilities such as bridges and roads.

The *constable* functioned as a "little sheriff" in the colonial towns and cities. Like the sheriff, the constable was responsible for a broad range of civil as well as criminal duties. At first, the constable's office was elective in most areas, but it gradually evolved into a semiprofessional appointive office. While in many areas, people sought to evade service as a constable, in Boston the office became a desirable and potentially lucrative position.[8]

The *watch* resembled the modern-day police in certain respects. Members of the watch were responsible for protecting the city at night from fires, crime and disorder, and suspicious persons. Boston created its watch in 1634. In keeping with the English tradition of collective responsibility, service on the watch was the duty of all male citizens. Watchmen were essentially drafted for duty, and as the years went by, men increasingly sought to evade this responsibility. Originally, the watch was exclusively a nighttime activity, although eventually some of the larger cities instituted a day watch.[9]

The Quality of Law Enforcement

The quality of service provided by the sheriff, the constable, and the watch was extremely poor. Very quickly, inefficiency, corruption, and political interference emerged as American traditions. There was never a golden age of efficiency and integrity in American law enforcement.

With respect to *police protection,* the existing institutions were ill-equipped to prevent crime or apprehend offenders. Only the watch had crime prevention as part of its mission. The sheriff and constable were *re*active agencies, responding only to criminal complaints brought to them. Furthermore, all three agencies lacked the personnel to effectively apprehend criminals.

Order maintenance was also a problem. The colonial cities were filled with disorder, and organized rioting was a frequent form of political action. The watch functioned only at night and was ill-equipped to deal with major disorders. The sheriff and constable, the only officials on duty during the day, also had extremely limited capacity. Colonial newspapers were filled with complaints about crime, disorder, and rioting.

The concept of *service,* in the modern sense, did not exist for colonial law enforcement agencies. The sheriff and the constable carried out various civil responsibilities for local government but did not exist to provide direct services to individual citizens.

Law enforcement was relatively inefficient in the settled areas along the Atlantic coast. In the sparsely settled frontier areas inland, it was virtually nonexistent until the nineteenth century. Frontier communities were forced to rely on their own resources for basic protection and law enforcement. This necessity contributed to the American tradition of vigilantism. Citizens took the law into their own hands because often there was no official law at all.[10]

Colonial law enforcement agencies also developed a tradition of corruption very early. Many citizens evaded nightwatch duty, often by paying someone else to serve for them. Sheriffs and constables were paid through a system of fees, with a prescribed fee for such tasks as serving a subpoena, testifying in court, maintaining a prisoner in jail, and so forth. In the larger communities, the office of sheriff or constable could be the source of considerable income. Rather than public servants, officers were often entrepreneurs, using the office for personal gain. Finally, the records of colonial courts are filled with cases of alleged misconduct. Citizens responded in kind, and court records also indicate widespread citizen disrespect and abuse of officials.[11]

As local officials, law enforcement agents were important political figures. In Virginia and North Carolina, for example, sheriffs were appointed by the governor only upon the recommendation of the county courts. The courts, meanwhile, were controlled by the wealthy elite. Because of its responsibilities for collecting taxes and supervising elections, the sheriff's office was the most important local political office.

THE CREATION OF THE MODERN POLICE

Breakdown of the Old System

The law enforcement institutions established during the colonial period continued after the American Revolution with little change. The larger cities—Boston, New York, Philadelphia—were forced to expand the size of their watch systems, but these still remained small and inefficient.

The old system broke down in the 1830s and 1840s. As in Britain, a wave of riots and disorders swept American cities. The cause of the disorders was the revolutionary transformation of American society, including urbanization, industrialization, and immigration. The largest cities had grown into huge complexes, creating a crisis in all public services. Industrialization had altered the daily pattern of work and created extremes of wealth and poverty. Finally, immigration brought to the United States people of different ethnic and religious backgrounds. Many of the riots were clashes between different ethnic groups: the newly arrived German or Irish Catholics versus the established Anglo-Saxon Protestants. Economic problems generated disorder as banks were attacked by rioters. Americans used violence to settle questions of morality: rioters objecting to new medical practices attacked hospitals. Finally, race was a source of disorder: white rioters attacked abolitionists and free black citizens in Northern cities.[12]

The First American Police

Existing institutions appeared inadequate to the task of maintaining order. Abraham Lincoln warned in 1838 of the "increasing disregard for law which pervades the country."[13] When Americans sought to create a new and more effective system of law enforcement, they found two models available. One was the slave-patrol system that existed in the South. For example, Charleston, South Carolina, had a slave patrol of about 100 officers as early as 1837. Other Southern communities maintained similar systems to police the slaves.[14] The other model was the London Metropolitan Police.

In Boston, major riots in 1834, 1835, and 1837 brought about the creation of a new police force in 1838. Yet, with only nine officers, the new force was a token gesture at best. By 1846 it had grown to only thirty officers. Police protection was more an idea than a reality. Creation of the New York City police was stimulated by both the 1834 riots and a spectacular crime, the murder of Mary Cecilia Rogers in 1841. Political stalemate prevented the establishment of the new police until 1845. With 800 officers, it was a much larger force than Boston's. Events in Philadelphia followed a more erratic course. Between 1833 and 1854 the city experimented with several different arrangements before finally settling on a London-style police force.[15]

The delay in creating police forces in New York and Philadelphia reflected public uncertainty. The resemblance of the police to a standing army aroused memories of the British colonial army. Political groups feared that rival factions would gain control of the new institution. And all factions shared a reluctance to bear the cost of this new social institution.

In copying the London Metropolitan Police, Americans borrowed selectively. The London Metropolitan Police was a highly *centralized* agency of the national government. The citizens of London had no direct political influence over the department. American police departments, in contrast, were radically *decentralized*. Not only were they agencies of city government, but effective control was exercised at the neighborhood and ward level.

The London police were highly *professional* in that commissioners were chosen because of their proven administrative experience and could implement policies without regard for political pressure. The American police, in contrast, were extremely *unprofessional*. Democratic politics dictated that any citizen could hold public office. Police administration was a job for amateurs, not experienced professionals. The combination of amateurism at the top and constant political pressure at all levels guaranteed that American policing would develop along different lines than the London police.[16]

AMERICAN POLICING IN THE NINETEENTH CENTURY

The Influence of Politics

The quality of American police service in the nineteenth century could hardly have been worse. The police were completely unprofessional and police work was dominated by corruption and inefficiency. The source of these problems was *politics*. Local government was viewed primarily as a source of opportunity—for jobs, for profit, for social mobility, for corruption. Control of local government was available to any group that could control a sufficient number of votes. Effective control, moreover, was exercised at the neighborhood and ward level. Mayors and chiefs of police had little real power; power lay with city councilmen and police captains at the neighborhood level. Politics influenced every aspect of policing: personnel standards, law enforcement priorities, corruption, and police "reform."[17]

Police Personnel

Selection standards for police personnel were nonexistent. Officers obtained their jobs through political contacts. A person's age, health, or moral character were no barrier to employment. In addition, new officers received no formal training. An officer would be handed his badge, baton, and the manual of department rules and sent out on the street. A few departments attempted to provide formal training (for example, Cincinnati in 1888), but they were the exceptions. The first textbook on policing was not published until 1909.

The job of police officer was highly desirable, since it paid more than most blue-collar jobs. In 1880 most big cities paid their police about $900 a year; a factory worker could expect to earn only about $450 a year. There was no job security, however, and officers lost their jobs when a rival political party gained control. Civil service protection did not emerge until the end of the century.

Because the selection of police officers was a product of political patronage, the composition of police forces reflected the turbulent ethnic group politics of American cities. Jobs as police officers were prizes that each group sought to keep for itself. The appointment of Barney McGinniskin, the first Irish-American police officer in Boston, created a major political crisis in 1851. Soon, however, the Irish gained control of most American police departments. German-Americans were strong in Cleveland, Cincinnati, Milwaukee, and St. Louis. Other groups fought for their share of patronage appointments. Blacks managed to gain a foothold in Chicago and a few other cities because of their political support from the Republican party.

Appointment to the police force was more than just a job. For immigrant groups it was an important step up the social scale. To wear the uniform and represent the law meant that both the individual and the group had arrived. Older immigrant groups fought the appointment of officers from new immigrant groups to prevent them from gaining this important measure of social status.[18]

Police Work

In terms of law enforcement, order maintenance, and service, police work was hopelessly inefficient. Officers patrolled on foot and their ranks were spread very thin. Chicago officers were responsible for patrolling beats of three and four miles in length. In many cities the police did not even attempt to patrol all parts of the city. Finally, police officers habitually evaded their responsibilities, spending much of their time in saloons and barbershops. Robert Peel's concept of preventive patrol was an idea rather than a reality.

The primitive state of technology blocked effective management and contributed to the decentralized nature of police administration. It was difficult for supervisors to control their officers. The early call box, from which patrol officers were required to call in, was easily sabotaged.[19] Officers could not easily summon backup help in case of major emergencies. Finally, the chief of police could not effectively command and control his subordinates; precinct captains were often completely autonomous.

Technology also affected the ability of the police to respond to public needs. There was no way a citizen could quickly summon the police in the event of a crime or an emergency. As a result, people expected little of the police. Disorder was a fact of life that people simply lived with. Even if some method of summoning the police had existed, it would have done little good. Officers did not see themselves as professionals with an obligation to serve the public efficiently and impartially.

The police faced considerable hostility from the public. The first officers were treated with ridicule and contempt. Throwing rocks at the police or taunting them in some other fashion was a popular sport for youth gangs. Individuals often resisted arrest (between 60 and 80 percent of the arrests involved drunks), and police officers responded by subduing them with force. The tradition of police brutality was a product of the twin problems of citizen disrespect and unprofessional officers.

Initially, American police officers were not armed. As late as 1880 the police of Brooklyn (then an independent city of 500,000 people) were unarmed. In some cases, weapons were optional or carried at the discretion of a sergeant. Beginning in the

Civil War years, police firearms became more prevalent. The police adopted weapons as standard equipment in response to the rising level of violence around them. Police conduct, in short, was largely a response to citizen conduct.

The police were an important social-welfare institution in the nineteenth century. Until about 1900, when other institutions were created to deal with the problem, police departments provided lodging, and in some cases breakfast, to homeless people.[20] Philadelphia lodged over 100,000 people a year during the 1880s. This is an excellent illustration of how the American police often acquired responsibility for miscellaneous social services.

Corruption and Politics

Police corruption was a direct product of political influence. It was not limited to the police, however; the entire criminal justice system and all of city government was pervaded by corruption. Mark Haller argues that corruption was one of the main functions of local government.[21] In other words, it was not an irrational phenomenon but served important social purposes.

Nonenforcement of the law was the primary area of corruption. The police obtained payoffs for permitting gambling, prostitution, and illegal liquor sales to flourish. Money from regular payoffs was divided among the officers in the area, including the supervisors. Corruption also extended to internal personnel practices. Officers often had to pay for promotions with bribes. The cost of obtaining a promotion was paid for by the greater opportunities for graft.

Nonenforcement of the law had important political significance. Control of alcohol consumption was the major issue in local politics. Sobriety and temperance was a badge of respectability for many people of Protestant and Anglo-Saxon background. They sought to impose their morality on other groups, especially the Irish and Germans, by controlling or outlawing drinking. At the same time, the neighborhood saloon was the focal point of the political machines. The attack on the saloon was also an attack on working-class political power. By controlling the police and not enforcing the laws, working-class immigrant groups were able to nullify the laws.

Police "Reform"

The failure of the police to enforce the laws was the mainspring of police "reform" in the nineteenth century. Reform movements had a special character. The main issue involved the question of which group would control the police department—the idea of police professionalism had not yet arrived. Little effort was given to raising personnel standards, providing training, or improving management techniques. The reformers usually represented the respectable groups in society: the middle class and the native-born Americans. They sought to wrest control of the police from the working-class, immigrant political machines. Because the machines were extremely effective, the reformers enjoyed only minor success.[22]

The struggle for control of the police resulted in experiments in new forms of governance. At one time or another in the nineteenth century virtually every police department was governed by a commission whose members were appointed by the governor, the mayor, or some other process. New York was the first to try this approach in 1853. Four years later, the commission was reorganized and the power to appoint commissioners was given to the state legislature. Thus, New York City lost direct control of its own police department. During the last half of the nineteenth century American police departments experimented with every conceivable type of commission: local, state, appointive, elective. Cincinnati alone made ten changes in the form of administrative control between 1859 and 1910. Each political faction sought some formula that would give it control over the police department. The struggle only increased the extent of political influence over American policing.[23]

Impact of Reform   Reform had only minimal impact on the quality of policing. Control often passed from one political faction to another, but with little effect on personnel standards or police practices. Police departments did grow in size and strength. Improvements in the call box facilitated communications and the advent of the horse-drawn police wagon made arrests much easier.

Curiously, however, as police departments grew, arrests declined. Erik Monkkonen found a steady decline in arrest rates in major American cities between 1860 and 1920. This was mainly a result of a sharp decline in the number of arrests for offenses against the public order: drunkenness, disturbing the peace, and so on. It is not clear, however, *why* this decline occurred. Some historians argue that American cities became more orderly and that the actual number of offenses declined. Monkkonen argues that the police redefined their role in society, focusing on the control of criminal behavior rather than the control of the lower class in general.[24]

THE ORIGINS OF POLICE PROFESSIONALISM

In the first years of the twentieth century a new generation of leaders embarked on a campaign to professionalize the American police. This movement was part of the much broader reform movement known as progressivism. The progressives attacked economic problems (trust busting, railroad regulation), social-welfare problems (child labor, housing conditions), and local government along with many other issues. They sought to modernize social institutions to meet the needs of modern society. Police reform was simply one part of this larger movement.

Two of the most prominent leaders of the police professionalization movement were Richard Sylvester and August Vollmer. The American police had been without an effective professional organization. One police chiefs' convention was held in 1871, but the National Chiefs of Police Union, later renamed the International Association of Chiefs of Police, was not established until 1893. Sylvester was superintendent of the District of Columbia police from 1898 to 1915 and president of the IACP from 1901 to 1915. As head of the IACP he transformed it into the leading voice of police professionalism and the vehicle for disseminating new ideas in policing.[25]

August Vollmer was even more famous than Sylvester. He served as chief of police in Berkeley, California, from 1905 to 1932. His most notable contribution was promotion of the idea of higher education for police officers. Vollmer hired college graduates as Berkeley police officers and organized the first college-level police science courses at the University of California in 1916. He traveled widely, preaching the gospel of police professionalism, and served as a consultant to many police departments. He was the main author of the Wickersham Commission report on the police in 1931.[26]

The Reform Agenda

The leaders of the police professionalism movement agreed on a basic agenda. The overall goal was to "get politics out of the police and get the police out of politics." The first item on the reform agenda involved hiring experienced executives to run police departments. They often looked to the military or private industry for such leaders. To further curb the influence of politics, police executives should enjoy job security and be guaranteed their jobs for several years.

The second item on the reform agenda involved centralizing command and control within the department. The reformers advocated closing many of the precinct stations and installing centralized records systems at headquarters. This was a technique for breaking the political power of ward politicians.

Raising personnel standards was the third item on the agenda. Vollmer took the lead by emphasizing higher education for police officers. This was a radical idea at a time when most police officers lacked even a high school diploma. Slowly, other departments began to insist on minimal entry standards. Persons with bad health, criminal records, or serious mental problems were gradually weeded out by the new criteria. New York led the way, with formal training for police beginning in the 1890s.

A fourth item on the agenda was the development of specialized units. Through the nineteenth century, police departments were very unspecialized; usually, they were divided into patrol officers and detectives. In the first years of the twentieth century, however, new specialties appeared: vice, traffic, juveniles, records, training, and so forth. As a result, police departments became increasingly complex bureaucracies. Managing the organization itself became an important task.

The final item on the reform agenda was the development of a sense of mission. The leaders of the professionalization movement fought hard to establish the idea that the police, like other professions, had a special mission or calling: to protect and serve the public in an efficient and impartial manner. The idea of a mission meant taking seriously the task of law enforcement. This, in turn, put added emphasis on training in specialized crime-fighting techniques and units (such as vice). August Vollmer also promoted the idea that the police mission included crime prevention. The police should seek to help juveniles who were on the brink of crime.

Women Police Juvenile work became the domain of female police officers. Until now policing had been an exclusively male occupation, with the exception of a few matrons to guard women in the local jail. The first American policewoman was Lola Baldwin in Portland, Oregon, in 1905. The most important individual was Alice Stebbins Wells, appointed to the Los Angeles Police Department in 1910, who organized and lead the International Association of Policewomen in 1915. The work of the organization bore fruit; by 1919 over sixty police departments employed female officers, and by 1925 the number had risen to 144. Women officers were almost exclusively confined to juvenile or clerical work. They did not enter the ranks of patrol officers until the late 1960s.[27]

Accomplishments and Failures Professionalization progressed erratically. Some departments—Milwaukee, Cincinnati, Berkeley—established high standards of professionalism. Others remained mired in corruption and inefficiency. Vollmer spent one year (1924) as head of the Los Angeles police before giving up in despair and returning to Berkeley. Chicago seemed especially resistant to reform. In Philadelphia, a reform administration made exceptional progress between 1911 and 1915, but most of these advances were wiped out when the old political machine regained control of the city government.

By 1920 the reformers had succeeded in establishing the *ideal* of police professionalism, even if only a few departments lived up to it. They had also created, in the IACP and other professional associations, the vehicle for continued reform. The reform agenda remained unchanged until the 1960s. Police reform also had its limitations. The individual police officer was the "forgotten person" of professionalization. Most reformers had contempt for ordinary police officers. They placed all of their hopes in strong administrators. As a result, officers did not gain a voice in policing and retreated into an isolated and alienated subculture. Also, the reformers' success in centralizing command and control transformed police organizations into highly centralized and isolated bureaucracies. By the 1960s this was recognized as a major police problem.

The reformers were also responsible for increasing the militarism of the American police. In the nineteenth century, the police had been distinctly unmilitaristic— sloppy, ill-disciplined, poorly managed. To inject needed discipline and to enhance the idea of a police mission, the reformers turned to the military model. Departments instituted military-style drill and added marching bands. The police mission came to be understood as a war on crime, an idea that often alienated the police from the public.

New Forms of Law Enforcement

In the first decade of the twentieth century two important new law enforcement agencies were created: the state police and the federal Bureau of Investigation.

State police agencies had existed in the nineteenth century but had not played a major role in the law enforcement field. The Texas Rangers were created in 1835. Other states maintained small offices with a few agents. Pennsylvania introduced a new era with the creation of the Pennsylvania State Constabulary in 1905. It was a highly centralized, militaristic agency, reflecting the ideas of the reform agenda. Business interests welcomed the constabulary, since they had found both the local police and the militia to be unreliable during strikes. Organized labor bitterly attacked it, however, denouncing its agents as "cossacks."[28] Eventually, other states created similar law enforcement agencies, though few were as militaristic as Pennsylvania's. These agencies fell into two categories: highway patrols, with limited jurisdiction; and state police, with general law enforcement powers.

Until 1908 the federal government had had only limited investigatory or law enforcement capabilities. Private detective agencies were sometimes used under contract, a practice that generated controversy. President Theodore Roosevelt asked Congress to create a federal law enforcement agency, but Congress refused: several congressmen were being prosecuted for fraud, and Congress was reluctant to give the executive branch additional investigative power. In fact, Congress passed a law forbidding the Justice Department from borrowing agents from the Secret Service or any other federal agency. Faced with this opposition, Roosevelt simply waited for Congress to adjourn and then created the Bureau of Investigation by executive order.[29]

In its first twenty-five years, the Bureau of Investigation (it was renamed the Federal Bureau of Investigation in 1934) had a troubled history. Agents apparently opened the mail of one senator who had opposed its creation. In 1919 it was directly involved in the illegal round-up, detention, and deportation of alleged radicals, and it was involved in a number of scandals in the 1920s.

THE DEVELOPMENT OF AMERICAN POLICING, 1920–1960

In the four decades between 1920 and 1960, police professionalization made slow but steady progress. At the same time, however, new problems emerged. Progress in professionalization was offset by higher public expectations about the quality of police service. The most important development was a revolution in police work brought about by changes in technology.

The Revolution in Police Work

Three technological innovations brought about a revolution in American police work between 1920 and 1960: the patrol car, the two-way radio, and the telephone.[30]

The *patrol car* made its first appearance just before World War I. Several cities competed for the honor of adopting it first. In the 1920s the patrol car was in widespread use—the police had to use the automobile to keep up with the citizens and criminals who were themselves using it. At the same time, motorized patrol seemed to promise more efficient coverage of the steadily growing American cities. By the 1950s most departments converted exclusively to motorized patrol. Foot patrol remained common only in the densely populated cities of the Northeast.

While the patrol car promised to increase police efficiency, it had other unintended consequences. It removed the officer from the street and ended informal contacts between officers and law-abiding citizens. The police became increasingly isolated and police-community relations suffered. To many people, especially racial minorities, the police seemed like an alien occupying army.

The second technological innovation, the *two-way radio,* became a common feature in the late 1930s. It promised to solve one of the oldest problems in police administration. Now supervisors could maintain continuous contact with patrol officers. Not only could they guarantee that the officers were in fact on duty, they could also dispatch them quickly to the scene of a crime or problem. Patrol officers devised ways of evading continuous supervision, but it was no longer possible to completely avoid one's duty for extended periods of time.

The third innovation was the *telephone*, which was patented in 1877 and had spread throughout American society. By itself it had little impact on the police, but in conjunction with the two-way radio and the patrol car it completed the communications link between citizen and patrol officer. It was now possible for a citizen to summon the police and have them respond relatively quickly.

The result was a revolution in public expectations. Technology made it easier to summon the police, and citizens increasingly did so. Over the space of a single generation, from the late 1930s to the 1950s, citizens became socialized into the habit of "calling the cops." The police were caught on the horns of a dilemma. Their work load skyrocketed in volume and altered in content. The more professional police departments made a fetish of rapid response. Calls for service, meanwhile, became increasingly dominated by requests to deal with minor disorders. Police departments had to work harder just to maintain the same level of service.

The Emergence of O. W. Wilson

In this context of technological innovation and demands for greater efficiency, O. W. Wilson emerged as the leading expert on police administration. A protégé of August Vollmer, he carried on his mentor's campaign for police professionalism. Wilson's great contribution involved formulas for the efficient use of motorized patrol. He first developed his ideas as police chief in Wichita, Kansas, from 1928 to 1939. He wrote an influential pamphlet on patrol-car allocation and was a tireless advocate of the one-officer car. Two one-officer cars were twice as efficient as one two-officer car, he argued, with no loss of officer safety. Wilson served as professor and dean of the School of Criminology at Berkeley from the late 1930s through 1960, when he was appointed superintendent of the Chicago Police Department.[31]

Wilson was the principal author of the International City Management Association's text, *Municipal Police Administration,* and in 1950 he published the first edition of his enormously influential text, *Police Administration.* This became the "bible" on the subject, and its precepts trained an entire generation of police officials. To the end, Wilson stressed efficiency in organizational structure, patrol allocation, and communication.

The Wickersham Commission

In 1929, President Herbert Hoover appointed the National Commission on Law Observance and Enforcement to study the American criminal justice system. More widely known as the Wickersham Commission, after its chairperson George Wickersham, the commission devoted two of its fourteen reports to the police.

The most sensational of all the Wickersham Commission reports was Report 11, *Lawlessness in Law Enforcement.* It thoroughly examined and exposed the problem of police brutality. The report concluded that "The third degree—the inflicting of pain, physical or mental, to extract confessions or statements—is extensively practiced." It found that the police commonly used beatings, threats, protracted questioning, and illegal detention. Some of the more bizarre techniques used to extract confessions included holding a suspect out a third-story window by his ankles, or forcing a murder suspect to stand in the morgue with his hand on the victim's body. The chief of the Buffalo police simply said "to hell with" the Constitution.[32]

Public concern about police brutality had been rising since the turn of the century. Magazines devoted an increasing number of articles to it, while victims of police misconduct brought suits in increasing numbers. The Wickersham Commission report created a sensation and aroused public opinion even more. The leaders of American policing were deeply embarrassed: the stories of widespread brutality damaged their claim that policing was a profession. This public pressure forced police departments to take steps to eliminate the worst kinds of misconduct. Brutality was not eliminated, by any means, but the Wickersham Commission report was a watershed. After 1931 brutality became the exception rather than the rule.

Report 14 of the Wickersham Commission, *The Police,* dealt with police administration. Written principally by August Vollmer, it restated the agenda of police professionalization.[33] The need for expert leadership, centralized administrative control, and higher personnel standards was reaffirmed. While it contained nothing new, the report gave the professionalization movement an additional boost. By the 1930s a new generation of police officials had reached leadership positions. O. W. Wilson was the best example of this group. Unlike the first generation of reformers, these men did not have to fight to establish the legitimacy of the idea of professionalism. They could take it for granted and build upon the initial accomplishments. Their work was assisted by a network of professional organizations—the IACP, the California Peace Officers' Association, and the Bureau of Municipal Research in New York City.

The FBI and the "War on Crime"

The FBI emerged as another powerful voice for police professionalism in the 1930s. In its early years, the Bureau had been riddled with scandal. J. Edgar Hoover was appointed director of the Bureau in 1924, and he proceeded to clean up the agency while reducing its size. For nearly ten years Hoover presided over a small and unobtrusive agency. All that changed in the early 1930s.

The years of the great depression were marked by fears of a national crime wave. The gangland wars in Chicago during the late 1920s, the highly publicized exploits of John Dillinger, Pretty Boy Floyd, Bonnie and Clyde, and others, and the sensational kidnapping and murder of the son of Anne and Charles Lindbergh all contributed to the crime-wave scare.[34]

Hoover responded by seeking and obtaining expanded authority and resources for the Bureau. A series of federal laws in 1934 gave the Bureau jurisdiction over new areas of criminal activity (for example, interstate flight to avoid prosecution; shipment of stolen property across state lines). The size of the Bureau also grew. Even more important, Hoover became a master of public relations. FBI press releases touted the exploits of its agents in tracking down criminals. In many cases the Bureau inflated the significance of people who were little more than minor criminals.[35]

The FBI also gained jurisdiction over two important functions. In 1930 it gained responsibility for the new Uniform Crime Reports system. Despite its many weaknesses, the UCR was the first national system of crime statistics in American history. The symbolic role of the FBI was important. Local police departments sent their reports to the Bureau in Washington, and the FBI had the privilege of announcing the annual crime rate figures. In this respect, the FBI became the unofficial voice of American policing. In 1935 the Bureau opened the National Police Academy, where it provided training for police officers in local departments. With the academy and with the FBI crime lab, opened in 1932, the Bureau established itself as the new leader in police professionalism.

Professionalism had special meaning for Hoover and the FBI. Professional cops were tough, fearless crime fighters. Moreover, they were well trained and utilized the latest scientific crime-fighting techniques. In particular, they were expert sharpshooters. In its press releases and training programs, the Bureau advanced this image of police professionalism. As a consequence, the crime-fighting or law enforcement aspects of the police role overshadowed all others. The order maintenance and service aspects of the police role sank to second-class status. Officers derided them as not being "real" police work.

This dramatic shift in the role image of the police occurred at the same time that the content of *actual* police work was moving in the opposite direction. Technological innovations resulted in the police being more and more involved in minor disputes and emergencies. The police were increasingly becoming peacekeepers while their public image emphasized crime fighting. Experts did not fully recognize the inconsistency between image and reality until the 1960s. Another disturbing aspect of the FBI's brand of professionalism was the emphasis on firearms, which had traditionally been a relatively minor part of policing. At first, the American police were not armed at all. Even by the early twentieth century, firearms were not emphasized; in the 1930s, the firearm became the symbol of policing.

California Professionalism

California had been a leader in the movement for police professionalism since the early days of August Vollmer's career. From the late 1930s through the 1950s, California established itself as the clear leader among the forty-eight states. Vollmer's protégés spread throughout the state, carrying on his work. The California Peace Officers' Association was a first-rate professional organization, surpassing the IACP in many respects. Education continued to receive great emphasis. The first under-graduate law enforcement program was established at San Jose State College in 1931; with O. W. Wilson as dean (1950–1960), the School of Criminology in Berke-ley became the leader in the field. California also developed a system of regional training for police officers in the late 1930s.

By the 1950s the most famous California police official was William Parker, chief of the Los Angeles police. Parker assumed control of the scandal-ridden department in 1950 and quickly transformed it into an efficient, corruption-free agency. Even Parker's severest critics admitted that Los Angeles cops were honest. Within a few years the department was nationally recognized as the most professional in the entire country.[36]

Parker transformed the Los Angeles police through a combination of authoritar-ian administrative practices and intensive public relations. He centralized command and control within the department and tolerated neither corruption nor dissent. Offi-cers who questioned his policies soon found their careers blocked. As critics pointed out, an officer could be severely reprimanded for damaging a patrol car but go unpunished for shooting and killing a citizen.

Parker's public relations campaign included skillful manipulation of the media. He cooperated closely with the producers of the popular television show, *Dragnet*. The show equated the Los Angeles police with the relentless, efficient, and quiet professionalism of Sergeant Joe Friday. Through a glossy annual report and numer-ous public speeches, Parker touted the accomplishments of the Los Angeles police. He continually emphasized the crime-fighting role, portraying the police as the "thin blue line" between civilization and chaos. He attacked court decisions that limited police powers (notably the *People v. Cahan* decision in 1955, in which the California Supreme Court invoked the exclusionary rule).[37] Finally, he regarded all critics as "subversives" or communist sympathizers—an argument that found a receptive audience in the cold war atmosphere of the 1950s.

Parker's accomplishments were significant. He quickly transformed a large and corrupt department into a model of efficiency and honesty. In that sense he proved that corruption could be eradicated. Meanwhile, Chief Wyman Vernon was achiev-ing similar results in Oakland, California. Parker also succeeded in instilling Los Angeles officers with a sense of mission. The price of these achievements, however, was high. In the long run, the authoritarian management style was incompatible with true professionalism. Carried to extreme, it excluded due process from personnel management.

Even more important, Parker's style of professionalism was incapable of dealing with the growing police-community relations problem. Relations between the police and the black community became increasingly strained during the 1950s as a result of both the steady migration of blacks to the big cities and the growing momentum of the civil rights movement. Black citizens were no longer willing to tolerate indig-nities at the hands of the police. Parker, however, turned a deaf ear to complaints voiced by black community leaders. Critics of the police, he charged, undermined law enforcement and were probably the unwitting "dupes" of the Communists.

Early Warnings

The police received early warnings about two problems that would eventually explode into major crises in the 1960s. One involved police-community relations. The other involved police unionism.

Relations between the police and the black community erupted into violence between 1915 and 1919, and again in 1943. The early period was marked by a violent riot in East St. Louis, Illinois, in 1917, and followed by a series of riots in several cities, notably Chicago, in 1919. Subsequent investigations revealed that the police were guilty of racial discrimination before the riots, discriminatory arrests during the riots, and in some cases active participation in the riots themselves. Nothing was done to improve police-community relations at that time.[38]

The modern police-community relations movement developed in the wake of another series of riots in 1943. The most serious riot occurred in Detroit, where it disrupted wartime production, but other major riots occurred in New York and Los Angeles. In most cities across the country, local committees were formed to bridge the gap between minority-group communities and the police. A number of police departments (Boston, Milwaukee, Richmond, California, and so on) instituted training programs in race relations. The effort was small, but it represented a significant beginning. There were no riots after 1943, but the police-community relations movement remained alive. Beginning in 1955 Michigan State University and the National Conference of Christians and Jews sponsored an annual workshop on police-community relations. The St. Louis police instituted the first police-community relations unit in 1957.

The second emerging problem involved rank-and-file police officers and police unionism in particular. The more the police thought of themselves as professionals who had made a lifetime career choice, the more they thought in terms of an organized effort to defend their interests. Fraternal associations and police unions were inevitable consequences of professionalism.[39]

Fraternal groups first appeared in the nineteenth century. They were primarily social clubs, but many offered some tangible benefits, such as group insurance plans. The police first turned to unionism during World War I, when the cost of living more than doubled in a few years. When the American Federation of Labor agreed to charter police unions, sixty-five local unions immediately applied. One of those was the Boston police union; their application set the stage for a dramatic and violent confrontation.

The 1919 Boston police strike is perhaps the single most famous event in American police history. Boston officers began agitation for a raise in 1917. The maximum salary of $1400 a year for a patrol officer had not changed since 1898. When the officers' demand for a $200-a-year raise was rejected, they voted to turn their social club into a union and join the AFL. Police Commissioner Edwin U. Curtis responded by suspending the leaders of the organization. Attempts at mediation failed, and on September 9, 1919, 1117 of Boston's police officers went out on strike, leaving only 427 on duty.[40]

Violence and disorder erupted in the city. In addition to vandalism and property destruction, there were personal attacks on both striking and nonstriking officers. While Governor Calvin Coolidge dragged his feet in mobilizing the militia, volunteers provided emergency police protection. After a day and a half, the militia finally arrived. Governor Coolidge gained a national reputation for his statement that "There is no right to strike against the public safety by anybody, anywhere, at any time." The strike quickly collapsed, and all of the strikers were dismissed from their jobs.

The national reaction to the Boston police strike was swift and extreme. Newspapers carried lurid accounts of violence and anarchy. Police unions, identified with communism and chaos, quickly collapsed across the country. All that remained over the next twenty years were such groups as the Fraternal Order of Police.

During World War II the police again turned to unionism, and for the same reason: lagging salaries in an inflationary wartime economy. Beginning in 1943 the new unions enjoyed brief success. Within four years, however, they had been crushed by a combination of unfavorable court decisions and firm opposition by administrators.

Police personnel problems festered during the late 1940s and 1950s. Salaries continued to fall behind those paid in private industry. The authoritarian style of management departments denied officers any voice in the management of policing. In 1960, Richard A. Myren sounded a prophetic warning.[41] Police departments were failing to effectively utilize their personnel.

THE POLICE CRISIS OF THE 1960s

The police crisis that erupted with a fury in the 1960s consisted of several different elements: new expectations about police performance, political protests against racial discrimination and the Vietnam war, and a sharp rise in the rate of violent crime. The American police officer, particularly the officer on the beat in the big cities, stood at the center of each of these problems.

The U.S. Supreme Court was the major instrument of the new public expectations about police performance. In a series of landmark decisions, referred to collectively as the due process revolution, the Court established specific guidelines for police procedures. In each case the Court ruled in favor of the individual citizen rather than the police.

In *Mapp v. Ohio* (1961), the Court invoked the exclusionary rule. Evidence obtained through an unreasonable search and seizure was excluded from use at trial. The exclusionary rule already applied to federal proceedings (since *Weeks v. United States,* 1914) and in about half of the states. The Court's decision in *Mapp* applied the Fourth Amendment of the Constitution by way of the Fourteenth Amendment, which held that no state shall "deprive any person of life, liberty, or property without due process of law." Application of the Bill of Rights to the states was the most significant aspect of the due process revolution.[42]

The police protested the *Mapp* decision, but even more controversial decisions were yet to come. In *Escobedo v. Illinois* (1964) the Court ruled that a suspect was entitled to legal counsel while in police custody, once the questioning became accusatory. An even greater storm of protest followed the *Miranda v. Arizona* decision in 1966. The Court ruled that the police had to advise suspects that they had a right to remain silent, that anything they said could be used against them, that they had a right to an attorney, and that an attorney would be provided if they could not afford one.

These decisions had several consequences. First, they defined new standards for police procedures. The Court took up these issues mainly because the police had failed to develop their own standards. Second, the decisions dramatically increased public awareness of the details of police procedure. Heightened awareness increased public expectations about the quality of police conduct. Police officers were now expected to conform to constitutional standards. This, in turn, stimulated the third major consequence. The decisions forced police departments to raise their personnel standards. In the years that followed, departments across the country raised recruitment standards, improved training, and provided more specific procedures for officers on the street.[43]

The civil rights movement imposed additional demands upon the police. As the momentum of the movement escalated (the sit-ins of 1960 marked a major turning point), black citizens were less willing to suffer abuses at the hands of the police. In both the South and the North civil rights demonstrations brought protesters into direct confrontation with the police. The cry of police brutality covered everything from verbal insults to physical abuse. For many blacks, the cop on the street became the symbol and tangible scapegoat for a systematic pattern of racial discrimination in the United States.

The frustration of Afro-Americans finally exploded into violent disorders in 1964. A riot broke out in New York City after an off-duty police officer shot and killed a black youth. Riots also erupted in other cities that summer. In 1965 an even more serious riot broke out in the Watts section of Los Angeles. It was sparked by a routine traffic stop. With continued rioting in 1966 and 1967, the long hot summer of urban disorders appeared to have become an established tradition. Most of the riots were precipitated by an incident involving the police. The 1967 Detroit riot, the worst one of all, started after the police raided an after-hours bar.[44]

The Police Examined

The riots focused national attention on the big-city police officer. Two national studies examined the police in detail: the President's Commission on Law Enforcement and Administration of Justice (1965–1967) and the National Advisory Commission on Civil Disorders (1967–1968).

The report of the President's Crime Commission, *The Challenge of Crime in a Free Society* (1967), was the first comprehensive study of the American criminal justice system since the 1931 Wickersham Commission. Moderate in its approach, the commission reaffirmed the traditional agenda of police reform. It called for higher personnel standards, improved management, and greater use of science and technology to solve police problems. Personnel standards received considerable attention. Existing salaries were not adequate to attract qualified recruits, and most departments were below their authorized strength. The commission recommended that the police actively recruit college graduates and recommended that eventually all police officers should possess a college degree.[45]

The commission handled controversial matters with great caution. It avoided taking a stand on recent Supreme Court decisions and barely mentioned the problem of police corruption. The commission charted some important new directions in the study of the police. It sponsored the first detailed research on the day-to-day work of patrol officers. These field studies (published as Albert Reiss's *The Police and the Public* and Donald Black's *The Manners and Customs of the Police)* were a landmark event which touched off an explosion of research on the American police.[46]

The commission also acknowledged the disturbing fact that some of the best police departments also had serious police-community relations problems. This marked the beginning of a reexamination of the agenda of police professionalism. The commission tentatively endorsed the concept of team policing as an alternative to the traditional approach.

The report of the National Advisory Commission on Civil Disorders (popularly known as the Kerner Commission, after its chairman, Otto Kerner) repeated many of the recommendations of the President's Crime Commission, only in more forceful terms. President Johnson appointed the commission in the summer of 1967, following the major riots in Newark, New Jersey, and Detroit. Its report appeared in the spring of 1968. One chapter dealt directly with police-community relations, while two others dealt with aspects of the administration of justice.[47]

The commission found "deep hostility between police and ghetto communities as a primary cause of the disorders."[48] Five problem areas needed attention. Routine police operations needed to be changed "to ensure proper individual conduct and to eliminate abrasive practices." Like the President's Crime Commission, the Kerner Commission found that "many of the serious disturbances took place in cities whose police are among the best led, best organized, best trained and most professional in the country."[49] Without naming it, the commission was clearly referring to the Los Angeles Police Department. Aggressive patrol—a style of policing that resulted in frequent police-citizen contacts—appeared to be a problem. The commission also noted that motorized patrol removed the officer from the street and alienated the police from ordinary citizens.

Other recommendations included providing more police protection for ghetto residents (who were the most frequent victims of crime), developing effective mechanisms for handling citizen complaints, policy guidelines for police officers (particularly in the area of use of deadly force), and greater community support for the police. Increased hiring and promotion of minority-group officers was an important way to gain community confidence and support.

The impact of the two commission reports was mixed. Some of the recommendations were implemented, and in the 1970s there was considerable progress in areas such as the development of policy guidelines and the use of discretion. Efforts were made to improve police-community relations: virtually every big-city police department created a special police-community relations unit, but their effectiveness remained unproven, however, and police-community relations remained tense through the 1970s. Rioting ended as suddenly as it had started. The last major riots occurred in the spring of 1968, following the assassination of Martin Luther King. There were no major riots until the one in Miami in 1980.

Other Police Problems

Police-community relations was only one of several problems that exploded in the mid-1960s. At the same time, the police were embroiled in the protests over the Vietnam war. Antiwar protesters borrowed confrontation tactics from the civil rights movement, using sit-ins, demonstrations, and sustained occupation of college campus buildings. The inevitable result was direct conflict with the police. The student occupation of buildings at Columbia University in the spring of 1968 ended with a bloody clash with the New York City police. At the Democratic party convention in Chicago in August the Chicago police ran wild, freely assaulting demonstrators, journalists, and bystanders alike.[50]

Hostility between the police and young white Americans was further deepened by the development of a youth counterculture in the late 1960s. Along with long hair and rock music, drug usage became one of the badges of membership in the counterculture. The result was the emergence of extensive drug usage, with a drug traffic industry to supply it. The use of illegal drugs accompanied an outlaw mentality and hostility to the police among young, white, middle-class Americans.

Finally, the crime rate rose dramatically in the 1960s. Between 1960 and 1970 the crime rate per 100,000 persons doubled. Particularly disturbing was the increase in violent crime; the robbery rate nearly tripled in the same period. The rise in violent crime not only increased the workload of the police and made their work more dangerous, it created enormous public pressure for the police to "do something" about crime.

The police found the Supreme Court a convenient scapegoat. They blamed the *Mapp, Escobedo,* and *Miranda* decisions for "handcuffing" them in their efforts to combat crime. This view won considerable support among white middle-class adults and conservatives generally. The attacks on the police generated a law-and-order backlash. Congress responded by passing the Omnibus Crime Control and Safe Streets Act of 1968. The law created the Law Enforcement Assistance Administration (LEAA), to provide financial assistance to criminal justice agencies.

POLICING IN THE 1970s and 1980s

Law Enforcement Assistance Administration

The new LEAA proved to be a financial bonanza for the American police, although its long-term contributions to the improvement of policing remain in doubt. From 1965 to 1967, LEAA was preceded by the Office of Law Enforcement Assistance, which supported much of the work of the President's Crime Commission. OLEA sponsored the field studies of police patrol and the innovative Family Crisis Intervention Unit with the New York City police, but it operated with an annual budget of only $7 million. LEAA began with a budget of $63 million in 1969 and reached a peak of $895 million in 1975.[51]

Born in an era of police crisis, LEAA devoted a disproportionate amount of its funds to law enforcement. Critics quickly charged that other components of the criminal justice system were neglected, and that too much money was being spent for exotic hardware. Many departments used LEAA funds to improve their communications technology and purchase bizarre antiriot equipment. (The equipment arrived just as the riots ended.)

The Research Revolution

LEAA funds were largely (but not completely) responsible for a police research revolution. Social scientists had largely neglected the police until the mid-1960s. By the 1970s research on the police turned into a flood. More was known about basic police operations and the effectiveness of particular innovations.[52]

The research revolution, based on college and university campuses, was partly supported by the Law Enforcement Education Program (LEEP). Designed to encourage criminal justice personnel to obtain college educations, LEEP fostered the development of criminal-justice programs on college campuses. The number of undergraduate-degree programs increased from 39 in 1967 to 376 in 1977. As a result, the educational-attainment levels of American police officers rose significantly. By 1975 the National Manpower Survey found an educational generation gap between younger and older officers.[53]

LEAA funding for research was paralleled, on a smaller scale, by the Police Foundation. A private foundation, it was created in 1970 with a $30-million dollar grant from the Ford Foundation. Its board of directors included police administrators, scholars, and public officials. The Police Foundation sponsored some of the most innovative research in the 1970s.

The research revolution can be viewed in terms of a handful of its most notable achievements. These include studies of police patrol, criminal investigation, team policing, and the use of policewomen on patrol.

The Kansas City Preventive Patrol Experiment   The Kansas City Preventive Patrol Experiment evolved out of the work of the President's Crime Commission. The commission sponsored the first observational studies of patrol but noted that little was known about patrol effectiveness. With $1 million dollars from the Police Foundation, and the support of Police Chief Clarence Kelley, the Kansas City Police Department undertook a scientific experiment on the effectiveness of patrol (see Chapter 5). The experiment compared patrol districts that had normal levels of patrol, saturation patrol, and no routine patrol (only direct response to calls for service). The researchers found no significant difference in the amount of crime, the level of citizen satisfaction, or police morale.[54] The Kansas City study was a landmark in American policing. Although it had certain flaws, it represented a new level of sophistication in thinking about the basic police operation of preventive patrol.

The Criminal Investigation Process   With LEAA funding, the Rand Corporation undertook an extensive study of the criminal investigation process. Their findings punctured most of the myths surrounding detective work. Of those crimes that were solved, most were solved by information gathered by the first officer to respond to the scene of the crime. Follow-up investigations by detectives were extremely unproductive. Detectives spent most of their time on paperwork and gave most crimes only superficial attention (see Chapter 6).[55] The Rand study stimulated new thinking about how police departments could effectively carry out investigations. One alternative was to combine patrol and investigative tasks through team policing.

Team Policing   Endorsed by the President's Crime Commission, team policing became the fad of the early 1970s. Pioneered by the British police, the concept involved assigning a team of officers to a definite geographic area on a permanent basis. The team would be responsible for all police services (patrol, investigation, juvenile, etc.) in the area. Presumably, this arrangement would enhance the officers' knowledge of and commitment to the area. This, in turn, would improve police-community relations. Officers would develop policy relevant to their area, and this participation would enhance officer morale.

The effectiveness of team policing remained in question (see Chapter 4). An early study by the Police Foundation found that team-policing experiments were beset by poor planning and confusion about their objectives. Not all experiments included all the key elements of the concept. The willingness to experiment with team policing, however, indicated the receptiveness of many police departments to innovation.[56]

Policewomen on Patrol   A major change in the role of policewomen occurred in the late 1960s. The President's Crime Commission suggested that greater utilization of women officers could help solve the personnel crisis. Meanwhile, female officers themselves, influenced by the women's movement, actively sought patrol duty. The first American policewomen to perform routine patrol were two officers in Indianapolis, Indiana, in 1968.

Many police officials argued that female officers could not handle the tasks of patrol duty effectively. According to this traditional "macho" perspective, policing required physical strength and a tough masculine attitude. Studies by the Police Foundation and LEAA, however, found that female officers were just as effective in carrying out routine patrol duty as were comparable male officers (see Chapter 11).[57]

New Developments in American Policing

Police Unions   Attempts to organize police unions had been defeated on two occasions in the past, but in the late 1960s unionism finally triumphed. Within a few years officers in most large police departments were represented by unions (the principal exceptions were in southern cities).

Several factors contributed to the triumph of police unionism. Police officers were angry and alienated and saw unions as a solution to their problems. Police salaries had fallen to relatively unattractive levels by the mid-1960s. In addition, officers resented the authoritarian style of management that prevailed in both the professional and unprofessional departments. Unions gave them a voice in police management that they had been denied. Finally, police officers were angry about the Supreme Court decisions, the riots and criticisms of the police, and the fact that they seemed to be singled out as the scapegoat for all the ills of society (see Chapter 12).[58]

Police unions had a dramatic effect on American policing. They effected a hidden revolution in police administration by gaining a voice in many administrative matters. By the 1970s police chiefs could not take decisive steps without consulting or negotiating with the local union. This created a crisis for the police professionalization movement. Since the turn of the century, police reform had been based on the leadership of strong-willed police executives. The story of professionalization was the story of Vollmer in Berkeley, Wilson in Wichita, Parker in Los Angeles, Vernon in Oakland, Kelley in Kansas City, and others. Unions made this style of reform difficult, if not impossible. Further professionalization would have to involve the unions. By the early 1980s a new style of reform has yet to be worked out.

Thus far, attempts to organize a single national union of police officers have failed and most unions are independent locals. Many are affiliated with the Fraternal Order of Police or the International Conference of Police Associations (ICPA), but these national organizations have little effective control over their members. In other ways, however, the unions contributed to the improvement of the police. They fought for and won substantial improvements in salaries and benefits. Police jobs became very attractive, and departments were able to raise their recruitment standards. Also, by giving police officers a sense of control over their jobs, the unions dramatically improved morale. Finally, the unions put an end to many of the arbitrary and capricious personnel practices that existed in a number of departments.

SUMMARY: AMERICAN POLICING IN THE 1980s

American law enforcement in the 1980s is still dominated by the past. The tradition of localism prevails, and responsibility for law enforcement is divided among almost 20,000 separate agencies. A pattern of uneven development prevails among these agencies. Some of the largest departments could be described as reasonably professional, but most of the smaller departments are still characterized by low personnel standards and archaic management practices. The spread of mandatory statewide training for all police officers is an encouraging development; in particular, it has raised personnel standards in very small departments.

The big-city police have shown themselves, in many cases, to be receptive to change and improvement. Experiments with team policing, new strategies of participatory management, and a greater willingness to be candid about their strengths and weaknesses are hopeful signs. In 1975, James Q. Wilson wrote: "A few police departments in this country have shown themselves to be remarkably innovative, experimental, and open to evaluative research. There are not as yet many prosecutors or courts about which one can say the same thing."[59]

Despite these promising steps, many problems remain. The police cling to the fiction that they can effectively reduce crime if only they had the necessary powers and resources. A growing body of evidence suggests that there is little the police can do to either stop crime or apprehend a greater percentage of criminals. While some departments are open to innovation, the majority continue to go about their business in the traditional way.

Corruption has been reduced or eliminated in some departments but remains a problem in many others. Police-community relations also continue to trouble the police. The focus of minority-group relationships has shifted to equal employment opportunity. The hiring of minority-group officers has lagged behind the representation of minorities in individual communities. Detroit and Washington, D.C., made considerable progress, but most others fail to act until they are sued for employment discrimination.

As the police entered the 1980s, the major problem looming over all others was the financial crisis. Inflation took its toll on policing in several respects. Taxpayers revolted against paying more for public services. At the same time, police officers have demanded continued salary increases so they can keep pace with inflation. Police chiefs and city officials find themselves in a terrible bind. Many big-city departments have laid off large numbers of police officers (the New York Police Department declined by 26 percent in the mid-1970s) and now seek greater productivity from fewer officers. The hiring freeze, meanwhile, has made it impossible for departments to correct the imbalance in female and minority representation.

Finally, the research revolution in policing created a new dilemma. Experts knew far more about the police by the 1980s but had fewer answers about how to improve the police. Many old solutions had been exposed as wishful thinking. There was no reason to believe that more education, by itself, would improve the performance of police officers, or that the consolidation of small departments would yield greater efficiency. But a solid core of evidence, for example, about ways to reduce the use of deadly force, has offered some promise for the future.

REVIEW

1 What were the major contributions of the English heritage to American law enforcement?

2 Describe briefly the institutions of law enforcement in colonial America.

3 What social factors contributed to the creation of the modern police?

4 Indicate the principal differences between the London Metropolitan Police and the American urban police.

5 Discuss the impact of politics on policing in the nineteenth century.

6 What were the major items on the agenda of police professionalization in the early twentieth century?

7 Explain how technological innovations revolutionized police work.

8 Discuss the impact of the Wickersham Commission reports on the police.

9 Indicate the various factors that contributed to the police crisis of the 1960s.

10 What were the most important new aspects of policing in the 1970s and 1980s?

REFERENCES

1 Samuel Walker, *A Critical History of Police Reform* (Lexington: Lexington Books, 1977).
2 David R. Johnson, *American Law Enforcement: A History* (St. Louis: Forum Press, 1981), pp. 1–8.
3 Raymond B. Fosdick, *European Police Systems* (Montclair: Patterson Smith, 1972).
4 T. A. Critchley, *A History of Police in England and Wales,* 2nd ed. rev. (Montclair: Patterson Smith, 1972), chap. 1.
5 Critchley, *A History of Police in England and Wales,* chap. 2.
6 Allan Silver, "The Demand for Order in Civil Society: A Review of Some Themes in the History of Urban Crime, Police, and Riot," in *The Police: Six Sociological Essays,* ed., David J. Bordua (New York: John Wiley, 1967), pp. 12–13.
7 Samuel Walker, *Popular Justice* (New York: Oxford University Press, 1980), pp. 11–13.
8 Roger Lane, *Policing the City* (New York: Atheneum, 1971), chap. 1.
9 Ibid.
10 Walker, *Popular Justice,* pp. 31–33.
11 Douglas Greenberg, *Crime and Law Enforcement in the Colony of New York, 1691–1776* (Ithaca: Cornell University Press, 1976).
12 Richard Hofstadter and Michael Wallace, eds., *American Violence: A Documentary History* (New York: Vintage Books, 1970).
13 Walker, *Popular Justice,* p. 57.
14 Robert F. Wintersmith, *Police and the Black Community* (Lexington: Lexington Books, 1974), pp. 17–21.
15 Lane, *Policing the City;* James F. Richardson, *The New York Police: Colonial Times to 1901* (New York: Oxford University Press, 1970); Samuel B. Warner, *The Private City* (Philadelphia: University of Pennsylvania, 1971).
16 Wilbur R. Miller, *Cops and Bobbies: Police Authority in New York and London, 1830–1870* (Chicago: University of Chicago, 1977).
17 Walker, *A Critical History;* Robert Fogelson, *Big City Police* (Cambridge: Harvard University Press, 1977).
18 Robert K. Merton, *Social Theory and Social Structure* (New York: The Free Press, 1968), pp. 126–136.
19 Jonathan Rubinstein, *City Police* (New York: Ballantine Books, 1974), pp. 15–21.
20 Erik Monkkonen, *Police in Urban America, 1860–1920* (Cambridge: Cambridge University Press, 1981), pp. 86–109.
21 Mark H. Haller, "Historical Roots of Police Behavior: Chicago, 1890–1925," *Law and Society Review,* 10 (Winter 1976): 303–324.
22 Walker, *A Critical History,* pp. 25–28.
23 Raymond B. Fosdick, *American Police Systems* (Montclair: Patterson Smith, 1972), pp. 76–117.
24 Monkkonen, *Police in Urban America.*
25 Walker, *A Critical History,* pp. 56–61.
26 Gene E. Carte and Elaine H. Carte, *Police Reform in the United States: The Era of August Vollmer* (Berkeley: University of California Press, 1975).
27 Walker, *A Critical History,* pp. 84–94.
28 Ibid., pp. 75–78.
29 Sanford J. Ungar, *FBI* (Boston: Little, Brown, 1976), pp. 39–40.
30 Walker, *A Critical History,* pp. 134–137.

31 William J. Bopp, *O. W.: O. W. Wilson and the Search for a Police Profession* (Port Washington, N.Y.: Kennikat Press, 1977).

32 U.S., National Commission on Law Observance and Enforcement, vol. 11, *Lawlessness in Law Enforcement* (Washington, D.C.: U.S. Government Printing Office, 1931).

33 U.S., National Commission on Law Observance and Enforcement, vol. 14, *The Police* (Washington, D.C.: U.S. Government Printing Office, 1931).

31 Walker, *Popular Justice,* pp. 183–186.

35 Ungar, *FBI,* pp. 54–63.

36 Paul Jacob, *Prelude to Riot* (New York: Vintage Books, 1968), pp. 13–60.

37 William Parker, *Parker on Police* (Springfield: Charles C Thomas, 1957), pp. 113–123.

38 Samuel Walker, "The Origins of the American Police-Community Relations Movement: The 1940's," in *Criminal Justice History: An International Annual,* vol. I (New York: John Jay Press, 1980), pp. 225–246.

39 Sterling Spero, *Government as Employer* (Carbondale: Southern Illinois University, 1972), pp. 245–294.

40 Francis Russell, *A City in Terror—in 1919—The Boston Police Strike* (New York: Viking Press, 1975).

41 Richard A. Myren, "A Crisis in Police Management," *Journal of Criminal Law, Criminology, and Police Science* 50 (March–April 1960): 600–604.

42 Archibald Cox, *The Warren Court* (Cambridge: Harvard University Press, 1968).

43 Walker, *Popular Justice,* pp. 229–232.

44 National Advisory Commission on Civil Disorders, *Report* (New York: Bantam Books, 1968).

45 President's Commission on Law Enforcement and Administration of Justice, *The Challenge of Crime in a Free Society* (New York: Avon Books, 1968).

46 Albert Reiss, *The Police and the Public* (New Haven: Yale University, 1971); Donald J. Black, *The Manners and Customs of the Police* (New York: Academic Press, 1980).

47 National Advisory Commission on Civil Disturbances, *Report,* chaps. 11–13.

48 Ibid., p. 299.

49 Ibid., p. 301.

50 National Commission on the Causes and Prevention of Violence, *Rights in Conflict* (New York: New American Library, 1968).

51 Walker, *Popular Justice,* pp. 236–238.

52 David J. Farmer, "The Research Revolution," *Police Magazine* (November 1978): 64–65.

53 U.S., Department of Justice, *The National Manpower Survey of the Criminal Justice System,* vol. 2, *Law Enforcement* (Washington, D.C.: U. S. Government Printing Office, 1978).

54 George L. Kelling et al., *The Kansas City Preventive Patrol Experiment: A Summary Report* (Washington, D.C.: The Police Foundation, 1974).

55 Peter W. Greenwood et al., *The Criminal Investigation Process,* vol. 1, *Summary and Policy Implications* (Santa Monica: Rand Corporation, 1975).

56 Lawrence W. Sherman et al., *Team Policing: Seven Case Studies* (Washington, D.C.: The Police Foundation, 1973).

57 Peter B. Bloch and Deborah Anderson, *Policewomen on Patrol: Final Report* (Washington, D.C.: The Police Foundation, 1974); Joyce Sichel et al., *Women on Patrol: A Pilot Study of Police Performance in New York City* (Washington, D.C.: Department of Justice, 1978).

58 Hervey A. Juris and Peter Feuille, *Police Unionism* (Lexington: Lexington Books, 1973).

59 James Q. Wilson, *Thinking about Crime* (New York: Basic Books, 1975), p. 97.

CHAPTER **2**

CONTEMPORARY POLICE SYSTEMS

THE POLICE INDUSTRY

The purpose of this chapter is to present an overview of American law enforcement and describe the unique features of its various components. We shall adopt the industry perspective developed by Ostrom, Parks, and Whitaker.[1] This perspective offers a picture of the totality of police services and provides an alternative to the traditional approach, which focuses on single agencies.

Defining Our Terms

This chapter discusses those agencies that provide *basic police services*. These include law enforcement (the detection of crime and the apprehension of criminals), the prevention of crime (preventive patrol), and order maintenance (resolution of disputes, etc.).[2]

This definition is necessary because of the complexity surrounding the terms *police officer* and *peace officer*. These legally designated titles are defined by statute. Iowa law designates eight categories of peace officer, the last being a catchall: "all other persons so designated." California statutes specify more than thirty different occupations with the status of either police officer or peace officer.[3]

In California and many other states correctional officers hold police officer status. In the broadest sense, they are part of the law enforcement industry. In this chapter, however, we shall use a more limited approach, focusing only on those agencies where police services are the primary mission.

Components of the Industry

Police services are provided by three levels of government: federal, state, and local. The local level of government contains two major subcomponents: municipal and county agencies. In addition there are various other local law enforcement agencies, such as constables, coroners, and special-district police (school districts, campus police, park police, etc.). The private security industry is the final component.

Nearly 20,000 separate government agencies provide police protection. In fiscal year 1979 they employed a total of 644,073 full-time employees at a cost of almost $14 billion. Private security firms employ an estimated 500,000 people at a cost estimated between $6 and $12 billion (precise estimates do not exist and estimates vary considerably).

A Complex Enterprise

Law enforcement in the United States is a large, complex, and tremendously varied enterprise. Federal, state, county, and municipal law enforcement functions are quite different from each other. At the same time, there is great variety among agencies at the same level of government. The big-city police department in New York or Los Angeles is worlds apart from the small-town police force. Even metropolitan departments vary according to their style of management, level of professionalism, and image in the community.

An appreciation of the variety of law enforcement and the hazards of generalization is one of the keys to understanding the American police. Unfortunately, there is a serious imbalance in the available literature: most of the research and popular literature focuses on urban police departments, while, as Lee Brown points out, "there is a dearth of information on the role of the sheriff."[4]

SIZE AND SCOPE OF THE INDUSTRY

Police and the Criminal Justice System

The police are the largest component of the criminal justice system. As Figure 2.1 indicates, police protection accounted for over half (55 percent) of the total expenditures by government agencies for criminal justice services in fiscal year 1979. Meanwhile, police protection accounted for 57 percent of all full-time criminal justice system employees (see Figure 2.2).

The Number of Agencies

Police services are provided by 19,691 separate government agencies. This high figure is a result of the decentralization of law enforcement responsibilities in the United States. This country stands in sharp contrast to other countries in the world. England, with a population of 46 million people (about one-fourth the size of the United States), has a total of 39 law enforcement agencies.[5]

The exact number of law enforcement agencies in the United States has been a matter of some controversy. The President's Commission on Law Enforcement adopted the traditional estimate of 40,000 in 1967.[6] More recent surveys by the Census Bureau and the U.S. Department of Justice indicate that the actual number is only half of the traditional estimate—thus providing one example of the general lack of reliable data on the American police.

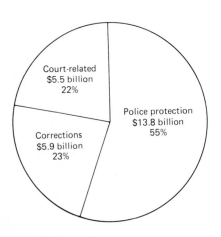

FIGURE 2.1
Total criminal justice expenditures, by system component, 1979. *(U.S. Department of Justice, Sourcebook of Criminal Justice Statistics—1981, Washington, D.C., Government Printing Office, 1982, p. 4.)*

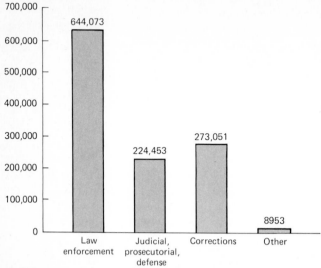

FIGURE 2.2
Full-time employees, by criminal justice system component, 1979. *(U.S. Department of Justice, Sourcebook of Criminal Justice Statistics—1981, Washington, D.C., Government Printing Office, 1982, p. 19.)*

The Number of Personnel

In fiscal year 1979 government agencies employed a total of 644,073 persons on a full-time basis in the area of police protection. Police personnel figures are complex and must be read with some care if meaningful comparisons are to be made.

The first important distinction is between *full-time* and *part-time* employees. Many of the small law enforcement agencies in rural areas rely heavily on part-time employees, who may not necessarily receive the same salaries or be eligible for the same benefits. Also, heavy use of part-time employees often indicates a low level of professionalism.

Another important distinction is *full-time equivalent* (FTE) employees. Two part-time employees, both working 20 hours a week, equal one FTE employee.[7]

A second important distinction is between *sworn* officers and *nonsworn* civilian employees. Statistics on full-time employees usually include both sworn officers and civilians; these figures, therefore, do not tell us how many police officers are available for duty with an agency.

A third distinction is between the *authorized* and the *actual* strength of an agency. A city police department may be authorized to employ 600 officers, for example. Yet, there are rarely 600 officers actually on the payroll. The number drops because of retirements, resignations, and terminations. Because of financial problems, many agencies do not fill existing vacancies and remain below authorized strength.

The Distribution of Agencies and Personnel

Law enforcement agencies and personnel are not evenly distributed. Table 2-1 shows that 74.6 percent of all full-time employees are employed by local governments. Federal employees account for only 11.2 percent of the total.

The overwhelming majority of law enforcement agencies employ only a small number of people. Table 2-2 shows that 155 local agencies employ 300 or more sworn officers, while 10,085 local agencies employ less than 10 sworn officers. Yet the 155 large agencies employ nearly half of all sworn officers, while the 10,085 small agencies employ less than 10 percent of all sworn officers. In short, the typical law enforcement agency in the United States is a small-town police department with fewer than ten employees. The typical law enforcement officer, on the other hand, works for a big city police department.

Patterns of Growth

Law enforcement was a growth industry during the 1960s and 1970s in terms of both expenditure and employment. According to the U.S. Department of Justice, total government expenditures on police protection doubled (up 126 percent between 1971 and 1979 alone, rising from $6.1 billion a year to $13.8 billion. The total number of law enforcement personnel, however, increased only 24.9 percent (from 515,691 to 644,073) in the same time period. The difference reflects the financial impact of improvements in police salaries and fringe benefits.[8]

Total law enforcement costs increased at a slower rate between 1971 and 1979 than costs for all other components of the criminal justice system. Public-defender costs grew by 364.6 percent, legal services and prosecutorial costs increased 235.4 percent; corrections costs increased 161.3 percent; and judicial expenditures grew by 149.5 percent.

Amedeo R. Odoni computed growth trends for big-city police departments between 1959 and 1973. He divided the cities into two groups: Group A, the thirteen

TABLE 2-1
FULL-TIME EMPLOYEES BY LEVEL OF
GOVERNMENT, 1979

Level of government	Total agencies	% of total agencies
Federal	72,561	11.3
State	90,779	14.1
Local	480,733	74.6
Total	644,073	100.0

Source: U.S., Department of Justice, *Expenditure and Employment Data for the Criminal Justice System 1979* (Washington, D.C.: U.S. Government Printing office, 1982), p. 37.

TABLE 2-2
STATE AND LOCAL LAW ENFORCEMENT AGENCIES BY NUMBER OF SWORN OFFICERS AND LEVEL OF GOVERNMENT, MARCH 31, 1977

Level of government	Total agencies	Medical examiners/ coroners[1]	Other related agencies	Total agencies	Number of agencies, by number of sworn officers									
					1	2 to 4	5 to 9	10 to 24	25 to 49	50 to 99	100 to 199	200 to 299	300 and over	Not available
Total	19,691	1,683	395	17,613	1,658	4,405	4,210	4,095	1,673	862	362	111	201	36
State	980	56	254	670	22	53	113	227	99	50	30	21	46	9
Local	18,711	1,627	141	16,943	1,636	4,352	4,097	3,868	1,574	812	332	90	155	27
County	4,999	1,599	60	3,340	157	735	859	843	349	211	105	25	45	11
Municipal	11,703	28	80	11,595	1,360	3,221	2,784	2,432	954	467	195	62	108	12
Township	1,811	—	1	1,810	111	381	415	522	239	115	25	—	—	2
Special district and independent school district	198	—	—	198	8	15	39	71	32	19	7	3	2	2

Source: U.S., Department of Justice, Justice Agencies in the United States: Summary Report 1980 (Washington, D.C.: U.S. Government Printing Office, 1980), p. 7.

cities with 2000 or more police employees; and Group B, twenty cities with 650 to 1800 police employees. The number of *uniformed officers per capita* increased by 34 percent for Group A and 41 percent for Group B in that period. In certain cities, the size of the department doubled. The Atlanta police department increased from 620 to 1455 sworn officers, while Kansas City increased from 721 to 1307 officers. Total expenditures rose 235 percent for Group A cities and 218 percent for Group B cities.[9]

Explaining the Growth   Several factors account for the increases in police expenditure and employment during the 1960s and 1970s. The most important was the political response to the "crime problem." The real increase in the crime rate, together with public reaction to riots and political protests in the 1960s generated a law-and-order mood. Politicians responded to pressure to "do something" by granting increases in both personnel and salaries to law enforcement. According to former police chief Jerry Wilson, political pressure was the main factor behind the growth of the Washington, D.C., metropolitan police force from 2236 officers in 1955 to 4982 in 1973.[10]

Improvements in police salaries were the result of two factors. First, police salaries had fallen to a relatively low and uncompetitive level by the mid-1960s.[11] Much of the subsequent increase was simply a matter of catching up. Second, the emergence of strong police unions in the late 1960s led to continued improvements in both salaries and fringe benefits. The cost of fringe benefits generally equals about one-third of the basic salary.

MUNICIPAL POLICE

Municipal or city police are the largest and most important component of American law enforcement. They earn this status by virtue of their size, role, public image, and political salience. In 1979, nearly three-quarters of all full-time police employees (480,733 of 644,073) were employed by municipal agencies. Mention the word "police," and most people think of a cop patrolling a city street. Most news stories about the police involve those in the big cities.

The role of the municipal police is more complex and controversial than the role of other law enforcement agencies. City police perform a wide range of law enforcement, order maintenance, and service functions. City police are on call twenty-four hours a day and respond to all the social problems that other public and private agencies either cannot or will not handle.

The city police are primarily responsible for maintaining order and preserving the peace in an infinite range of unpredictable and ambiguous situations. As a result, the police are at the center of chronic social problems. Very often a police officer is the first to respond to incidents involving alcoholism, drug abuse, family problems, and other miscellaneous kinds of "disorderly" behavior. The police are in direct contact with poor people and the problems arising from poverty. Finally, the police are at the center of the problem of racism and racial discrimination.

Big-City Focus

The municipal police are also the most important element of American policing in terms of public image and political significance. This is largely the result of the prominence of the small number of very large police departments. Events involving the police in New York City, Chicago, Washington, D.C., or Los Angeles are *national* news items.

A few giant agencies dominate the municipal law enforcement picture. The largest—in a class by itself—is the New York City Police Department, with 24,408 sworn officers (1978) and another 5,000 civilian employees. (Because of the city's financial troubles the department has been shrinking significantly; in the early 1970s it numbered nearly 30,000 sworn officers.) Chicago, the second largest department, has 13,020 sworn officers. Philadelphia has 8209 officers, while Los Angeles has 6979. Even Dallas, with 1997 sworn officers, is among the very large departments.[12]

The very big departments dominate serious scholarly thinking about the police. *Most of the research on American law enforcement pertains to big-city departments.* And even that body of data is heavily skewed toward a few departments, primarily New York City, Chicago, Los Angeles, Philadelphia, Boston, and Washington. Much less is known about medium-sized agencies, and almost nothing is known about policing in small-town America.

In one of the few such existing studies, Galliher et al. examined 269 agencies in communities with populations of 50,000 or less in a Midwestern state. They found that the role of the police in the small community differed substantially from the big-city context. Crime was not a major problem. The majority of complaints received by small-town police departments involved minor disturbances. Complaints about traffic problems accounted for 25 percent of all calls. Public disturbances accounted for 19 percent, while family disturbances represented 18 percent, and "stray dogs" another 11 percent of all calls.[13]

Because of the enormous variety of city policing it is almost impossible to make broad generalizations. Perhaps the flavor is best conveyed through a series of profiles of different police departments.

New York City

Because of its size, traditions, and media prominence, the New York City Police Department is unique. It is twice as large as Chicago's, the second largest department, and three times as large as Philadelphia's. Its annual budget of $800 million is equal to half of the combined budgets of the next twelve largest departments.

The NYCPD is rich in tradition. It has a notorious history of corruption and political influence. The scandal investigated by the Knapp Commission in the early 1970s was only the latest in a series of major scandals extending back through the nineteenth century. The chief executive is the police commissioner, who is appointed by the mayor. Although they officially have a term of five years, commissioners average less than three years in office. Appointments (and removals) of commissioners are largely the result of political considerations.

Because of its size, the NYCPD has an incredibly complex bureaucratic structure. It fragments into a set of mini-empires, feudal baronies, and cliques. While commissioners come and go frequently, the lower levels of the department are extremely resistant to change. In *Target Blue,* Robert Daley provides a vivid picture of Commissioner Patrick V. Murphy's limited ability to command and change the department.[14]

The working environment of the NYCPD is equally complex. Although New York does not have the highest crime *rate* in the country, it does have an enormous *volume* of crime. In 1978 the NYCPD was faced with 1503 homicides, 74,029 robberies, and 164,447 burglaries. Meanwhile, the racial, ethnic, and cultural variety of the city presents the police with infinitely complex problems in order maintenance and community relations. Finally, with New York City the media capital of the country, the NYCPD is constantly in the national spotlight.

Ashland, Nebraska

Halfway across the country—and practically in another world from the NYCPD— is the Ashland, Nebraska, police department. With three sworn officers (part-time employees bring it to five FTEs), Ashland is in many respects typical of the American municipal police.[15]

Crime is not a serious problem in Ashland, a city of 2278 people, about 25 miles from Omaha, the major metropolitan center in the state. In 1974 there were a total of twenty-seven index crimes, including three burglaries, two assaults, and nineteen larcenies. There were no murders, rapes, or robberies. The Ashland police cleared four of the twenty-seven crimes.

Order maintenance is the major police activity in Ashland. And given the extremely homogenous population, even this is a relatively easy task. There are no ghettos or pockets of extreme poverty in Ashland. The major threat to disorder is teenage hot-rodding.

Gordon, Nebraska

Not all small cities are as peaceful as Ashland, however. Superficially, Gordon, Nebraska, resembles Ashland. Located in the northwest part of the state, it has a population of 2268 and a police department of six sworn officers.

But Gordon is located a few miles south of the Rosebud Indian Reservation in South Dakota, and it has a serious problem in police-community relations involving Native Americans. In 1974 the Gordon police made 578 arrests, most of whom were Indians. Most of the arrests were alcohol-related: 411 for drunkenness, 30 for liquor-law violations, and 71 for driving under the influence.

Tensions between the Gordon police and the Indian community reached crisis proportions in 1979 when Joanne Yellow Bird won a damage settlement of $300,000 for being beaten in the Gordon jail. She was pregnant at the time of the beating and lost the child as a result.[16] In short, racial problems are not confined to the big cities.

The police in small towns where there is a racially heterogeneous population face serious police-community relations problems.

Lakewood, Colorado

Lakewood, a rapidly growing suburb of Denver, attempted to establish a service-oriented police department in the 1970s. According to James Q. Wilson, the service orientation is characterized by a "high level of apparent agreement among citizens on the need for and definition of public order." It is found primarily in homogenous, middle-class suburbs such as Lakewood.[17]

To achieve the service model, the Lakewood police adopted many innovations. Officers wore civilian-style blazers and were termed *agents*. This was an attempt to avoid the traditional military model of American policing. The department aggressively recruited persons with college educations. In 1973, of 177 agents, 11 had graduate degrees, 76 had bachelor's degrees, and another 64 were in their third or fourth year of college. Between 1970 and 1980 eight agents left to become police chiefs in other cities, while three left to enter graduate school.[18]

The Lakewood police adopted team policing as an alternative to the traditional style of organizing and delivering police services (see Chapter 4 for a description and analysis of team policing). The department also emphasized positive police-community relations, adopting the philosophy that "every agent is a 'community relations' officer."

Lakewood's experiments ran into some difficulties.[19] Eventually, the civilian blazers were abandoned in favor of a more traditional uniform. The term *agent* was also replaced by a more traditional rank designation. Finally, the team policing approach was substantially reorganized in 1973. Despite these difficulties, the Lakewood experience demonstrates an innovative approach to policing. The community context favored innovation. Lakewood was a new community, which was not incorporated until 1969. As a result, there was no tradition-encrusted police department, and it was possible to start from scratch. As a relatively homogenous suburban community, there was a high degree of consensus about the proper form of law enforcement.

THE COUNTY SHERIFF

The county sheriff occupies a unique place in American law enforcement. This uniqueness involves both the legal status and the role of the office. In important respects the sheriff is very different from other law enforcement agencies.[20]

Today there are an estimated 3340 county sheriff departments. Like municipal police departments, most of these are in rural areas and have fewer than ten sworn officers.

Legal Status

The legal status of the sheriff is unique. The office is mandated in the constitutions of thirty-five states and mentioned in the constitutions of two other states. The term of office and the method of selection are also specified by many of these state constitutions. As a result, major changes in the office of sheriff would require a constitutional amendment—a lengthy and difficult process.

The second unique aspect of the sheriff's office is that it is elective in all but two of the fifty states. (Sheriffs are appointed by the governor in Rhode Island; and by the chief justice of the supreme court in Hawaii.)

As an elected official, the sheriff is an extremely important figure in local politics. In many rural areas the sheriff is the most powerful political figure. To secure election, candidates must develop political followings. The policies of a sheriff's office often reflect the need to return favors to political supporters. Finally, as an elected official the sheriff enjoys a degree of independence from other officials. Police chiefs, in contrast, must answer to those who appoint them.

A Unique Role

The role of sheriff is unique because the office serves all three components of the criminal-justice system. In addition to being a *law enforcement official,* with the traditional responsibilities of providing police protection, the sheriff is an *officer of the court.* Sheriffs serve warrants and subpoenas and provide protection for the courts. Finally, the sheriff is a *corrections officer* with responsibility for maintaining the county jail.

The correctional responsibilities of the sheriff are experiencing change. In most states, the sheriff is still the county jailer, but in Connecticut, Delaware, Hawaii, and Rhode Island, state departments of corrections manage the jails. In many of the large cities of other states responsibility for the jail has been transferred to a separate agency: in New York City a municipal department of corrections manages the jail; in Omaha, a county department of corrections runs the jail.

Variations

Not all sheriff departments are alike. Lee Brown developed a typology of four different models, according to their responsibilities.[21] The *full-service* model carries out law enforcement, judicial, and correctional duties. The *law enforcement* model (such as Multnomah County, Oregon) carries out only law enforcement duties, with other duties assumed by separate civil-process and correctional agencies. The *civil-judicial* model involves only court-related duties (for example, Connecticut and Rhode Island). Finally, the *correctional-judicial* model (San Francisco County) involves all functions except law enforcement.

There are also important variations in the organizational structure of sheriff departments. In a number of urban areas, city and county governments have been consolidated, either completely or in part. In San Francisco, Denver, and Nashville, city police departments have law enforcement responsibility for the entire city-county area. In Jacksonville (Duvall County, Florida) and Las Vegas (Clark County, Nevada) the sheriff commands a unified law enforcement agency for the entire city-county area. Other variations also exist.[22]

The consolidation of municipal and county agencies is a response to problems arising from urbanization. In the colonial era of American history, the sheriff was the principal law enforcement agent. As cities grew, municipal police departments assumed primary responsibility for the urban areas. Sheriffs' departments and municipal police departments coexist in most urban areas today. The result is a fragmentation of the law enforcement effort, lack of coordination, and overlapping jurisdiction.

OTHER LOCAL AGENCIES

The local picture is complicated by the existence of additional agencies with some law enforcement responsibilities. The three most important of these are the constable, the coroner, and various special-district police agencies.

The Constable

Like the sheriff, the constable is an office whose roots can be traced back to colonial America. The constable exercised law enforcement powers on the neighborhood or community level. In certain respects, the constable resembles the sheriff, with the power to make arrests, serve warrants, and so forth.

Urbanization and the consequent growth of city police departments have stripped the constable's office of most of its functions. Today it is largely a relic of the past. The Advisory Commission on Intergovernmental Relations found the constable to be "of minor importance" and recommended abolishing the office. Its law enforcement functions could be assumed by other agencies and its judicial functions assumed by lower courts.[23]

The Office of Pennsylvania Courts found many serious problems with the office of constable in its 1977 report. There were simply "too many constables," who were "not adequately supervised." Pennsylvania constables were elected to six-year terms from townships, boroughs, or wards. No minimum qualifications for the office existed. Constables received a basic fee of $5.00 for such tasks as serving warrants, subpoenas, or civil process, or for protecting the polls and providing occasional security for local judges. The constable in Fulton County received a total of $87 in 1975, while a constable in Pittsburg who specialized in traffic warrants earned $50,000.[24]

The continued existence of the constable is an excellent illustration of how institutional change in the United States often fails to keep pace with social change. The office of constable remains even though most of its primary functions have been taken over by other, larger agencies.

The Coroner

Because of its investigative responsibilities, the coroner is often regarded as a law enforcement agent by the Census Bureau and the Justice Department. There are an estimated 1683 coroners or medical examiners in the United States. In twenty-six states the coroner is an elected official; nineteen of those states provide for a coroner in the state constitution.

The Advisory Commission on Intergovernmental Relations endorsed two reforms. Some states have retained the coroner's office but provided it with a qualified medical staff. Other states have abolished the office and replaced it with a state (or in some cases local) medical examiner. Lack of medical expertise, investigative skills, and legal training are the most serious problems with the office of coroner.[25]

Special-District Police

In many local areas special-district law enforcement agencies have been established to provide police services to particular institutions and/or geographic areas. The most common of these are transit, housing, park, public school, and campus police forces. The 1977 *Expenditure and Employment Data* report identified a total of 167 special-district agencies and several hundred campus police departments.[26]

New York City has a separate transit police force, with over 2800 officers, a Housing Authority police force, with more than 1400 officers, and the Port Authority police, with 1200 officers. By the late 1970s there were plans to merge these agencies with the New York City Police Department. The Los Angeles school district employs over 300 full-time officers, while the Chicago Board of Education employs 112 full-time officers and at least as many part-time persons. The Metropolitan Transit Police Force in Washington, D.C., represents a unique example of an agency whose responsibilities cover three different political jurisdictions. The metro police force of about 200 officers has law enforcement responsibilities in Maryland, Virginia, and the District of Columbia.[27]

Special-district forces illustrate one of the major problems in American policing. These agencies are created to provide extra police services for a particular institution or area. While they relieve the primary law enforcement agency of a major burden of responsibility, they create additional problems of communication and coordination.

STATE AGENCIES

State governments also perform law enforcement functions. Nominally, the attorney general is the chief law enforcement officer in each state. Apart from limited investigatory duties, however, attorneys general are primarily prosecutors. The basic police functions of patrol, investigation, and public safety are performed by a separate agency, usually called either the highway patrol or state police.

State police agencies are relatively new, compared with other law enforcement agencies. The first modern state police was the Pennsylvania State Constabulary, created in 1905. Earlier forms included the Texas Rangers, established in 1835, and a small number of state law enforcement agents in certain New England states.[28]

Considerable variation exists among state law enforcement agencies with regard to role and mission, and administrative structure.[29]

Role and Mission

With respect to role and mission, state law enforcement agencies fall into two broad categories. The first is the *highway patrol,* defined by the IACP as a "state law enforcement agency with a uniformed field patrol. Police services restricted to or concentrated on traffic, vehicle, and highway related activities."[30] Highway patrols are found in twenty-five states: Alabama, Arizona, California, Colorado, Florida, Georgia, Iowa, Kansas, Minnesota, Mississippi, Missouri, Montana, Nebraska, Nevada, North Carolina, North Dakota, Ohio, Oklahoma, South Carolina, South Dakota, Tennessee, Texas, Utah, Washington, and Wyoming.

The second category, referred to as the *state police,* is defined by the IACP as agencies with "a uniformed field patrol force. Responsible for general police services." These are found in twenty-three states: Alaska, Arkansas, Connecticut, Delaware, Idaho, Illinois, Indiana, Kentucky, Louisiana, Maine, Maryland, Massachusetts, Michigan, New Hampshire, New Jersey, New Mexico, New York, Oregon, Pennsylvania, Rhode Island, Vermont, Virginia, and West Virginia.

The essential difference, in short, is whether the agency's role and mission includes general police powers throughout the state or whether it is restricted to highways and related matters. These differences reflect political decisions concerning the appropriate kind of state law enforcement. The roles and missions of state agencies are specified by statute. Various political factors enter into the creation of these agencies. Opposition from local law enforcement agencies, for example, serves to define a more restricted role and mission for the state police in some states. Opposition from particular interest groups is also important. Because the Pennsylvania State Constabulary was perceived as an antilabor agency, many other states restricted the power of their state police in labor disputes.

The two categories of highway patrol and state police are extremely general. Within each category, many variations exist. The Colorado Highway Patrol, for example, has no jurisdiction in labor disputes. Nine other states restrict the jurisdiction of their agency regarding labor disputes in some respect. Seven states restrict the law enforcement powers of state police within cities.

Administrative Structure

Considerable variation also exists in the administrative structure of state law enforcement agencies. One report found that "almost every possibility" exists.[31] Several states have an umbrella agency containing a number of different departments responsible for various services. The New Jersey Department of Public Safety includes eight divisions: Division of Law, State Police, Division of Motor Vehicles, Division of Alcohol Beverage Control, Division of Criminal Justice, Division of Consumer Affairs, Police Training Commission, and State Athletic Commissioner.

Other states maintain a completely autonomous agency. A few states have several agencies with various law enforcement responsibilities. In Nevada the Highway Patrol coexists with investigators from the Attorney General's Office and the state Department of Law Enforcement Assistance, which provides crime lab, criminal investigation, and training services.

Law Enforcement Services

State law enforcement agencies provide a variety of different services. Great variation exists from state to state, and all agencies do not provide a full range of services.

General Patrol   In the rural areas of most, but not all, states the police engage in general preventive patrol. Responsibility is *concurrent* with local agencies in the sense that both agencies share the responsibility.

Traffic Enforcement   In about half of the states enforcement of traffic laws and patrol of the main highways is the primary responsibility of the state law enforcement agency.

Criminal Investigation   State laws vary in the assignment of responsibility for investigation of general crimes, organized crime, and narcotics offenses. In some instances, a separate agency has responsibility for a particular category of crime.

Criminalistics   Criminalistics (crime lab) services are provided at the state level in almost every state. This is generally the only source of technical assistance for small agencies unable to maintain their own crime lab.

Training   Mandatory training for all police officers in a state is an increasingly common practice. In a number of states, the training of officers in small departments is handled by the state law enforcement agency.

FEDERAL LAW ENFORCEMENT AGENCIES

The federal component of the law enforcement industry is relatively small but more complex than is generally recognized. There is no agreement about the exact size of federal law enforcement activities. The 1977 *Expenditure and Employment Data* report estimates that there are 73,559 full-time federal employees engaged in police protection, at a cost of $1,959,000 per year. Federal activities account for about 15 percent of all expenditures for police protection.[32] A report by the General Accounting Office, however, estimates a much higher level of federal activity. According to the GAO there are a total of 169,625 employees engaged in police protection at an annual cost of $2.6 billion.[33]

The discrepancy between these estimates arises from different interpretations of the meaning of law enforcement. In the broadest sense, the terms *law enforcement* or *police* refer to the general regulatory functions of government. By this definition, virtually all government agencies exercise some police power.

A narrower definition of law enforcement is more appropriate for the purposes of this book. We are concerned with those agencies for whom protection, investigation, or enforcement is the primary mission. This also includes federal agencies that maintain sizable enforcement divisions. The U.S. Postal Service, for example, is not primarily a law enforcement agency. The Postal Inspectors Division, however, is an important federal law enforcement unit. At the extreme end of the scale there are several small federal law enforcement units. The separate U.S. Supreme Court Police Force employs 273 people. There is also a separate National Gallery of Art Protection Staff.

The bulk of federal law enforcement is carried out by nine agencies located in four departments. The Federal Bureau of Investigation is the largest and most important. As Table 2-3 shows, it is one of four agencies within the Department of Justice. The U.S. Customs Service, located within the Department of the Treasury, is the second largest. Postal inspectors with the U.S. Postal Service, a separate government corporation, is the third largest. The U.S. Marshals Service, with 94 marshals and about 18,000 deputies, has an extremely complex role. Its officers have both law enforcement and court-related duties and are assigned to several different federal justice agencies.

Role and Mission

The role and mission of each federal agency is specified by statute. Federal law indicates the particular laws that officers of a given agency are to enforce. In this respect the role of federal agents is far less complicated than that of municipal police. Federal agents do not have the ambiguous and difficult order-maintenance responsibility of municipal police. They are not called upon to respond to vague "disturbance" calls, where it is often the officer's task to determine exactly what is occurring and to make difficult discretionary decisions.

The role and mission of the FBI, however, has long been a matter of controversy. The Bureau was created in 1908 over the objections of Congress, which feared a national police force. Under the directorship of J. Edgar Hoover (1924–1972), the

TABLE 2-3

EXPENDITURE AND EMPLOYMENT DATA OF MAJOR FEDERAL LAW ENFORCEMENT AGENCIES, 1977

Agency	Expenditures	No. employees
Department of Justice		
Federal Bureau of Investigation	$463,751,000	19,310
Drug Enforcement Agency	158,224,000	4,019
Immigration and Naturalization Service	64,488,000	3,876
Department of the Treasury		
Customs Service	$341,337,000	13,378
Bureau of Alcohol, Tobacco and Firearms	118,443,000	3,982
Secret Service	111,611,000	3,574
Internal Revenue Service	109,728,000	4,686
Postal Service	113,590,000	5,472
General Services Agency		
Office of Federal Protective Service Management	82,949,000	3,401

Source: U.S., Department of Justice, *Expenditure and Employment Data For the Criminal Justice System, 1977* (Washington, D.C.: 1977), pp. 40–41.

FBI concentrated its efforts on investigating alleged "subversives" and apprehending bank robbers and stolen cars. Critics charged that the FBI ignored white-collar crimes, organized crime, and violations of the civil rights of minorities. After Hoover's death it was discovered that in the pursuit of subversives, the FBI committed many crimes itself. Finally, in the late 1970s under the directorship of William Webster, the FBI launched an aggressive campaign against white-collar and organized crime.[34] In short, the role and mission of an agency is not simply a matter of statute. As the case of the FBI indicates, the enforcement priorities of an agency can be shaped by administrative discretion.

American Indian Tribal Police

A unique component of the law enforcement industry is the American Indian tribal police. Although subject to a repressive reservations policy, American Indians retain significant degrees of autonomy from state and federal governments. On many reservations separate tribal governments are responsible for making and administering tribal law. This involves a separate tribal criminal justice system. According to the Justice Department there are 208 such American Indian tribal criminal justice agencies, including 62 law enforcement agencies. The largest number are located in two states: fourteen in New Mexico and thirteen in Arizona.[35]

THE PRIVATE SECURITY INDUSTRY

The private security industry is an important component of the law enforcement universe. While public law enforcement agencies deliver services to the public at large, some private citizens and businesses are able to purchase additional police services directly. Businesses, for example, purchase additional protection through security guards. Some residential areas contract for patrol services from private security agencies, thus supplementing the preventive patrol of the local police.

The private security industry is large and growing, but its exact size is not known. There are an estimated 4000 private agencies, but that figure is constantly changing. Moreover, many people employed by private security agencies are part-time or short-term employees. Kakalik and Wildhorn estimated that a total of 429,000 persons work in the private security field, of whom 292,000 regarded it as their primary occupation.[36]

Although no precise figures are available, it is generally believed that expenditures for private security doubled in the 1970s. One estimate calculated that total private security expenditures rose from $2.9 billion in 1968 to $6.35 billion in 1978. The rise in crimes against persons and property, together with increased fear of crime, are the main causes of the growth of the private security industry.

Problems

The private security industry is beset with many problems similar to those facing public law enforcement agencies. The most serious involves the quality of personnel.

Private security employees generally have minimal education and little or no training. Typically, employment in private security is the last resort for individuals unable to find other jobs or the temporary first resort for young persons who have not yet established careers for themselves. Turnover is extremely high.

As a consequence, private security faces a number of serious operational problems. Misuse of force is a major problem; employees often lack the background, training, and supervision to effectively guide their judgment in making arrests, conducting searches, or exercising physical or deadly force.

The problems associated with the industry have spurred the movement toward licensing and regulation. State laws could establish minimum recruitment and training standards and guidelines for the exercise of police powers.

THE FRAGMENTATION ISSUE

The fragmentation of responsibility is one of the dominant characteristics of the American law enforcement industry. This fragmentation is rooted in the basic structure of the American political system. Under the U.S. Constitution the national government exercises only those powers which have been delegated to it. The bulk of administrative responsibility lies with the state and local governments. Local communities jealously guard their prerogative to maintain and deliver basic social services. The localist orientation is especially strong with respect to public schools and law enforcement.

Some critics have long argued that the fragmentation of law enforcement responsibility is one of the principal barriers to effective, efficient, and professional policing. The President's Commission on Law Enforcement summarized this perspective in 1967: "A fundamental problem confronting law enforcement today is that of fragmented crime repression efforts resulting from the large number of uncoordinated local governments and law enforcement agencies."[37] Figure 2.3, which shows the geographic distribution and relative size of the eighty-five agencies serving the Detroit metropolitan area, illustrates the fragmentation issue.

According to the critics, several problems result from fragmentation:

Lack of Coordination   Criminals do not respect political boundaries. In the commission of a crime or crimes they may travel from one city or state to another. The same criminal may commit a series of crimes in neighboring communities. The absence of a mechanism to ensure efficient communication and coordination of effort between law enforcement agencies, the critics argue, hinders the crime-repression effort.

Duplication   Overlapping jurisdiction is also a consequence of fragmentation. A particular rural area may be the responsibility of both the county sheriff and the state police for police patrol. This duplication of effort, the critics charge, is not the most cost-effective way to deliver police services to the public. A single agency could provide the same level of services at a reduced cost.

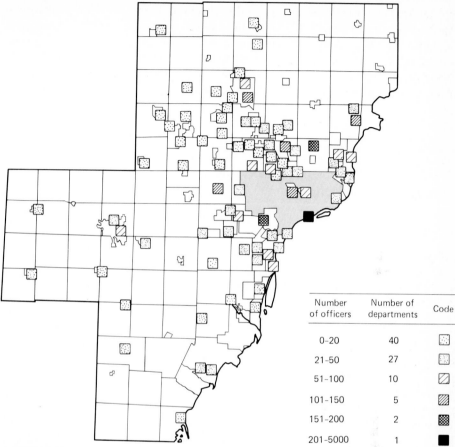

FIGURE 2.3
Size and distribution of law enforcement agencies, Detroit metropolitan area. *(President's Commission on Law Enforcement and Administration of Justice, Task Force Report: The Police, Washington, D.C., 1967, p. 69.)*

Number of officers	Number of departments	Code
0-20	40	
21-50	27	
51-100	10	
101-150	5	
151-200	2	
201-5000	1	

Lack of Uniform Standards As a result of political decentralization, local units of government in the United States are generally free to provide the kind of services they see fit. There is no central coordinating mechanism to enforce uniform standards. Many critics argue that this has impeded the progress of police professionalization. In England, on the other hand, local police agencies are regularly inspected by the national government. And since local agencies receive approximately half their annual budget from the national government, uniform standards can be effectively enforced.

In other areas of government services, standards are enforced indirectly. Educational institutions, for example, must meet accreditation criteria. Public school teachers must fulfill certain requirements in order to be certified. In some states social workers are certified, just as lawyers and doctors are licensed by the state.

The development of mechanisms to ensure uniform standards for law enforcement agencies has begun to appear. More than forty states now require formal training of all police officers. The Justice Department has recently funded a project to develop accreditation standards for all law enforcement agencies. But for the most part, law enforcement agencies today are subject to little or no outside control. Compliance with recognized professional standards is strictly voluntary.

Proposed Solutions

The problems associated with fragmentation may be attacked in one of several ways. The International City Management Association's *Local Government Police Management* suggests three approaches:[38]

1 A unified system merging functional components while preserving the separate identities of all participants
2 A unified system with one jurisdiction contracting with another for complete police services
3 A unified system through establishment of a new governmental entity to provide areawide police services

The third approach is the most radical, since it involves the consolidation of existing units of government into a single entity. It is also the most controversial and the one that faces the most serious obstacles. Local units of government jealously guard their autonomy; residents and taxpayers fear loss of control over their public-service agencies. Consequently, relatively little progress has been made in the direction of consolidation over the years.

Contracting for services, the second approach, is less drastic, and there has been considerable progress in this direction. Small units of government may contract either for complete police services or simply for particular services. This approach encounters much less political opposition, since local residents retain control over services through the contract.

Merging functional components (communications, training, records, etc.) is also a partial approach that encounters less political opposition. *Local Government Police Management* cites the example of the Genesee County Communications Center. In Michigan, the city of Flint police department, the Genesee County Sheriff's Department, the state police, and many small departments in the area maintain a common communications center for receiving citizen calls and dispatching police officers.

As a result of consolidation and contracting, the number of local law enforcement agencies has been declining. The Bureau of Justice Statistics eliminated more than 1000 local agencies from its list between 1975 and 1977.[39]

Fragmentation Reconsidered

Experts in the field of public administration first identified the fragmentation problem in the late 1920s. Over the next fifty years consolidation of services became a standard part of the agenda of modern police reform. Virtually every major commission report and text in the field has recommended some form of consolidation.[40]

Despite the experts' attacks on fragmentation, there was virtually no empirical evidence to substantiate the existence of a problem or to assess its seriousness. The first attempt to investigate the question was undertaken by Ostrom and associates at the Indiana University Workshop in Political Theory and Policy Analysis. Their findings challenged prevailing assumptions.[41]

Ostrom, Parks, and Whitaker examined the delivery of police services in eighty medium-sized (1.5 million people or less) metropolitan areas. In these areas they identified 1827 individual agencies or "producers" of police services.

They found "a much richer network of interrelationships among agencies, and a much higher use of auxiliary services in general, than we would have expected." Contrary to popular belief, "Informal interagency assistance is common," and "strict duplication of services is almost nonexistent in the production of direct police services" in the metropolitan areas they studied. With respect to patrol, for example, they found that informal arrangements by which agencies coordinated, shared, or alternated responsibility were common, and small agencies routinely had access to auxiliary services such as crime laboratories maintained by larger agencies.

More importantly, they found that larger units were not necessarily more efficient. With respect to patrol: "Larger departments do *not* translate their relative personnel advantage into as high an on-street presence as do small- to medium-sized agencies." In short, small agencies may be more efficient in the delivery of the basic police service of preventive patrol.

REVIEW

1 What are the dominant characteristics of the American law enforcement industry?

2 What percentage of the total expenditures for criminal justice does law enforcement account for?

3 What is the size of the typical law enforcement agency in the United States?

4 Explain the difference between "full-time" and "full-time equivalent" employees.

5 Describe how the Lakewood, Colorado, police department originally differed from the typical city police department.

6 What are the two basic types of state law enforcement agencies?

7 Identify the five largest federal law enforcement agencies. In what departments of the federal government are they located?

8 What problems result from the fragmentation of American law enforcement?

9 Describe three possible solutions to law enforcement fragmentation.

10 According to Ostrom, Parks, and Whitaker, how serious is the fragmentation problem?

REFERENCES

1 E. Ostrom, Parks, and Whitaker, *Patterns of Metropolitan Policing* (Cambridge: Ballinger Publishing, 1978), pp. 3–4.

2 U.S., Department of Justice, *Expenditure and Employment Data for the Criminal Justice System, 1977* (Washington, D.C.: U.S. Government Printing Office, 1979), pp. 427–431.

3 *California Penal Code,* Part 2: "Of Criminal Procedure," Title 3, Chapter 4.5.

4 Lee P. Brown, "The Role of the Sheriff," in *The Future of Policing,* ed., Alvin W. Cohn (Beverly Hills: Sage Books, 1978), pp. 227–228.

5 T.A. Critchley, *A History of Police in England and Wales,* 2nd ed. rev. (Montclair: Patterson Smith, 1972), chaps. 9, 10.

6 President's Commission on Law Enforcement and Administration of Justice, *The Challenge of Crime in a Free Society* (New York: Avon Books, 1968), p. 239.

7 U.S., Department of Justice, *Expenditure and Employment Data,* p. 428.

8 U.S., Department of Justice, *Trends in Expenditure and Employment Data for the Criminal Justice System, 1971–1977* (Washington, D.C.: U.S. Government Printing Office, 1980).

9 Amedeo Odoni, "Recent Employment and Expenditure Trends in City Police Departments in the United States," *Journal of Criminal Justice* 5 (Summer 1977): 119–147.

10 Jerry V. Wilson, *The War on Crime in the District of Columbia, 1955–1975* (Washington, D.C.: Department of Justice, 1978).

11 President's Commission on Law Enforcement and Administration of Justice, *Task Force Report: The Police* (Washington, D.C.: U.S. Government Printing Office, 1967), pp. 133–134.

12 U.S., Department of Justice, *FBI Uniform Crime Reports, 1978* (Washington, D.C.: U.S. Government Printing Office, 1979), pp. 230–313.

13 John F. Galliher et al., "Small-Town Police: Troubles, Tasks, and Publics," *Journal of Police Science and Administration* 3 (March 1975), 19–28.

14 Robert Daley, *Target Blue: An Insider's View of the N.Y.P.D.* (New York: Dell Books, 1974).

15 Nebraska Commission on Law Enforcement and Criminal Justice, *Crime in Nebraska: Uniform Crime Reports—1979,* (Lincoln: Nebraska Commission on Law Enforcement and Criminal Justice, 1979).

16 *Omaha World-Herald,* August 3, 1979.

17 James Q. Wilson, *Varieties of Police Behavior* (New York: Atheneum, 1973), p. 200.

18 City of Lakewood, Department of Public Safety, *A Special Report* (Lakewood, Co.; Author, 1973).

19 Dorothy Guyot, "Bending Granite: Attempts to Change the Rank Structure of American Police Departments," *Journal of Police Science and Administration* 7, no. 3 (1979), 273–274.

20 National Sheriffs' Association, *County Law Enforcement: An Assessment of Capabilities and Needs* (Washington, D.C.: Author, n.d.)

21 Brown, "The Role of the Sheriff," pp. 237–240.

22 National Sheriffs' Association, *County Law Enforcement,* p. 31.

23 Pennsylvania, Administrative Office of Pennsylvania Courts, *The Constables of Pennsylvania: A Critical Survey, 1976* (Philadelphia: Author, 1977).

24 Ibid., pp. 1–2.

25 U.S. Advisory Commission on Intergovernmental Relations, *State and Local Relations* *in the Criminal Justice System* (Washington, D.C.: U.S. Government Printing Office, 1971), p. 28.

26 U.S., Department of Justice, *Expenditure and Employment Data, 1977,* pp. 399–425.

27 Martin Hannon, "The Metro Transit Police Force: America's First Tri-State, Multi-Jurisdictional Police Force," *FBI Law Enforcement Bulletin* 47 (November 1978), pp. 16–22.

28 Bruce Smith, *The State Police* (New York: Macmillan, 1925).

29 International Association of Chiefs of Police, Division of State and Provincial Police, *Comparative Data Report, 1974* (Gaithersburg, Md.: IACP, 1975).

30 Ibid., p. 36.

31 Ibid., p. 39.

32 U.S., Department of Justice, *Expenditure and Employment Report, 1977,* pp. 37–41.

33 *The New York Times,* October 14, 1975, p. 24.

34 Sanford J. Ungar, *FBI* (Boston: Little, Brown, 1976); James Q. Wilson, "The Changing FBI—The Road to Abscam," *Public Interest* 59 (Spring 1980), 3–14.

35 U.S., Department of Justice, *Justice Agencies in the United States: Summary Report 1980* (Washington, D.C.: U.S. Government Printing Office, 1980), p. 23.

36 James S. Kakalik and Sorrel Wildhorn, *The Private Police: Security and Danger* (New York: Crane Russak, 1977).

37 President's Commission on Law Enforcement, *Task Force Report: The Police,* p. 68.

38 Bernard L. Garmire, ed., *Local Government Police Management* (Washington: International City Management Association, 1977), p. 39.

39 U.S., Bureau of Justice Statistics, *Justice Agencies in the United States: Summary Report, 1980* (Washington, D.C.: U.S. Government Printing Office, 1980), p. 6.

40 President's Commission on Law Enforcement, *Task Force Report: The Police,* chap. 4; U.S. Advisory Commission on Intergovernmental Relations, *State and Local Relations,* pp. 17–20; U.S. National Advisory Commission on Criminal Justice Standards and Goals, *Police* (Washington, D.C.: U.S. Government Printing Office, 1973), pp. 73–76.

41 Ostrom et al., *Patterns of Metropolitan Policing.*

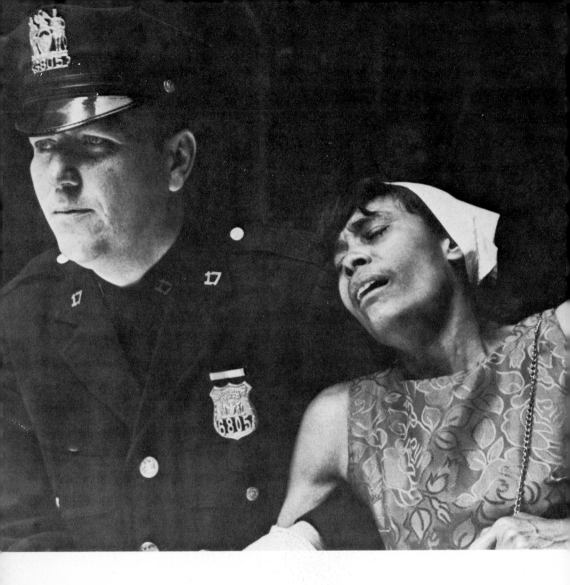

CHAPTER 3

THE POLICE ROLE

IMAGE AND REALITY

"For what social purpose do police exist?," asks Jerome Skolnick.[1] The most basic questions surrounding the police involve their *role* in society. Why do we have police? What are they supposed to do? What do they do that other social agencies do not do? What tasks do they perform on a day-to-day basis?

Too often, oversimplified answers are provided for these questions. Some argue that the police "enforce the law," or that they "protect and serve." These answers are much too simple, and they obscure the incredibly complex role that the police play. The American Bar Association argues that "the police should be recognized as having complex and multiple tasks to perform."[2] Herman Goldstein warns that "anyone attempting to construct a workable definition of the police role will typically come away with old images shattered and a new-found appreciation for the intricacies of police work."[3]

The Need For Answers

A clear understanding of the police role—and an appreciation of its complexity—is not an abstract, philosophical matter. It relates directly to practical, day-to-day problems of policing. Bernard Garmire suggests that "once we know what the police are to do, then we can address the three critical problems of police recruitment, training and leadership."[4]

With respect to *recruitment,* we cannot know what kind of person to recruit— what kind of person is likely to do well in policing—until we have a good understanding of what the job involves. Police recruitment has generally proceeded on the assumption that certain characteristics yield good police officers. Yet, these assumptions have rarely been tested.

With respect to *training,* it is necessary to know what kinds of tasks and situations an officer will encounter in order to design a meaningful training program. For years, training programs ignored the issues of race relations and human relations. Contemporary training programs fail to deal with many situations and problems that police officers routinely encounter.

With respect to *leadership,* supervisors cannot make basic decisions unless they have a clear understanding of what the police are to do. Leaders must be able to plan, to set goals and objectives, to direct their personnel in the pursuit of those goals, and to evaluate performance. Along the same lines, the public cannot evaluate the performance of a police department unless it has a clear sense of the department's purpose.

THE CRIME-FIGHTER IMAGE

One of the greatest obstacles to understanding the American police is the crime-fighter image. Many people believe that the role of the police is confined to law enforcement: the prevention of crime, the detection of crime, and the apprehension of criminals. In this view, all other tasks are secondary. Non-crime-related tasks are seen as not being "real" police work. In its most extreme form, the crime-fighter image views the police as an "army," a "thin blue line," fighting a "war on crime."

The crime-fighter model is not an accurate description of the police role. It does not describe what police officers actually do on a day-to-day basis. Research has confirmed the fact that police officers typically spend only about 20 percent of their time on law enforcement–related activities.[5] The typical officer rarely makes a felony arrest. The crime-fighter model also fails to describe what the police are *supposed* to do. By law and by political direction, society has mandated that the police undertake many tasks, only some of which relate to law enforcement.

Sources of the Crime-Fighter Image

The crime-fighter image exerts a powerful grip on the public imagination. Many people accept it as a description of reality; this public misunderstanding creates many problems and inhibits improvements in policing.

The crime-fighter image is widespread because it is created and perpetuated by three powerful sources: the entertainment media, the news media, and the police themselves.

The Entertainment Media   Police stories are consistently popular items in the entertainment media. Television cop shows offer violence and fast-paced action. Movies are able to offer even greater levels of violence, sex, and action. In television, movies, and fiction alike, the mystery story allows the audience to watch the skilled detective solve the crime. *Dragnet,* perhaps the most famous television cop show of all time, presented Sergeant Joe Friday as the model of the relentlessly efficient detective who always got his man.[6]

One study of television cop shows identified the following "glaring inaccuracies" in the image of the police.[7]

1 "An overemphasis on violence and action in solving crimes"
2 An "overemphasis on technological sophistication in solving crimes"
3 Not recognizing the role played by citizens in helping the police
4 An exaggerated impression of the "success of the police in apprehending criminals"
5 An "overestimation of violent street crime, which serves as a justification for the police to resort to violence"
6 An "overemphasis on 'gimmickery' to make the improbable seem routine"
7 An extreme "contempt for constitutional rights"

With respect to the legality of police practices, another study found that television cops routinely violate the constitutional rights of citizens. A survey of fifteen prime-time cop shows identified "43 separate scenes in which serious questions could be raised about the propriety of the police action."[8] These incidents included twenty-one clear violations of constitutional rights, seven omissions of constitutional rights, and fifteen instances of police brutality and harassment. In other words, actual police performance in America today may be much better than the image presented on television.

The entertainment media concentrate on the law enforcement aspects of policing because it offers the basic elements of a good story: action, drama, mystery. A crime provides a dramatic event, and the apprehension of the criminal provides a good resolution to the drama. Other aspects of police work do not have the same elements of drama. Much police work is boring and uneventful; many situations are routine, low-level, undramatic disputes. The police find themselves involved in many ongoing problems, such as chronic alcoholism and family problems, that do not have dramatic resolutions.

The News Media   The news media also overemphasize the law enforcement aspects of policing. A crime—particularly a major crime—is a newsworthy "event." The news media in the United States concentrate on such dramatic events. A police raid or an arrest provides good film footage for television news. Both the electronic media and the print media fail to adequately cover ongoing problems. And much of police work involves ongoing problems rather than dramatic events.

The Police Themselves   The police themselves are also responsible for perpetuating the idea that their role is primarily law enforcement. Police department annual reports contain crime-related data almost exclusively: crimes reported, arrests, property recovered. Little data is presented on non-crime-related activities.

The Los Angeles Police Department cultivates the crime-fighter image more aggressively than others. The department's annual report portrays itself as the "thin blue line" between civilization and anarchy. One chart purports to show a correlation between a rising crime rate and court decisions which, it claims, hinder police work and "rip at the fabric of law enforcement."[9]

Why do the police choose to present a distorted image of their own role? The concept of a profession includes the idea of an important *mission*. Law enforcement provides the image of such an important mission: catching dangerous criminals, protecting the public safety. It is also highly specific. There is a specific problem (crime) and a specific duty (catch the criminal). The other aspects of policing do not have these same elements. The resolution of petty disputes does not appear to be nearly as important. Nor is it as specific: it is hard to identify the problem and difficult to specify the proper duty.

Peter Manning argues that the American police have consciously manipulated their image as crime fighters. The emphasis on law enforcement did not begin until the 1930s. This emphasis is, in part, related to the professionalization of the police. Like other professions, the police sought to stake out their area of expertise. In this case it was crime. Staking out an area of expertise is also one technique for denying the expertise of other groups. The police sought to become the sole experts on the subject of crime.[10]

Consequences of the Crime-Fighter Image

The crime-fighter image has serious consequences for the public, police departments, and individual officers.[11]

The *public* suffers in several ways. First, the crime-fighter image creates unrealistic expectations about the ability of the police to prevent crime and apprehend criminals. The entertainment media in particular create the impression that the police are highly successful. Yet the aggregate clearance rate for index crimes does not exceed 20 percent; taking into account unreported crime, the actual clearance rate is closer to 10 percent. Also, there is no conclusive evidence that police patrol effectively deters crime. Victims of crime often blame the police for allowing crime to occur and failing to apprehend criminals.

Second, because the crime-fighter image presents an inaccurate picture of police work, it prevents an informed public debate about police resources and policies. Without an understanding of what the police actually do, the public cannot intelligently discuss how police use existing resources, how resources might be reallocated or increased, or how police handle particular problems.

Police departments suffer for the same reasons noted above. Executives cannot provide effective leadership for the full range of police activities when attention is focused on only one of those activities. Within policing, crime fighting receives the rewards and high status. The detective bureau is the sought-after assignment. The big arrest is the rewarded activity. Effective planning and supervision can only take place when there is a balanced understanding of the full range of police activities.

Finally, the crime-fighter image harms *individual police officers.* Officers suffer from what is termed "role conflict." Many enter law enforcement as a career expecting it to be an exciting job, filled with the rewards of apprehending dangerous criminals. They soon find that their job is routine, boring, and filled with many petty incidents. Morale suffers because of this conflict between their expectations about the police role and the role they actually experience.[12]

THE POLICE ROLE: COMPLEX AND AMBIGUOUS

A Definition of Role

Milton Yinger defines role as "a unit of culture; it refers to the rights and duties, the normatively approved patterns of behavior for the occupants of a given position."[13] Role has both a sociological and a psychological dimension. *Sociologically,* it refers to a position in the social structure. The police are a formal institution in society with certain powers and responsibilities. *Psychologically,* it refers to attitudes and beliefs about that position. People believe certain things about the police and expect certain kinds of behavior from the police. Police officers themselves internalize certain attitudes and beliefs about their job.

In actual encounters between police and citizens, the sociological and psychological dimensions interact in complex ways. A family disturbance is a good example. Police officers respond to the disturbance because, sociologically, they possess the power to intervene, to enforce the law, and to maintain order. Psychologically, however, the attitudes and behavior of all the individuals involved vary. An officer who believes his job involves crime fighting may regard this incident as trivial. He may leave the scene as quickly as possible, doing as little as possible. Another officer, believing his job to be social service–oriented, may spend a great deal of time at the scene, attempting to counsel the disputing parties. One of the parties involved may view the police role in society as oppressive and respond to the individual officer in a hostile fashion. Another, with a positive image of the police role, may respond in a very different fashion.

Role Conflict   The incident described above illustrates the phenomenon of role conflict. The officer experiences *internal* role conflict when faced with a task that is inconsistent with his or her expectations about the job, and *external* role conflict when faced with citizens who have different expectations about how the officer should handle the situation.[14]

Role conflict is also illustrated by police juvenile units. In some respects the juvenile officer is expected to play a *support* role. The officer's job is to establish friendly relations with juveniles and, in a helpful manner, provide advice and counsel in an effort to lead them away from criminal activity. But in other respects the officer is expected to play a *control* role—to control crime and delinquency through strict law enforcement. Infractions are to be dealt with by arrest.[15]

In a particular encounter, it is often unclear—to both juvenile and police officer—which role the officer is playing.

The Enacted Police Role

Until recently, few attempts were made to describe the police role accurately. Police officials preferred to use vague generalities such as "protect and serve." The public accepted uncritically the crime-fighter image portrayed by the media.

Discussions of the police role are often confused because it possesses three different dimensions. First, there is the official, *prescribed role.* Statutes specify the duties and responsibilities of the different law enforcement agencies. Whether or not they perform all these duties and responsibilities is another question. Second, there is the *preferred role,* what people think the police ought to do. Different people, however, have different ideas about what role they would prefer the police to play. Some would prefer a strict law enforcement role. Others would prefer a social-service role. Finally, there is the *enacted role,* what the police actually do. The enacted role may bear little relationship to either the officially prescribed or the preferred role.[16]

The American Bar Association's *Standards Relating to the Urban Police Function* has identified eleven elements of the enacted police role:

1 to identify criminal offenders and criminal activity and, where appropriate, to apprehend offenders and participate in subsequent court proceedings

2 to reduce the opportunities for the commission of some crimes through preventive patrol and other measures

3 to aid individuals who are in danger of physical harm

4 to protect constitutional guarantees

5 to facilitate the movement of peoples and vehicles

6 to assist those who cannot care for themselves

7 to resolve conflict

8 to identify problems that are potentially serious law enforcement or governmental problems

9 to create and maintain a feeling of security in the community

10 to promote and preserve civil order

11 to provide other services on an emergency basis[17]

Problems The ABA list provides a useful starting point for describing the enacted police role. It illustrates the point made by Robert diGrazia, former police commissioner of Boston: "The police role cannot be characterized by one or two simple tasks. Rather the role of the police in this country is far more varied and complex than is commonly recognized." The police role is complex and ambiguous in at least three major ways.[18]

First, it involves a wide *variety* of tasks. Only a few of those tasks deal directly with law enforcement. Many deal with providing emergency and nonemergency services to the community.

Second, there is often a *conflict* between different tasks. The police are responsible for maintaining civil order (item 10) but are also responsible for protecting constitutional guarantees (item 4). In the case of a demonstration or a picket line, the officer often has to make difficult choices about balancing the rights of demonstrators or pickets with the need to preserve order.

In the case of a criminal investigation, the officer is faced with a conflict between the need to gather evidence efficiently and arrest suspects (item 1) and the need to respect the constitutional rights of people (item 4), who as suspects are still innocent until proven guilty. This conflict—often described as a conflict between the crime-control and due process models—involves one of the most common controversies about the police role.[19] Which task should receive greater emphasis—crime control or protection of constitutional rights?

Third, the police role is *ambiguous* because the proper course of action is not always clear. How should the police assist those who cannot assist themselves (item 6)? Frequently, the police arrest chronic alcoholics to protect them against possible danger (muggers, severe weather, etc.). Yet is this a proper use of the criminal law? Even more difficult are the tasks of resolving conflict (item 7) and maintaining order (item 10). How are these to be accomplished? What is the most effective course of action? Simply identifying the task does not tell the officer what to do. For the most part, officers answer these questions on an ad hoc situational basis, using their discretion to treat each situation as a unique case.

Analyzing Police Tasks

To understand the various police tasks, it is useful to group them into different categories. For example, of citizen complaints radioed to police cruisers in Syracuse, New York, during one week in 1966, grouped according to information-gathering, service, order-maintenance, and law-enforcement activities. Only 10.3 percent of the calls related to law enforcement tasks. Other researchers, using similar categories, have obtained similar findings.[20]

Analyzing police tasks in this fashion permits us to discuss the police role intelligently. It facilitates informed planning about department priorities and the allocation of personnel. Training programs can be modified to provide recruits with an accurate picture of the kind of work they will be doing. Particular units of the training program can be developed to cover the different activities.

The Police as Peacekeepers

It is the consensus of expert opinion that the police role should be seen as peacekeeping rather than crime fighting. The peacekeeping role can be seen both in terms of how police officers spend their time and how they respond to particular situations. The police spend only about 10 percent of their time on strictly law enforcement-related duties (other researchers have put the figure closer to 20 percent). Bayley and Mendelsohn argue that the police "spend most of their time interceding and rendering assistance in nonpunitive ways. They interrupt behavior many more times than they punish it."[21]

Michael Banton, who was perhaps the first to identify and label the peacekeeping role, reached his conclusion not on the basis of how an officer spends his time but on "how he responds when he has to deal with offenses." According to Banton, "the most striking thing about patrol work is the high proportion of cases in which policemen do *not* enforce the law." The police rarely punish, in the sense of making an arrest; most often they mediate, counsel, or warn the individuals involved.[22] Chapter 7 explores the issue of police discretion in detail.

The idea of the police as peacekeepers is a matter of controversy. Many people, including many police officers, cling to the idea of the police as crime fighters. Patrick V. Murphy, former commissioner of police in New York City, accepts the peacekeeping concept. He argues that "The policeman is the most important social worker we have. Often it is far better to settle an argument or disperse a crowd and move on than to make an arrest." By contrast and typical of the traditional point of view is a comment made by a Philadelphia police inspector to the President's Crime Commission: "once a police officer becomes a social worker he isn't any good anymore as a policeman."[23]

SHAPING THE POLICE ROLE

The police role has evolved without any rational planning. Historically, the police acquired responsibilities simply because no other agency existed to perform particular tasks. Today, the police role is shaped by a variety of social, political, legal and administrative factors. The ABA identified five major factors, including: (1) the legislative mandate of the police; (2) the right to use force; (3) the investigative ability of police agencies; (4) the twenty-four hour availability of police service; and, (5) social and political pressures on the police from the community.[24]

Legislative Mandate

The police are an agency of government, created and controlled by law. The logical starting point for understanding the police role is to examine the statutes that create law enforcement agencies. Legislative mandates cover a wide range of human behavior and empower the police to intervene in many peoples' lives. The mandate to maintain order is very broad. A crime is a specific act, but "order" is a condition. The distinction between order and disorder is extremely ambiguous.[25] This permits the police to intervene in situations where they choose to. Even more important it allows citizens to request police intervention, even in situations that do not constitute serious disorder.

As was discussed in Chapter 2, major differences exist between the legal mandates of the municipal police, country sheriffs, state police, and federal law enforcement agencies. The municipal police have the broadest authority with responsibility for law enforcement, order maintenance, service, and information. As a result, their role is the most complex and the most ambiguous.

County sheriffs have a very different mandate. In most jurisdictions the sheriff is a law enforcement official, serves the courts in a wide range of civil and criminal proceedings, and functions as a correctional official with responsibility for the county jail. In many areas the responsibility of the sheriff for order maintenance and service is quite limited.

State and federal law enforcement agencies have much more clearly defined mandates. For example, in many states the responsibilities of the state police are limited to highway and traffic problems. The FBI can act only where federal statutes authorize them to act. Neither state nor federal agencies have the order-maintenance and service responsibilities of the municipal police.

The legislative mandate of particular agencies can be altered by revising the law. A good example is the package of federal laws passed in 1934 which greatly expanded the powers of the FBI. It is also possible to narrow or abolish an agency's mandate altogether. The Advisory Commission on Intergovernmental Relations, for example, "recommends that states abolish the office of constable and transfer its duties to appropriate lower court systems."[26]

Authority to Use Force

Egon Bittner argues that the legal authority to use force is the core of the police role, the single factor that defines their role and distinguishes them from other occupations.[27]

Force includes several different police powers. At the extreme, it includes the power to use deadly force, to legally take another person's life. It also includes the right to use physical force. Finally, it includes the power to deprive people of their liberty—to stop and question people and to make arrests.

The authority of the police to use force is not unlimited. Bittner identifies three general limitations. First, it is limited by law: the right to use deadly force, for example, is limited by state law and by the Constitution as interpreted by the Supreme Court. Second, officers may use force only in the performance of their job. They are not justified in using force to settle strictly private disputes. Finally, officers may not use force "maliciously or frivolously." They may not arrest, harass, or abuse citizens for sheer spite or amusement.[28]

As Bittner points out, the importance of the authority to use force does not involve its *actual* use. What is important is the *potential* to use it. He argues that "There can be no doubt that this feature of police work is uppermost in the minds of people who solicit police aid or direct the attention of the police to problems, that persons against whom the police proceed have this feature in mind and conduct themselves accordingly."[29]

The authority to use force, in other words, is the key element in the social psychology of the police role. People call the cops because something is happening that they do not like, and they want the police to use their authority to stop it. Individuals who are confronted by the police respond to their authority: they either defer respectfully or challenge that authority. Recognition of police authority, the capacity to use coercive force, is the key part of all police-citizen encounters. The individual police officer recognizes his or her own capacity to use force and uses it accordingly.

Bittner's theory helps explain why the police are routinely involved in such a wide range of activities. The American habit of calling the cops is an attempt to use the power of the police for one's own ends. People seek to enlist the police on their side. They call the cops whenever they feel there is a "problem" about which "someone" should "do something." These situations are not always ones where the police have legitimate (that is, legal) authority to act. For example, the police are often called to what are essentially civil disputes (landlord-tenant disputes, child-custody disputes, etc.).[30]

The capacity to use force distinguishes the police from other public and private agencies. Social workers and educators do not possess similar powers. People do not call them to intervene in problem situations. Nor do they have the power to intervene or to force solutions.

Police Investigative Abilities

The police are uniquely equipped to investigate problems and situations. Unlike any other social agency, the police have the training and experience to conduct investigations into sensitive or private matters. Consequently, when someone in power feels the need to have certain information, they routinely turn to the police. This may occur even though there are no legal grounds for such an investigation. Some of the worst abuses of power involve investigations into essentially political matters.

Twenty-Four-Hour Availability

Herman Goldstein points out that "many problems coming to the attention of the police become their responsibility because no other means has been found to solve them. They are the residual problems of society." The police role is extremely complex, in short, because no other agency exists to handle many situations.[31]

The police are often the *initial contact* between social agencies and social problems. Typically, the police receive a call about a "disturbance." Once they arrive at the scene, they discover that it is a problem involving mental illness, or alcoholism, or some other social problem. In many instances the police *label* the problem and *refer* it to the appropriate agency. In other instances they do nothing more than attempt to restore order. The police handle problems when no other agency is available, problems that have not yet been labeled, and problems that have been labeled but for which no official agency exists.

The growing complexity of the police role is, in part, a result of the police effort to increase their availability. Since the 1930s, police reform has stressed increased responsiveness to citizen calls for service. New communications technology—the telephone, the two-way radio, the patrol car—made it possible for the police to respond quickly.

Disadvantages   Disagreement exists concerning the advantages and disadvantages to the police of their twenty-four-hour availability.[32] The primary disadvantages involve questions of efficiency. Miscellaneous service calls constitute the bulk of the police workload. Some experts argue that this diverts critical police time and resources away from genuinely serious threats to life and property. Some departments have begun to respond selectively to calls for service, either postponing or not responding at all to certain nonemergency calls (see Chapter 5).

Others argue that the large number of miscellaneous duties hinders the development of police professionalism. One characteristic of a profession is responsibility for a clearly defined area of expertise. The police, however, handle anything and everything. It is difficult if not impossible to specify a precise area of expertise.

Advantages   There are certain advantages to twenty-four-hour availability. Providing miscellaneous services increases police contact with the public. In many ways this generates good will and promotes positive police-community relations. Also, contact with the public increases the police officer's knowledge about the community. This knowledge can be translated into more effective police work after a crime has been committed. Contacts with specific individuals, for example, may prove useful in a criminal investigation.

The twenty-four-hour availability of the police may also be the most economical way for society to provide miscellaneous emergency and nonemergency services. There are many problems that demand attention. If the police did not have responsibility for them, another agency might have to be created. Savings in the police budget would be more than offset by the added expenses of a new agency. Finally, the police are an efficient way to handle emergencies because many situations are not clearly labeled at first. Often, when a call is received it is not until after a police officer arrives that the exact nature of the problem is known.

Community Pressures

The role of the police varies from community to community according to the different pressures that are brought to bear on them. These community pressures take several different forms.

Community Characteristics   The social and economic characteristics of a community exert a powerful influence on the police. The effect of this influence is most evident when we compare a small town or suburban community with a metropolis.

Many small towns and most suburban communities lack many of the social and economic problems of urban areas. The population is often homogenous and generally middle-class. There are no large concentrations of poverty, and there are no great racial or ethnic differences. Also, in the small communities social relations are more personal and informal. There is generally a consensus on public expectations about law enforcement and order maintenance. The police have the relatively easy job of enforcing this consensus.

The big cities have the worst of this country's social problems. There is poverty and the social ills associated with poverty: crime, delinquency, family breakdown, mental illness, drug abuse, etc. A major part of the role of the police in the metropolis involves coping with these social ills. In addition, the big cities have racially and ethnically diverse populations. The role of the police involves mediating between different lifestyles and conflicting expectations about law enforcement and order maintenance.

Political Culture   James Q. Wilson argues that each community has a distinct political culture—local tradition of expectations about government and local government agencies. Police corruption flourishes where the local political culture tolerates it. In his study of police corruption, Lawrence Sherman cites examples (notably Oakland) where the police department succeeded in reducing corruption in city government and, thereby, altering the local political culture.[33]

Public-Interest Groups   The role of the police is shaped by the pressure applied by particular groups within the community. There are a wide variety of pressure groups; their relative influence varies from community to community.

The more important of these include: (1) business and labor groups, which can exert strong influence over such issues as the policing of vagrants in business districts and police handling of labor disputes; (2) civil rights groups, which can influence how city government responds to the police-community relations problem and to particular race-related incidents; (3) neighborhood groups, which can influence law enforcement policy in particular areas; (4) the media, which can influence public opinion about the police through vigorous investigative reporting (in New York City, for example, the Knapp Commission investigation of police corruption was credited to the investigative work of David Burnham, reporter for the *New York Times*); and (5) the police union, which in some cities (notably Boston and New York City) has emerged as a powerful force in local politics, influencing policy with respect to police-community relations in particular.

Administrative Policy

The ABA list of factors that shape the police role ignored the impact of administrative policy. The role of an agency can be shaped by policy decisions made by the chief executive. The best example of administrative leadership shaping the role of an agency is J. Edgar Hoover's career as director of the FBI from 1924 to 1972. The FBI's mandate comes from federal statutes, but Hoover chose to interpret that mandate in a particular way. Under his leadership the Bureau gave special emphasis to bank robbery, kidnapping, and alleged political subversion. Critics charged that the Bureau virtually ignored organized crime, white-collar crime, and violations of federal civil rights laws (especially involving blacks in Southern states). The FBI's role in these areas, in short, was minimal. Not until 1979, with Abscam and other programs, did the Bureau assume a larger role in white-collar crime.[34]

THE POLICE AND SOCIAL CONTROL

The police are part of the social-control network of society. Morris Janowitz defines social control as "the capacity of a society to regulate itself according to desired principles and values." In this sense, social control is not the same as repression or enforced conformity. Janowitz comments, "The problem is whether the processes of social control are able to maintain the social order while transformation and social change take place."[35] In a democratic society the police have the responsibility to protect and maintain the process of social change. The ABA identified protection of constitutional guarantees as one part of the police role. This includes protection of the right to demonstrate, picket, engage in free speech, etc.

The Limits of Police Capability

The social-control capacity of the police is a subject of great controversy. Much of the debate focuses on the deterrent effect of police patrol. Does routine police patrol deter crime? That is, does it influence people to not commit crime? Traditional patrol theory, derived from the principles of Robert Peel, maintains that a police presence does effectively deter crime. Contemporary police management experts, such as O. W. Wilson, accept this view. Other experts, however, question the deterrent effect of the police. The Kansas City Preventive Patrol Experiment, for example, raised serious questions about the effect of patrol (see Chapter 5).

To a great extent, police effectiveness depends upon the willingness of people to be controlled. The 1977 blackout in New York City dramatized the point. Electric power failed in New York and remained out for twenty-five hours, beginning at 9:35 P.M. on July 13. Vandalism and looting erupted throughout the city. The eventual losses totaled nearly $150 million. The police arrested 3800 people but could not stop the general lawlessness. Two journalists commented that the incident confirmed "how impossible is the task of controlling people who do not consent to be controlled."[36] An understanding of the police role begins with a recognition of their limited capacity to control behavior.

A Multisystems Perspective

Society maintains social control through many different means. An important distinction can be made between primary and secondary agents of control. The family is the most important primary agent of social control. In the family unit, the individual learns the acceptable patterns of behavior. The individual is further socialized by peer groups, community groups, and religious organizations. The role of the police should be viewed from a multisystems perspective; that is, they function as part of several systems of social control.

The Criminal Justice System   The police are a part of the criminal justice system. Through the decision to arrest or not arrest, they determine the workload for the rest of the system. In a more fundamental sense, the police play a key role in the allocation of justice. Even where cases are immediately dismissed by the prosecutor, the individual has been "punished" by the indignity of arrest, the temporary deprivation of liberty, the disruption of personal life, and the fact of an arrest record. Failure to arrest where illegal behavior in fact occurs, on the other hand, means that the behavior has been officially condoned.

The interaction of the police with the other components of the criminal-justice system is complex. The police not only affect the other components but are affected by them. Police officers often express great frustration over what they view as the leniency of prosecutors and judges. This frustration affects their morale and, ultimately, their behavior. Police officers are reluctant to make arrests when they know that successful prosecution is unlikely.

The Social-Welfare System   The police are also a part of the social-welfare system—in many respects, the most important part. They are often the first contact that official agencies have with social problems such as delinquency, family problems, drug abuse, alcoholism and mental illness. The police frequently label social problems and refer them to other agencies.[37]

Police relations with social-welfare agencies are problematic because they lack the formal connection that exists in their relationship with the criminal justice system. In some cases a close and cooperative relationship exists. In other cases, it is filled with conflict. Programs such as the Family Crisis Intervention Unit, developed in New York City, are designed to develop closer cooperation. Such programs involve training to ensure that police officers make referrals of social problems to the appropriate agency.[38]

The Political System   Politics is the process by which public policy is determined, resources are allocated, and power distributed and maintained. The police are an integral part of the political system in both tangible and symbolic ways.[39]

Although declining in importance, jobs on the police force are a part of the political role of the police. Prior to the advent of civil service, politicians rewarded their friends with jobs on the police force. In the nineteenth century this was one of the most important aspects of policing. Today, as a result of civil service, politicians are not able to control appointments as in the past.

The police are also important as symbols of the political system. They are the most visible manifestation of power and authority in society. Attitudes toward the police are, to a great extent, determined by peoples' attitudes toward the political system generally. Arthur Niederhoffer describes the police officer as "a 'Rorschach' in uniform." People project upon the officer their attitudes about a wide range of issues.[40]

Because of their political significance, control of the police is an important issue in local politics. The most direct form of political control is through the appointment of the top police official, the commissioner, public-safety director, or chief. In most cities, the mayor has the power to appoint this top official. Leonard Ruchelman identified three different models of police politics. New York City in the 1950s and 1960s was characterized by a continuing struggle for control between the mayor and the police department ("Mayor-Police War"). In Philadelphia, meanwhile, the police commissioner effectively controlled the mayor on important policy questions ("Police Cooptation of the Mayor"). Eventually, former police commissioner Frank Rizzo was elected mayor, enhancing even further the political power of the police. In Chicago, Mayor Richard Daley effectively controlled the police department ("Mayor Ascendant").[41] Following Daley's death, however, subsequent mayors of Chicago were less able to maintain tight control over the police.

Police-community relations is a major arena for the struggle for control over the police. The concept of "civilian review," for example, represents an attempt by the black community to assert some control over the police. The police successfully resisted civilian review, particularly in New York City and Philadelphia, through their political power.

Politics can have an important effect on day-to-day police operations. Pressure from elected officials can force the police to divert resources to a particular problem. Typically, political pressure results in a crackdown on prostitution or public drunkenness. The crackdown is often a temporary one and ends as soon as the political pressure disappears.

The concept of police professionalism is based on the idea of eliminating such political influence. Police agencies should be run by nonpartisan experts whose expertise is based on training and experience. Autonomy, the ability to make decisions on the basis of independent professional judgment, is one of the key elements of all professions. As Ruchelman points out, however, an autonomous bureaucracy wields considerable political power.[42] In many big cities unions representing public workers have become extremely powerful political forces.

CLARIFYING THE POLICE ROLE

Many experts recognize the need to clarify the police role. Herman Goldstein, for example, argues that the police role must be redefined before other police problems can be dealt with. The major problems resulting from the complexity and ambiguity of the police role include:

1 *Public misunderstanding.* Most citizens do not have an accurate understanding of police responsibilities and activities. They accept at face value the crime-fighter role image presented by the media. As a result, they do not understand either the limited capacity of the police to control crime or the many noncriminal responsibilities of the police.

Lacking an accurate understanding of the police role, citizens cannot contribute in a meaningful way to public debate about the effective utilization of police resources. Responsible police planning begins with clear directions from the citizenry about priorities for law enforcement and order maintenance.

2 *Police officer role conflict.* Police officers themselves accept the crime-fighter image, and this results in role conflict. Officers soon discover that little of their time is spent on strictly law enforcement activities. As a result, morale and the quality of police service suffer. Officers downgrade the importance of the many noncriminal activities they are called upon to perform.

3 *Police planning.* Effective management of police agencies involves planning about goals, objectives, tactics, and the utilization of resources. Agencies cannot undertake meaningful planning without having an accurate understanding of the basic role of the police. Acceptance of the crime-fighter image results in a distortion of the management process.

4 *Personnel management.* Police departments cannot effectively manage their personnel without a clear understanding of their role. In order to recruit, train, and supervise officers it is necessary to know what job they are expected to perform. The reward system in American police departments overemphasizes law enforcement functions and fails to recognize, through training and rewards, other functions.

Proposed Solutions

Proposed solutions to the problems surrounding the police role include three alternatives: the development of formal policy statements; role specialization; and role redefinition.

Formal Policy Statements The National Advisory Commission on Criminal Justice Standards and Goals (1973) recommends that police departments develop formal statements setting forth their role (see Exhibit 3.1).

The advantage of formal policy statements, according to the commission, is that "police employees have a model, and members of the public have a standard by which to measure police performance."[43] In short, such statements would enhance accountability: individual officers would be accountable for their handling of particular situations, and agencies as a whole would be accountable to the public for their overall performance.

Policy statements should not be rigid or inflexible. The National Advisory Commission recommends that statements undergo regular review and be revised as circumstances dictate.

Exhibit 3.2 represents a statement of policy concerning pornography adopted by the Dayton, Ohio, police department. The statement reviews the legal aspects of pornography and the role of both citizens and the police. It contains a candid statement about the problem of limited police resources and explicitly declares that it is not the role of the police to act as a "community censor." The statement is a clear directive to officers about how to act and notifies citizens about what to expect.[44]

EXHIBIT 3.1

Standard 1.1

The Police Function

Every police chief executive immediately should develop written policy, based on policies of the governing body that provides formal authority for the police function, and should set forth the objectives and priorities that will guide the agency's delivery of police services. Agency policy should articulate the role of the agency in the protection of constitutional guarantees, the enforcement of the law, and the provision of services necessary to reduce crime, to maintain public order, and to respond to the needs of the community.

1 Every police chief executive should acknowledge that the basic purpose of the police is the maintenance of public order and the control of conduct legislatively defined as crime. The basic purpose may not limit the police role, but should be central to its full definition.

2 Every police chief executive should identify those crimes on which police resources will be concentrated. In the allocation of resources, those crimes that are most serious, stimulate the greatest fear, and cause the greatest economic losses should be afforded the highest priority.

3 Every police chief executive should recognize that some government services that are not essentially a police function are, under some circumstances, appropriately performed by the police. Such services include those provided in the interest of effective government or in response to established community needs. A chief executive:

a Should determine if the service to be provided has a relationship to the objectives established by the police agency. If not, the chief executive should resist that service becoming a duty of the agency;

b Should determine the budgetary cost of the service; and

c Should inform the public and its representatives of the projected effect that provision of the service by the police will have on the ability of the agency to continue the present level of enforcement services.

d If the service must be provided by the police agency, it should be placed in perspective with all other agency services and it should be considered when establishing priorities for the delivery of all police services.

e The service should be made a part of the agency's police role until such time as it is no longer necessary for the police agency to perform the service.

4 In connection with the preparation of their budgets, all police agencies should study and revise annually the objectives and priorities which have been established for the enforcement of laws and the delivery of services.

5 Every police agency should determine the scope and availability of other government services and public and private social services, and develop its ability to make effective referrals to those services.

Source: National Advisory Commission on Criminal Justice Standards and Goals, *Police* (Washington, D.C.: Author, 1973), p. 12.

EXHIBIT 3.2

Dayton, Ohio, Police Department Policy Statement on Pornography

The following policy establishes the Department's position regarding the initiation and investigation of alleged pornography.

I Background Information
  A. The Police Dilemma
    As police officers, we are sworn to uphold the Constitution of the United States as well as the statutes of the State. In the determination of pornography, the question is usually whether the material is protected by the Constitution or is unlawful under the State statutes.
    It is not realistic to expect us to make proper decisions in this area where the courts throughout the nation have been particularly unsuccessful in developing an enforceable standard.
    By means of this policy the Department intends to fulfill its obligations to the Constitutional protections of the First Amendment and its obligations to support the State statutes.
  B. Community Morals
    It is inaccurate and unrealistic to assert that Police Officers embody a "Moral sense of Community." Policemen should not be expected to determine what adults may see or read or perform as a community censor.
    It is essential that community citizens become directly involved in litigation in which such matters are resolved, and that determinations as to prosecutions for pornography not be left exclusively in our hands.
  C. Police Resources
    The Department's manpower position is continuing to deteriorate due to austerity at a time when our community is plagued with violent crime, narcotics, and property

crime. It is not justifiable for the Department to regularly allocate police resources to investigate and prosecute persons for such a low-priority problem as pornography.

II. The Citizens' Role
  A. Citizens who believe they have observed a statute being broken are responsible for coming to the Organized Crime Unit of the Department.
  B. The citizen-complainants must be prepared to establish probable cause to support their allegation that a violation has occurred and must be willing to sign affidavits for the purpose of securing arrest and/or search warrants.
  C. The citizen or citizens must be prepared to testify in all judicial proceedings relative to the alleged violation.

III. The Police Role
  A. The Department's Organized Crime Unit is responsible for rendering assistance to citizen-complainants.
  B. Citizen-complainants are to be assisted in the preparation of affidavits, consulting with the prosecutor and the securing of arrest and search warrants.
  C. Departmental officers are to execute all warrants and to assist the citizen-complainant in the collection and preservation of evidence.

Successful police operations require an active partnership between community citizens and police officers. It is hoped that this policy with its shared responsibilities for both citizen-complainants and the police department will further the development of such a partnership.

Source: U.S., Department of Justice, *Improving Police/Community Relations* (Washington, D.C.: Author, 1973), p. 84.

Policy Development   Who should develop policy statements for police departments? Is it the responsibility of the police chief? Should other members of the
department, including patrol officers, participate? Or should elected officials develop
policy for the police department? To what extent should ordinary citizens have an
opportunity to contribute?

These questions focus on one of the central problems concerning the police in a
democratic society: Who controls the police and who determines police policy? There
are no easy answers to these questions. The present situation is unacceptable. Most
police departments have no formal policy governing basic operations. In practice,
policy is made by officers on the street: when they exercise their discretion to arrest
or not arrest they are making policy. Two problems result. First, it is a *hidden* policy-
making process, with no open review. Second, it results in *inconsistent* policy, since
there is nothing to ensure uniformity among different police officers.[45]

The National Advisory Commission recommends that "The police role must be
determined at the local level by the police chief executive." Yet at the same time the
chief should "provide for maximum participation in the policy formulation process."
Input should be solicited "from all levels within the agency" and "from outside the
agency as appropriate—from other government agencies, community organizations,
and the specific community affected."[46]

The National Advisory Commission's approach has been supported by other
groups, including the President's Commission on Law Enforcement (1967) and the
American Bar Association.[47]

Role Specialization   An alternative approach to clarifying the police role
involves role specialization. The police department would be divided into two or more
units, each responsible for particular tasks. This approach recognizes the fact that
the police perform many different tasks. It seeks to eliminate much of the confusion
and ambiguity by designating responsibility for particular tasks.

The President's Commission on Law Enforcement proposed a form of role specialization in 1967. Its report recommended that "Basic police functions, especially
in large and medium-sized urban departments, should be divided among three kinds
of officers, here termed the 'community-service officer,' the 'police officer,' and the
'police agent.'"[48]

The *community-service officer* (CSO) would be an apprentice between the ages
of 17 and 21. The CSO would not have full law enforcement powers (that is, power
of arrest, authority to use deadly force, etc.) and would work under the supervision
of a regular police officer. The CSO would be responsible for primarily nonemergency service-related tasks. This concept is modeled after other professions where
the less critical tasks are delegated to paraprofessionals.

The *police officer* would perform most of the patrol, investigation, and enforcement tasks currently handled by the police. In particular, the police officer would be
responsible for law enforcement and order maintenance functions requiring the exercise of police authority.

The *police agent* would be a more specialized law enforcement official, concentrating on a particular area of enforcement. The agent might specialize, for example,

in homicide investigation or juvenile work. This approach is also modeled after other professions where practitioners develop specialties (doctors become pediatricians, surgeons, psychiatrists, etc.). It allows individuals to gain expertise based on years of practice and continued training. It also fosters the development of a greater sense of professionalism based on mastery of a particular specialty.

Despite the commission's recommendation, few departments have experimented with the role-specialization concept. The police department in Worcester, Massachusetts, experimented with the CSO concept. Their *police service aides* were responsible for nonemergency, noncriminal service calls. This included taking reports on crimes already committed, handling transportation assignments, and providing information and miscellaneous service to citizens. An evaluation of the experiment found that the PSAs handled 24.7 percent of all calls directly and assisted in another 8.2 percent of the calls. Citizens, PSAs, and regular police officers expressed satisfaction with the experiment. The evaluators termed it a success.[49]

The role-specialization approach has advantages and disadvantages. The first advantage, as the Worcester experiment indicates, involves reduction of the workload for regular police officers. Presumably this allows them more time to work on more serious problems. Second, the CSO approach serves as an effective recruitment device. Individuals who perform well as CSOs can be promoted to the rank of full police officers. Third, the police agent concept permits greater specialization, which presumably fosters both greater effectiveness and professionalism.

The major disadvantage is that the role-specialization approach fails to eliminate the basic problems surrounding the police role. Police officers are called to situations without knowing the exact nature of the problem. The officer enters the scene and must first determine what is happening. In this sense, the police officer is a catch-all position. Role specialization permits other specialists (the CSO and the police agent) to handle those situations whose nature is known in advance, but this is not the case with most situations.

Redefining the Police Role   The most challenging proposal for clarifying the police role has been made by Herman Goldstein. The author of *Policing a Free Society* and principal author of the ABA report on *The Urban Police Function,* Goldstein served as administrative assistant to Superintendent O. W. Wilson with the Chicago police in the early 1960s. The main issue, according to Goldstein, is how we *think* about the police. The crime-fighter image is an inaccurate and inappropriate description of what the police do and ought to do. He proposes viewing the police as an "Agency of Municipal Government Housing a Variety of Functions." He argues that it is "essential to break through the confining criminal justice framework" and recognize the broad responsibilities of the police. David Farmer agrees, suggesting that we think of the police as "community managers."[50]

Goldstein's approach is essentially a *theoretical* one, but it has important practical implications. The recruitment and training of police officers emphasizes the law enforcement function. Typically, officers receive extensive training in criminal procedure and departmental procedures for arrest. Little training is done with regard to different social problems that officers encounter. Not only do officers fail to get the needed training, but the training curriculum reinforces the idea that law enforcement is the primary function of the police.

The evaluation of individual officers and entire police departments also has a law enforcement emphasis. Departmental records, reflected in annual reports, are almost exclusively devoted to crime. There is no way to effectively account for the department's performance in other areas. Nor is there any way to effectively evaluate the performance of individual officers in the noncriminal area.

Although it is a challenging concept, Goldstein's proposal has its problems. The basic problem is that it overlooks Bittner's point about the right of the police to use force. Recognition of this power shapes public perception of the police and, as Bittner suggests, accounts for why people call the police in the first place. To view the police as just another agency of government blurs this important distinction and evades many of the problems that result from it.[51]

Reducing the Military Image   An alternative to Goldstein's approach involves simply reducing the military image of the police, since the crime-fighting image goes hand in hand with the militaristic image.

Changing police uniforms is one way to reduce the militaristic image. The Menlo Park, California, police department reported a successful experiment in having officers wear civilian-style blue blazers rather than traditional police uniforms. Changing both the uniforms and the rank designations is another approach. The police in Lakewood, Colorado, attempted both, although they reverted back to more traditional uniforms and titles after encountering difficulties.[52]

Another way to reduce the militaristic nature of police departments is to alter the formal structure of the department and the authoritarian command system. Team policing, in its pure form, includes both of these changes. (Team policing is discussed in detail in Chapter 4.)

REVIEW

1 Describe the elements of the crime-fighter image of the police.

2 Why is the crime-fighter image an inaccurate description of the contemporary police?

3 Define the concept of *role*.

4 According to the American Bar Association, what are the current responsibilities of the police?

5 What percentage of citizen calls are related to law enforcement, order maintenance, and service tasks?

6 How do legislative bodies shape the police role?

7 According to Egon Bittner, the capacity to use force is the core of the police role. Why?

8 In addition to the criminal justice system, what other systems of social control are the police a part of?

9 Give an example of how formal policy statements can clarify the police role.

10 How does Herman Goldstein suggest we redefine the police role?

REFERENCES

1 Jerome Skolnick, *Justice without Trial* (New York: John Wiley, 1967), p. 1.
2 American Bar Association, *Standards Relating to the Urban Police Function* (Chicago: American Bar Association, 1973), p. 7.
3 Herman Goldstein, *Policing a Free Society* (Cambridge: Ballinger, 1977), p. 21.
4 Barnard L. Garmire, "The Police Role in an Urban Society," *The Police and the Community*, ed., Robert F. Steadman (Baltimore: Johns Hopkins University Press, 1972), p. 3.
5 Albert Reiss, *The Police and the Public* (New Haven: Yale University Press, 1971), p. 96.
6 Doris Graber, "Evaluating Crime-Fighting Policies: Media Images and Public Perspective," in *Evaluating Alternative Law-Enforcement Policies*, eds., Ralph Baker and Fred A. Meyer, Jr. (Lexington: Lexington Books, 1979), pp. 179–199; John H. Culver and Kenton L. Knight, "Evaluating TV Impressions of Law Enforcement Roles," Ibid., pp. 201–212.
7 John H. Culver and Kenton L. Knight, Ibid., pp. 207–209.
8 Stephen Arons and Ethan Katsch, "How TV Cops Flout the Law," *Saturday Review*, March 19, 1977, p. 13.
9 Los Angeles Police Department, *Annual Report*, 1977, pp. 5–6.
10 Peter K. Manning, *Police Work* (Cambridge: MIT Press, 1977), chap. 4.
11 Goldstein, *Policing a Free Society*, pp. 29–31.
12 J. Milton Yinger, *Toward a Field Theory of Behavior* (New York: McGraw-Hill, 1965), pp. 99–100.
13 Ibid.
14 Ibid.
15 National Institute for Juvenile Justice and Delinquency Prevention, *Police-Juvenile Operations*, Vol. 2 (Washington, D.C.: U.S. Government Printing Office, 1977), pp. 3–10.
16 Elmer Johnson, "Police: An Analysis of Role Conflict," *Police* (January–February, 1970), 47–52.
17 American Bar Association, *Standards*, p. 53.
18 Robert DiGrazia, "A Message from the Commissioner," Boston Police Department, *Annual Report*, 1975.
19 Herbert Packer, *The Limits of the Criminal Sanction* (Stanford: Stanford University Press, 1968), chap. 8.
20 James Q. Wilson, *Varieties of Police Behavior* (New York: Atheneum, 1973), p. 18.
21 David H. Bayley and Harold Mendelsohn, *Minorities and the Police* (New York: Free Press, 1969), pp. 68–69.
22 Michael Banton, *The Policeman in the Community* (New York: Basic Books, 1964), p. 127.
23 Robert Daley, *Target Blue* (New York: Dell Books, 1974), p. 4; President's Commission on Law Enforcement and Administration of Justice, *Field Studies* IV, "The Police and the Community," Vol. II (Washington, D.C.: U.S. Government Printing Office, 1967), p. 139.
24 American Bar Association, *Standards*, pp. 46–47.
25 Wilson, *Varieties of Police Behavior*, p. 21.
26 U.S. Advisory Commission on Intergovernmental Relations, *State-Local Relations in the*

Criminal Justice System (Washington, D.C.: U.S. Government Printing Office, 1971), p. 28.

27 Egon Bittner, *The Functions of the Police in Modern Society* (Washington: National Institute of Mental Health, 1970), pp. 36–47.

28 Ibid., p. 37.

29 Ibid., p. 40.

30 Egon Bittner, "Florence Nightingale in Pursuit of Willie Sutton: A Theory of the Police," in *The Potential for Reform of Criminal Justice,* ed., Herbert Jacob (Beverly Hills: Sage Publications, 1974), pp. 17–44.

31 Herman Goldstein, "Improving Policing: A Problem-Oriented Approach, *Crime and Delinquency* 25 (April 1979): 243.

32 Richard A. Myren, "The Role of the Police," in *The Changing Police Role,* ed., Roy R. Roberg (San Jose: Justice Systems Development, 1976), pp. 19–26.

33 Wilson, *Varieties of Police Behavior,* pp. 233–271; Lawrence W. Sherman, *Scandal and Reform: Controlling Police Corruption* (Berkeley: University of California Press, 1978).

34 Sanford J. Ungar, *FBI* (Boston: Little, Brown, 1976).

35 Morris Janowitz, "Sociological Theory and Social Control," *American Journal of Sociology* 81 (July 1975): 82–85.

36 *Police Magazine* 2 (January 1979): 35–44.

37 Goldstein, *Policing a Free Society,* chap. 4.

38 Morton Bard, *Training Police as Specialists in Family Crisis Intervention* (Washington, D.C.: U.S. Government Printing Office, Department of Justice, 1970).

39 Goldstein, *Policing a Free Society,* chap. 6.

40 Arthur Niederhoffer, *Behind the Shield: The Police in Urban Society* (Garden City: Anchor Books, 1969), p. 1.

41 Leonard Ruchelman, *Police Politics: A Comparative Study of Three Cities* (Cambridge: Ballinger Publishing, 1974).

42 Ibid., p. 94.

43 National Advisory Commission on Criminal Justice Standards and Goals, *Police* (Washington, D.C.: U.S. Government Printing Office, 1973), p. 13.

44 U.S., Department of Justice, *Improving Police/Community Relations* (Washington, D.C.: U.S. Government Printing Office, 1973), p. 84.

45 K. C. Davis, *Police Discretion* (St. Paul: West Publishing, 1975), pp. 38–41.

46 National Advisory Commission, *Police,* p. 49.

47 President's Commission on Law Enforcement and Administration of Justice, *The Challenge of Crime in a Free Society* (New York: Avon Books, 1968), pp. 265, 272; American Bar Association, *Standards,* pp. 71–74.

48 President's Commission on Law Enforcement, *The Challenge of Crime,* pp. 274–277.

49 James M. Tien and Richard C. Larson, "Police Service Aides: Paraprofessionals for Police," *Journal of Criminal Justice* 6 (Summer 1978): 117–131.

50 Goldstein, *Policing A Free Society,* pp. 33–42; David J. Farmer, "The Future of Local Law Enforcement: The Federal Role," in *Crime and Justice in America,* eds., John T. O'Brien and Marvin Marcus (New York: Pergamon Press, 1979), p. 93.

51 Bittner, *Functions of the Police,* pp. 39–42.

52 James H. Tenzel, Lowell Storms, and Harvey Sweetwood, "Symbols and Behavior: An Experiment in Altering the Police Role," *Journal of Police Science and Administration* 4 (1976): 21–28.

CHAPTER **4**

ORGANIZATION AND
MANAGEMENT

75

Police services are delivered to the public through organizations. The quality of police service, or professionalism, depends to a great extent on how well a particular agency is organized and managed. The purpose of this chapter is to (1) describe the dominant features of American law enforcement organizations, (2) identify the major strengths and weaknesses of prevailing organizational styles, (3) critically evaluate contemporary standards of professional organization and management, and (4) discuss alternative organizational styles that have been proposed and tested.

THE MODERN BUREAUCRACY

Charles Perrow argues that organizations are "tools"; they are a means by which a certain task or tasks can be accomplished.[1] The respected text on *Municipal Police Administration* defines the purpose of organization as "the arrangement and utilization of total resources of personnel and materiel in such a way as to make easier and to expedite the attainment of specified objectives in an efficient, effective, economical, and harmonious manner."[2]

American law enforcement organizations are *bureaucracies*. They are not unique in this respect. Virtually all large organizations in modern society are bureaucracies. This includes private corporations, government regulatory agencies, universities, and so on. Thus, American law enforcement organizations share many characteristics—including both strengths and weaknesses—with other bureaucracies.

Law enforcement agencies in the United States are remarkably similar in terms of structure and management process. The only major differences are between the large and the very small departments: the large agency is a complex bureaucracy, arranged in a hierarchical fashion and managed by means of an authoritarian style of command.

Bureaucracy Defined

A bureaucracy includes the following elements:

1 A complex organization, performing many different tasks in pursuit of a common goal

2 The placement of particular specialized tasks into separate compartments (or "bureaus")

3 A hierarchical organizational structure, with a division of labor between workers, first-line supervisors, and head supervisors

4 A clear chain of command by which information flows upward through the organization and commands flow downward

5 Written rules for the performance of duties, designed to ensure uniformity and consistency

6 Career paths by which personnel move upward through the organization in an orderly fashion[3]

Bureaucracy is the dominant organizational form in modern society because it is viewed as being the most efficient means of accomplishing organizational goals. The primary achievement of bureaucracy is in being able to perform many specialized tasks simultaneously and to coordinate them in such a way as to achieve consistency of performance in the pursuit of a common goal.

Criticisms of Bureaucracy

Bureaucracy is widely regarded as a problem in modern society. The term "bureaucracy" is often used as an epithet (as in "It's all a bureaucratic mess"). According to Perrow, "The conventional criticisms of bureaucracy fall into two categories. First, they are said to be inflexible, inefficient, and in a time of rapid change, uncreative and unresponsive." The second major criticism is that bureaucracies "stifle the spontaneity, freedom, and self-realization of their employees."[4]

American police organizations have been accused of being uncreative and unresponsive to social change, particularly with regard to police-community relations. And they have been accused of failing to utilize the talents of rank-and-file police officers and failing to offer sufficient opportunities for career advancement.[5]

James Q. Wilson refers to the widespread discontent with modern organizations as the "bureaucracy problem." The key issue in this problem is "getting the front-line worker . . . to do 'the right thing'."[6] The main purpose of bureaucracy is precisely that: to get employees to do the right thing, to ensure consistent standards of performance.

The study of law enforcement organizations should focus on two aspects of the bureaucracy problem. First, it should examine the extent to which current organizational arrangements achieve the goal of ensuring consistent satisfactory performance. Second, it should examine the extent to which the bureaucracy itself is a part of the problem. That is, to what extent do current organizational arrangements impede good performance?

Principles of Organization

The modern bureaucracy is built around a set of principles of organization. Essentially the same set of principles have been applied to private corporations, the military, and other governmental organizations.

The leading exponent of applying the principles of organization to law enforcement organizations was O.W. Wilson. His textbook, *Police Administration,* first published in 1950, influenced an entire generation of police administrators. Wilson's principles of organization, as stated in the 1977 edition, are as follows:[7]

> **1** Tasks, similar or related in purpose, process, method, or clientele, should be grouped together in one or more units under the control of one person. In order to facilitate their assignment, these tasks may be divided according to (a) the time, (b) the place of their performance, and (c) the level of authority needed in their accomplishment.

2 Specialized units should be created only when overall departmental capability is thus significantly increased; they should not be created at the expense of reduced control and decreased general interest.

3 Lines of demarcation between the responsibilities of units should be clearly drawn by a precise definition of the duties of each, which should be made known to all members so that responsibility may be placed exactly. Such definition avoids duplication in execution and neglect resulting from the nonassignment of a duty.

4 Channels should be established through which information flows up and down and through which authority is delegated. These lines of control permit the delegation of authority, the placing of responsibility, the supervision of work, and the coordination of effort. Lines of control should be clearly defined and well understood by all members so that all may know to whom they are responsible and who, in turn, is responsible to them. Exceptions to routine communication of information through channels should be provided for emergency and unusual situations.

5 Structure and terminology should facilitate the understanding of the purposes and responsibilities of the organization by all its members.

6 Each individual, unit, and situation should be under the immediate control of one, and only one, person, thus achieving the principle of unity of command and avoiding the friction that results from duplication of direction and supervision.

7 The span of control of a supervisor should be large enough to provide economical supervision, but no more units or persons should be placed under the direct control of one person than he or she is able to manage.

8 Each task should be made the unmistakable duty of someone; responsibility for planning, execution, and control should be definitely placed on designated persons.

9 Supervision should be provided for every member of the organization and for every function or activity. (If the supervision is not immediately available at the actual level of execution, it should be obtainable through referral to a predesignated authority.)

10 Each assignment or duty should carry with it commensurate authority to fulfill the responsibility.

11 Persons to whom authority is delegated should be held accountable for the use made of it and for the failure to use it.

From Theory to Practice

The application of Wilson's principles of organization is illustrated by Figure 4.1 which represents the organizational chart of the Omaha, Nebraska, police department. The department has about 560 sworn officers, and the organizational chart represents the result of thirteen years of "reform" involving the application of Wilson's principles.

The chart illustrates the principle of the grouping of similar tasks. Six different units report directly to the chief. Each unit consists of a particular type of task or tasks: uniform field services, criminal investigation, technical services, administrative services, inspectional services, and community relations. Patrol services are subdivided according to time (A, B, and C shifts) and place (by sectors and patrol areas).

The degree of specialization represents a compromise between the needs of the job and the resources of the department. Criminal investigation, for example, is divided into four general areas of activity. There is a sufficient volume of work to create a separate homicide and assault unit, but there is neither sufficient demand nor resources to specialize further (larger departments, with more resources and a higher volume of work often have separate homicide units).

The chart clearly indicates the lines of demarcation of responsibility for each unit and the channels of communication for information and commands. Each unit is headed by one officer and there is a rational pattern of assignment of unit heads: bureaus are commanded by deputy chiefs, sections are commanded by captains (with some exceptions), units are commanded by lieutenants. The span of control is limited: the chief directly commands six subordinates; the Uniform Field Bureau and Criminal Investigation heads directly command four subordinates each, etc.

The structure makes it possible to pinpoint responsibility and hold particular individuals accountable for particular successes or failures, such as an especially high clearance rate for a particular crime, or a failure in patrol coverage at a particular time and place.

The Quasi-Military Style

American law enforcement organizations are frequently characterized as being quasi military because they share certain characteristics in common with military organizations. According to Egon Bittner, "the conception of the police as a quasi-military institution with a war-like mission plays an important part in the structuring of police work in modern American departments."[8]

The most visible similarities between the police and the military are the use of uniforms and rank designations such as sergeant, lieutenant, and captain, which are borrowed from the military. The police and the military are the only two organizations in American society legally authorized to use coercive (including deadly) force.

The quasi-military nature of the American police also refers to the authoritarian style of command. Like the military, decisions are made by top commanders and communicated to lower-ranking personnel in the form of orders. Failure to obey orders can result in disciplinary action. The management process, in other words, is not democratic in nature. There is no discussion or debate about policy involving personnel at the lower ranks.

Criticisms of the Quasi-Military Style Many experts regard the quasi-military style as the source of numerous police problems. They argue that the authoritarian style of command is fundamentally at odds with the democratic principles of American society and has a detrimental effect on lower-ranking personnel. Rank-and-file police officers are treated like robots whose duty is simply to follow orders. This approach, it is argued, fails to provide sufficient job satisfaction for police officers.[9]

The authoritarian style of command is seen by critics as being incompatible with professionalism. In other occupations, professionalism is based on peer review. The performance of individual practitioners is judged by other practitioners. Individual practitioners are expected to exercise their own professional judgment in their work. The authoritarian, quasi-military style limits professional judgment through a rigid command-and-control system.[10]

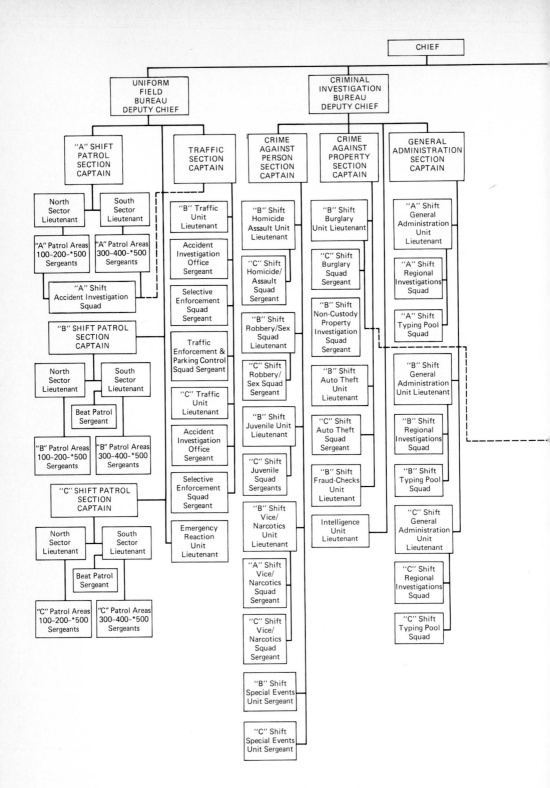

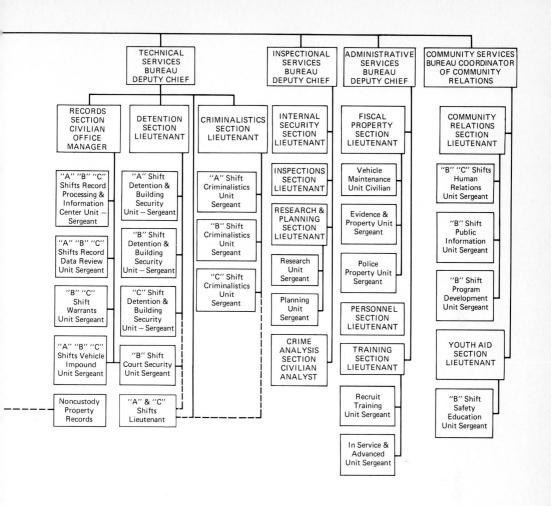

FIGURE 4.1
Organizational chart. *(Omaha Police Division, Standard Operating Procedures, vol. 1, 1980.)*

Finally, critics argue that the quasi-military style encourages a war-on-crime mentality among the police. This outlook encourages officers to view criminals as "the enemy" and to think that any tactic is justified in fighting the enemy. Critics point out that the police, unlike the military, are created to serve a civilian population and that all civilians, including criminal suspects, retain basic constitutional rights. The war-on-crime mentality tends to blur the distinction between criminal suspects and law-abiding citizens.[11]

Organization and Professionalism

The nature of American police organizations is directly related to the dominant conception of American police professionalism. As Jerome Skolnick argues, professionalism acquired a special meaning in American policing. It is fundamentally different from the meaning of professionalism in other occupations.[12]

Police professionalism has been defined in terms of managerial efficiency. This primarily involves the application of the principles of organization set forth by O. W. Wilson. The professional police department is one with a rational organizational chart, a clear chain of command, and a centralized command-and-control style. One of the major goals of professionalization is the subordination of the individual officer to a strict set of controls, usually in the form of written operating procedures.

In their histories of the American police, Fogelson and Walker argue that this style of professionalism developed as a strategy to eliminate the corruption and inefficiency that prevailed in the nineteenth century. The process of professionalization involved the slow but steady application of the principles of organization first articulated by August Vollmer and then more fully developed by O. W. Wilson.[13]

Professionalization versus Bureaucratization Professionalism is not always compatible with the bureaucratic organizational form. Professionalism involves the exercise of individual judgment. The individual practitioner acquires professional skill through an extensive period of formal training. The professional has a monopoly on expertise, and outsiders are not considered qualified to evaluate performance. Only other professionals—peers with similar training and expertise—are able to evaluate performance.

Bureaucracy takes a very different approach. It seeks to subject the individual worker to a strict set of formal controls. These controls include rules of procedure, formal evaluation of performance by supervisors, and the right of clients to appeal decisions. The bureaucrat works "by the book," while the professional works on the basis of discretion.

The development of American police organizations has involved a process of bureaucratization rather than professionalization. This has included the growth of more complex organizational structures and more specific rules and procedures to control police discretion. Critics such as Skolnick argue that the bureaucratic form is incompatible with true professionalism. Alternative organizational forms, such as team policing and the democratic model, are intended to introduce a truer form of professionalism into American policing. These alternatives are discussed later in this chapter.[14]

Management

The organizational chart depicts the formal structural elements of the organization. The day-to-day dynamics of the organization depend upon how it is managed. There are different styles of management. Textbooks such as O. W. Wilson's *Police Management* offer prescriptions for the proper approach, and courses on organization and management are taught in most criminal justice or law enforcement college programs.

The Functions of Management   The primary functions of management include planning, organizing, coordination, and control.[15] Planning involves determining the basic goals of the organization, establishing priorities, and developing strategies for attainment of the established goals. Organizing involves primarily arranging the personnel and resources of the organization to facilitate the achievement of established goals. Coordination involves ensuring that all parts of the organization work together harmoniously to achieve the common set of goals. Control involves delegating responsibility for particular tasks and maintaining an effective system of supervision to ensure that tasks are performed in a satisfactory manner.

The delegation of responsibility is one of the key elements in the management process. The modern bureaucracy, which involves the simultaneous performance of many different specialized tasks, depends upon the delegation of responsibility to lower-ranking personnel. How much responsibility is delegated and how it is delegated is one of the central issues in management theory.

Management Styles   Four different styles of management can be identified.[16] One is the *exploitative-authoritative* style, in which leaders do not trust their employees and motivate them primarily through threats and coercion. Most of the communication in the organization flows downward; employees are expected to follow orders with little opportunity for input. J. Edgar Hoover's leadership is an example of the exploitative-authoritative style. Many observers believe that William Parker adopted a similar approach with the Los Angeles Police Department.[17]

A second style is characterized as *benevolent-authoritative*. This approach is less extreme than the previous one. Power is concentrated at the top of the organization, but there is some opportunity for two-way communication. Discipline includes some positive rewards and attention to the needs of employees.

A third approach is the *consultative* style. This is a more open management system. Leaders demonstrate trust in their employees by allowing them some participation in management decisions. There is effective communication between all levels of the organization. While basic policy decisions are made at the top, responsibility for implementation rests with employees at lower levels.

The fourth approach, the *participative-group* style, is an extreme version of the consultative style. There is a high degree of trust among members of the organization. Decisions are made in a participatory manner involving employees from all levels. Leaders assume responsibility primarily for coordinating the activities of the organization as a whole.

Shanahan, Hunger, and Wheelen examined management styles in police departments in 1976. They surveyed 171 police officials attending the FBI's National Police Academy in January 1976. The subjects were asked to describe their own organization in terms of eight different dimensions:

1 Leadership processes
2 Motivational forces
3 Communication processes
4 Interaction-influence processes
5 Decision-making processes
6 Goal-setting (or ordering) processes
7 Control processes
8 Performance goals and training

The results indicated that the officers placed their departments at about the midpoint of the consultative style of management. This represented a significant change from a 1974 survey, which placed most departments in the upper range of the benevolent-authoritative style.[18] The survey suggests that the stereotype of the quasi-military police department may be exaggerated and that American police departments may be more open, with greater consultation and flow of communication than is generally believed.

CIVIL SERVICE FORMAT

Personnel systems are an important added dimension of the formal arrangements of American police organizations. Most agencies are governed by some form of civil service personnel system. Civil service is based on the idea that personnel decisions should be based on objective qualifications rather than favoritism, with written specifications for the recruitment, promotion, and discipline of personnel.

Civil service was designed to eliminate the influence of partisan politics in public employment. By the 1820s American politics was based on the spoils system: victorious politicians rewarded their friends with government jobs. Civil service was designed to end these abuses. The Pendleton Act of 1883 introduced civil service procedures to employment with the federal government. In that same year New York became the first state to impose such procedures on local governments. The New York City Police Department was the first to operate under a civil service system.[19]

Contemporary Civil Service Systems

Personnel practices in local government today are typically governed by formal procedures specified either by state law or local ordinance. In 80 percent of the cities surveyed by the Justice Department, ultimate authority over personnel procedures rests with a *board* or *commission* consisting of three to five persons. Board members are typically appointed by the chief executive (mayor or city manager) of the government unit for a specified term. The board sets basic policy and hires a *personnel director* to administer policy on a day-to-day policy.

Civil service boards are responsible for the following aspects of personnel policy:[20]

1 Development of job descriptions and pay scales
2 Development of recruitment criteria
3 Development and administration of recruitment tests
4 Certification of qualified applicants
5 Development of promotional criteria
6 Development and administration of promotional tests
7 Development of disciplinary procedures
8 Final review of disciplinary appeals

The purpose of these procedures is to ensure that decisions are based on qualifications and merit (e.g., test scores) rather than favoritism. Civil service procedures were designed to limit the personal discretion of top police officials. An important consequence, however, is that the ability of top officials to reward excellence is also limited. A police chief cannot suddenly promote an officer who has performed well. This *lack of administrative flexibility* in personnel decisions is an important aspect of police organizations.

Rank Structure

Another dimension of the inflexibility is the rank structure. Civil service systems specify the various ranks, the job descriptions of each rank, and the procedures for promotion or demotion.

Dorothy Guyot points out that there are two different types of rank systems: rank-in-job and rank-in-person. Under a *rank-in-job* system, an employee carries a title and responsibilities while assigned to a particular job; if demoted or reassigned, the employee loses both the title and the responsibilities. In private industry, for example, a person might be promoted to assistant vice president for marketing. That employee loses the title and the responsibilities if demoted or reassigned. Management has considerable flexibility in making these decisions.[21]

Police departments, under civil service procedures, use a *rank-in-person* system. Under this system, the employee carries the title almost permanently. An officer promoted to the rank of sergeant retains that title until either promoted or demoted. And civil service procedures make promotion and demotion exceptionally difficult. Furthermore, while holding the rank of sergeant, the employee is restricted to those tasks defined as sergeant's tasks in job descriptions. As a result, a police chief or other top official cannot promote, demote, or reassign officers at will.

Guyot argues that "an impressive list of management problems . . . are exacerbated by the prevailing rank structure of police departments." Because the structure is sanctioned by civil service law (and reinforced by union contracts), trying to change personnel procedures in American police departments is like "bending granite" according to Guyot.[22]

The major problems imposed on police organizations by civil service systems may be summarized as follows:

1 Lack of management *flexibility* in personnel decisions, especially the limited ability to promote and demote.

2 Lack of *incentives* for individual officers: exceptional performance cannot be easily rewarded through promotion or pay increases.

3 *Insularity:* since departments generally promote only from within, there is an absence of fresh perspective and new ideas.

INFORMAL POLICE ORGANIZATION

The organizational chart and civil service procedures constitute the *formal* aspects of police organizations. The actual day-to-day operations, however, are affected by important *informal* aspects. The distinction between formal arrangements and informal procedures is characteristic of most large organizations.

Reiss and Bordua point out that "In principle and in rhetoric, a police organization is one characterized by strict subordination, by a rigid chain of command, and more doubtfully, by a lack of formal provision for consultation between ranks."[23] But they warn against an uncritical acceptance of this view. Actual operations may be very different. Guyot suggests that "Within police departments, as in any formal organization, there are subdivisions, hierarchies, status groupings, and other formal arrangements. There are also informal relationships, cliques, friendship patterns, and temporary collaborations." A police department, Guyot continues, "is not a sack of potatoes."[24] There are important distinctions to be made between individuals and groups within the department.

Work-Group Analysis

One way to analyze the informal arrangements inside a department is through work groups. Individuals performing the same task and working together on a daily basis form identifiable groups. Different groups often compete with each other for status and rewards.

The detective force constitutes one of the most important work groups within a police department. Traditionally, detectives have enjoyed the highest status, especially in relation to patrol officers. Not only is criminal investigation viewed as "real" police work, but detectives enjoy the considerable privileges of working in civilian clothes and being free to manage their own time. Patrol duty is generally regarded as a low-status assignment.[25]

Rivalry between different work groups impairs the efficiency of police work. In his participant-observer study of the Philadelphia police, Rubinstein found that patrol officers and detectives compete rather than cooperate. Each officer jealously guards his or her own information about criminal activity. Sharing information creates the possibility that another officer or unit might get the credit for an important arrest.[26]

Other forms of information do not flow through the organization by way of the proper channels. Lower-ranking officers, for example, withhold information about problems that might embarrass them in the eyes of their supervisors. Sergeants often cover up mistakes by officers under their command because it would reflect poorly on their own performance. At the same time, information flows to friends in the organization, even though these people would not normally receive such information through the regular channels. Gossip is a process by which sensitive information is passed to people who would not or even should not have it.

Cliques

Police departments are also pervaded by groups of friends, commonly called "cliques." These patterns of friendship may be rooted in shared experience. The folklore of policing consistently affirms that police officers develop extremely close relationships with their partners. Often this is the result of shared danger and the bonds of trust that develop when two or more people find that they must rely solely on each other in dangerous situations. Some observers suggest that police officers have closer relationships with their partners than with their spouses.

Friendship patterns assume a larger importance in the internal politics of the department. Westley found that a police chief routinely faces difficult or sensitive tasks. The chief is forced to "maintain a group of favorites within the department whom he can depend on to handle delicate assignments."[27] Thus, there exists an informal channel of communication and command that is unrelated to the formal channels indicated by the organizational chart. The chief maintains this informal structure of communication and command by rewarding friends. One of the most important rewards available is assignment to the high-status duty of detective. Enemies can be punished by assignment to low-status duties of records or training. Assignment to various duties (as opposed to promotion in rank) is generally not governed by civil service procedures.

EVALUATING ORGANIZATIONAL STRUCTURES

The effectiveness of prevailing organizational arrangements is a matter of debate. Two basic schools of thought exist. The dominant school adheres to the principles of O. W. Wilson. According to this view, continued improvement in policing depends upon the application and refinement of Wilson's principles. While there is some disagreement over details of organization and management, there is a consensus about the value of a centralized bureaucratic structure. The alternative school of thought argues that the centralized bureaucracy has become an impediment to progress. Members of this school offer various proposals for decentralizing the structure of law enforcement organizations.

The debate between these two schools of thought hinges on evaluations of the prevailing form of organizational arrangements. In the following section we review the positive and negative features of these arrangements.

Positive Contributions

The centralized, quasi-military, bureaucratic form of organization developed as a solution to the problems of the nineteenth-century police. Fogelson and Walker argue that it was a strategy to both reduce external political control and impose internal discipline.[28] To a great extent, it succeeded in achieving many of its goals; the contrast between American police departments in 1900 and 1980 is striking. This is not to say that all problems have been eliminated, but remarkable progress is evident.

Improvement is particularly notable in the area of police officer behavior. Physical brutality and corruption are two problems that have been greatly reduced. The 1931 Wickersham Commission report found that brutality—the third degree—was a pervasive part of American policing.[29] By the 1970s, despite many allegations of brutality, only isolated instances of misuse of physical force were proven. A number of departments also succeeded in reducing—and in some cases virtually eliminating—corruption.

The use of deadly force provides a recent example of how bureaucratic procedures impose controls on police officer behavior. James Fyfe's study of police shootings in New York City illustrates how two techniques of bureaucratic control—written policy guidelines and administrative review of individual incidents—helped reduce firearms incidents by 35 percent.[30]

Similar techniques have been used to control police behavior in other areas of police work. In many cases, police departments have been forced to develop their own internal controls as a result of external pressure. The Supreme Court's decision in the *Miranda* case, for example, forced departments to provide guidelines and better training and supervision for its officers.

Improvement is also evident in the area of professional autonomy. The most blatant forms of political interference have been eliminated. Recruits are selected on the basis of modest levels of qualifications and subjected to steadily increasing amounts of training. Officers reaching the higher command levels have a reasonable amount of experience and have demonstrated at least some level of competence.

Perhaps most important, policing has developed a sense of professional identity. Police work is seen as a career with a mission. That mission involves the duty to protect and serve the public in a fair and impartial manner. Finally, law enforcement officials have a commitment to their own continued professional development.

Negative Features

Criticism of the prevailing form of organization emerged in the 1960s. Richard Myren wrote a prophetic article on police management in 1960, anticipating many subsequent critics. Jerome Skolnick questioned the prevailing concept of police professionalism in 1967. Egon Bittner and others challenged the appropriateness of the quasi-military style.[31]

According to the critics, the negative features of current organizational arrangements fall into four categories: the quasi-military style, police-community relations, police officer morale, and communication and control.

The quasi-military style, as we have already noted, encourages a war-on-crime mentality that allows officers to view citizens as the enemy. It also encourages an authoritarian approach to management which is contrary to the idea of professionalism as it exists in other occupations.[32]

The centralized bureaucratic police organization, according to the critics, is unable to respond effectively to the police-community relations problem. Like many large bureaucratic organizations, police departments tend to turn inward. The organization becomes defensive in the face of criticism. Isolation from and indifference to the clients is seen as one of the inherent problems of modern bureaucracy.[33] Innovative approaches to policing are required. Yet police departments seem unable to institute significant change. As Perrow notes, the inability to change in the face of a changing environment is seen as one of the major problems of the modern bureaucracy.[34]

Low morale among rank-and-file officers is also a major problem. Many critics view the organizational arrangements as the source of this problem. Morale suffers in part because rank-and-file officers have little opportunity to participate in the direction of their work. Officers are expected to follow orders, not make policy. Ironically, this problem is often most severe in the more professionalized departments; these departments usually have the most elaborate forms of bureaucratic control, which subject the officers to detailed rules of procedure.

The personnel systems of police bureaucracies are generally punishment-centered.[35] Officers can be punished for violating established procedures, and the rules of procedure are often very extensive. Yet there are few ways in which an officer can be rewarded for good performance. Police personnel systems have generally failed to develop procedures for evaluating routine police performance and identifying and rewarding good performance. In the punishment-centered bureaucracy, officers tend to concentrate on staying out of trouble.

Finally, morale suffers because existing personnel systems provide only limited opportunities for career advancement. All officers enter at the rank of police officer and advance either by assignment to criminal investigation or by promotion to higher rank. Detective assignments are few in number. Promotional opportunities are equally scarce. Under existing civil service systems officers must serve a certain number of years in rank before becoming eligible to take a promotional exam. And in most departments, seniority counts heavily toward promotion.[36] Thus, many officers face the prospect of remaining at their present rank for many years with little or no prospect for career advancement.

The final criticism is that they do not fulfill their own objectives, particularly with regard to communication and control. According to Wilson's principles, communication flows through the organization in an efficient and orderly manner. Information flows upward and command flows downward. Because the organization is structured in a rational way, each person has access—or the ability to gain access—to needed information.

In actual practice, as we have already seen, this is not necessarily the case. Sometimes information is deliberately withheld from superiors by their subordinates.[37] Frequently, top officials do not know what is going on in their own organization. At the same time, important information can be withheld from subordinates. In departments managed in the exploitative-authoritarian style, top officials control and manipulate their subordinates by selectively withholding important information.[38]

Equally serious, information does not necessarily flow smoothly across the organization in a lateral direction. As Rubinstein points out patrol officers jealously guard information on criminal events, hoping to make a successful arrest rather than share it with detectives. It is not clear that officers on one shift communicate with officers on other shifts assigned to the same area. The LEAA report on *Crime Analysis in Support of Patrol* concluded that most departments do not make effective use of the various data that are collected.[39]

Gerald Caiden argues that many departments suffer from "overbureaucratization."[40] In these cases, the structure and procedures are so complex that they interfere with efficient operations. Communication is difficult because there are too many specialized units. Decision making is inhibited because there are so many levels of authority that it takes a long time to obtain approval of any decision.

Excessive paperwork (red tape) is another feature of overbureaucratization. An emphasis on written records is one of the main features of the modern bureaucracy. Written records are a technique designed to ensure accountability of individual employees and provide documentation of overall performance of the organization. At some point, however, paperwork becomes dysfunctional. Preparation of reports consumes too much time and diverts time and energy from an employee's basic task. Police officers regularly complain about excessive paperwork.

Contemporary police organizational arrangements also do not necessarily achieve their objectives in terms of control. In theory the bureaucratic structure and process provide close supervision of all employees. The concept of the "span of control" is designed to ensure that one supervisor is not responsible for too many people.[41] In actual practice, however, close supervision in American police departments is largely a matter of appearance. Officers generally work alone or in pairs. The style of supervision varies from sergeant to sergeant. In some cases there is close supervision; in other cases there is virtually none.[42]

The primary technique of control involves written rules and records. Rules of procedure provide guidelines for officers, while written records provide evidence of activity. Several problems result from this system. This approach, as we have already noted, is punishment-centered. Officers are more likely to be punished for violating a rule than rewarded for performing well. Also, rules invite evasion. Officers can become more concerned with evading the rules than with performing well. Rules that are too detailed become unworkable.

TEAM POLICING

By the late 1960s, discontent with the shortcomings of the quasi-military organizational form stimulated a search for alternatives. Unquestionably, the catalyst for this search was the police-community relations crisis. Four years of rioting (1964–1968) in urban centers focused public attention on the police and focused professional attention upon the organizational form.

Frances Bish points out that "Proposals for organizational reform generally imply some assumed relationship between organizational arrangements and performance. By altering organizational arrangements, it is hoped that we can, somehow, improve public service delivery and/or otherwise 'make citizens better off'."[43] Recent proposals for organizational reform fall into several categories. At one extreme is the call for radically restructuring departments and decentralizing command responsibility. A less extreme approach is the concept of team policing. More moderate reforms call either for decentralizing responsibility within the existing organizational framework or developing a more consultative management style.

Team policing emerged as a fad in American policing in the 1970s. Borrowed from the English,[44] it was first attempted in the United States by the Syracuse police department in 1968. By 1974 as many as 60 police departments had attempted some version of team policing.[45]

It is important to note that many police departments often applied the *label* to changes that represented only slight variations from traditional practice. As a result, there is much confusion about team policing and its impact. True team policing is indicated by the program elements discussed below. Particular team-policing experiments should be evaluated in terms of the extent to which they contain all or most of these program elements.

The LEAA National Evaluation Program report on *Neighborhood Team Policing* identified four different types of team-policing programs:[46]

1 *Basic patrol teams,* involving "the reorganization of departments into teams responsible for basic preventive patrol, radio dispatch service and traffic duties." Team responsibilities do not include criminal investigation or community relations.

2 *Patrol-investigative teams,* with follow-up responsibilities for criminal investigation.

3 *Patrol–community service teams,* with responsibilities for community relations.

4 *Full-service teams,* as the name suggests, involves giving responsibility for all basic police services (patrol, investigation, community relations) to decentralized, geographically based teams.

The full-service team approach, often called "neighborhood team policing," is the most complex and important type of team policing.

Neighborhood Team Policing

Neighborhood team policing consists of the following program elements:[47]

1 *Decentralization.* Major decisions about police policy regarding law enforcement, order maintenance, service, and community relations are to be made by middle-level supervisors in charge of particular teams.

2 *Geographic focus.* Teams are assigned to particular geographic areas, previously recognized as neighborhoods with some degree of self-identity. The geographic focus is enhanced by the stability of assignment of police officers. Officers remain assigned to a particular team for extended periods of time.

3 *Unity of police services.* Under the full-service approach, the team assumes responsibility for all basic police services in the area. For example, follow-up investigations are handled by team members, not by specialists working out of police headquarters.

4 *Team or task-force decision making.* Decisions about policy and specific operations are made by team members on the basis of a high degree of group interaction.

5 *Community input.* The team engages in a high degree of interaction with residents of the neighborhood, and policy reflects the input of citizens.

Anticipated Advantages   Neighborhood team policing is designed to deal with all the major criticisms of the traditional quasi-military organizational form. The decentralized, neighborhood focus, together with increased community input, is designed to improve police-community relations. In theory, the team members will be able to develop policy that reflects the special needs of the neighborhood.

At the same time, the morale of police officers is expected to improve, since they will have greater participation in the decision-making process and, it is argued, will become more fully professional.

Finally, communication within the department will be improved. Important policy decisions will be made within the team, and information will not have to flow through an extended chain of command. It is also anticipated that this improved communication will enhance the effectiveness of the department in carrying out its responsibilities. Patrol officers, who are in effect the eyes and ears of the department, will be able to utilize the information they gather about the neighborhood. Presumably, information will flow more freely, and this will have a positive impact on policy.

Evaluating Team Policing

In theory, team policing appears to be the answer to many serious problems. How effective is it in practice?

Answering this question is difficult, in part, because many of the experiments labeled "team policing" fail to contain all the main program elements. Sherman, Milton and Kelley evaluated seven team-policing experiments for the Police Foundation. Only two—in Holyoke, Massachusetts, and Venice (a section of Los Angeles), California—included most of the program elements. Others either did not plan or planned but failed to include important elements.[48]

Evaluation of team policing is also difficult because of a lack of meaningful data. The National Evaluation Project report found "many gaps in our knowledge about team policing." For example, "None of the Basic Patrol Teams have collected the kinds of evaluative information which would make it possible for us to judge whether or not the program was effective."[49] The Police Foundation report also concluded that "The data are far too scant" to determine whether team policing had a significant effect on crime, community relations, morale, or productivity.[50]

Cincinnati COMSEC Experiment   The most thoroughly evaluated team-policing project is the Community Sector Team Policing Experiment (COMSEC) in Cincinnati, Ohio. The evaluators reported that "no easy conclusions" could be drawn about COMSEC. Positive accomplishments in some areas were balanced by problems in other areas.[51]

COMSEC was launched in March 1971, but it was not a success. It was reorganized in March 1973 with the cooperation of the Police Foundation. The formal evaluation of COMSEC lasted from March 1973 until September 1975. The COMSEC experiment was carried out in Police District 1, which has a resident population of 35,000 (out of a total city population of 500,000) but attracts an estimated 250,000 persons each day to the central business district. This area accounts for 25 percent of the reported crime in the city.

Under COMSEC, Police District 1 was divided into six sectors, each with its own team. These six sectors included:

1 Two predominantly black, high-crime, low-income residential areas
2 A low-income, mixed residential and business area
3 A predominantly white, middle-class residential area
4 A racially mixed (black and Appalachian white), low-income, high-crime, largely residential area
5 The central business district of Cincinnati

The impact of team policing on different kinds of neighborhoods could therefore be evaluated.

COMSEC contained the basic elements of neighborhood team policing: "Responsibility for essentially all police services within a given neighborhood was delegated to a team of officers who were rarely reassigned." Moreover, "The program stressed informal interaction and increased communications among team members." The program had two main goals: "To reduce crime and to improve police-community relations."

With respect to *crime,* COMSEC "was more successful in reducing burglary than policing in other parts of the city, and did as well in controlling other kinds of crime." With respect to *police-community relations,* citizen satisfaction with police services remained at the already high pre-COMSEC level. Fewer citizens felt "very unsafe" walking at night in their neighborhoods, and citizens believed that the police were more responsive to their calls for service. With respect to police officer *morale,* "officers reported positive changes in the breadth of their jobs . . . in their independence, and in their influence over decisions."

However, many of these gains were lost at the end of eighteen months. The COMSEC experiment coincided with a corruption scandal in the Cincinnati police department. Although no officers assigned to COMSEC were implicated in the scandal, the Police Foundation evaluators believed that the scandal (which did implicate the chief of police) adversely affected the project. Morale within the experiment declined, and crime appeared to be increasing toward the end.

Implementing Team Policing

The Police Foundation study of seven team policing experiments identified three major problems that caused experiments to either fail altogether or achieve only partial success.

1 Mid-management of the departments, seeing team policing as a threat to their power, subverted and, in some cases, actively sabotaged the plans.

2 The dispatching technology did not permit the patrols to remain in their neighborhoods, despite the stated intentions of adjusting that technology to the pilot projects.

3 The patrols never received a sufficiently clear definition of how their behavior and role should differ from that of a regular patrol; at the same time, they were considered an elite group by their peers who often resented not having been chosen for the project.[52]

In other words, team-policing experiments suffered from a lack of effective planning. Often goals were not clearly formulated by project leaders; in other cases goals were not communicated to middle-management supervisors and patrol officers. As a result, some officers felt confused and uncertain, while others felt threatened.

The problems related to dispatching technology were potentially more serious. In retrospect, it is clear that a highly centralized organization cannot be suddenly decentralized. Genuine decentralization may require not only extensive planning but also substantive and expensive changes in the technology of command and control.

Team policing represents an attempt to reorient the role of police officers. Here again, serious problems were encountered. In part it is difficult to change the orientation of employees who have been socialized into a certain role concept, especially when that concept is supported by a lengthy tradition of police history. Moreover, the attitudes and behavior of police officers are related to their career expectations. Team-policing projects were sabotaged in some cases by middle-level officers who felt their careers were threatened by the new approach to policing.

Team Policing and Accountability

The evaluators of COMSEC noted a more serious problem related to accountability. As the experiment progressed, some top police officials had second thoughts about team policing. "Although they wanted to be responsive to the community and also to provide their officers with a more satisfying work experience, senior officers feared that with the promised autonomy and reduction in central control, their officers might become less productive or even corrupt."[53]

In short, "autonomy and control were competing issues." The COMSEC experience, and team policing in general, dramatizes the inherent dilemmas of police accountability in a democratic society. Autonomy is a strategy for achieving greater responsiveness to the public. Yet centralized control is a device for ensuring conformity to the law.

There are limits to how much responsiveness to the public is tolerable. A majority of the public, for example, might demand suppression of the rights of a minority; yet this would be unconstitutional. Under team policing, different teams might develop very different law enforcement policies. One team, for example, might take a hard line on vice offenses, while another might take a tolerant approach. Given the concept of equal protection of the laws, can such divergent policies be permitted?

With regard to police performance standards, team policing dramatizes a similar dilemma. Centralized control has been a strategy for eliminating corruption, controlling discretion, and generally raising standards. The price, however, has been paid in terms of officer morale. Team policing, in its attempt to improve morale by reducing centralized control, raises the possibility of a parallel reduction in accountability.

The Democratic Model

John Angell has proposed a more radical version of team policing which he calls the democratic model. It remains a theoretical concept since it has not been adopted by any American police department.[54] Angell proposes a radical decentralization of police organizations, accompanied by new techniques for accountability and control of police officer behavior. In many important respects, the democratic model is closer to the style of professionalism that is found in other occupations.

Under the democratic model a police department would be divided into three basic sections. The *General Services Section* would be responsible for basic police services; it would be subdivided into teams assigned to particular geographic areas. The *Coordination and Information Section* would provide a minimal amount of centralized management; policy making, however, would remain with the General Services Section. Finally, a *Specialized Services Section* would make available specialists in certain areas (juvenile, traffic, criminal investigation) as needed and as requested by teams in the General Services Section.

The concept is especially democratic with respect to personnel policies. Angell proposed abolishing rank designations and rigid pay scales. "The General Services Section would consist entirely of police generalists, who would have equal rank and would have no formally assigned supervisor. The leadership is expected to develop situationally as the circumstances dictate. In other words, team members can determine who will lead them, and the person who occupies the leadership role may change as the situation changes." Additionally, salaries would be flexible and pay increases would be based on merit. The evaluation of an officer's performance would be made by other team members.

The democratic model involves restructuring police organizations along the lines of other professions. The abolition of hierarchy and substitution of team decision making and peer review are intended to achieve certain goals. First, it would allow officers greater participation in decision making. Second, it would allow greater opportunities for career development. Individual officers could specialize in areas where they found themselves to be competent. Presumably, greater job satisfaction would result. Third, peer review of performance would produce an effective system of self-discipline. Officers would be responsible for the performance of other team members. This would move the police in the direction of other professions, where there is a collective sense of responsibility for the overall performance of the profession.

Angell's proposal raises many challenging questions.[55] Because no department has adopted the democratic model, there is no evidence on how well it might work. One basic question involves implementation: Would it be possible to convert an existing department to the democratic model? Important features of most police departments are sustained by law (for example, civil service systems) or by legally binding union contracts. Large organizations are extremely resistant to change.[56] A related implementation question involves individual police officers. Would it be possible to reorient a group of veteran officers to a new system of job performance and discipline? The democratic model involves not just a different formal structure but a different set of expectations and behaviors as well.

Another basic question involves the same problems of accountability raised by team policing. With decision making about policy radically decentralized into geographic teams, would there be a sufficient degree of consistency between different teams in one urban community? Or does radical decentralization create a problem of great differences in policy and practice from one neighborhood to another? A related accountability problem involves the conduct of individual officers. Angell's proposal calls for professional peer review. What happens, however, if peer review fails? What mechanisms do the public have to seek effective review of police performance?

Patrol Decentralization

Several police departments have adopted some of the elements of team policing by decentralizing authority over patrol operations. Wayne A. Kerstetter examined patrol decentralization experiments in five cities: Los Angeles; Santa Ana, California; Hartford, Connecticut; Charlotte, North Carolina; and Portland, Oregon. He points out that "the decentralization of authority is the key structural element in team policing." The cases studied involved decentralization of authority to determine:

1 The number of police officers to work each shift
2 The particular duty assignments of these officers
3 The enforcement tactics, strategy, and priorities (within certain limits)[57]

Los Angeles Basic Car Plan   The most significant experiment in patrol decentralization involved the Basic Car Plan in the Los Angeles Police Department. It was particularly important considering the size of the department (about 8000 sworn officers), its political visibility, and its reputation as a department with one of the most highly centralized command structures. Gerald Caiden called the Basic Car Plan "the most comprehensive and radical [decentralization] of any large-scale urban police force anywhere in recent history." Daniel Skoler called it "an important and historic [step] for American police technology."[58]

The Basic Car Plan represented a modified version of neighborhood team policing. Each "basic car" was permanently assigned to a certain geographic neighborhood.

Regional commanders were given a high degree of authority over particular duty assignments and enforcement tactics. Meanwhile, existing police districts were consolidated into regional bureaus and placed under the command of deputy chiefs. Each deputy chief had a high degree of autonomy and was, in effect, the chief of police for that area. Finally, central headquarters was reorganized, and some support operations were decentralized into the regional bureaus.

The decentralization of the Los Angeles police did not happen all at once. Instead, it occurred over a six-year period, often on a trial-and-error basis. The turning point was a speech by Chief Ed Davis to the 1970 IACP convention. He told his fellow chiefs that "The managers in police service have been carrying the ball for too long. It is time that they started being the coach, helping their men learn how to block and tackle, how to run with the ball, and how to stay in shape."[59] In short, top managers should be responsible for overall policy and direction but middle managers should assume responsibility for operational decisions.

Evaluation   Kerstetter evaluated patrol decentralization experiments in five communities, including Los Angeles. He conducted in-depth interviews with chief executives, senior managers, and middle managers and supplemented these interviews with observation of police operations and attendance at community meetings.

The most important impact of decentralization seemed to occur in the area of police-community relations. In the view of police managers, decentralization "facilitated responsiveness to the community by identifying, both within the department and for the community, one person who was to be held responsible for policing a particular area." In short, decentralization enhanced accountability.[60]

A second area of impact involved organizational development. Decentralization appeared to help middle managers (lieutenants and captains) develop the skills necessary for their new responsibilities. Decision making was facilitated because decision makers were closer to the street-level problems. Decentralization appeared to improve morale by providing greater opportunities for career development among younger officers.

With respect to crime, the impact of patrol decentralization was difficult to assess. Kerstetter's survey did not involve a detailed analysis of the variables affecting changes in criminal activity. He did find, however, that police managers believed that decentralization led to greater police-citizen cooperation and that this facilitated crime prevention and apprehension.

Decentralization is not without its costs. Kerstetter found that it led to a sense of fragmentation and that officers felt they were part of separate departments rather than a single, cohesive unit. There also appeared to be a problem with respect to consistency of policy and standards. The problem mainly focused on small issues, such as different units' policies toward tardiness and uniforms.

Finally, decentralization introduced the inevitable problems of coordination and control. Information did not flow smoothly among different geographic units. The development of different operational strategies for different areas is one of the primary goals of decentralization. Coordination between units, however, becomes problematic. This is aggravated by the fact that decentralization involves the deliberate loss of management control by top level managers. This problem is inherent in all decentralization or team-policing strategies. The techniques for balancing top-level control and lower-level autonomy need to be developed.

Task-Force Policy Making

An alternative approach to changing the decision-making process in police organizations is the use of policy-making task forces. The formal structure of the organization remains unchanged and ultimate authority for decisions remains with the same officials. But the task-force approach involves officers from different ranks in making policy recommendations.

The most notable example of the use of task forces occurred in Kansas City. In 1971, Chief Clarence Kelley established four planning task forces in the Kansas City Police Department. They represented the three patrol districts and one special operations unit. Each task force was directed to identify "critical problems" in their respective areas and to propose solutions. Consultants from the Police Foundation played a major role in developing the task-force approach and working with the four task forces.[61]

The task-force approach is based on the principle of involving rank-and-file personnel in the policy-making process. In Kansas City "The decision to establish these task forces was based on the beliefs that the ability to make competent planning decisions existed at all levels within the department and that if institutional change was to gain acceptance, those affected by it should have a voice in planning and implementation."[62]

This approach addresses itself to several problems related to traditional police organization decision making. Recognition of competence among lower-ranking personnel is an alternative to the traditional top-down decision-making process in the modern bureaucracy. The direct involvement of lower-ranking personnel affords them greater job satisfaction. Not only does this result in higher morale, but it prepares individuals for eventually assuming the responsibilities of higher rank. Finally, involvement of lower-ranking personnel creates a higher probability that innovations will be accepted within the organization. The Police Foundation evaluation of team-policing experiments found that in many cases the officers who were to carry them out did not understand the goals and procedures of team policing. They had been excluded from the planning process.

Weisbord, Lamb, and Drexler refer to task forces as "collateral organizations." A task force coexists within the existing organization. It utilizes the same personnel but focuses on a specific problem that does not fall neatly within the jurisdiction of an existing unit. Many problems, for example, cut across the jurisdictional lines indicated by the organizational chart. Weisbord, Lamb, and Drexler argue that a task force involves people with three different kinds of competence:[63]

    1 Those with formal authority over the problem
    2 Those with the skill and knowledge needed to solve it
    3 Those most affected by the problem or its solution

Task forces not only increase democracy in the organization by opening up the decision-making process but offer the prospect of more efficient and effective operations through flexible use of existing personnel.

Summary: Changing Organizations

Large organizations are difficult to change. As Perrow points out, critics view resistance to change as one of the major problems with bureaucracies. Despite the great interest in changing and improving police organizations, relatively little is known about the change process.

Jack R. Greene points out that planned change in police organizations can be of three different types. The first involves improving the quality of individual personnel; the second involves restructuring the organization; and the third involves changing the climate within the organization. Greene argues that each approach "makes certain assumptions about how change will occur as well as the kind and type of outcome." Too often, reformers have failed to specify the type of change they seek to bring about. Also, change has been evaluated in terms of the outcome (usually the impact on the crime rate) rather than the process. Further research on the change process in law enforcement is needed.[64]

REVIEW

1 What are the characteristics of the modern bureaucracy?

2 List the principles of organization that underlie the contemporary law enforcement organization.

3 Indicate the major problems with the quasi-military style of police organization.

4 How does management style affect the operations of a law enforcement agency?

5 Discuss the impact of civil service systems upon contemporary law enforcement organizations.

6 What are cliques and how do they affect the day-to-day operations of a police department?

7 Discuss the major positive and negative features of the organizational style of American law enforcement agencies.

8 Describe the principal elements of team policing.

9 What are the major objectives of Angell's democratic model of law enforcement organization?

10 What are the potential advantages of using task forces in law enforcement policy making?

REFERENCES

1 Charles Perrow, *Complex Organizations: A Critical Essay* (Glenview: Scott, Foresman, 1972), p. 14.

2 International City Management Association, *Municipal Police Administration,* 7th ed. (Washington, D.C.: Author, 1971), p. 17.

3 Perrow, *Complex Organizations,* p. 4.

4 Ibid., pp. 6–7.

5 John E. Angell, "Toward an Alternative to the Classic Police Organizational Arrangements: A Democratic Model," *Criminology* 9 (1971): 185–206.

6   James Q. Wilson, *Varieties of Police Behavior* (New York: Atheneum, 1973), pp. 2–3.

7   O. W. Wilson and Roy C. McLaren, *Police Administration,* 4th ed. (New York: McGraw-Hill, 1977), pp. 73–74.

8   Egon Bittner, *The Functions of the Police in Modern Society* (Washington, D.C.: National Institute of Mental Health, 1970), p. 52.

9   Ibid., pp. 58–59.

10   Jerome Skolnick, *Justice without Trial* (New York: John Wiley, 1966), pp. 235–239.

11   Bittner, *Functions of the Police in Modern Society,* chaps. 7–8.

12   Skolnick, *Justice without Trial,* pp. 235–239.

13   Robert Fogelson, *Big City Police* (Cambridge: Harvard University Press, 1977); Samuel Walker, *A Critical History of Police Reform* (Lexington: Lexington Books, 1977).

14   Angell, "Toward an Alternative to the Classic Police Organizational Arrangements."

15   Bernard Garmire, ed., *Local Government Police Management* (Washington, D.C.: International City Management Association, 1977), pp. 122–123.

16   Gerald W. Shanahan, et al., "Organizational Profile of Police Agencies in the United States," *Journal of Police Science and Administration* 7 (September 1979): 354–355.

17   Sanford J. Ungar, *FBI* (Boston: Little, Brown, 1976); Paul Jacobs, *Prelude to Riot* (New York: Vintage Books, 1968), pp. 13–60.

18   Shanahan et al., "Organizational Profile," 356.

19   U.S., Department of Justice, *Civil Service Systems: Their Impact on Police Administration* (Washington, D.C.: U.S. Government Printing Office, 1979), p. 4.

20   Ibid., pp. 45–51.

21   Dorothy Guyot, "Bending Granite: Attempts to Change the Rank Structure of American Police Departments," *Journal of Police Science and Administration* 7, no. 3 (1979): 253–284.

22   Ibid.

23   Albert Reiss and David J. Bordua, "Environment and Organization: A Perspective on the Police," in *The Police: Six Sociological Essays,* ed. David J. Bordua (New York: John Wiley, 1967), p. 48.

24   Dorothy Guyot, "Police Departments Under Social Science Scrutiny," *Journal of Criminal Justice* 5 (Summer 1977); 109.

25   William A. Westley, *Violence and the Police* (Cambridge: MIT Press, 1970), pp. 38–39.

26   Jonathan Rubinstein, *City Police* (New York: Ballantine Books, 1973), pp. 121–122, 138, 148–149, 200–201.

27   Westley, *Violence and the Police,* p. 23.

28   Fogelson, *Big City Police;* Walker, *A Critical History of Police Reform.*

29   Samuel Walker, *Popular Justice* (New York: Oxford University Press, 1980), pp. 173–177.

30   James Fyfe, "Administrative Interventions on Police Shooting Discretion: An Empirical Examination," *Journal of Criminal Justice* 7 (Winter 1979): 309–323.

31   Richard Myren, "A Crisis in Police Management," *Journal of Criminal Law, Criminology, and Police Science* 50 (March–April, 1960): 600–604; Skolnick, *Justice without Trial;* Bittner, *Functions of the Police in Modern Society.*

32   Bittner, *Functions of the Police in Modern Society,* chaps. 7–8.

33   Angell, "Toward an Alternative to the Classic Police Organizational Arrangements."

34   Perrow, *Complex Organizations,* p. 6.

35   John H. McNamara, "Uncertainties in Police Work: The Relevance of Police Recruits' Backgrounds and Training," in *The Police: Six Sociological Essays,* ed. David J. Bordua (New York: John Wiley, 1967), pp. 177–178.

36 Guyot, "Bending Granite."

37 Rubinstein, *City Police,* pp. 121–122, 138, 148–149, 200–201.

38 Westley, *Violence and the Police,* pp. 23–30.

39 U.S., Department of Justice, National Evaluation Program, *Crime Analysis in Support of Patrol, Phase 1 Report* (Washington, D.C.: U.S. Government Printing Office, 1977).

40 Gerald E. Caiden, *Police Revitalization* (Lexington: Lexington Books, 1977), pp. 11–17.

41 Wilson and McLaren, *Police Administration,* pp. 81–83.

42 John P. Clark and Richard E. Sykes, "Some Determinants of Police Organization and Practice in Modern Industrial Democracy," in *Handbook of Criminology,* ed. Daniel Glaser (Chicago: Rand McNally, 1974), p. 473.

43 Frances Bish, "The Limits of Organizational Reform" (Paper presented at the Workshop in Political Theory, Indiana University, 1976), p. 5.

44 Samuel G. Chapman, ed., *Police Patrol Readings,* 2nd ed. (Springfield: Charles C Thomas, 1970), chap. 5.

45 Alfred I. Schwartz and Sumner N. Clarren, *The Cincinnati Team Policing Experiment: A Summary Report* (Washington, D.C.: Police Foundation, 1977), p. 2.

46 U.S., Department of Justice, National Evaluation Program, *Neighborhood Team Policing* (Washington, D.C.: U.S. Government Printing Office, 1977), pp. 10–13.

47 L. W. Sherman, C. H. Milton, and T. V. Kelly, *Team Policing: Seven Case Studies* (Washington, D.C.: Police Foundation, 1973), pp. 3–7.

48 Ibid., p. 7.

49 U.S., Department of Justice, National Evaluation Project, *Neighborhood Team Policing,* p. 40.

50 Sherman et al., *Team Policing,* p. 107.

51 Schwartz and Clarren, *Cincinnati Team Policing Experiment,* p. 9.

52 Sherman et al., *Team Policing,* pp. 91–96.

53 Schwartz and Clarren, *Cincinnati Team Policing Experiment,* p. 7.

54 Angell, "Toward an Alternative to the Classic Police Organizational Arrangements."

55 L. W. Sherman, "Middle Management and Police Democratization: A Reply to John E. Angell," *Criminology* 12 (February 1975): 363–377; John E. Angell, "Organizing Police for the Future: An Update on the Democratic Model," *Criminal Justice Review* 1 (Fall 1976): 35–51.

56 Mary Ann Wycoff and George L. Kelling, *The Dallas Experience: Organizational Reform* (Washington, D.C.: Police Foundation, 1978).

57 Wayne A. Kerstetter, "Patrol Decentralization: An Assessment," *Journal of Police Science and Administration* 9 (March 1981): 48.

58 Caiden, *Police Revitalization,* pp. 276–277; Daniel Skoler, *Organizing the Non-System* (Lexington: Lexington Books, 1977), p. 66.

59 Caiden, *Police Revitalization,* p. 275.

60 Kerstetter, "Patrol Decentralization," 51.

61 Thomas Sweeney, *Changing Police Organizations: Four Readings* (Washington, D.C.: National League of Cities, 1973), pp. 13–29.

62 George L. Kelling et al., *The Kansas City Preventive Patrol Experiment: A Summary Report* (Washington, D.C.: Police Foundation, 1974), pp. 6–7.

63 Marvin Weisbord, Howard Lamb, and Allan Drexler, *Improving Police Department Management Through Problem-Solving Task Forces* (Reading, Mass.: Addison-Wesley, 1974), p. 16.

64 Jack R. Greene, "Organizational Change in Law Enforcement," *Journal of Criminal Justice* 9, no. 1 (1981): 79–91.

5

PATROL: THE BACKBONE OF POLICING

As O. W. Wilson argued, patrol is "the backbone of policing."[1] The majority of police officers are assigned to patrol and, in that capacity, deliver the bulk of police services to the public. The marked patrol car and the uniformed patrol officer are the most visible manifestations of the police in the eyes of the public.

Patrol is extremely important in other respects. It exerts a formative experience on all police officers. New officers begin their careers assigned to patrol duty. Under prevailing personnel practices, all officers undergo this experience. "Street experience" is one of the shared experiences of the police subculture. Officers argue that people who have not had this "street experience"do not know what police work is "really like."

Patrol duty, however, suffers from low status within the police department. The National Advisory Commission on Criminal Justice Standards and Goals pointed out that "The patrolman is usually the lowest paid, least consulted, most taken for granted member of the force. His duty is looked on as routine and boring."[2] Career advancement in policing involves getting out of patrol duty, either by assignment to the detective bureau or by promotion to higher rank. Enhancing the status of patrol duty and improving the morale of patrol officers are seen by some experts as the most critical problems facing the police today.

The purpose of this chapter is to explore five aspects of police patrol: (1) its function, (2) its organization and delivery, (3) its dominant features, (4) its effectiveness, and (5) its improvement.

THE FUNCTION OF PATROL

Since the time of Robert Peel, patrol has been the core of police work. Peel's major innovation was the idea of a continuous police presence throughout civil society, organized and delivered by means of regular patrol over a fixed beat by uniformed officers.

The basic purposes of patrol has not changed since 1829: the deterrence of crime; the maintenance of a feeling of public security; and twenty-four-hour availability for service to the public.

The *deterrence* of crime has been traditionally viewed as the most important function of patrol. According to O. W. Wilson, patrol is designed to create "an impression of omnipresence" which will eliminate "the actual opportunity (or the belief that the opportunity exists) for successful misconduct."[3]

Police management experts over the course of many decades have devoted their attention to increasing the effectiveness of this deterrent function. From the late 1930s through the 1960s, O. W. Wilson was the leading expert on the use of rational and scientific techniques for effective patrol deployment.

For nearly 150 years the deterrent effect of police patrol was taken for granted. Officials simply assumed that the presence of police patrol throughout the community did, in fact, deter criminal conduct. Scientific experiments to test this proposition did not occur until the 1970s.[4]

Maintaining *public security,* the second function of patrol, is closely related to the first. The omnipresence of the police through patrol is designed to create in the minds of law-abiding citizens the feeling that the police are at work deterring crime and available in case of emergency. Police work depends greatly on public perceptions about the police. It is not so much a matter of what the police actually do as what people think they are doing. The omnipresence of the police is designed to increase the perception that the police are doing their job and, as a consequence, justifying the tax dollars the public spends on police protection.

The third function of patrol, *availability for service,* involves many different tasks. As a technique of deployment, patrol represents an extreme case of the decentralization of government service. Patrol officers are deployed throughout the community on a neighborhood basis. This technique is designed to increase the speed at which they can respond to requests for service.

The services rendered by patrol officers are limitless. Patrol officers respond after a crime has been reported, attempt to maintain order in potentially dangerous situations, render emergency services to persons in need, and are available to provide information about any and every kind of problem to citizens.

ORGANIZATION AND DELIVERY OF PATROL SERVICES

The organization and delivery of patrol services refers to the manner in which a police department places patrol officers in the field. This involves six related issues:[5]

1 The number of sworn officers available for duty (usually measured in terms of the ratio of officers per population)
2 The allocation of sworn officers to patrol duty
3 The distribution of patrol officers according to time of day and territory
4 The type of patrol used (foot, car, one-officer, two-officer)
5 The style of patrol tactics (aggressive, passive)
6 The style of patrol supervision.

Number of Sworn Officers

The number of sworn officers per population varies considerably from city to city. Figure 5.1 represents FBI data on the average number of police department employees and range in number of employees per 1000 inhabitants. The data clearly indicate the enormous variation, even within cities of the same size. The average for all cities is 2.5 per 1000 (this refers to total employees, not sworn officers). It is highest (3.4) in the large cities where crime is the most serious problem. Curiously, the smallest cities have both the highest and lowest number of officers per population.

Two questions are raised by the variations indicated in Figure 5.1. First, why do such wide variations exist? The National Manpower Survey concluded that "Despite the number of social and economic variables tested, a large portion of the variation in police population ratios remains unexplained."[6] High ratios correlate most strongly with high robbery rates, apparently reflecting public concern over "high-fear" crimes. The second question is whether or not a high ratio of police per population has an effect on the crime rate. Experts are generally in agreement that, by itself, the number of officers per population has no effect on crime.

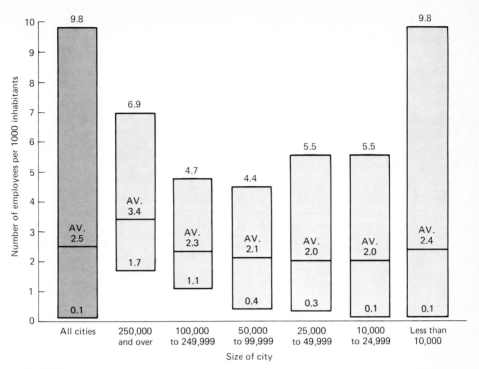

FIGURE 5.1
Average number of police department employees, and range in number of employees, per 1000 inhabitants, by size of city, 1978. *(Federal Bureau of Investigation, Uniform Crime Reports, 1978, p. 231.)*

Allocation of Officers to Patrol

Allocation refers to the proportion of officers in the department assigned to patrol duty. Considerable variation in allocation patterns is evident. In most departments more than half of all officers are allocated to patrol duty; yet some departments allocate only 40 percent, while others allocate as many as 80 percent of their officers to patrol. Generally, the larger departments are able to allocate only about 60 percent of their officers to patrol. Because of their size, more officers are needed for administrative and support duties.

Distribution of Patrol Officers

The distribution of patrol officers is defined as the "assignment of a given number of personnel according to area workload, time or function."[7] Professional police management has traditionally emphasized the rational distribution of patrol officers according to a workload formula.

Differences in patrol workload vary primarily according to geography and time of day. Low-income neighborhoods are the busiest police patrol areas. Victimization surveys indicate that crime is most heavily concentrated in these areas. In 1978 the victimization rate for violent crimes was 56.3 per 1000 in households with a family income of less than $3000, but only 29.6 per 1000 in households with a family income of between $15,000 and $24,999.[8] Low-income people also make greater use of the police for noncriminal matters. The poor in general are high consumers of public services: public schools, public transportation, social services, etc.[9]

The patrol workload also varies according to the time of day. Most serious crimes occur at night, while family fights and other disturbances are also concentrated in the evening. Figure 5.2 indicates the variation in patrol car "runs" in the Omaha Police Division according to shift.

The different shifts also vary in their impact upon officers' lives. The evening shift (4:00 P.M. to midnight) not only has the heaviest workload but is the most disruptive of an officer's personal life. It is usually considered the least desirable assignment. The night shift (midnight to 8:00 A.M.) usually divides into two periods. The first few hours are often very busy, but after 2:00 or 3:00 A.M. there is little or no activity at all. Many officers regard this as the most boring assignment. The day shift (8:00 A.M. to 4:00 P.M.) is the least disruptive of an officer's personal life and offers a relatively light workload. A large number of the calls are nondangerous follow-up calls.

A rational approach to patrol distribution, then, dictates a concentration of patrol officers in the evening shift. Surprisingly, many departments do not follow this practice. A 1975 study of 321 departments found that half had equal numbers of officers assigned to all shifts. The 1978 *Police Practices* survey confirmed this fact. Many departments also fail to reorganize patrol beats to follow changes in the geographic distribution of the population and criminal activity.[10] A Rand Corporation study of patrol in 1971 found one department that "has never been reorganized."[11] Failure

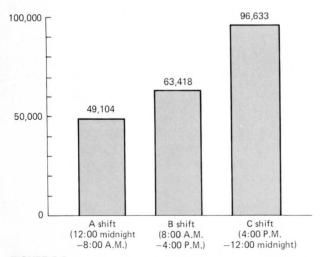

FIGURE 5.2
Cruiser car runs by shift, Omaha, Nebraska, 1979. *(Omaha Police Division, Annual Report, 1979.)*

to adjust to the changing social environment is one characteristic of an unprofessional department.

Type of Patrol

The dominant type of patrol is by *automobile*. The second (although much less important today) is *foot* patrol. Other specialized forms of patrol exist but are of marginal importance. These include motorcycle, bicycle, horse, and helicopter types of patrol.

The *Police Practices* survey found that more than 90 percent of all beats were handled by motor patrol. Foot patrol accounted for less than 10 percent.[12] Motor patrol first appeared around the time of World War I. By the late 1930s and 1940s, police management experts stressed the importance of motor patrol as a means of increasing efficiency. The International City Management Association found that the number of cities using motor patrol increased from 840 in 1946 to 1000 in 1954 and 1334 in 1964.[13]

The change from foot to motor patrol over the course of several decades had a revolutionary impact on American policing. On the one hand it fulfilled the expectations of the management experts by allowing more efficient patrol coverage. Police departments were able to cover more areas more frequently and to respond more quickly to calls for service.

Motor patrol had other unforeseen consequences, however. William A. Westley pointed out in 1950 that "In contrast to the man on the beat, the man in the car is isolated from the community." The President's Commission on Law Enforcement noted that "The most significant weakness in American motor patrol operations today is the general lack of contact with citizens except when an officer has responded to a call. Forced to stay near the car's radio, waiting an assignment, most patrol officers have few opportunities to develop closer relationships with persons living in the district."[14]

The efficiency of motor patrol in terms of coverage involved a trade-off in terms of community relations. Police officers had few contacts with ordinary citizens in nonconflict situations; most conflicts were in problematic crime-related or order-maintenance situations. Few people noticed this change in policing until the riots of the 1960s dramatized the problem of police-community relations. In response to the crisis, experts began to rethink the value of foot patrol and some cities expanded or reinstituted foot patrol.

One-Officer versus Two-Officer Cars

A major issue in patrol management involves the question of whether to staff cars with one or two officers. Management experts waged a long battle in favor of one-officer cars. Given the fact that 80 to 90 percent of police budgets are consumed by salaries, the one-officer car is far more efficient. Two one-officer cars can provide twice the coverage as one two-officer car.

Rank-and-file officers generally tend to favor two-officer cars. Safety is the primary consideration. Officers feel more secure handling potentially dangerous situations with a back-up officer available. Some research, however, questions the idea that two-officer cars necessarily afford greater safety.[15]

The arguments in favor of the one-officer car have generally prevailed. The International City Management Association reported a significant shift from two-officer to one-officer cars between 1946 and 1964, as indicated in Table 5-1.

The use of two-officer patrol cars (or two-officer foot patrols), while limited, is found primarily in the more dangerous, high-crime areas. Even O. W. Wilson, the chief advocate of one-officer cars, conceded that "there are sections of many cities in the United States in which it would be foolhardy for a police administrator to deploy police officers in one-man cars or on foot by themselves."[16]

In summary, considering all the factors involved—allocation and distribution of patrol officers and type of patrol—tremendous variation exists from department to department. Table 5-2 compares deployment patterns in Detroit and Dallas. Detroit uses a significant number of foot patrols and a high proportion of two-officer patrols. Dallas, on the other hand, uses very few foot patrols and relies primarily on one-officer patrols.

TABLE 5-1
TRENDS IN THE USE OF ONE-OFFICER AND TWO-OFFICER
PATROL CARS, 1946–1964

	Two-officer only (%)	One-officer only (%)
1946	36.3	18.0
1954	23.3	19.8
1964	5.0	41.0

Source: President's Commission on Law Enforcement and Administration of Justice, *Task Force Report: The Police* (Washington, D.C.: U.S. Government Printing Office, 1967), p. 55.

TABLE 5-2
PATROL BEAT ASSIGNMENTS, DETROIT AND DALLAS

	Motor		Foot		Total
	One officer	Two officer	One officer	Two officer	beats
Detroit					
Day	30	120	0	37	187
Evening	18	125	0	32	175
Night	0	110	0	20	130
Dallas					
Day	85	37	7	0	129
Evening	101	54	7	0	162
Night	47	40	3	0	90

Source: Adapted from Police Foundation, *Police Practices: The General Administrative Survey* (Washington, D.C.: Author, 1978).

The Cost of Patrol

Patrol is the most expensive element of police service. The cost of maintaining one patrol car on duty twenty-four hours a day can run as high as $300,000 per year.

The most expensive aspect of patrol (and of all police services) is the cost of maintaining full-time personnel. In the terminology of economists, patrol is labor-intensive, relying primarily on personnel rather than labor-saving equipment. Starting salaries for police officers averaged $15,159 in 1980, while maximum salaries averaged $19,066. Added to this is the cost of fringe benefits which now equal 30 to 35 percent of base salaries. Officers make additional money through overtime duty.

The issue of patrol officer *availability* further increases the cost of patrol. At a minimum, staffing one patrol beat requires three officers (one for each shift). Yet an officer is not available seven days a week, fifty-two weeks per year. According to commonly used formulas, each officer is entitled to 115 days off per year (weekends or the equivalent) plus 14 days of regular vacation. In addition, officers average 3.8 sick days per year and 2.2 days of injury leave per year. Thus, each officer must be relieved of duty by another officer for 135 days of each year. The availability factor is then computed according to the following formula:

$$\frac{365 - 135}{365} = \frac{230}{365} = .63 \text{ availability factor.}$$

Since each of the three officers assigned to a beat are available only 63 percent of the time during the year, it requires a total of 4.8 officers to maintain continuous patrol on one beat for a full year.[17]

DOMINANT FEATURES OF PATROL WORK

Little was known about day-to-day police patrol work until the 1960s. The President's Crime Commission sponsored one of the early field studies of patrol work. Other studies also appeared in the mid-1960s. These studies provide an overview of the patterns of police patrol work in an urban setting.[18]

Mobilization

Mobilization refers to the process by which a patrol officer comes into contact with a citizen (an "encounter"). Mobilizations fall into two general categories. *Calls for service* involve a request for police service by a citizen. *On view* refers to an encounter or activity initiated by the officer.

Albert Reiss's *The Police and the Public* involved field studies in three large cities (Boston, Chicago, and Washington, D.C.) during the summer of 1966. Researchers observed a total of 5360 mobilizations. Of these, "81 percent originated with citizens telephoning the police for service and the department dispatching a one- or two-man beat car to handle the incident. Fourteen percent originated on the initiative of police while patrolling an area, and 5 percent originated when a citizen mobilized the police in a field setting."[19]

Because the telephone is the primary means by which the police are mobilized, *citizen discretion* is the major determinant of the police workload. Victimization surveys indicate that only about half of all crimes are reported to the police. The reporting of crimes is influenced primarily by citizens' evaluation of the seriousness of the crime and the probability that the police will be able to solve it. A citizen's overall evaluation of the local police department, however, does not appear to influence the decision to report a crime.[20]

Victimization surveys have examined citizen reporting of crimes. Little is known about the factors that influence citizen requests for police service in noncriminal matters.

The ease of requesting police service through the telephone has produced a long-term shift in public expectations. The more available police service, the more citizens become accustomed to using that service. Table 5-3 indicates trends in the number of patrol-car dispatches by the Omaha police department between 1969 and 1979.

Part of the increase can be attributed to the installation of a 911 emergency phone number in the early 1970s. This shows that by increasing the sophistication of their communications technology and by encouraging the public to request service, the police succeed in increasing their own workload and straining their available resources.

The Role of the Dispatcher

The dispatcher plays a key role in shaping the nature of police work. Typically, the dispatcher receives only fragmentary information from the citizen requesting police service. The dispatcher then interprets the information and relays it to a police officer. In the process, important decisions are made: whether or not it is an urgent call, etc. George Antunes and Eric Scott argue that "in the link between a call for service and the arrival of a responding patrol officer, the complaint operator is the key deci-

TABLE 5-3
PATROL-CAR DISPATCHES, OMAHA
POLICE DIVISION, 1969–1979

Year	Dispatches
1969	143,531
1971	194,843
1973	209,260
1975	218,498
1977	205,918
1979	204,155

Source: Omaha Police Division, *Annual Report,* 1969, 1971, 1973, 1975, 1977, 1979.

sion maker in the police bureaucracy."[21] The recruitment, training, and supervision of dispatchers, then, is an important factor in the quality of service rendered by a police agency.

Types of Calls

Research consistently indicates that the vast majority of calls do not involve a criminal incident.[22] However, in a study comparing calls for service Reiss found that 58 percent of all requests for police service involved a criminal matter *as defined by the citizen.* Yet in the same time period the police recorded only 17 percent of patrol car dispatches as involving criminal events, while 83 percent were recorded as noncriminal in nature.[23]

Two factors explain this apparent discrepancy. First, it indicates that "many citizens have only a vague understanding of the difference between civil, private, and criminal matters."[24] They call the police to handle situations in which the police have no legitimate jurisdiction. The responding officer faces the difficult task of explaining why no action can be taken. Police departments in some cities, notably New York and Oakland, have adopted guidelines for handling domestic disturbances. Second, patrol officers exercise enormous discretion, even in those situations where they do have legitimate authority to act. By choosing to handle a domestic disturbance by means of a warning rather than an arrest, the responding officer in effect classifies an incident as order maintenance instead of law enforcement.

These data confirm the fact that the police officer is essentially a peacekeeper. Crime, though a constant preoccupation, represents only a small part of what a patrol officer actually does. The President's Crime Commission estimated that "an individual patrol officer can expect an opportunity to detect a burglary no more often than once every 3 months and a robbery no more often than once every 14 years."[25]

Use of Patrol Time

Recent studies have explored the question of how patrol officers use their time. The basic distinction is between "committed" and "uncommitted" time or between being "out of service" and "in service." While handling a call the officer is out of service and is committed. In other words, the officer is not available to handle another call for service. During uncommitted time the officer is in service and is available for calls.

Richard Larson estimated that the average call took about thirty minutes of an officer's time (based on ten minutes of travel time and twenty minutes for handling the call itself). Based on the number of calls per day in Kansas City, Larson then estimated that the average officer spent 16.7 percent of his or her time handling calls. Other studies have reached similar conclusions.[26]

Estimates of the average amount of committed time masks important differences between patrol beats. Officers assigned to high-crime areas will spend more time handling calls than officers in low-crime areas. Officers assigned to the evening shift will be busier than officers assigned to the other two shifts (see Figure 5.2).

Data from the Kansas City Preventive Patrol Experiment provided estimates of how officers spend their uncommitted time. Reiss had previously found that patrol results in few on-view contacts with citizens. Table 5-4 shows the percentage of both uncommitted time and total patrol time that Kansas City police spent on different categories of activity.

Patrol duty, in short, is not an exciting, action-packed assignment. It is often boring, with extended periods of time filled by trivial activities. A significant amount of time is filled with activities completely unrelated to police work.

Evasion of Duty

Despite the fact that the two-way radio provides for constant monitoring of patrol-officer activities, officers are in fact able to evade work. According to Jonathan Rubinstein, the simplest technique is to delay reporting the completion of a call. The dispatcher assumes that the officer is still busy with the call until receiving an in-service report. In this way the officer is able to create some free time. Police officers have also devised ways of sleeping on duty (known as "cooping" in New York City). One technique is to have one officer remain awake, monitoring the radio, while other officers in other cars sleep.[27]

THE EFFECTIVENESS OF PATROL

How effective is routine police patrol? Does it accomplish its basic function of deterring crime? Are different patrol strategies more effective than others?

TABLE 5-4
PATROL OFFICER'S USE OF TIME, KANSAS CITY

Category	Noncommitted time (%)	Total time (%)
Mobile Police–Related Looking for suspicious cars, people, stolen autos, traffic violations, training new officers, watching buildings, residences, etc.	23.54	14.20
Non-Police-Related Eating, resting, people watching, sleeping, personal errands, etc.	25.47	15.36
Stationary and Contact Personnel Police–Related Report writing, surveillance, traffic enforcement, discussing cases, etc.	26.01	15.69
Residual Traveling from station, court, etc.	24.98	15.06

Source: George L. Kelling et al., *The Kansas City Preventive Patrol Experiment: A Summary Report* (Washington, D.C.: Police Foundation, 1974), p. 42.

In 1967 the President's Crime Commission observed that "resources and talent for proper research have not been devoted in any great extent to discovering and analyzing the relationship between police patrol and deterrence."[28] The deterrent function had been an unexamined assumption. The commission helped to stimulate new thinking about police patrol, which led to sophisticated experiments to test its effectiveness. The Kansas City Preventive Patrol Experiment (1972–1973) introduced a new era in police thinking.

Early Experiments

The initial experiments with alternative patrol tactics did not yield scientifically valid evidence about the effectiveness of either normal patrol or possible alternatives.[29] These early experiments were poorly planned, often implemented in haste, and lacked research designs necessary for a scientific experiment.

Operation 25   The first experiment was "Operation 25" conducted by the New York City Police Department in 1954. For four months the NYCPD doubled the number of patrol officers in the Twenty-fifth Precinct (a high-crime area in the East Harlem section of Manhattan). Prior to the experiment many of the foot-patrol beats had been unstaffed. Using primarily new officers just out of the Police Academy, all beats were staffed during the four-month experiment.

According to official records, crime appeared to drop as a result of the experiment. Muggings dropped from a total of sixty-nine in the same period a year before to only seven; auto thefts declined by two-thirds (from 78 to 24); homicide, however, remained the same.

Operation 25 was not a valid experiment, because it relied entirely on official reports and did not control for possible fluctuations in the reported crime rate that might have been unrelated to the increase in patrol officers. Also the experiment dramatized the *displacement* problem. No attempt was made to discover if criminal activity was simply shifted into neighboring areas which still had the normal amount of police patrol.

The British Beat Patrol Experiments   Using four cities, the British police experimented with variations in patrol in the mid-1960s. Over a series of four-week periods the number of officers on foot patrol was varied from zero to four.

The Home Office, which sponsored the experiment, concluded that the number of crimes reported decreased significantly when the number of patrol officers was increased from zero to one. Some police presence, in other words, appeared to make a difference. Further increases in patrol intensity—changing from one to two, three, or four officers on a beat—did not appear to yield additional reductions.

New York City: Twentieth Precinct   In 1966 the New York City Police Department undertook another experiment, attempting to control for some of the limitations of Operation 25. In the Twentieth Precinct, the number of patrol officers was increased by 40 percent. The New York City Rand Institute, which evaluated the experiment, sought to control for the possible displacement phenomenon by measuring crime in two neighboring precincts.

The experiment produced a 33 percent reduction in street robberies, a 49 percent reduction in auto theft, and a 49 percent reduction in grand larcenies "visible from the street." No significant increases in crime were reported in the neighboring precincts. The experiment did rely on crimes reported to the police and, therefore, did not control for fluctuations in the reporting rate unrelated to increases in police patrol.

The New York Subway Experiment   Because of a serious increase in the number of crimes on the New York subway system, in 1965 the city more than doubled the number of police patrols on the subway (from 1200 to 3100). The effect of this increase was analyzed after the fact by researchers from the Rand Corporation.

The additional officers were deployed between the hours of 8:00 P.M. and 4:00 A.M. Every train and subway station had at least one officer on duty during that time period. Initially, there was a short-term decline in serious crime. Within two years, however, crime began to increase again at a rapid rate. By 1970 there were six times as many robberies as had occurred in 1965 before the additional police were deployed.

The researchers discovered a "phantom" effect. Crimes declined during hours of the day when there were no additional officers on duty. Presumably, potential criminals believed that the police presence had been increased for those hours.

Unfortunately, it was subsequently discovered that the transit police deliberately manipulated their crime data to demonstrate a deterrent effect. Jan M. Chaiken, who conducted the after-the-fact evaluation, argues that a deterrent effect "would have been observed even if the data were scrupulously correct," and that the manipulation only "distorted" the apparent effect.

This event dramatized the hazards of using official data. Not only do police reports record only reported crimes but they are subject to manipulation, either through inefficiency or deliberate falsification. Reporters for Washington, D.C., newspapers, for example, found the Washington police deliberately manipulating crime reports in order to achieve a "reduction" in crime in 1970–1971.[30]

The Kansas City Preventive Patrol Experiment

The Kansas City Preventive Patrol Experiment is a landmark event in the history of American policing.[31] It was the first comprehensive and scientific experiment designed to measure the effectiveness of traditional police patrol. Although critics identified flaws in its methodology and have challenged its findings, the experiment raised thinking about patrol to a new level.

Origins   The origins of the Kansas City experiment are nearly as important as the experiment itself. Clarence Kelley, then chief of police in Kansas City, established four task forces in the department to develop ideas for improving policing. The task forces included rank-and-file officers and represented a creative approach to participatory management. The combination of an innovative and charismatic police chief and rank-and-file participation was a key ingredient in the experiment.[32]

The South Patrol Division Task Force identified five problem areas that deserved greater attention. However, the task force then confronted the problem of limited resources. The department could give additional attention to the five problem areas only by reducing the number of officer-hours spent on routine patrol. At this point a significant thing happened. Some of the members of the task force "questioned whether routine preventive patrol was effective, what police officers did while on preventive patrol duty, and what effect police visibility had on the community's feelings of security." The experiment was designed to discover whether officers could be freed from routine patrol duty and made available for other assignments.

Once the department decided to undertake the experiment, it received important assistance from the Police Foundation. The foundation provided not only the expertise to design a scientifically controlled experiment but also the necessary funding. The experiment represented an excellent example of collaboration between a reform-oriented police department, a private foundation, and academic researchers.

The Experiment The experiment began on July 19, 1972, but within a month it was clear that experimental conditions were not being maintained. It was temporarily suspended and then resumed on October 1, 1972. The experiment ran for 12 months, ending on September 30, 1973.

Fifteen of the twenty-four beats in the South Patrol Division were selected for the experiment (nine were eliminated as being unrepresentative of the area). "The 15 beats in the experimental area were computer matched on the basis of crime data, number of calls for service, ethnic composition, median income and transiency of population into five groups of three each." The three beats in each group were assigned different levels of police patrol:

1 *Reactive:* "no preventive patrol as such. Police vehicles assigned these beats entered them only in response to calls for service. Their noncommitted time (when not answering calls) was spent patrolling the boundaries of the reactive beats or patrolling in adjacent proactive beats."

2 *Proactive:* the five proactive beats were assigned two or three times the normal number of marked police vehicles.

3 *Control:* the five control beats were assigned the normal level of patrol (one car per beat).

Figure 5.3 represents a schematic diagram of the beats in the experimental area.

The use of fifteen different beats within one area of the city helped in part to control for the displacement phenomenon noted in previous experiments with intensive patrol. This did not completely eliminate the possibility of displacement, since criminal activity could shift to a different patrol division in another area of the city.

The research team used twenty different data sources and produced findings in thirteen major areas. Part of the significance of the Kansas City experiment was the use of so many different data sources and the exploration of such a wide variety of issues.

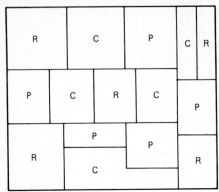

P = proactive
C = control
R = reactive

FIGURE 5.3
Schematic representation of the fifteen-beat experimental area, Kansas City Preventive Patrol
Experiment. *(George L. Kelling et al., The Kansas City Preventive Patrol Experiment: Final
Report, Washington, D.C., Police Foundation, 1974, p. 9.)*

The thirteen major findings may be grouped into three general areas:

Crime
    Community victimization
    Departmental reported crime
    Rates of reporting crime to the police
    Arrest trends
Community perceptions and attitudes
    Citizens' fear of crime
    Protective measures used by citizens
    Protective measures used by businesses
    Community attitudes toward the police and the delivery of police services
    Businesspeople's attitudes toward the police and the delivery of police services
    Citizen attitudes toward the police as a result of encounters with the police
    Estimation of citizen-police transactions
Police department practices
    Police response time
    Traffic incidents

The data sources included extensive community surveys of both citizens and businesspeople; observations of police-citizen encounters by trained observers; interviews
with citizens and police officers; and official departmental records. Unlike previous
experiments, the Kansas City study used the new "victimization" technique to
attempt to measure actual criminality rather than crimes reported.

Findings   The Kansas City experiment found that variations in the level of patrol made little difference in any of the areas tested. The major findings included:

> *Finding 1: Victimization:* The Victimization Survey found no statistically significant differences in crime in any of the 69 comparisons made between reactive, control and proactive beats.
>
> *Finding 5: Citizen fear of crime:* Citizen fear of crime was not significantly affected by changes in the level of routine preventive patrol.
>
> *Finding 8: Citizen attitudes toward police:* Citizen attitudes toward police were not significantly affected by alterations in the level of preventive patrol.
>
> *Finding 12: Response time:* The amount of time taken by police in answering calls for service was not significantly affected by variations in the level of routine preventive patrol.[33]

Implications   The Kansas City experiment challenged traditional assumptions of routine police patrol. The deterrent effect of policing was apparently not weakened by the elimination of routine patrolling. Citizen fear of crime and citizen attitude toward the police were also not affected. The ability of the police to respond to calls for service was not affected.

Joseph D. McNamara, chief of the Kansas City police in 1974, warned that "A great deal of caution must be used to avoid the error that the experiment proved more than it actually did." He added that "One thing the experiment did not show is that a visible police presence can have no impact on crime in selected circumstances." McNamara stressed the point that the experiment seemed to show that police officers' uncommitted time (about 60 percent of their time on duty) could be used more effectively, most likely in activities with more specific objectives than routine patrol.[34]

George Kelling, director of the experiment and principal author of the final report, added that it would be a mistake to conclude that patrol was completely unnecessary or that police departments could manage with far fewer resources. He argued that "the experiment has demonstrated that the time and staff resources do exist within police departments to test solutions" to the many complex and interrelated problems of police service.[35]

Criticisms   Richard C. Larson found serious flaws in the research design of the experiment. He noted that when patrol cars in the reactive beats entered the area in response to calls, they made a visible police presence. In the eyes of citizens and potential criminals this was the same as routine patrol. Larson also pointed out that police vehicles from other specialized units (who were not part of the experiment) operated in the reactive beats, thereby creating a visible police presence. Larson found other differences in the reactive beats: officers undertook a higher rate of self-initiated activities (such as vehicle stops); used sirens and lights more often in responding to calls; and there was a higher incidence of two or more cars responding to a call for service.[36]

The experiment, in short, was not perfect. The conclusions that can be drawn from it must be tentative. At best, it seems to indicate that possibilities exist for more flexible and creative approaches to the use of patrol officers. To date, only one attempt has been made to replicate the Kansas City experiment. A similar study in Albuquerque, New Mexico, reached essentially similar conclusions.[37]

The Effectiveness of Foot Patrol

In the late 1960s renewed interest in foot patrol emerged. This development was mainly a result of the police-community relations crisis. It appeared that the patrol car had isolated the patrol officer from the community, reducing or eliminating informal contacts between officers and law-abiding citizens. Consequently, some departments added additional foot-patrol beats as part of their police-community relations programs.

The Police Foundation evaluated the effectiveness of foot patrol in selected New Jersey cities between 1977 and 1979. *The Newark Foot Patrol Experiment* sought to measure its impact on crime, arrest rates, and community attitudes. It found that "Generally, crime levels . . . are not affected [by foot patrol] for residents or commercial respondents at a significant level." However, foot patrol did have a significant effect on the attitudes of residents in the area. "Consistently, residents in beats where foot patrol was added see the severity of crime problems diminishing in their neighborhoods at levels greater than the other two areas." Residents of the foot-patrol areas felt that the safety of their neighborhoods had increased.[38]

IMPROVING POLICE PATROL

Because of the importance of the patrol function, substantial improvement in policing must involve patrol. Gerald Caiden argues that "Police revitalization begins with patrol."[39] Efforts to improve the effectiveness of routine police patrol can be divided into two general categories: traditional and new. The traditional approach is associated with the work of O. W. Wilson and dominated police thinking from the late 1930s through the 1960s. The new approaches emerged in the 1970's and are built upon the new knowledge base about the nature of patrol. Pressure for greater efficiency in patrol increased in the late 1970s as local governments experienced severe financial constraints.

Traditional Approach

The traditional approach to improving the efficiency of routine patrol accepted uncritically the basic assumptions of patrol: it deterred crime, reassured the public, and allowed the police to respond quickly to requests for service.

The principal objectives of the traditional approach were threefold: (1) maintain maximum coverage, (2) distribute patrol officers in a rational manner, and (3) reduce response time.

Coverage   Maintaining coverage involved maximizing the impression of patrol omnipresence. Thus the police should cover every area of the city and should appear to patrol each area as frequently as possible. With this objective in mind, O. W. Wilson and others lead the fight for replacing foot patrol with motor patrol and using one-officer rather than two-officer cars. Both tactics would allow the department to cover the maximum amount of area.

Distribution   Professional police management has traditionally emphasized the rational distribution of patrol officers according to workload demands. O. W. Wilson was the pioneer in this field, experimenting with distribution formulas in the late 1930s and publishing a pamphlet on the *Distribution of Police Patrol Force* in 1941. Revised versions were developed by the Field Operations Division of the IACP in 1959 and by Wilson's colleague, Roy C. McLaren, in the 1960s.[40]

Three basic distribution formulas are available. The first is *simple distribution,* which distributes patrol officers according to the size of the patrol district and the calls for police service. A second approach involves using a *hazard formula.* Calls for police service are not all equally serious. A "hazard score" is computed for each patrol district by assigning different points to different types of calls for service and then determining the total number of points for each district. A third approach is the *allocation-by-objective* formula. This approach differs from the hazard formula by taking into consideration multiple objectives, as patrol visibility, the percentage of time each unit is out of service, travel time, and other measures of actual police performance.[41]

Richard C. Larson has been the leading advocate of more sophisticated patrol-distribution formulas, including the allocation-by-objective approach. Gerald Caiden, however, argues that Larson's models are self-defeating because they are too sophisticated for police departments to implement.[42]

Response Time   Traditional approaches assume that a speedier police response would (1) increase the chances of apprehending an offender and (2) foster a positive attitude toward the police on the part of the citizens who summoned them.

In its *Task Force Report: Science and Technology,* the President's Commission on Law Enforcement argued that "short response time correlates with ability to make an arrest." Its data indicated that in emergency situations response time averaged 4.1 minutes in calls where an arrest was made and 6.3 minutes in calls where the crime remained uncleared. In "nonemergency but urgent" situations, average response time was 5.3 minutes where arrests were made and 7.8 where the crime remained uncleared.[43]

The National Advisory Commission on Criminal Justice Standards and Goals recommended that "urban area response time . . . under normal conditions should not exceed 3 minutes for emergency calls, and 20 minutes for nonemergency calls." The Commission stated that "when the time is cut to 2 minutes, it can have a dramatic effect on crime."[44]

Total response time (from the moment of the crime to the arrival of the first police officer) consists of three basic components: (1) the time between the crime and the

moment the citizen calls the police; (2) the time required for the police to process
the call (answer the phone, obtain details from the citizen, dispatch a patrol car);
(3) travel time from the moment the patrol car receives the dispatch until it arrives
at the scene.

Recent research questions the value of emphasizing quick response time. Data
from Kansas City indicates that improved response time by the police does not
increase the chances of making an arrest. The most important delay, researchers
found, was the time it took the citizen to call the police. Delays often lasted as long
as an hour. Many citizens call other people (friends, family, etc.) before calling the
police. In this matter, as in others, citizen discretion is a major constraint on the
police.[45]

The traditional approach to improving patrol is not irrelevant. Many police
departments have yet to adopt even the simplest formulas for rationally distributing
patrol officers. Improvements in communications technology can help police departments cope effectively with increasing calls for service. But the traditional approach
was based on unexamined assumptions about patrol. The research of the past fifteen
years—notably the empirical studies of patrol work and the Kansas City patrol
experiment—have led to new thinking about improving patrol.

New Approaches

LEAA surveyed the major new approaches in the area of patrol: The authors
reviewed the existing literature on all aspects of patrol operations, including reports and evaluations of innovative programs, and made site visits to twenty-six
police departments. They report two major new approaches to improving patrol efficiency.[46]

Managing the Service-Call Workload   Traditionally, police departments sought
to respond as quickly as possible to all requests for service. Distinctions were made
between emergency, nonemergency but urgent, and all other nonemergency. But it
was always assumed that a sworn officer would respond as quickly as possible to each
and every request.

A report by the Police Executive Research Forum on *Differential Police Response
Strategies* found that police departments could make more efficient use of patrol
resources by analyzing requests for service, establishing priorities, and providing different responses according to the seriousness of the incident and other relevant
factors.[47]

The LEAA report described one approach in detail, which recommended dividing
calls for service into three categories: type A, in which time was critical and an
immediate response was needed; type B, which required the presence of a sworn
police officer but where time was not critical; and type C, where time was not critical
and where the presence of a sworn officer was not necessary. It was estimated that
type A calls represented only 15 percent of all calls.

Type B calls could be handled by "stacking." Patrol officers would respond only when they had completed other duties (such as directed patrol, see below). Type C calls could be handled by a variety of different methods. The citizen could be referred to another agency. Reports could be taken over the phone (especially in the case of "cold" property crimes where there was little likelihood of clearance). The citizen could be encouraged to file a report by mail or by visit to the police station. Table 5-5 indicates the priority guidelines developed by the Kansas City police department.

Police Aides   An alternative method of handling low-priority calls is through the use of nonsworn personnel. Many tasks do not involve the need for a sworn police officer. The President's Crime Commission recommended the creation of a community service officer (CSO) job classification to handle many of these routine tasks. Sworn officers would be freed for more critical tasks.[48] (For further discussion, see Chapter 3.)

Directed Patrol   As the name suggests, directed patrol involves providing patrol officers with specific directions for patrol activities. The traditional approach to patrol provides officers with only the general instruction to maintain patrol coverage, watch for suspicious persons or events, and respond to calls for service. Directed patrol involves instruction to look for specific persons or types of crime or to patrol certain areas intensively.[49]

The key element of directed patrol is crime analysis. Through sophisticated analysis of crime data for particular areas, police managers can develop specific patrol tactics. Patrol officers carry out these assignments during uninterrupted blocks of time when they are freed from responsibility for responding to service calls. In this respect, the concept of directed patrol builds upon the findings of the Kansas City patrol experiment, together with the idea that calls for service can be either stacked or handled by other personnel.

Community-Oriented Policing   The San Diego Police Department undertook a variation of directed patrol with its community-oriented policing (COP) experiment. Supported by the Police Foundation, the COP program began in 1973. The concept rested on the "assumption that each patrol beat or community within a city has unique social and law enforcement problems that can only be adequately addressed when patrol officers have a clear understanding of these problems." Each officer, then, was directed to develop a "beat profile," analyzing the unique social characteristics of the area.[50]

To implement the program, the San Diego Police Department also undertook extensive training and developed new methods of evaluating patrol officers. Officers were encouraged "to develop analytical and planning skills and to adapt their patrol activity to beat conditions." Community-oriented policing is a form of directed patrol because it gives patrol officers a specific task to accomplish—to develop systematic information about the assigned beat—rather than to simply engage in random, undirected patrol.

TABLE 5-5
CALL PRIORITIZATION GUIDELINES, KANSAS CITY POLICE DEPARTMENT

Type of call	Type of response	Type of call	Type of response
Homicide		*Fire or Disaster*	
Homicide	Immediate	Fire	Immediate
Suicide / attempt	Immediate	Explosion	Immediate
Dead body	Immediate	*Intoxicated Person*	
Sex Offenses		Person down, injured	Immediate
Rape / attempt	Immediate	Intoxicated	Delay
Molestation	Walk / phone in	*Disturbance*	
Indecent act	Walk / phone in	Disturbance	Immediate
Robbery		Investigate trouble	Immediate
Robbery / attempt	Immediate	Mental	Immediate
Strongarm / attempt	Delay*	Noise (specify)	Delay or refer to city prosecutor's office
Assaults			
Shooting	Immediate	*Traffic*	
Cutting	Immediate	Handle traffic	Delay
Other assault	Walk / phone in	Check traffic lights and barricade	Immediate or notify public works
Burglary		Obstruction in street	Immediate or notify public works
Residence	Delay		
Nonresidence	Delay	Illegally parked	Delay
Larceny		*Traffic Accident*	
Larceny / attempt	Walk / phone in	Accident, property damage	Walk / phone in or delay
Holding person for	Immediate		
Purse snatch / attempt	Walk / phone in	Investigate, injury	Immediate
		Fatality	Immediate
Auto Theft		*Alarm*	
Stolen / attempt	Walk / phone in	Holdup	Immediate
Attempt to locate	Walk / phone in	Burglar	Immediate
Recovered stolen	Delay		
Miscellaneous Report		*Self-Initiated Duties*	
Animal bite	Delay	Traffic violation	Immediate
Loss	Walk / phone in	Assignments	N / A
Recovered property	Delay	Building check	Delay
Destruction of property	Walk / phone in	Car check	N / A
		Foot patrol	N / A
Open door or window	Immediate	Warrant / subpoena	Delay
		Car chase	N / A
Fraud	Walk / phone in	Listing	Delay
Suspicious		Pedestrian check	N / A
Person	Immediate	Residence check	Delay
Prowler	Immediate		
Car prowler	Immediate	*Juveniles*	
Occupant, parked car	Immediate	Lost juvenile	Immediate
		Disperse group	Delay
Ambulance		Holding	Immediate
Investigate need	Immediate		
Ambulance en route	Immediate		

(continued)

TABLE 5-5   (continued)
CALL PRIORITIZATION GUIDELINES, KANSAS CITY POLICE DEPARTMENT

Type of call	Type of response	Type of call	Type of response
Miscellaneous		*Miscellaneous*	
Check abandoned car	Delay	Animal	Delay
		Lost/senile	Immediate
Wires down	Immediate	Assist motorist	Delay
Explosive device	Immediate	Open fire hydrant	Delay
Gambling game	Delay	Fireworks	Delay
Target shooters	Immediate		

*All calls marked "DELAYED" will be answered immediately if the incident is in progress, suspects are in the area or are known, and there is danger to human life or of property destruction.
Source: U.S., Department of Justice, *Improving Patrol Productivity*, vol. 1, *Routine Patrol* (Washington, D.C.: Author, 1977), p. 75.

Summary

In the past decade there has been considerable creative thinking and experimentation with respect to management of the patrol function. Although the American police have a reputation for being resistant to change, a few departments have been notably receptive to new ideas. At this point, however, there is no conclusive evidence about the effectiveness of the different proposed innovations. According to John Heaphy of the Police Foundation, "more is known about what *does not* work in police patrol than about what does. It is clear that patrol resources could and should be better directed, but the question of how to accomplish this is far from being resolved."[51]

REVIEW

1 What are the major functions of police patrol?

2 What factors should be taken into account in the distribution of patrol officers?

3 Discuss the relative advantages of one-officer versus two-officer patrol cars.

4 Indicate the relative frequency of the different types of requests for police service.

5 Approximately what percentage of their time do patrol officers spend in service?

6 Describe the research design used by the Kansas City Preventive Patrol Experiment.

7 What were the major findings of the Kansas City experiment?

8 What impact does response time have on the ability of the police to clear crimes?

9 Describe two approaches to the efficient management of the police service-call workload.

10 How does directed patrol differ from traditional patrol?

REFERENCES

1 O. W. Wilson and Roy C. McLaren, *Police Administration,* 4th ed. (New York: McGraw-Hill, 1977), pp. 320–321.

2 U.S., National Advisory Commission on Criminal Justice Standards and Goals, *Police·* (Washington, D.C.: U.S. Government Printing Office, 1973), p. 189.

3 Wilson and McLaren, *Police Administration,* p. 320.

4 Jan M. Chaiken, "What Is Known about Deterrent Effects of Police Activities," in *Preventing Crime,* ed. James A. Cramer (Beverly Hills: Sage, 1978), pp. 109–136.

5 James Q. Wilson and Barbara Boland, *The Effect of the Police on Crime* (Washington, D.C.: U.S. Department of Justice, 1979).

6 U.S., Law Enforcement Assistance Administration, *The National Manpower Survey of the Criminal Justice System,* vol. 2, *Law Enforcement* (Washington, D.C.: U.S. Government Printing Office, 1978), p. 37.

7 Wilson and McLaren, *Police Administration,* p. 657.

8 U.S., Department of Justice, *Criminal Victimization in the U.S., 1978* (Washington, D.C.: U.S. Government Printing Office, 1980), p. 27.

9 David H. Bayley and Harold Mendelsohn, *Minorities and the Police* (New York: Free Press, 1969), p. 63.

10 Kevin Krajick, "Does Patrol Prevent Crime?" *Police Magazine* (September 1978), 5–16; John Heaphy, ed., *Police Practices: The General Administrative Survey* (Washington, D.C.: Police Foundation, 1978).

11 James S. Kakalik and Sorrel Wildhorn, *Aids to Decision-Making in Police Patrol,* vol. 1 (Santa Monica: Rand Corporation, 1971), p. 87.

12 Heaphy, *Police Practices,* p. 11.

13 President's Commission on Law Enforcement and Administration of Justice, *Task Force Report: The Police* (Washington, D.C.: U.S. Government Printing Office, 1967), p. 55.

14 Ibid., p. 54; William A. Westley, *Violence and the Police* (Cambridge: MIT Press, 1970), p. 35.

15 Chicago Police Department 1963 Training Report, "One-Man Patrol Cars," 1963, in *Police Patrol Readings,* 2nd ed., ed. Samuel G. Chapman (Springfield: Charles C Thomas, 1970), pp. 212–220.

16 Wilson and McLaren, *Police Administration,* p. 337.

17 Gerald E. Caiden, *Police Revitalization* (Lexington: Lexington Books, 1977), p. 107.

18 U.S., National Advisory Commission, *Police,* p. 204.

19 Albert Reiss, *The Police and the Public* (New Haven: Yale University Press, 1971).

20 Ibid., p. xiii.

21 Ibid., pp. 65–70; U.S., Department of Justice, *The Police and Public Opinion* (Washington, D.C.; U.S. Government Printing Office, 1977).

22 George Antunes and Eric J. Scott, "Calling the Cops: Police Telephone Operators and Citizen Calls for Service," *Journal of Criminal Justice,* 9, no. 2 (1981): 165–180.

23 Reiss, *Police and the Public,* p. 73.

24 Ibid., p. 77.

25 President's Commission on Law Enforcement and Administration of Justice, *Task Force Report: Science and Technology* (Washington, D.C.: U.S. Government Printing Office, 1967), p. 12.

26 Richard C. Larson, "What Happened to Patrol Operations in Kansas City? A Review of the Kansas City Preventive Patrol Experiment," *Journal of Criminal Justice* 3, no. 4 (1975): 273.

27 Jonathan Rubinstein, *City Police* (New York: Ballantine Books, 1974), pp. 117–119.

28 President's Commission on Law Enforcement and Administration of Justice, *The Challenge of Crime in a Free Society* (New York: Avon Books, 1968), p. 249.

29 Chaiken, "What Is Known about Deterrent Effects of Police Activities?", James Q. Wilson, *Thinking About Crime* (New York: Basic Books, 1975), chap. 5.

30 David Seidman and Michael Couzens, "Getting the Crime Rate Down: Political Pressure and Crime Reporting," *Law and Society Review* 8 (Spring 1974): 457–493.

31 George L. Kelling, et al., *The Kansas City Preventive Patrol Experiment: Final Report* (New York: Police Foundation, 1974).

32 Ibid., pp. 6–8.

33 Ibid., pp. 20–39.

34 Ibid., pp. v–vi.

35 Ibid., pp. 48–49.

36 Larson, "What Happened to Patrol Operations in Kansas City?"

37 *Criminal Justice Newsletter,* August 27, 1979, p. 4.

38 Police Foundation, *The Newark Foot Patrol Experiment* (Washington, D.C.: Author, 1981), pp. 4–5.

39 Caiden, *Police Revitalization,* p. 107.

40 Wilson and McLaren, *Police Administration,* pp. 656–671.

41 Joseph Ferreira, Jr., "Comparing Patrol Unit Allocation Methods," in *Patrol Deployment,* ed. Richard C. Larson (Lexington: Lexington Books, 1978), pp. 183–221.

42 Caiden, *Police Revitalization,* p. 111.

43 President's Commission on Law Enforcement and Administration of Justice, *Task Force Report: Science and Technology* (Washington, D.C.: U.S. Government Printing Office, 1967), p. 9.

44 National Advisory Commission, *Police,* p. 193.

45 U.S., Department of Justice, *Response Time Analysis: Executive Summary* (Washington, D.C.: U.S. Government Printing Office, 1978).

46 U.S., Department of Justice, *Improving Patrol Productivity,* vol. 1, *Routine Patrol* (Washington, D.C.: U.S. Government Printing Office, 1977), p. 15.

47 Michael T. Farmer, ed., *Differential Police Response Strategies* (Washington, D.C.: Police Executive Research Forum, 1981).

48 President's Commission on Law Enforcement and Administration of Justice, *The Challenge of Crime,* pp. 275–276.

49 U.S., Department of Justice, *Improving Patrol Productivity,* chap. 4.

50 John E. Boydstun and Michael E. Sherry, *San Diego Community Profile: Final Report* (Washington, D.C.: Police Foundation, 1975).

51 John Heaphy, *The Municipal Yearbook, 1979* (Washington D.C.: International City Management Association, 1979), p. 257.

CHAPTER **6**

POLICING PEOPLE

Police work involves a wide range of situations and tasks. The purpose of this chapter is to examine in detail several of the more common situations: the domestic dispute; policing juveniles; policing skid row; criminal investigation; policing crimes of vice; and traffic enforcement.

DOMESTIC DISPUTES

The domestic dispute or family disturbance is a recurring situation for the police. According to James Q. Wilson, "family trouble" accounted for 7.3 percent of citizen complaints radioed to police cars in Syracuse, New York. Cumming, Cumming, and Edell found that "disputes" accounted for 7.9 percent of the situations handled by the police. Precise figures are difficult to obtain. Often the police receive only a complaint about "disorder," or "noise," or "trouble" at a certain address. The police officer who responds to the call does not necessarily specify that it was a domestic dispute in the official report.[1]

From the perspective of the police officer, domestic disputes are far more important than their absolute number. They are extremely unpredictable, difficult to handle, and frustrating. With nothing more than a complaint about "trouble" at a certain address, the officer arrives on the scene with little or no knowledge about the nature or the seriousness of the problem. The officer's first task is to determine the exact nature of the dispute: its seriousness, cause, principal offender, and the best disposition.

Police officers dislike domestic disputes because they can be extremely dangerous. According to the FBI, 30 percent of all assaults on officers occurred during "disturbance" calls (see Table 6-1). Disturbance calls also accounted for 10.7 percent of all police officers killed in the line of duty.

American Domestic Violence

Recent research has revealed that interpersonal violence is a frequent occurrence in the American home. Child abuse and spouse abuse are now recognized as serious problems. Murray Straus estimates that between 50 and 60 percent of all spouses are the victims of abuse. Only about 10 percent of all incidents are reported to the police. Finally, nearly one in five (18.6 percent) of all murders occur between family members.[2]

Violent crime within the family (murder or assault) is often the end result of a long history of domestic conflict. The Police Foundation discovered that in 85 percent of the domestic homicides in Kansas City the police had made at least one previous call to that address. In 50 percent of the domestic homicides, the police had made five or more previous calls.[3]

The Black Study

Donald Black has undertaken the most detailed study of domestic disputes. He analyzed 317 cases which he defined as "true disputes," meaning that they involved a

TABLE 6-1
LAW ENFORCEMENT OFFICERS ASSAULTED, 1978*

Type of activity	Total	Percent
Responding to "disturbance" calls (family quarrels, man with gun, etc.)	17,117	30.5
Burglaries in progress or pursuing burglary suspects	921	1.6
Robberies in progress or pursuing robbery suspects	729	1.3
Attempting other arrests	12,253	21.8
Civil disorder (riot, mass disobedience)	925	1.6
Handling, transporting, custody of prisoners	7,078	12.6
Investigating suspicious persons or circumstances	4,594	8.2
Ambush—no warning	264	.5
Mentally deranged	976	1.7
Traffic pursuits and stops	6,085	10.8
All other	5,188	9.2
Total	56,130	100.0†

*9150 agencies; 1978 estimated population 180,948,000
†Because of rounding, percentages may not add to total.
Source: U.S., Department of Justice, *FBI Uniform Crime Reports, 1978* (Washington, D.C.: U.S. Government Printing Office, 1979), p. 304.

request for the police to exercise some authority. These 317 cases included neighbor complaints about "noise" (30 percent of the total), situations where a woman was injured or threatened by a man (19 percent), disputes over property or money (14 percent), other kinds of physical fights (11 percent), requests that someone be removed from the premises (13 percent), child custody disputes (4 percent), and situations where someone was locked out of a residence or afraid to enter (5 percent).[4]

Disputes vary in terms of seriousness. In 26 percent of the cases the police had no legal grounds for taking any action. In another 9 percent of the cases there was evidence of some violation of the civil law (for example, a child custody situation). Slightly more than half of the cases involved a violation of the law: 37 percent involved misdemeanors and 18 percent involved felonies. Violence had occurred or had been threatened in 43 percent of the cases, and 17 percent involved a weapon.

Police Response   Police officers dislike domestic disputes not only because of the uncertainty and danger but also because of a sense of futility about what they can do. Donald Black quoted one officer as saying, "I hate those goddamn [domestic disputes]. There's not a thing you can do with them." Black also found that some officers deliberately drove slowly in response to domestic dispute calls in the hope that the dispute would resolve itself before they arrived.[5]

Black identified four different styles of control that police officers use to assert their authority in a domestic dispute: *penal* (condemnation or punishment); *compensatory* (persuading one person in the dispute to make restitution); *therapeutic* (providing help to an individual); or *conciliatory* (seeking a settlement of the dispute). The choice of a particular style involves an important exercise of police discretion. Police officers adopted a penal style in 22 percent of the total situations. The most frequent response (45 percent) was to use a combination of conciliatory and penal styles. Usually, this involved an attempt to settle the dispute while threatening punishment (possible arrest) for one or more of the disputants.[6] Table 6-2 shows the main variables involved in the officers, decision to use their arrest power or adopt an alternative style.

The Question of Race   The racial dimension of police response to domestic disputes is extremely important but very complex. Black found that the police are "more coercive toward blacks than toward whites" and that they devote "more time and energy to the disputes of whites than to those of blacks." Evidence of racial bias included the fact that "on a number of occasions the police frankly expressed their lack of concern for the problems of blacks."[7] The issue is complicated by the fact

---

TABLE 6-2
FACTORS INFLUENCING POLICE DISPOSITION OF DOMESTIC DISPUTES

Race
   1. The police devote more time and energy to the disputes of whites than to those of blacks.
   2. The police are more coercive toward blacks than toward whites.

Social Class
   3. The police devote more time and energy to the disputes of middle-class people than to those of lower- and working-class people.
   4. The police are more conciliatory and therapeutic toward middle-class people, more penal toward lower- and working-class people.

Household Status
   5. The police favor heads of household when they have disputes in their own dwellings.
   6. The police are more conciliatory as the parties to a household dispute are more equal, and they are more penal as the parties are less equal.

Age
   7. The police favor adults when they have disputes with juveniles.
   8. The police are more conciliatory toward adults, more penal and moralistic toward juveniles.

Intimacy
   9. The police are more likely to comply with complainants as the relational distance between the disputants increases.
   10. The police are more conciliatory as the parties to a dispute are more intimate, and they are more penal as the parties are more relationally distant.

Organization
   11. The police favor groups when they have disputes with individuals.
   12. The police are more conciliatory toward groups, more penal toward individuals.

Legitimacy
   13. The police are more penal and coercive as their authority is accorded less legitimacy, but only to a point, when they may withdraw.

Source: Donald Black, *The Manners and Customs of the Police* (New York: Academic Press, 1980), p. 187.

that black officers are apparently more likely to arrest black suspects than are white officers. Black suggests that black officers may be better able to relate to the black victims of violence or threatened violence. Thus, they may arrest black *suspects* more often in order to protect the black *victim*.

Family Crisis Intervention

The concept of family crisis intervention involves training police officers in special techniques for handling domestic disputes. The fact that many disputes are repeaters and that many result in murder or other serious violence indicates the need for more effective police response.

Dr. Morton Bard, a psychologist at City University of New York, pioneered the concept of family crisis intervention. Working with the New York City Police Department and with financial support from the Office of Law Enforcement Administration, Bard developed a special Family Crisis Intervention Unit (FCIU) in 1966.[8]

The FCIU included eighteen officers from New York's Thirtieth Precinct who received special training in psychology and the techniques of dispute resolution. Beginning in May 1967 the officers were deployed in three 6-member teams where they functioned as "generalist-specialists": they handled the normal work of patrol officers but were dispatched to all family-dispute calls. According to Bard, the "project sought to demonstrate the effective utilization of selected police officers in a program of crime prevention and preventive mental health." The program emphasized referral of citizens to community social service agencies.

A twenty-month evaluation of the project produced mixed findings. The FCIU handled 1388 incidents involving 962 families. The Twenty-fourth Precinct, which served as a control group, handled only 492 incidents involving 484 families. Not only were there more incidents, but there was a higher proportion of "repeat" calls in the FCIU area. However, homicides increased in the Thirtieth Precinct (the FCIU area) and decreased in the Twenty-fourth Precinct. The program directors expressed their conclusions in very cautious terms. It was their "impression" that an FCIU program "*may* serve to reduce the occurrence of family assaults and family homicides" and "*may* have a positive effect on police-community relations" (emphasis added).[9] The New York City FCIU project was not continued when funds from the federal grant ran out. Since then only a few police departments have attempted similar experiments.

In a subsequent experiment, supported by the Police Foundation, Morton Bard tested the use of three different approaches to handling domestic disputes. Police officers in Norwalk, Connecticut, compared the disposition of disputes through the use of "authority," "negotiation," and "counseling." The officers viewed the negotiation and counseling approaches more favorably after using them, while they viewed the authority approach less favorably.[10] The experiment did not draw any conclusions about the effectiveness of the different approaches in reducing domestic violence, but Bard did argue that it demonstrated the possibilities for effective collaboration between police and social scientists in dealing with routine police problems.

New Legal Considerations The crisis-intervention approach, which received a great deal of publicity in the 1960s and early 1970s, emphasized alternatives to the use of arrest (that is, mediation, counseling, referral). This rested on the assumption that arrest resulted in negative consequences for the citizens involved.

By the late 1970s, the social and legal climate changed significantly. Women's groups raised the issue of women as the victims of spouse abuse. Groups in New York City and Oakland sued the police for failing to protect battered women. The New York City Police Department settled the case *(Bruno v. Codd)* out of court in 1978 by agreeing to make arrests in situations where there was reasonable cause to believe that felonious assault had occurred. A similar suit against the Oakland police *(Scott v. Hart)* produced a similar settlement.[11] The new legal climate, in short, indicated a presumption in favor of arrest wherever there was evidence of violent assault.

POLICING JUVENILES

Policing juveniles presents difficult problems for the police. The main problem involves disagreement about the proper police role. One school of thought maintains that the police should adopt a strict *law enforcement role* toward juveniles: police should concentrate their efforts on violations of the criminal law and should make arrests when they encounter violations.

Another school of thought maintains that the police should adopt a *crime prevention role:* police officers should be concerned with assisting juveniles and should function primarily as social workers. Officers, according to this view, should seek to protect and rehabilitate juveniles who have committed a minor offense or who seem likely to commit a violation. The crime prevention role stresses handling juveniles through informal means; counseling is preferable to arrest. Arrest should be used only as a last resort and in cases of serious offenses.[12]

The IACP recommends a middle-of-the-road policy, combining the law enforcement and crime prevention roles: "Most police departments operate juvenile programs that combine the law enforcement and delinquency prevention roles, and the police should work with the juvenile court to determine a role that is most suitable for the community."[13]

For the officer on the street, the result of the combined approach is often role confusion (see Chapter 3). A recent report on police-juvenile operations pointed out that "Crime prevention can be viewed as 'social work,' a role which police often see as taking time away from what they consider to be their primary role—the apprehension of criminals."[14] Officers fear that if they adopt a friendly and helpful attitude in one situation they will not be taken seriously when the situation calls for a stricter law enforcement position.

Juvenile work is primarily located within two different parts of the police organization. Patrol officers routinely encounter juveniles and juvenile problems as part of their normal duty. Most large police departments also maintain a separate juvenile unit. These special units bear a variety of names: juvenile division, youth division, crime prevention division, etc. The separate juvenile unit normally adopts a clear crime prevention role. Patrol officers experience more confusion over the choice between the law enforcement and crime prevention roles.

O.W. Wilson defined the specific responsibilities of the separate juvenile unit as follows:[15]

1 The suppression and prevention of delinquent and criminal behavior by youths. Various codes define juvenile delinquency in terms of acts committed by persons under a certain age limit, usually sixteen to eighteen, but the youth division will find that there is so much overlapping of ages among participants in delinquent acts, particularly in gang activities, car thefts, and burglaries, that they are justified in concerning themselves with persons of all ages up to twenty-one when those over the statutory juvenile age but under twenty-one are involved with younger offenders.

2 The processing of youth arrests. When juveniles, minors with juveniles, and minors engaged in gang activities are taken into custody by any unit of the department, the youth-division personnel should be available to assist in the specialized handling of these cases.

3 The preparation and presentation of court cases. Youth-division personnel should present in court only those cases which have been completely investigated, and each case must be as ready for presentation as it is possible to make it.

4 The diversion of offenders out of the criminal justice system and adjustment of cases. When the best interests of the community and the individual are served by adjusting cases without resorting to court action, youth-division personnel should accomplish this by turning the offender over to his or her parents or other authorized adult and, where feasible, obtaining the assistance of appropriate community agencies.

5 The surveillance of amusement parks, recreation centers, schools, special events, and other places where youth problems are likely to develop. The youth division must maintain a liaison with the licensing section of the vice division in order that appropriate action may be taken against licensed establishments that contribute to juvenile delinquency.

6 The provision of intelligence relating to youthful offenders, with particular emphasis on gang membership and activities. The youth division should maintain a file on all known offenders and exchange information with the patrol and detective divisions and other crime-prevention agencies in the city as well as with the court.

7 The exercise of supervision over police efforts to deal with "status offenders"— youths who have not committed a crime per se but who are by statute given status as potential wards of the juvenile court. In this category are truants, runaways, children who are abandoned or abused by their parents, and so on.

Police-Juvenile Encounters

Encounters between patrol officers and juveniles are often problematic. The behavior of the juveniles is often legally ambiguous, involving potential but not necessarily actual serious lawbreaking. The role of the police officer is equally ambiguous in the sense that it is not clear whether the officer is adopting the law enforcement or the crime prevention role.

Another problem involves conflict over lifestyles. Werthman and Piliavin found that juvenile gangs regard the street corner as a "private place." This is where they engage in recreation with their friends. Gang members erect "transparent walls" between themselves and others using the streetcorner. Violation of this space is regarded as an actual "trespass."[16]

The use of public areas as private space is more common among low-income people. Middle-class juveniles also engage in the same practice, however. Teenagers frequently "cruise" the streets and use parks or commercial parking lots as party areas. These practices—which they regard as harmless recreation—bring them into conflict with other people who have different standards of public behavior. Police officers face the problem of mediating between these conflicting expectations. The fact that juveniles frequently operate their stereos at a loud volume and consume alcohol or drugs in violation of the law gives the police a pretext for intervention.

Police intervention in these disorder situations is difficult and frustrating. The officer often encounters hostile or belligerent behavior. Overreaction by the officer creates the possibility of a major, violent incident. Even if the officer succeeds in quieting or dispersing the crowd, the problem will probably reappear the next day, often in the same place. Werthman and Piliavin argue that in dealing with juvenile gangs, the officer must balance three competing interests—the rule of law, neighborhood practices, and the image of authority—without over- or underreacting.

Most encounters between the police and juveniles involve minor offenses. Only 5 percent of the encounters studied by Black and Reiss and 9 percent of those studied by Lundman et al. involved felonies. "Rowdiness," meanwhile, accounted for 60 percent and 44 percent of the encounters in the two studies, respectively.[17]

Disposition

Police officers respond to an encounter in one of several different ways. The most common response is for the officer to simply talk with the person or persons involved (either in the form of friendly counseling or stern warning or even possible threat of arrest) and leave the scene. If the officer takes the juvenile into custody, three options are available. The person can be released outright (often called "street release") with no formal record made, referred to a social-welfare agency (common in diversion programs), or referred to the juvenile court for formal processing.

Several factors influence disposition. The seriousness of the suspected offense is a major influence. Most felonies result in an arrest, while misdemeanors rarely do. Black and Reiss found that 15 percent of all encounters resulted in arrest; for Lundman et al. the figure was 16 percent. The demeanor of the juvenile is also important. Several studies have indicated that juveniles who exhibit disrespect for the police are more likely to be arrested. Police also respond to the wishes of the complaining party, especially an adult. Where the complaining adult wants the police to make an arrest, the police usually comply.[18]

Race. Whether or not systematic racial discrimination exists in police handling of juveniles is a matter of controversy. Early studies by Goldman and Piliavin and Briar indicated that the police were more likely to stop, question, and arrest black juveniles. Black and Reiss disagree, finding no evidence of systematic discrimination. It is true that more blacks are arrested than whites, relative to their numbers in the population. Black juveniles are arrested for more serious offenses, however. When the variable of offense seriousness is controlled, according to Black and Reiss, no systematic discrimination is found. Lundman et al. also suggest that black adults more often ask the police to arrest the suspect than do white adults, and that the police comply with these requests.[19]

Diversion Programs

In the late 1960s "diversion" emerged as a popular alternative in police handling of juveniles. Diversion may be defined as a formal program to temporarily delay prosecution, or send suspects into a "lower" level of the criminal justice system altogether. Diversion programs often involve referring the person to a social-service or treatment program rather than to juvenile court.

The concept of diversion received strong endorsement from the President's Crime Commission in 1967. The commission argued that "The formal sanctioning system [court] and pronouncement of delinquency should be used only as a last resort."[20] Labeling theory in criminology argues that individuals are more likely to continue lawbreaking activity once they have been officially designated delinquents. Diversion programs were intended both to avoid the labeling process and to provide more effective treatment of the suspect's needs (through job training, drug or alcohol abuse treatment, etc.).

Diversion was not a new idea in the 1960s. Police officers had traditionally practiced a form of diversion by simply talking to juveniles and releasing them. The so-called new diversion in the late 1960s involved the development of more formal processes of referral and treatment.[21]

Although popular, police diversion programs have not conclusively demonstrated their effectiveness. Examining nine evaluations of diversion programs, Gibbons and Blake concluded that there was "insufficient evidence" for any "confidence in diversion arguments and contentions."[22] Other critics have suggested that although diversion may bring more individuals under some form of social control, it carries its own form of labeling, and the decision to divert needs to be governed by due process guarantees.

SKID ROW

Alcohol-related offenses comprised 31.3 percent of all arrests in 1978—more than arrests for all seven index crimes. Many of these are repeat arrests of chronic alcoholics on skid row. Policing skid row is an important part of routine police work.

The term *skid row* describes both an identifiable geographic part of the city and a distinct part of the social structure. In other words, skid row is both a place and a way of life.[23]

Geographically, skid row is usually located in the inner city, near the central business district. Large cities may have several skid rows; Chicago, for example, has five different areas. Skid row is the home of society's chronic alcoholics. Also located in the area are the various services used by this population: bars and liquor stores, cheap flophouses and hotels, day-labor employment agencies, and social-service agencies such as the Salvation Army or church-related missions where skid row inhabitants can obtain baths, meals, and lodging.

The skid row inhabitant is typically a male with weak family or other social ties who works irregularly at best, is in poor health, and is a chronic alcoholic. Because they do not have strong ongoing relationships to other people (family, friends, job, etc.), skid row inhabitants are described as being "undersocialized." Economically, they survive by taking occasional day labor or by panhandling. They are routinely victimized by outsiders: they are exploited economically as a source of cheap labor, and are often the victims of robbery and assault.

Policing Skid Row

The police approach skid row primarily as a problem in peacekeeping.[24] In practice, this involves several objectives. One of the primary goals is to *contain the boundaries* of skid row. Skid row inhabitants, with their shabby dress, unshaven faces, and foul odor, are aesthetically offensive to the middle class. Panhandling is regarded as a major nuisance. Businesspeople are particularly concerned about keeping "bums" away from their stores because they are likely to scare away customers. Consequently, the police engage in a pattern of selective enforcement. The presence of the bum is generally tolerated on skid row but subject to arrest outside its boundaries. In this manner, the police define the geographic boundaries of skid row. (Occasionally, skid row is relocated completely through urban renewal.)

A second goal of the police is to *keep the peace* within skid row. Egon Bittner found that police officers develop "an immensely detailed factual knowledge" of the area. Like other police beats, skid row has its own normal routine. This includes a somewhat stable population (although there is a high rate of turnover) and an established routine to daily life. The officer knows when something abnormal is happening in the area.

The arrest of a skid row inhabitant usually has little to do with strict culpability. The person is not arrested because he or she has done something wrong but because the arrest serves some other purpose. One traditional purpose of arrest is simple protection. Skid row inhabitants are often helpless because of inebriation and their weak physical condition. They are easy prey for muggers (some of whom attack for the "fun" of it rather than for money), and some are so completely drunk that they are in danger of death through exposure to snow or rain. Arrest is simply a means of protecting the person.[25]

Arrests are also made for essentially aesthetic reasons. This occurs when the skid row inhabitant moves outside the boundaries, but it occurs within skid row as well. There are certain limits to unsightliness even in the relatively tolerant environment of skid row.

Periodic arrests also serve as reminders of police presence. The police "keep the peace" by reminding the inhabitants that they are tolerated only so long as they do not violate the norms of skid row. These norms include refraining from violence and overly aggressive panhandling.

Finally, arrests are made upon a specific complaint from a citizen. Skid rows are often located in or near warehouse districts or other low-rent commercial areas. People using the area for normal business activities may complain about a particularly offensive "bum."

Police Attitudes Police attitudes toward skid row inhabitants are complex. Generally, officers take a tolerant and even parental attitude, regarding them as children who cannot care for themselves. Arrest for protection reflects this approach. But officers also regard skid row inhabitants with contempt. Like middle-class society generally, they view skid row bums as weak and morally flawed people who have willfully "chosen" this way of life. Hence, they do not deserve any respect. Bums, then, are often the victims of police abuse, both verbal and physical. Because they have such weak contacts with normal society, skid row bums are basically defenseless against police abuse.

Changing Practices

Police practices toward skid row and alcohol-related offenses have been changing during the past twenty years. Though still sizable in number, alcohol-related arrests currently represent a much lower percentage of total arrests than previously. Between 1969 and 1978, arrests for drunkenness declined by nearly half.[26]

This trend reflects different influences. The rising volume of index crimes has prompted police to devote more time and resources to these more serious offenses. There has also been a trend toward decriminalization of the offense of public drunkenness. Decriminalization reflects mixed motives. In part it involves a due process consideration that drunkenness is a *condition* and not itself a criminal *act*. At the same time, some cities have experimented with *diversion,* referring chronic alcoholics to treatment centers rather than processing them through the criminal justice system.[27]

CRIMINAL INVESTIGATION

Criminal investigation is the most glamorous aspect of policing. Most police officers regard detective work as "real" police work, comparing it to the unfocused mission of patrol duty. Assignment to the detective bureau is one of the most prized rewards in an officer's career. The detective also dominates the public image of policing.

The Appeal of Detective Work

Detective work enjoys high status among police officers because of several features that make it a more attractive and satisfying assignment than patrol duty.[28]

Detectives are expected to exercise greater initiative and are freed from much of the direct supervision experienced by patrol officers. The opportunity for self-initiated activity offers greater job satisfaction. Freedom from direct supervision allows officers to control their own time and set their own pace of work (it also affords much greater opportunities to "goof off" on the job). Detectives work in civilian clothes, which enhances their sense of individuality.

The nature of the work also offers opportunities for greater job satisfaction. Detective work has a specific mission: apprehending the offender. An arrest represents tangible evidence of a job well done. The quality of work can also be measured in terms of the number of arrests, the importance of a particular arrest (for example, an arrest related to a highly publicized crime), and the percentage of arrests resulting in conviction. This contrasts sharply with patrol duty, which largely involves peace-keeping, where there is no final result or other tangible evidence of a job well done.

Finally, detective work is consistent with the crime-fighter image of the police. It offers the officer who accepts the crime-fighter role model a more satisfying self-image.

The Myth   The image of detective work bears little relationship to the realities of criminal investigation. According to popular belief, the detective is a "clever, imaginative, perseverant, streetwise cop who consorts with glamorous women and duels with crafty criminals." Herman Goldstein identifies the mystique of the detective as the belief that (1) criminal investigation is exciting, "a real science," and more important than patrol work; (2) the detective possesses "difficult-to-come-by qualifications and skills"; and (3) that "a good detective can solve any crime." In fact, there is little basis for any of these assumptions.[29]

The media play an important role in shaping the myth of the detective. From Sherlock Holmes to *Dragnet* and *Kojak,* detective stories have been an extremely popular form of entertainment. The importance of the media image lies in its influence on both the public and the police. Goldstein observes that "Many of the techniques employed by detectives today are more heavily influenced by a desire to imitate stereotypes than by a rational plan for solving crimes."[30]

The media image of detective work also creates unreasonable public expectations. Believing that good detectives can solve most crimes, the citizen-victim becomes frustrated and angry when the police fail to solve the crime he or she suffered. As Goldstein points out, "the capacity of detectives to solve crimes is greatly exaggerated."[31]

The Reality   Contrary to popular belief, detective work is neither glamorous nor exciting. According to Harold Pepinsky, "Most detectives spend the bulk of their time at their desks, going through papers and using the telephone."[32]

The Rand Corporation study is the most thorough analysis of detective work. Peter Greenwood and associates surveyed 153 police departments by mail and conducted interviews with officials at 29 departments. The report punctured many of the myths surrounding detective work. Actual detective work is superficial, routine, and non-productive: "many reported felonies receive no more than superficial attention from investigators" and "most minor crimes are not investigated" at all. Only 30 percent of all residential burglaries and 18 percent of all larcenies are worked on by detectives. The bulk of detective work involves "reviewing reports, documenting files, and attempting to locate and interview victims."[33]

Other problems with detective work include a tendency to collect more physical

evidence than can be effectively used and a failure to communicate well with prosecutors in developing cases. Also, detectives fail to notify crime victims about the
progress of cases, leading to considerable public dissatisfaction.

Investigating a Crime

The process of investigating a crime involves several different steps performed by at
least three different units within the police department: patrol officers, detectives,
criminalistics technicians. The two major stages of the investigation process are the
preliminary investigation and the follow-up investigation.

Preliminary Investigation   The preliminary investigation is normally the responsibility of the patrol officer who is the first to arrive at the scene of the crime. The
five major responsibilities include: (1) arresting any suspect or suspects, (2) providing
aid to any victims needing immediate medical attention, (3) securing the crime scene
to prevent loss of evidence, (4) collecting all relevant physical evidence, and (5) pre-
paring a preliminary report.[34] The preliminary investigation is extremely important.
Recent research has found that most crimes are cleared because of arrests or evidence collected by the first officer on the scene.[35]

Detective Unit   Once the responding officer has completed the preliminary investigation, the case is assigned to the detective bureau for the follow-up investigation.
In all but the smallest departments, the detective unit is separate from the patrol
unit. About 12 percent of all sworn officers in a department are normally assigned
to the detective unit.[36]

Detective units are organized differently, according to the size of the department
and the investigation workload. The smallest departments are completely unspecialized, with no separate detective unit at all. Medium-sized departments have a separate detective unit, but with no internal specialization: detectives handle all types
of crime. Larger departments specialize according to type of crime. Typically the
division is between crimes against persons and crimes against property. The very
largest departments, because of their size and workload, specialize even further, with
a separate homicide unit, robbery unit, and so on. Figure 6.1 indicates the organization of the criminal investigation bureau of the Omaha police department.

Two alternatives to the organization of detective units described above exist. One,
found in the largest police departments, decentralizes criminal investigation by geographic sector. Each geographic sector has its own detective unit. A second alternative is the team policing approach discussed in Chapter 4, with detectives working
closely with patrol officers in assigned geographic areas.[37]

Criminalistics   Technical specialists in investigation are normally located in a
separate administrative unit. They are available upon request to assist detectives in
the follow-up investigation. Only the larger police departments are able to maintain
their own criminalistics specialists. Smaller departments normally utilize the services
of either a neighboring large department or state police agency. Virtually all police

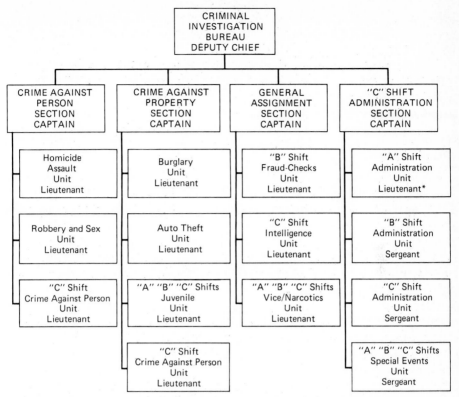

*Commanding Officer in charge of the Crime Against Person Section, Crime Against Property Section, General Assignment Section and the Administration Section of the "A" Shift

FIGURE 6.1
Organizational structure of the Criminal Investigation Bureau, Omaha Police Division. *(Omaha Police Division, Annual Report, 1979.)*

departments have technical services available to them through some form of cooperative arrangement.[38]

The Follow-Up Investigation The follow-up investigation includes the following steps: (1) interrogation of suspect or suspects, if arrested at the scene of the crime; (2) interview of witnesses; (3) search of the crime scene for physical evidence (at this point, criminalistics technicians may be brought in); (4) *modus operandi* review to determine if the crime is similar to others under investigation or resembles crimes committed by known suspects; (5) development of additional information from informants, contacts, official records, etc.; (6) preparation of reports.[39]

Case Screening All cases do not receive equal attention. Detectives screen cases, using either formal or informal methods. According to the Rand Corporation study of criminal investigation, most cases receive only superficial attention, with one day or less of investigation. Detectives routinely screen out those cases they are not likely to solve and devote their attention to cases where identification of a suspect seems likely.[40]

Traditionally, detectives screened cases informally, making judgments based on their own experience and intuition. Recently, however, police departments have begun to develop formal screening procedures. A Police Executive Research Forum survey found that 36 out of 49 departments used some formal screening procedure.[41]

Clearance Rates

The traditional measure of success for police with respect to crime is the *clearance rate.* According to the FBI, "Law enforcement agencies clear a crime when they have identified the offender, have sufficient evidence to charge him, and actually take him into custody, or in exceptional instances, when some element beyond police control precludes taking the offender into custody."[42] Figure 6.2 shows the clearance rates for the seven index crimes in 1977. Nationally, only 21 percent of all reported crimes are cleared. The clearance rate varies dramatically according to the type of crime. Interpersonal crimes of violence have a relatively high rate, while property crimes have an extremely low rate.

As a measure of performance, the clearance rate has several problems. First, the rate is based on official figures of *reported* crimes. Victimization surveys, however, indicate large numbers of crimes are not reported. In 1978 only 50.6 percent of all robberies were reported. The adjusted clearance rate, then, would be 13 percent. The

FIGURE 6.2
Crimes cleared by arrest, 1977. *(Federal Bureau of Investigation, Uniform Crime Reports, 1978, p. 176.)*

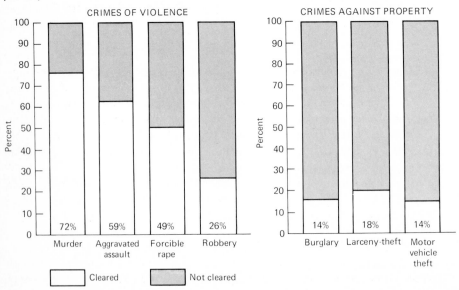

adjusted clearance rate for burglary would be 7 percent (based on a 46.9 percent reporting rate).[42]

The Rand Corporation study of criminal investigation identified other problems with official crime rates. Apprehension of the offender does not necessarily occur in the same reporting period as the crime. Thus, it would be possible to have three murders and four arrests in one year (one of the arrests being for a crime the previous year) which would yield a clearance rate of 133 percent. Also, police departments use different definitions of clearance. Some report as cleared only the crime for which the suspect was apprehended. Other departments "clear" additional crimes they believe the suspect committed even though the person is not formally charged with them. The Rand study concludes that "the clearance rate is generally unreliable as a measure" of police performance.[44]

"Solvability" Clearance rates vary for different crimes in large part because of the nature of the crime. Skogan and Antunes argue that "crimes differ in the extent to which they admit of solution." Clearance rates are generally low because, as the LEAA report on the New York City Street Crime Unit indicates, "most of the crimes are not at all susceptible to solutions." The size of the detective unit, the level of training, and the techniques used are largely irrelevant. The majority of the crimes that are cleared, Reiss and Bordua argue, "solve themselves in the sense that the violator is 'known' to the complainant or to the police at the time the crime initially comes to the attention of the police."[45]

Interpersonal crimes have relatively high clearance rates. The FBI reports that 72 percent of all murders are cleared. This is largely because in 56 percent of all murders the victim and the offender were acquainted with each other. Prior relationship between victim and offender also accounts for the high rates of clearance for aggravated assault and rape. The clearance rate for robbery is higher than for burglary because the victim is more likely to have a description of the offender. The lowest clearance rates are for those crimes (burglary, theft, auto theft) where there is no direct personal contact.

Crimes Cleared Most crimes are cleared as a result of work done by the responding officer. The most important determinant of whether or not a crime will be cleared is information about the identity of a prime suspect provided by the victim or witnesses. Table 6-3 presents an analysis of 1905 crimes that came to the attention of the Los Angeles Police Department in the summer of 1966. A suspect was named in 349 of those cases; 86.2 percent of those cases were eventually cleared. Only 11.6 percent of the cases where a suspect was not named were eventually cleared.

In short, follow-up investigations produced very few clearances. An Oakland, California, study concluded that "most robbery apprehensions are made as the result of immediate action by citizens and the police." Between 60 and 90 percent of all arrests were made by patrol officers.[46]

Productivity Measured in terms of arrests, the productivity of the police varies from department to department and from officer to officer. The Rand study found

TABLE 6-3
CRIMES CLEARED, BY SUSPECT NAMED OR NOT NAMED

Outcome	Number of cases	Suspect named	Suspect not named
Cleared	482	301	181
Not cleared	1423	48	1375
Total	1905	349	1556

Source: President's Commission on Law Enforcement and Administration of Justice, *Task Force Report: Science and Technology* (Washington, D.C.: U.S. Government Printing Office, 1967), p. 8.

that the amount of formal training, the procedures used, and the staffing and organization of investigative units had little impact on productivity.

The productivity of individual officers varies considerably. Riccio and Heaphy found that the number of arrests for index crimes ranged from a low of 2.18 to a high of 12.06 per officer. The Institute for Law and Society measured productivity in terms of "quality" arrests: those leading to a felony conviction. It found that a very small number of officers in the department accounted for an extremely high percentage of quality arrests. Out of 2418 police officers, 747 (31 percent) made no arrests that led to a conviction, while 368 officers (15 percent) made over half of the arrests that resulted in a conviction.[47]

Managing Investigations

The task of criminal investigation is generally not well managed, according to the Rand study. Criminal investigation textbooks concentrate on the technical aspects of the job: securing the crime scene, preserving physical evidence, conducting interrogations, etc. Little attention is given to planning, the development of clear goals and objectives, evaluating effectiveness, and supervising day-to-day work. The Rand study commented that "most investigators receive little substantive supervision on the performance of their jobs."

Federal Investigations In a study of the FBI and the Drug Enforcement Agency (DEA), James Q. Wilson analyzed criminal investigation as a task to be managed. Traditional thinking in the field of public administration, he argues, concentrated on the larger questions of the goals and resources of an agency. Insufficient attention has been given to the management of particular tasks.[48]

Wilson compared the means-oriented approach to criminal investigation used by the FBI with the goal-oriented approach of the DEA. The FBI traditionally emphasized the production of statistics: cases investigated, arrests made, convictions obtained, and stolen property recovered. This approach required agents to complete frequent, detailed reports of their activities. Wilson commented that "The practical question, of course, is whether the statistics employed accurately measure important things. For the most of its history FBI statistics did not meet this test." FBI statistics failed to distinguish important cases from minor cases and frequently inflated the value of recovered stolen property.

The DEA's approach set clear objectives for the number of arrests for each class of felony. The DEA strategy was to "work up," using Class 3 and 4 felony arrests as a way of obtaining more Class 1 and 2 felony arrests. Wilson found that this approach was not successful.

Both the FBI and the DEA are federal agencies. Criminal investigations in municipal police departments rarely utilize the kind of thinking found in those agencies. Little thought is given to long-range objectives and the tactics to be used in achieving them.

Improving Investigation Management   Several approaches have been developed to improve the management of criminal investigations. Skogan and Antunes emphasize the importance of citizen cooperation. In their view, citizens are coproducers of the kind of information that leads to arrests and convictions. They recommend that departments take steps to enhance the cooperation of citizens. In this respect, criminal investigation depends upon the quality of police-community relations for a given department.[49]

A second approach to improving productivity is to develop closer working relationships between patrol officers and detectives. In many instances, the two units compete rather than cooperate. Officers jealously guard their information and sources. In a competitive spirit, each officer hopes to achieve the "reward" of the important arrest.[50]

More efficient case screening is another way to improve the management of investigations. The Stanford Research Institute and the Police Executive Research Forum (PERF) developed a model for screening burglary cases. Under this system factors associated with each crime are assigned a certain number of points. The description or name of a suspect is worth nine points, an eye-witness report of the offense is worth seven points, usable fingerprints are worth seven points, and so on. Cases with more than ten points have a high probability of being cleared and are assigned for follow-up investigation. Cases with fewer than ten points do not receive follow-up investigation. Applying this system retrospectively to 12,000 cases, the researchers found that it would have successfully predicted the outcome (clearance or nonclearance) 85 percent of the time.[51]

The Rochester, New York, police department experimented with a team-policing approach to investigations. Each team consisted of thirty-six officers, thirty patrol officers and six detectives. The team was assigned to provide the full range of police services to a given geographic area on a twenty-four-hour basis. A four-month evaluation of the experiment in 1973 indicated that the team approach was three times more effective than the traditional approach in securing arrests for robbery and 50 percent more effective for burglary arrests. The report concluded that "a police department can improve its arrest and clearance rates by assigning detectives to work as part of police teams," rather than have them work independently in a centralized criminal investigation unit.[52]

POLICING VICE

Crimes of vice—prostitution, gambling, narcotics—present special problems for the police. These problems involve the nature of the criminal law, public attitudes toward vice crimes, and the practical problems of obtaining evidence.

The Law and Public Attitudes

American law labels a wide range of behavior as criminal. This tendency to deal with social problems (alcohol- and drug-related problems, for example) and questions of morality through the criminal law has created a crisis of overcriminalization. Many experts argue that American society has used the criminal law too frequently to deal with issues that could better be handled without the use of the criminal sanction.[53] The practical consequence for the police is that they face an enormous range of actual and potential criminal activity—far more than they can reasonably handle.

The problem is further complicated by ambivalent public attitudes about crimes of vice. In many instances the law making a particular behavior criminal is little more than a symbolic gesture. Legislators want to be on record as opposing a certain kind of behavior (prostitution, etc.) because it is "bad" or "wrong." They do not expect or necessarily want the law to be enforced.

Ambivalent public attitudes toward vice result partly from the pluralistic nature of our society. The population contains a wide range of races, ethnic groups, religions, and cultural lifestyles. Strong differences of opinion exist concerning the morality of commercial sex, gambling, and the use of "soft" drugs such as marijuana. The practical result for the police is that they face conflicting public pressure about which crimes to concentrate on. Certain groups want a tough policy toward gambling while others want a tolerant policy.

Investigating "Victimless" Crimes   Vice crimes are often considered essentially "victimless" crimes. Individuals participate in them voluntarily and there is no overt victim who has suffered some harm involuntarily. This creates a major law enforcement problem for the police. The lack of a victim or complaining party means that the police have to develop information about vice activities through their own initiative. Investigating victimless crimes and obtaining needed evidence leads the police to engage in often questionable tactics. Most vice crimes occur in private, and to obtain information or evidence the police may violate individuals' privacy.[54] Using wiretaps to investigate gambling operations is one example. Entrapment is another problem. The policing of prostitution and drug dealing often involves situations where the police induce the suspect into committing the offense.

Informants   To obtain information about suspected criminal activity, the police make use of informants. Persons who are either criminals themselves or who associate with criminals are extremely valuable sources of information. Police officers seek to develop a list of informants, individuals they can rely upon for accurate information.

The use of informants involves a number of serious problems. Jonathan Rubinstein observes that "Vice information is a commodity, and the patrolman learns that he must buy it on a restricted market."[55] To obtain information the officer must provide something in return. The most valuable commodity officers can provide is a promise of protection: they can agree to not arrest a person engaged in some form of criminal activity in exchange for information about other crimes and criminals.

This exchange with an informant brings the police into a business relationship with a criminal. By agreeing to not arrest a person, officers compromise their integrity. Some experts believe that the use of informants inevitably corrupts the police. The problem is compounded by the fact that police departments have traditionally provided no guidelines for the use of informants. Each officer is expected to learn how to use informants through word of mouth or personal experience.

Accounts of corruption in the New York City Police Department in the 1970s revealed that detectives maintained regular informants who were narcotics addicts by providing them with drugs. As a result, the officers found themselves in the role of drug dealers. Jerome Skolnick found that in "Westville" narcotics detectives generally allowed their informants to steal, while burglary detectives allowed their informants to engage in drug dealing.[56]

Vice and Police Corruption   Crimes of vice are a major source of police corruption. Enforcement efforts bring police officers into a close relationship with the criminal element. Vice crimes are the source of large profit, particularly gambling, and the criminals have an interest in protecting their business enterprise by corrupting officials.

Because of the enormous profits involved and the ambivalent public attitudes toward strict law enforcement, vice crimes create great temptations for corruption. They are part of the external environment that contributes to the existence of police corruption. (See Chapter 8 for a detailed discussion of this issue.)

Prostitution

As a business activity, prostitution is divided into two basic categories. Each one presents the police with a different problem in law enforcement.

Prostitutes may be classified as either call girls or streetwalkers. Call girls represent the upper end of the economic scale. They cater to a more affluent customer and generally make their arrangements through the telephone. As a result, their activities are much less visible to the public and to the police. The absence of public visibility means that there is less pressure for strict law enforcement. And because the women are not on the street, the police must use more initiative in trying to gather information about call-girl activity.[57]

Streetwalkers represent the low end of the economic scale. The women themselves are generally low-income, and prostitution is for them an easily entered profession. Because the women solicit on the streets, they present a very different problem for both the public and the police. Visibility generates public pressure for strict law enforcement. Periodically, there is an outcry from the media, elected officials, or moralistic civic leaders for a crackdown on prostitution.

The police respond to pressures for a crackdown by sweeping the street and arresting large numbers of suspected prostitutes. Police officers, however, recognize that their efforts are largely futile. In most cities, the normal penalty is a fine amounting to no more than a few hundred dollars or a short jail sentence. From the standpoint of the prostitute, this amounts to little more than a routine business expense. The women are usually back on the street, plying their trade, very soon afterward. In this respect, prostitution arrests are similar to arrests of chronic alcoholics. They are handled by means of revolving-door justice that imposes a small sanction and does not deal with the long-range problem.[58]

Obtaining evidence against suspected streetwalkers and pimps can present difficult legal problems. If the officer initiates the idea of sex for pay, he may be found to have engaged in entrapment. Because of the evidentiary problems, conviction can be difficult to achieve. A 1965 revision of the New York law regarding prostitution, which tightened the evidentiary requirements, resulted in an increase in streetwalker activity.[59]

Associated with prostitution are various ancillary crimes which represent a more serious problem. Patrons of prostitutes are occasionally robbed. Pimps, meanwhile, often maintain control over their prostitutes through intimidation and violence. In addition, selective enforcement has been a traditional part of police response to prostitution. Under the law, both prostitute and patron are guilty of the offense. In practice, police have traditionally arrested the woman but not the man. In recent years there has been greater pressure for equal enforcement of the laws.

Gambling

Gambling represents a particularly difficult problem for the police and the entire criminal justice system. The heart of the problem lies in ambivalent public attitudes toward gambling. On the one hand, the law prohibits most forms of gambling (with the exception of on-track horse-race betting, bingo, and legalized casinos in Nevada and New Jersey). On the other hand, a majority of Americans regard gambling as a legitimate form of recreation. Betting on athletic events is an established social custom. The "numbers" is an important part of daily life in many low-income neighborhoods.[60]

A Justice Department report on gambling law enforcement found that it is an extremely unattractive task for the police. Officers perceived that there is little public support for strict enforcement and that most people do not regard social gambling as a serious crime. Also, most officers felt that police department policies toward gambling enforcement were not clear. The officers themselves were generally left to work out an enforcement policy on their own.[61]

Gambling enforcement is a difficult and unrewarding task. Because social gambling takes place in private places and has no victims, information is difficult to develop. Detectives must rely either upon informants or wiretaps to gather information about gambling activities. Successful prosecution is also difficult to achieve. The use of wiretaps raises serious problems of the admissability of evidence. Even where prosecution is successful, the penalties are often very mild. The Justice Department report found that the typical fine amounted to only one or two days' profit for the gambling operation. In other words, it was little more than a small "tax."[62]

Police policies toward gambling create serious problems. The Justice Department report found that nonenforcement "does indeed seriously affect the way citizens judge their police department." A department's failure to suppress gambling contributes to negative evaluations of the department's overall performance. Significantly, nonwhites expressed greater interest in enforcement than did whites. This is probably because gambling (and other vice) enforcement has traditionally been tolerated by the police in nonwhite and low-income areas. Middle-class blacks, as a result, are more aware of gambling activities in their neighborhoods.

Gambling is also a major source of police corruption (see Chapter 8). The enormous profits from gambling activities are the principal source of income for organized crime. The corruption of law enforcement, in the context, becomes a tax that is paid to allow the gambling operation to continue.

Narcotics

The context of drug enforcement has been changing significantly over the past fifteen years. The extent of drug usage has steadily spread throughout society. Marijuana usage, for example, spread across college campuses in the mid-1960s and in the 1970s became increasingly popular among high school and even junior high school students. For a significant part of the population today, regardless of age, class, or race, marijuana is a popular recreational drug. The increased popularity of marijuana has been paralleled by increased usage of other addictive (heroin) and nonaddictive (cocaine) drugs.

The changing context of drug usage in the United States includes greater usage, more tolerant public attitudes, and a changing legal environment. Many areas have significantly reduced the penalties for possession of small amounts of "soft" drugs (for example, marijuana). At the same time some areas have sharply increased the penalties for drug trafficking. The 1973 New York drug law is the best example of the punitive approach.

Police practices have responded to the changing context. Possession of small amounts of marijuana is no longer a top law enforcement priority for most police departments. Narcotics enforcement tends to emphasize arrest of major drug dealers, and of dealers in heroin and cocaine in particular.

Part of the concern with heroin involves the addict-burglar connection. The police and the media argue that heroin addicts are responsible for a large percentage of burglaries, since they must steal to maintain their habits. Unfortunately, there is little evidence to substantiate the extent of the connection between heroin addiction and burglary. According to *Police* magazine, the junkie-burglar connection is largely myth. No one knows how many people actually use heroin in any community. Moreover, most of the heroin users are not addicted, and many users support their use without resort to predatory crime. Finally, it is not clear that addicts steal because they are addicts. Heroin usage may be one part of a criminal lifestyle and, in many cases, stealing precedes heroin usage.[63]

Police magazine also suggested that police activities did not curtail heroin usage. Law enforcement agencies typically approach the drug problem by attempting to arrest the major dealers and thereby "dry up" the supply. The DEA adopted a policy of "working up" the drug traffic ladder: arrests of small dealers, they assumed, would lead them to major dealers. On the whole, law enforcement strategies to suppress drug traffic have failed. Federal agents succeed in stopping only a small percentage of drugs brought into this country. The DEA policy of "working up" did not succeed, according to James Q. Wilson. State and local efforts have been equally unsuccessful.[64] In the face of this general failure, narcotics units of major police departments continue to go through the motions of enforcement.

Peter K. Manning characterizes drug enforcement as *The Narcs' Game*. Drug enforcement activities, he argues, are conducted for their "dramaturgical effect." The "big bust" is done for its impact on publicity rather than for its effect on the supply of drugs. Manning found that police departments lack any explicit policy with regard to drug enforcement. Individual agents are left on their own.[65] The big bust is widely publicized to maintain the impression that drugs are a serious problem in the community, and that the police are doing an effective job in attempting to suppress the drug traffic. Manning points out that many aspects of drug enforcement are not publicized. These include the mistakes, the small average size of most drug busts, the high cost of many drug buys, the number of raids that yield no drugs or arrests, and the drug "buy money" given to informants who then disappear.

As the title of his book suggests, Manning argues that narcotics enforcement is essentially a game. The police are unable to control drug traffic and do not even know how large or extensive it is. They approach it with no explicit policy and no meaningful measure of their own effectiveness. The rituals of drug enforcement (especially the big bust) are conducted primarily to maintain a public image of tough enforcement.

TRAFFIC

The enforcement of traffic laws is unique because it produces the broadest range of contact between the police and the public. For the most part, the average citizen is rarely in direct contact with a police officer. Criminal events and requests for police service involve a relatively small segment of the total population. Traffic law enforcement is the exception to this rule. Most adult citizens drive cars, and minor violations of traffic laws are common.

Traffic law enforcement is the source of low-level but significant friction between the police and the public. Citizens resent being stopped, asked to produce identification, and ticketed for what are often minor violations that do not greatly endanger the public safety. Because of this citizen resentment, police officers generally find traffic law enforcement a distasteful task and one that they often seek to avoid.[66]

Administration

Although responsibility for traffic law enforcement belongs to all officers, departments with more than 200 sworn officers generally maintain a separate traffic unit.

An average of about 7 percent of all officers are allocated to traffic units, although in some departments the figure is as high as 15 percent.[67]

The enforcement of traffic law violations varies widely from department to department. John Gardiner found that Dallas police officers wrote twenty times as many tickets as officers in Boston, even though both cities were approximately the same size at the time of the study. James Q. Wilson found similar variations in traffic law enforcement in his study of police discretion.[68]

High rates of traffic law enforcement are generally the result of a formal or informal departmental policy. Different motives produce tough enforcement policies. In some cases it can result from a conscious attempt to increase public safety. The policy may be determined by community pressure, the decision of elected public officials, or simply the initiative of the top police administrator. In other cases, however, a tough enforcement policy is mainly a management strategy to control the behavior of officers on the street. Because officers are not supervised by direct observation, management seeks other devices to ensure that they "produce." Traffic citations, which involve a written record of police officer initiative, are used as an index of production. Quotas on traffic citations are a means of ensuring that all officers are working.[69]

In some cases, the writing of tickets is the result of an individual officer's initiative. An officer with an aggressive working style may write large numbers of tickets for various reasons. It may be part of an effort to impress supervisors. On the other hand, it may be part of a crime suppression strategy. Traffic stops dramatically enhance the impression of a police presence. Officers are also able to gather useful information during a traffic stop, either by conversation or direct observation.

Recently there has been an upsurge of public concern about drunk driving. In many communities citizen groups have advocated tougher law enforcement in this area. Responding to the pressure, several states have enacted new laws with heavier penalties for drunk driving. The impact of these new laws depends on whether police officers choose to enforce them.

REVIEW

1 Why are domestic disputes an important aspect of policing?

2 Describe the concept of "family crisis intervention."

3 What is the nature of the role conflict in police-juvenile operations?

4 What factors influence the disposition of juvenile encounters by police officers?

5 Discuss the role of the police on skid row.

6 What are the principal myths of detective work?

7 Indicate the factors that contribute to the "solvability" of different kinds of crime.

8 Indicate ways in which the management of criminal investigations can be improved.

9 What are the major problems facing the police with respect to investigating crimes of vice?

10 How effective are the police in suppressing narcotics traffic?

REFERENCES

1 James Q. Wilson, *Varieties of Police Behavior* (New York: Atheneum, 1973), p. 18; Elaine Cumming, Ian Cumming, and Laura Edell, "Policeman as Philosopher, Guide and Friend," *Social Problems* 12, no. 3 (1965): 276–286.

2 Nancy Loving, *Responding to Spouse Abuse and Wife Beating: A Guide For Police* (Washington, D.C.: Police Executive Research Forum, 1980), p. 14.

3 The Police Foundation, *Domestic Violence and the Police* (Washington, D.C.: Police Foundation, 1977), p. 9.

4 Donald Black, *The Manners and Customs of the Police* (New York: Academic Press, 1980), pp. 119–120.

5 Ibid., pp. 146, 188–189.

6 Ibid., pp. 138–139.

7 Ibid., pp. 136–139.

8 Morton Bard, *Training Police as Specialists in Family Crisis Intervention* (Washington, D.C.: Law Enforcement Assistance Administration, 1970).

9 Ibid.

10 Morton Bard, *The Police and Interpersonal Conflict: Third-Party Intervention Approaches* (Washington, D.C.: Police Foundation, 1976).

11 Loving, *Responding to Spouse Abuse and Wife Beating*, pp. 36–37.

12 National Institute for Juvenile Justice and Delinquency Prevention, *Police-Juvenile Operations: A Comparative Analysis of Standards and Practices,* II (Washington, D.C.: U.S. Government Printing Office, n.d.) pp. 3–10.

13 R. Kobetz and B. Borsage, *Juvenile Justice Administration* (Gaithersburg, Md.: IACP, 1973), p. 112.

14 National Institute of Juvenile Justice, *Police-Juvenile Operations*, p. 3.

15 O. W. Wilson and Roy C. McLaren, *Police Administration*, 4th ed. (New York: McGraw-Hill, 1977), pp. 413–414.

16 Carl Werthman and Irving Piliavin, "Gang Members and the Police," in *The Police: Six Sociological Essays,* ed., David J. Bordua (New York: John Wiley, 1967), pp. 58–59.

17 Richard J. Lundman, et al., "Police Control of Juveniles: A Replication," *Journal of Research in Crime and Delinquency* 15 (January 1978): 78–79.

18 Ibid., 80–83.

19 Ibid., 83–84; Nathan Goldman, *Differential Selection of Juvenile Offenders for Court Appearance* (New York: National Council on Crime and Delinquency, 1963); Irving Piliavin and Scott Briar, "Police Encounters with Juveniles," *American Journal of Sociology* 70 (September 1964): 206–214; Donald Black and Albert J. Reiss, "Police Control of Juveniles," *American Sociological Review* 35 (February 1970): 63–77.

20 President's Commission on Law Enforcement and Administration of Justice, *The Challenge of Crime in a Free Society* (New York: Avon Books, 1968). p. 220.

21 Raymond T. Nimmer, *Diversion* (Chicago: American Bar Foundation, 1974), pp. 11–18.

22 Donald S. Gibbons and Gerald F. Blake, "Evaluating the Impact of Diversion Programs," *Crime and Delinquency* 22 (October 1976): 411–420.

23 Raymond T. Nimmer, *Two Million Unnecessary Arrests* (Chicago: American Bar Foundation, 1971), chap. 2.

24 Egon Bittner, "The Police on Skid-Row: A Study in Peace-Keeping," *American Sociological Review* 32 (October 1967): 694–715.

25 Wayne R. LaFave, *Arrest: The Decision to Take a Suspect into Custody* (Boston: Little, Brown, 1965), pp. 440–449.

26 Federal Bureau of Investigation, *Uniform Crime Reports—1978* (Washington, D.C.: U.S. Government Printing Office, 1979), p. 188.
27 Nimmer, *Two Million Unnecessary Arrests,* chaps. 5–7.
28 William A. Westley, *Violence and the Police* (Cambridge: MIT Press, 1970), pp. 36–44.
29 Herman Goldstein, *Policing a Free Society* (Cambridge: Ballinger, 1977), pp. 55–56.
30 Ibid., p. 55.
31 Ibid., p. 56.
32 Harold E. Pepinsky, "Police Decision-Making," in *Decision-Making in the Criminal Justice System: Reviews and Essays,* ed. Don Gottfredson (Washington, D.C.: National Institute of Mental Health, 1975). p. 27.
33 Greenwood, *Criminal Investigation Process,* p. 110.
34 George D. Eastman, ed., *Municipal Police Administration,* 7th ed. (Washington, D.C.: International City Management Association, 1971), pp. 134–136.
35 Greenwood, *Criminal Investigation Process,* p. 26.
36 Police Executive Research Forum, *Police Practices: The General Administrative Survey* (Washington, D.C.: Police Foundation, 1978), p. 9.
37 Peter B. Bloch and James Bell, *Managing Investigations: The Rochester System* (Washington, D.C.: Police Foundation, 1976).
38 Elinor Ostrom, et al., *Patterns of Metropolitan Policing* (Cambridge: Ballinger, 1977), chap. 7.
39 Eastman, *Municipal Police Administration,* pp. 136–137.
40 Peter W. Greenwood, et al., *The Criminal Investigation Process,* vol. 1, *Summary and Policy Implications* (Santa Monica: Rand Corporation, 1975).
41 Police Executive Research Forum, *Police Practices,* n.p.
42 FBI, *Uniform Crime Reports—1978,* p. 175.
43 U.S., Department of Justice, *Criminal Victimization in the United States, 1978* (Washington, D.C.: U.S. Government Printing Office, 1980), p. 72.
44 Greenwood, *Criminal Investigation Process,* p. 32.
45 Wesley G. Skogan and George E. Antunes, "Information, Apprehension and Deterrence: Exploring the Limits of Police Productivity," *Journal of Criminal Justice* 7 (Fall 1979): 219; U.S., Department of Justice, *New York City Police: Street Crime Unit* (Washington, D.C.: U.S. Government Printing Office, n.d.), p. 2; Albert Reiss and David J. Bordua, "Environment and Organization: A Perspective on the Police," in *The Police,* ed., David J. Bordua, p. 43.
46 Goldstein, *Policing a Free Society,* p. 56.
47 Lucius J. Riccio and John F. Heaphy, "Apprehension Productivity of Police in Large U.S. Cities," *Journal of Criminal Justice* 5 (Winter 1977): 271–278; U.S., Department of Justice, *Justice Assistance News* 2 (April 1981): 4–5.
48 James Q. Wilson, *The Investigators* (New York: Basic Books, 1978).
49 Skogan and Antunes, "Information, Apprehension and Deterrence," pp. 217–241.
50 Jonathan Rubinstein, *City Police* (New York: Ballantine Books, 1974), pp. 121–122, 138.
51 *Criminal Justice News,* February 4, 1980, pp. 4–5.
52 Bloch and Bell, *Managing Investigations.*
53 Norval Morris and Gordon Hawkins, *The Honest Politician's Guide to Crime Control* (Chicago: University of Chicago Press, 1970), chap. 1.
54 Arthur L. Stinchcombe, "Institutions of Privacy in the Determination of Police Administrative Practice," *American Journal of Sociology,* 69 (September 1963): 150–160.
55 Rubinstein, *City Police,* p. 381.
56 Jerome Skolnick, *Justice without Trial* (New York: John Wiley, 1967), p. 129.

57 Skolnick, *Justice without Trial,* p. 97.

58 LaFave, *Arrest,* p. 456.

59 Pamela A. Roby, "Politics and Criminal Law: Revision of the New York State Penal Law on Prostitution," *Social Problems* 17 (Summer 1969): 83–109.

60 U.S., Department of Justice, *Gambling Law Enforcement in Major American Cities* (Washington, D.C.: U.S. Government Printing Office, 1978), pp. 32–33.

61 Ibid., pp. 26–27.

62 Ibid., p. 28.

63 *Police Magazine* (November 1979): 42.

64 Wilson, *The Investigators.*

65 Peter K. Manning, *The Narcs' Game* (Cambridge: MIT Press, 1980).

66 Westley, *Violence and the Police,* p. 57.

67 Police Executive Research Forum, *Police Practices,* p. 9.

68 John A. Gardiner, *Traffic and the Police: Variations in Law Enforcement Policy* (Cambridge: Harvard University Press, 1969); Wilson, *Varieties of Police Behavior,* pp. 95–99.

69 Wilson, *Varieties of Police Behavior,* pp. 95–99.

CHAPTER **7**

POLICE DISCRETION

THE PROBLEM OF DISCRETION

Day-to-day policing involves a high degree of discretion. Roscoe Pound defined *discretion* as the "authority conferred by law to act in certain situations in accordance with an official's or an agency's own considered judgement and conscience."[1] Virtually all police activities involve situations where the officer is called upon to make a decision about the best course of action. These decisions are often critical life-and-liberty questions: whether or not to use deadly force; whether or not to make an arrest.

Evidence of police discretion is found in numerous studies of police behavior.

1 *Traffic citations.* John Gardiner found that police officers in Dallas wrote twenty times as many traffic tickets as police in Boston despite the fact that both cities had approximately the same population (700,000 in 1960). Meanwhile, in suburban Boston police in Cambridge wrote seven times as many tickets as police in neighboring Somerville.[2]

2 *Juvenile arrests.* In a study of four cities, Nathan Goldman found "a wide variation in rates of arrest in different communities. Arrests per thousand ranged from a low of 12.4 to a high of 49.7. Goldman also found tremendous differences in the proportion of arrests referred to juvenile court. Only 8.6 percent of arrested juveniles were referred in one city, while 71.2 percent were referred in another city.[3]

3 *Deadly force.* The Police Foundation found that the rate of police shootings of civilians ranged from a low of 4.2 shootings per 1000 officers in Portland, Oregon, to a high of 25 shootings per 1000 officers in Birmingham, Alabama.[4]

4 *Law enforcement policy.* K. C. Davis had a team of researchers telephone the twenty-one police district stations in Chicago to ask if they would be arrested for drinking in a public park. Officers at three of the districts said they would be arrested, four said they would probably be arrested, and eleven said that they would not or probably would not be arrested.[5]

Uncontrolled Discretion

Discretion is a major problem in American policing. The problem is not discretion itself but the fact that it is *uncontrolled*. Experts generally agree that a certain amount of discretion is a necessary and proper element of police work. As O. W. Wilson argued, police officers are not robots.[6] Human behavior is incredibly varied and complex, and police officers must respond to the unique characteristics of each situation. However, the fact that police officer discretion is uncontrolled contributes to a number of related problems.

Equal Protection of the Law   The American system of criminal justice is based on the ideal of equality before the law. The Constitution guarantees equal protection of the law to all citizens. This assumes that two people who have committed the same kind of act will be treated equally. The evidence clearly suggests, however, that the police do not necessarily handle similar situations in a similar manner. Some people are arrested while others are not, even though their behavior is roughly the same.[7]

Police-Community Relations Inconsistency in police behavior—or the *belief* that the police do not treat people equally—is a major cause of police-community relations problems. Minority groups argue that the police stop, question, frisk, and arrest minorities more often than whites. They also argue that minorities are more often the victims of physical force and deadly force than are whites (see Chapter 9).

Police Personnel Management The broad exercise of discretion by police officers raises the question of whether or not they are being adequately supervised. Sound management requires that personnel be given clear performance expectations and that their behavior be monitored to see if they are meeting those expectations. The lack of controls over police discretion undermines effective personnel management. A report on *The Police in the California Community* argued that "Properly developed and clearly articulated policies provide both the officer and the members of the community with standards against which behavior can be measured. This is extremely important, for unless such standards exist, it is extremely difficult to determine whether current practices are adequately meeting community needs."[8]

Law Enforcement Policy Planning A well-managed organization establishes clear policy setting forth its goals and objectives. In the case of policing, this might involve policy decisions about concentrating on certain crimes and deemphasis of other crimes. It might involve policies about the handling of juvenile problems that reflect the consensus of the community. Policy is translated into practice, however, only when the responsible officials act accordingly. The lack of effective controls over police discretion undermines the implementation of organizational policy.[9]

The Myth of Full Enforcement

Police officials are reluctant to publicly admit how widespread discretion is, particularly with respect to arrest. They prefer to maintain that police officers fully enforce all the laws. This has been called the "myth of full enforcement."

Several factors explain the continued existence of this myth. The first involves *legal considerations*. The law does not grant police officers the right not to enforce the law. In fact, the laws of most states define failure to enforce the law as a crime. K. C. Davis points out that Illinois police officers are potentially liable for a fine and imprisonment for up to five years if they fail "to perform any mandatory duty as required by law." In the case of *Bargain City v. Dilworth* (1960) the courts held that selective enforcement (enforcing the law against one party but not another) is unconstitutional under the equal protection clause of the Fourteenth Amendment.[10]

A second factor involves the *closed nature of police organizations*. Internal operations and decision making are almost entirely closed from public scrutiny. The police jealously guard this isolation, since it preserves their autonomy. Open acknowledgement of selective enforcement would invite public scrutiny. Questions of law enforcement priorities would become subjects for debate by public officials and citizens. The police would then have to account for their policies and the procedures by which policies were developed.[11]

A third factor involves the *image of police authority.* Police officers rely on the image of authority—the potential threat of arrest—to maintain control over situations. In their view, to admit that certain laws are not enforced would undermine their authority and make it difficult to handle encounters with the public.

Goldstein, Davis, and other experts argue that the myth of full enforcement cripples the development of professional policing. The most urgent need, in their view, is for candor. The police must openly acknowledge that discretion exists and then begin to develop procedures for its proper use.[12]

DISCRETION AND THE CRIMINAL JUSTICE SYSTEM

The issue of discretion is not confined to the police; it pervades the entire criminal justice system. As LaFave points out:

> It is helpful to look at the total criminal justice system as a series of interrelated discretionary choices, examining at each stage the extent to which discretion is and properly should be exercised, the criteria upon which the exercise of discretion is based, the nature and effectiveness of controls on it, and the effect of the exercise of discretion upon earlier and later stages of the process and upon the multiple objectives of the criminal justice system.[13]

The decisions of one component of the criminal justice system directly and indirectly affect other components. Thus, the study of police discretion directs our attention to how police decisions affect other components of the system *and* vice versa. Nathan Goldman, for example, reports that referrals to the juvenile court are affected by police officers' views of the court and their assessment of how the court would dispose of a case.[14]

The exercise of discretion also means that the police are allocating justice in the community. Police officers routinely make decisions affecting the life, liberty, and well-being of citizens. In short, they decide "who gets what" in the American political system. In one sense, the police are the real lawmakers. Judge Carl McGowan argues that "the police do in fact have a very real, though essentially negative, role in fashioning our substantive criminal law through their power of selective and discriminatory law enforcement."[15]

SOURCES OF POLICE DISCRETION

Police discretion is the result of many different factors. In any particular encounter between a police officer and a citizen one or more factors may influence the officer's decision. The relative importance of different factors may vary according to time, place, and circumstance.

The Work Environment

Police officers generally work alone or in pairs. Only occasionally do two or more officers appear at the scene of an incident. In the performance of basic tasks, then, the police officer does not have direct supervision. This work environment contrasts sharply with work in an office or factory. There, workers are subject to direct observation by supervisors and other employees. Joseph Goldstein characterizes the work environment of policing as one of "low visibility." Not only are officers free from direct observation by supervisors, but many encounters with citizens are not observed by other citizens (the domestic disturbance, for example, occurs within a private dwelling).[16]

The low visibility of the work environment encourages police discretion. Officers are not subject to direct orders, nor is there an effective means of reviewing their actions. Skolnick comments that "police work constitutes the most secluded part of an already secluded system [of criminal justice] and therefore offers the greatest opportunity for arbitrary behavior."[17] James Q. Wilson comments that in policing, "discretion increases as one moves *down* the hierarchy." The lowest-ranking officers make the most critical decisions.[18]

The Nature of the Criminal Law

Several features of criminal law contribute to police discretion. Some are inherent in the nature of law itself. Others are peculiar to American criminal law. The substantive criminal law is inherently vague. It identifies offenses and describes them in general terms. The application of these terms to a specific act is left to the discretion of the police officer. LaFave argues that "no legislature has succeeded in formulating a substantive criminal code which clearly encompasses all conduct intended to be made criminal and which clearly excludes all other conduct."[19]

Some categories of offenses leave more room for discretion than others. The "crime" of disorderly conduct demands the greatest exercise of discretion. Disorder, as Wilson points out, is a condition, not an act; people will disagree over what kind of conduct constitutes "disorder." Even the crime of assault requires the police officer to exercise discretion. Criminal codes specify different degrees of assault ("aggravated," "simple," etc.) and indicate the elements that characterize each degree. The police officer must exercise discretion in determining which degree of assault has occurred.[20]

A second aspect of the law that encourages police discretion is its "overreach"; it covers an extremely wide range of human behavior. American society has had a tendency to deal with social and medical problems, as well as questions of morality, through criminal sanctions. "Bad" conduct is made criminal. Many of these laws, however, are virtually unenforceable. In some cases, legislators have no realistic expectations that the laws will be enforced.[21]

As a consequence, basic questions about which laws to enforce are delegated to the police. Police discretion determines community law enforcement priorities. This process is largely hidden from public view. K. C. Davis argues that this is one of the important *positive* aspects of police discretion. The police are able to set more realistic enforcement priorities than legislators: "The common sense of the [police] officers very often prevails over the legislative excesses in the criminal legislation. . . . That is the police accomplishment."[22]

The Administration of Justice

The exercise of police discretion is influenced by considerations related to the administration of criminal justice. The most important consideration is *limited police resources.* The police do not have sufficient personnel or time to handle all the potential work that exists. A single arrest is a time-consuming event, involving the arrest itself, transportation of the suspect, booking, preparation of reports, court testimony, etc. Given the overreach of the criminal law. the police could not possibly arrest all violators.[23]

As a consequence of limited resources, the police develop law enforcement priorities. In many cases these are informal, developed by the individual officer. In other cases, supervisors will develop priorities and direct police officers accordingly. Rarely does a police department develop a formal, written policy about law enforcement priorities, however. Because these decisions are hidden from public view and made at such a low level, the chances of a lack of consistency are greatly increased.

Another consideration related to the administration of justice involves what has been called curbside justice. Police actions often involve an assessment of the "moral character" of the citizen and a judgment about what that person "deserves." An arrest is likely if the officer feels the person deserves punishment. Actions also reflect a prediction of the probable outcome of an arrest. Officers may choose not to arrest if they feel the arrest is unlikely to result in prosecution or conviction.[24]

The criminal justice system may also be used for reasons unrelated to prosecution. In *Arrest,* LaFave identifies several situations where arrests are made even though there is no realistic expectation of prosecution. Drunks, for example, are arrested for their own protection. The intoxicated person is open to injury from falling down, exposure, or muggers. Through arrest, the police can provide them with temporary protection. Because of changes in the law, however, this practice is becoming much less common.[25]

The Individual Officer

Factors associated with the individual officer also influence the exercise of discretion. The personal values of the officer, for example, can influence decision making. Some officers feel strongly about certain kinds of behavior and are more likely to arrest in those situations. Reiss argues that officers act on the basis of their "moral belief," at times deciding that *"the suspect is guilty and an arrest is therefore just"* [italics in original].[26]

One of the most important questions in policing is whether or not racial bias enters into discretionary-decision making. Reiss found contradictory evidence. Three-fourths of the officers studied expressed some form of racial prejudice. Yet Reiss was unable to identify a pattern of racially biased decision making. Using the same data, Donald Black was also unable to conclude that biased decision making exists.[27]

Officers' decisions are also based on considerations related to workload. James Q. Wilson argues that "with respect to routine police matters, *the normal tendency of the police is to underenforce the law"* [italics in original].[28] As a form of work, an arrest is difficult and time-consuming. It exposes the officer to potential resistance to arrest or complaints of misconduct. Officers often prefer to dispose of a situation without an arrest.

Career aspirations may influence an officer's decisions. Young, ambitious officers may work extremely hard, seeking to please the sergeant. If they believe the sergeant wants a large number of traffic citations or field interrogations, they will be likely to produce them. Veteran officers, on the other hand, who have given up hopes of promotion will be likely to produce much less.

Situational Factors

Police discretion is influenced by factors associated with each particular situation. The most thorough analysis of the situational factors in police discretion has been made by Black using data gathered for the President's Crime Commission.[29] According to his analysis, police discretion is not completely arbitrary. It is possible to predict with some confidence how officers will respond in given situations.

In the decision to make an arrest, legal factors are important. These include seriousness of the suspected offense and the strength of the evidence. Black concludes that "The probability of arrest is higher in legally serious crime situations than those of a relatively minor nature."[30] Where the evidence is weak, arrest is much less likely.

Factors related to both the complainant and the offender are also important. Black found that "arrest practices sharply reflect the preferences of citizen complainants."[31] When the complainant urged the officer to make an arrest, an arrest was very probable. The relationship between the complainant and the victim was also relevant. Arrests are far more likely where the two parties are strangers. Arrests are also more likely where the complainant occupies a higher social status than the offender. Finally, Black and others have concluded that the demeanor of the suspect is a very important factor: "The probability of arrest increases when a suspect is disrespectful toward the police."[32]

DECISION POINTS AND DECISION MAKERS

Discussions of police discretion focus on decisions made by patrol officers, with particular focus on the decision to arrest or not arrest. While this is a critically important area, it represents only part of the larger picture of police discretion. A balanced view of the subject takes into account the many different decision makers and decision points in policing.

Law Enforcement Priorities

A major decision point involves law enforcement priorities. What crimes will receive emphasis? How vigorous will the enforcement effort be? In many cases the decision maker is the top law enforcement executive.

One of the best examples of a conscious choice of law enforcement priorities involves the FBI. Under J. Edgar Hoover the FBI gave very low priority to organized crime and white-collar crime. Critics of the Bureau during the 1950s and 1960s were particularly upset over the failure of the agency to combat organized crime. During this period the Bureau did give particular emphasis to the recovery of stolen vehicles that had been transported across state lines. The decision to emphasize one type of crime and deemphasize another is an excellent example of executive discretion over law enforcement priorities.[33]

Other examples can be cited. According to Sherman, police corruption in Oakland, California, was substantially reduced because the police chief took a vigorous enforcement policy toward gambling and corruption in city government.[34] The attack on gambling is an example of administrative discretion. Variations in the rate at which police departments issue traffic citations is also an example of a choice of enforcement priorities.[35]

Investigative Techniques

The choice of techniques for investigating crimes or suspected crimes is also a discretionary decision. In some cases these decisions are made not by the top executive but by the supervisors of investigative bureaus.

Several examples of the discretionary choice of investigative techniques can be cited. A newspaper investigation revealed that Omaha, Nebraska, ranked fourth in the entire country in the use of wiretaps. According to population, Omaha was only the thirty-fifth largest city in the country. The large number of wiretaps represents decisions concerning law enforcement priorities (an attempt to suppress gambling) and the best techniques to implement policy.[36]

The FBI's Abscam investigation, with the primary reliance on the use of undercover agents posing as the representatives of wealthy Arabs, involved a choice of investigative techniques. The methods used by the FBI in this investigation are extremely controversial, since they raise questions about entrapment (the questions are still to be resolved by the courts).[37]

Patrol Officer Dispositions

By far the most numerous and most important discretionary decisions are those made by patrol officers. Discretion increases further down the police organizational hierarchy. Contacts between patrol officers and citizens are the primary way in which police services are delivered to the public.

Patrol officer dispositions involve a wide range of possibilities. These include the obvious decisions to arrest or not arrest, to use or not to use deadly force or physical force. But it also includes a wide range of alternatives for handling the numerous order-maintenance situations. An officer can choose verbal or nonverbal techniques. Verbal techniques range from gentle persuasion to threats. A study of the performance of male and female officers in New York City identified the following verbal and nonverbal techniques:[38]

Verbal techniques	Nonverbal techniques
Ordering	Official acts (e.g., arrest)
Requesting	Use of body without touch
Recommending	Physical contact
Reasoning	Gentle
Verbal manipulating	Rough
Threatening	Display of weapon
	Use of weapon

THE CONTROL OF DISCRETION

The Need for Control

Experts recognize the need to control police discretion. The President's Crime Commission, the National Advisory Commission on Criminal Justice Standards and Goals, and the American Bar Association standards project all recommend that police departments take immediate steps to control police discretion.[39]

The control of discretion is necessary for several reasons. Much police discretion is illegal, violating the principle of equal protection of the law. Unequal enforcement of the law—or the *belief* that enforcement is unequal—is one of the sources of police-community relations problems. The control of discretion is a necessary ingredient of effective personnel management. Departments need to provide their officers with specific performance guidelines. Finally, the control of discretion is necessary for meaningful planning about broader law enforcement priorities and community needs.

The Need for Candor   The first step in dealing with police discretion is candor, a frank admission that it exists. Traditionally, the police have denied that they exercise discretion. Herman Goldstein points out that police chiefs "balk at the suggestion that policy-making be done openly and that operating policies be published."[40] The National Advisory Commission, however, recommends that "Every police agency should acknowledge the existence of the broad range of administrative and operational discretion that is exercised by all police agencies and individual officers."[41]

Realistic Expectations   Realistic expectations are needed in attempting to deal with police discretion. Experts recognize that *discretion cannot be eliminated*. Discretion is inherent in police work. Laws and administrative directives can, at best, provide general guidelines for police officers. The individual officer will always have to exercise discretion in applying general guidelines to a specific situation. Moreover, discretion can be a positive feature of police work. Officers routinely confront difficult situations that call for delicate handling. The professional police officer, using good judgment, is in the best position to determine what the situation needs.

A realistic objective, then, is not to eliminate discretion but to limit and control it. Jerome Skolnick argues that there is a crucial difference between *delegated* and *unauthorized* discretion.[42] Delegated discretion is explicitly granted and limited by general guidelines. Unauthorized discretion is exercised without any authorization either by law or administrative directive.

Standard-Operating-Procedure Manuals

The National Advisory Commission recommends that departments develop and publish "comprehensive policy statements that publicly establish the limits of discretion, that provide guidelines for its exercise within those limits, and that eliminate discriminatory enforcement of the law." Exhibit 7.1 represents the complete recommendation by the commission.

EXHIBIT 7.1

Standard 1.3 Police Discretion

Every police agency should acknowledge the existence of the broad range of administrative and operational discretion that is exercised by all police agencies and individual officers. That acknowledgment should take the form of comprehensive policy statements that publicly establish the limits of discretion, that provide guidelines for its exercise within those limits, and that eliminate discriminatory enforcement of the law.

1 Every police chief executive should have the authority to establish his agency's fundamental objectives and priorities and to implement them through discretionary allocation and control of agency resources. In the exercise of his authority, every chief executive:

a Should seek legislation that grants him the authority to exercise his discretion in allocating police resources and in establishing his agency's fundamental objectives and priorities;

b Should review all existing criminal statutes, determine the ability of the agency to enforce these statutes effectively, and advise the legislature of the statutes' practicality from an enforcement standpoint; and

c Should advise the legislature of the practicality of each proposed criminal statute from an enforcement standpoint, and the impact of such proposed statutes on the ability of the agency to maintain the existing level of police services.

2 Every police chief executive should establish policy that guides the exercise of discretion by police personnel in using arrest alternatives. This policy:

a Should establish the limits of discretion by specifically identifying, insofar as possible, situations calling for the use of alternatives to continued physical custody;

b Should establish criteria for the selection of appropriate enforcement alternatives;

c Should require enforcement action to be taken in all situations where all elements of a crime are present and all policy criteria are satisfied;

d Should be jurisdictionwide in both scope and application; and

e Specifically should exclude offender lack of cooperation, or disrespect toward police personnel, as a factor in arrest determination unless such conduct constitutes a separate crime.

3 Every police chief executive should establish policy that limits the exercise of discretion by police personnel in conducting investigations, and that provides guidelines for the exercise of discretion within those limits. This policy:

a Should be based on codified laws, judicial decisions, public policy, and police experience in investigating criminal conduct;

b Should identify situations where there can be no investigative discretion; and

c Should establish guidelines for situations requiring the exercise of investigative discretion.

4 Every police chief executive should establish policy that governs the exercise of discretion by police personnel in providing routine peacekeeping and other police services that, because of their frequent recurrence, lend themselves to the development of a uniform agency response.

5 Every police chief executive should formalize procedures for developing and implementing the foregoing written agency policy.

6 Every police chief executive immediately should adopt inspection and control procedures to insure that officers exercise their discretion in a manner consistent with agency policy.

Source: National Advisory Commission on Criminal Justice Standards and Goals, *Police* (Washington, D.C.: U.S. Government Printing Office, 1973), p. 21.

EXHIBIT 7.2

Misdemeanor Possession of Marijuana by Students to Be Handled by Uniform Patrol Cars

GENERAL:

When calls are received from schools on students found in possession of misdemeanor amounts of marijuana, the Uniform Patrol car in the area shall be responsible for the investigation.

The Uniform Field Bureau Patrol car in the area shall be dispatched to meet the administrator or teacher who made the telephone call, whether the call comes in to "911" or through the Vice/Narcotics Unit.

In the event a Police Officer is dispatched to a situation where a third party (private security personnel, school administrator, etc.) is holding misdemeanor quantities of marijuana and alleges that another party (student, etc.) was in possession of it, the following procedure will be followed:

1 Information Report will be made stating all the facts presented.
2 The contraband (marijuana) will be seized by the Police Officer.
3 Property Reports shall be made with the same R.B. as the Information Report.
4 The property (marijuana) shall be turned in through the proper chain of custody.

Prosecution at a later date could be made in two ways:

1 Reports will be sent to the City Prosecutor for proper determination of filing charges.
2 The person (private security personnel, school administrator, etc.) alleging the act may proceed to the City Prosecutor's office for discussion or request of issuing a warrant against the party.

If the Police Officer finds marijuana on the party being detained he will:

1 Field release the party if under sixteen (16) years old.
2 Issue a citation for misdemeanor court if over sixteen (16) years old

No arrests will be made at the scene of the call by the Police Officer unless he has on site evidence of the misdemeanor violation where he could proceed for prosecution on his own direct testimony.

Source: Omaha Police Division, *Standard Operating Procedure Manual* (Omaha: Author, n.d.).

In professionally managed police departments, policy statements are collected in standard operating procedure manuals, which are distributed to all officers. The more professional departments have the most extensive and detailed manuals. Many small departments, however, have no manuals at all.

Exhibit 7.2 represents the Omaha Police Division's policy on handling misdemeanor possession of marijuana by students. It illustrates how a procedure manual provides guidance for officers in particular kinds of situations.

The Advantages of SOP Manuals   Written policy offers obvious advantages. It provides clear direction for working police officers. It indicates, in general terms at least, what they must do and what they may not do. Since it is in writing, there can be no dispute about departmental policy on that issue. Because policy directives are circulated to all sworn officers, they help ensure consistency of performance, which in turn promotes equal protection of the law. Written policy directives, then, provide the basis for effective supervision. Officers can be rewarded for following policy and disciplined for violations. Finally, written policy can help maintain good police-community relations. When citizens lodge complaints about police conduct, the complaint can be sustained or dismissed depending on whether the officer's actions conformed to policy.

Written directives are a fundamental element of modern management. The management of a large bureaucracy demands consistency of performance and the coordination of large numbers of personnel. The professionalization of the police has involved the application of these techniques to police organizations. Written policy directives eliminate the extreme forms of unregulated discretion.

The Limits of Procedure Manuals   Procedure manuals are not a cure-all. There are problems with most existing procedure manuals as well as certain inherent limitations in this approach.

Even in the best police departments, procedure manuals tend to emphasize *technique* rather than *policy*. Typically, manuals specify in great detail the mechanics of taking a suspect into custody and ignore the question of when to make an arrest. The problem of selective enforcement is not discussed.

Many important subjects are not covered by procedure manuals. The report on *The Police in the California Community* observed that "there are a number of areas where policy statements are either non-existent or are so poorly articulated that they are virtually ineffective." It found that 65 percent of the procedure manuals it examined had no policy statement regarding field interrogations, 37 percent had no policy on the use of nondeadly force, and 31 percent had no policy on the use of deadly force.[43] The Omaha police department has an extensive procedure manual filling five loose-leaf notebooks, but there is no reference to domestic disturbances or the proper use of informants.[44]

One of the major problems with existing procedure manuals is the process by which they are developed. Typically, procedures are developed only in response to a crisis. Peter Manning quoted a British police sergeant as saying that their procedure manual represented "140 years of screw ups. Every time something goes wrong, they make a rule about it."[45] This approach has been termed crisis management. When procedure manuals develop in this manner, they are often haphazard and unsystematic. Taken as a whole, the procedures do not represent systematic planning with consideration for basic goals and objectives.

Procedure manuals have certain inherent limitations. First, it is impossible to develop a procedure for every conceivable situation. In this respect manuals are like the criminal law itself. Second, there is a point of diminishing returns. When procedures become too detailed and too complex they are unmanageable. Officers are more likely to ignore than attempt to follow overly complex rules. Finally, the development of rules encourages willful evasion.

The Impact of Policy Statements

Evidence suggests that policy statements can have a significant impact on police behavior. An important case study is James Fyfe's analysis of the impact of a more restrictive policy on deadly force in the New York City Police Department.[46]

In 1972 the NYCPD issued Temporary Order of Procedure 237 (TOP 237), which directed that officers should use only the minimum amount of force necessary, that firearms should not be used where the lives of innocent bystanders might be threatened, and that warning shots were forbidden. The department also established a Firearms Discharge Review Board to review cases where an officer had discharged a firearm.

Fyfe analyzed firearms discharges between 1971 and 1975. As Table 7-1 indicates, the weekly mean number of discharges declined by about one-third. The most

TABLE 7-1
OFFICER-REPORTED FIREARMS INCIDENTS, NEW YORK CITY POLICE DEPARTMENT, 1971–1975

Reason for shooting	Pre-TOP 237	Weekly Mean	Post-TOP 237	Weekly Mean	Totals	Weekly Mean
Defense of life	65.8% (1016)	11.9	70.6% (1582)	9.0	67.9% (2598)	10.0
Prevent or terminate crime	21.4% (330)	3.9	4.6% (103)	0.6	11.3% (433)	1.7
Destroy animal	4.4% (68)	0.8	11.4% (255)	1.5	8.4% (323)	1.2
Suicide attempt	0.7% (11)	0.1	0.8% (18)	0.1	0.8% (29)	0.1
Accidental	3.6% (56)	0.7	9.0% (201)	1.2	6.7% (257)	1.0
Other	4.1% (63)	0.7	3.7% (83)	0.5	3.8% (146)	0.6
Totals	40.8% (1562)	18.4	59.2% (2265)	12.9	100.0% (1827)	14.7

Source: James J. Fyfe, "Administrative Interventions on Police Shooting Discretion: An Empirical Examination, *Journal of Criminal Justice* 7 (Winter 1979):317.

significant reduction occurred in the category of shootings to "prevent or terminate crime." These are usually the most controversial incidents, since there is no imminent threat to the life of the officer or other citizen. Fyfe also found that the reduction in the use of deadly force was not accompanied by an increased number of police officer injuries or deaths.

Fyfe concludes that "In the most simple terms, therefore, the New York experience indicates that considerable reductions in police shooting and both officer and citizen injury and death are associated with the establishment of clearly delineated guidelines and procedures for the review of officer shooting discretion."

An even more significant reduction in the use of deadly force occurred in Omaha. The number of firearms incidents dropped from an average of more than thirty a year (1971–1973) to less than ten a year (1977–1979) following the development of a more restrictive firearms policy.[47]

Administrative Rule Making

The leading authorities on the subject of police discretion recommend a systematic approach to the development of policy statements. K. C. Davis recommends adoption of the administrative rule-making process.[48]

Administrative rule making is practiced by all federal and many state government agencies. It is designed to fill in the gap between the law and practice. The laws creating government agencies usually provide only a general and often vague mandate. The agencies are left with enormous discretion in developing specific policy. Administrative rule making is designed to control this discretion.

The basis for administrative rule making is the federal Administrative Procedure Act of 1946. The key concept is the idea of "notice and comment." Agencies are required to give notice that they are developing a policy, solicit input from interested parties, and publish the policy as adopted. Proposed policies are published in the *Federal Register* and, once adopted, codified and published in the *Code of Federal Regulations* (CFR). Exhibit 7.3 represents the key section from the Administrative Procedure Act.

EXHIBIT 7.3

Excerpt, Administrative Procedure Act of 1946

After notice required by this section, the agency shall give interested persons an opportunity to participate in the rule making through submission of written data, views, or arguments with or without opportunity for oral presentation. After consideration of the relevant matter presented, the agency shall incorporate in the rules adopted a concise general statement of their basis and purpose.

Source: Administrative Procedure Act, 5 U.S.C. 553 (c).

Objectives of Rule-Making   K. C. Davis, the leading authority on the subject, argues that the objectives of administrative rule making are to confine, structure, and check discretion—not to eliminate it

Confining discretion, Davis explains, means "fixing the boundaries." Written policies should indicate where police officers may exercise discretion and where they may not. Policy regarding the use of deadly force is a good example. Discretion is confined when a policy clearly indicates that officers may not fire warning shots in the air or use deadly force against a person who has committed a misdemeanor. Discretion still exists, but it has been confined to a narrower range of situations.[49]

Structuring discretion means keeping "the manner of the exercise of discretionary power within the boundaries." The seven elements of structured discretion involve "open plans, open policy statements, open rules, open findings, open reasons, open precedents, and fair informal procedure."[50] Taking the example of the use of deadly force, in practice this would mean that the department would openly announce a plan to develop a policy, publish that policy statement, announce the rules governing application of the policy (that is, how an officer would be disciplined for improper use of deadly force), announce the findings in a disciplinary case, and so on.

One of the important consequences of this approach, according to Davis, Goldstein, and others, is the development of a general atmosphere of openness within police departments. This, they argue, would have a positive effect on police-community relations and help break down the isolated and defensive attitude among police officers.[51]

Checking discretion, Davis continues, involves the principle of "checks and balances," which is a fundamental part of constitutional government. Discretionary decisions are checked in the sense of being reviewed by other persons. Once discretion is openly acknowledged, general policy and its application to specific situations can be reviewed by a variety of different persons: supervisory officers, special internal units within the department, legislative committees, and so on. Discretion, then, is no longer hidden; it is openly discussed and reviewed both within and without the police department.[52]

Applying Rule Making to the Police   Realistically, can the technique of administrative rule-making be applied to the police? Some would argue that it cannot on the grounds that policing is a very different kind of activity from the work done by a government regulatory agency. Davis, Goldstein, and the National Advisory Commission suggest that it can. Davis goes even further, suggesting that the courts may even *require* the police to adopt rules. He cites recent cases where the courts have required other administrative agencies to adopt rules governing their discretionary decision making.[53]

The Texas Model Rules   The Texas Criminal Justice Council, in cooperation with the International Association of Chiefs of Police, has published a set of *Model Rules for Law Enforcement Officers*. Subtitled, *A Manual on Police Discretion,* this document provides an example of the kind of rules a police department might adopt.[54]

The Texas model rules sanction selective enforcement within the framework of certain guidelines. Chapter 6 provides that:

6.01. An officer is not obliged to make an arrest in every instance. He may in some circumstances, for good cause consistent with the public interest, decline to arrest notwithstanding the existence of probable cause to arrest. Among the factors which the officer may properly consider in determining not to arrest are:
(a) if the victim is not seriously interested in prosecution because:
    (1) he desires restitution only;
    (2) he is in a continuing relationship with the offender; or
    (3) he is in a family type relationship with the offender.
(b) if the offense complained of arose out of some underlying illegal activity engaged in by the offender and the victim;
(c) if the offender is or is willing to become an informant;
(d) if the offender can be referred to another agency which is better equipped to deal with the problem;
(e) if the actual damage done to persons or property is minimal;
(f) when an adequate civil remedy is available to the injured party;
(g) whether arrest would result in unnecessary harm to the victim or offender which would outweigh the risk of non-arrest.
6.02. When an officer declines to make an arrest he shall warn the offender
(a) that his conduct has come to official attention; and
(b) that he will be arrested if such conduct is continued or repeated.
6.03. Section 6.01 is not applicable to crimes of violence.
6.04. An officer shall be able to articulate the reason(s) for his failure to arrest a particular offender.

The model rules *confine* discretion by specifically not allowing nonenforcement in the case of violent crimes (Section 6.03). This provides guidance to police officers on the street and limits their discretion in one major area. The rules, in effect, make social policy: they are based on the assumption that a violent crime is a sufficiently serious act that requires arrest.

The rules specifically *prohibit* certain types of misuse of the arrest power:

6.07. In determining whether to arrest, the officer shall not consider the race, creed, religion, or any other arbitrary classification of the offender or victim.
6.08. An officer shall not arrest an offender for conduct which the officer has provoked.
6.09. An officer shall not make an arrest as a pretext to search for evidence of a totally unrelated crime.

Finally, the model rules provide that systematic nonenforcement of the law in certain categories must be based on general departmental policy:

6.10. Where it has been determined that certain criminal laws shall not be enforced, the officer shall not arrest for those offenses. This determination should be made only through an established departmental administrative rule-making procedure which provides for citizen participation and judicial review.

The Rule-Making Process The process by which rules are developed is as important as the rules themselves. Traditionally, police procedures have been developed by police chiefs with little or no formal consultation. The National Advisory Commission on Criminal Justice Standards and Goals recommends "maximum participation" by all interested parties in the development of rules and policy statements (see Exhibit 7.4).

Input from both citizens and rank-and-file police officers offers a number of potential benefits. The involvement of citizens, it is argued, can help to improve relations between the police and the public. Alienation from the police results from the fact that many segments of the public do not understand what police policy is or have no voice in its determination.

Involvement of rank-and-file police officers serves to enhance the professionalism of the police. One of the hallmarks of a profession is involvement in decision making on the most important issues. Doctors, for example, determine the standards of proper medical care. In contemporary police organizations, however, rank-and-file officers are expected to follow orders, not provide input into policy decisions.

EXHIBIT 7.4

Standard 2.2: Establishment of Policy

Every police chief executive immediately should establish written policies in those areas of operations in which guidance is needed to direct agency employees toward the attainment of agency goals and objectives.

1 Every police chief executive should promulgate policy that provides clear direction without necessarily limiting employees' exercise of discretion.

2 Every police chief executive should provide for maximum participation in the policy formulation process. This participation should include at least:

a Input from all levels within the agency—from the level of execution to that of management—through informal meetings between the police chief executive and members of the basic rank, idea incentive programs, and any other methods that will promote the upward flow of communication; and

b Input from outside the agency as appropriate—from other government agencies, community organizations, and the specific community affected.

3 Every police chief executive should provide written policies in those areas in which direction is needed, including:

a General goals and objectives of the agency;

b Administrative matters;

c Community relations;

d Public and press relations;

e Personnel procedures and relations;

f Personal conduct of employees;

g Specific law enforcement operations with emphasis on such sensitive areas as the use of force, the use of lethal and nonlethal weapons, and arrest and custody; and

h Use of support services.

Source: U.S. National Advisory Commission on Criminal Justice Standards and Goals, *Police* (Washington, D.C.: U.S. Government Printing Office, 1973), p. 53.

One consequence is alienation of rank-and-file officers from the rules themselves. Officers resent the *Miranda* and *Mapp* rules, in part because they were imposed on the police by the courts. Judge Carl McGowan argues that "It is a psychological truism that self-regulation tends to command a higher degree of observance by the regulated."[55] Police officers would be more likely to accept rules they had a hand in developing.

THE LIMITS OF REFORM

Despite the fact that the exercise of discretion is a basic problem in policing, there are severe limits to our ability to control it. In *Working the Street,* Michael K. Brown argues that "if there is a lesson to be learned from the experiences of the most recent generation of reformers, it is that simply enveloping policemen in a maze of institutional controls without grappling with the grimy realities of police work does not necessarily promote accountability and may only exacerbate matters."[56]

The "grimy reality" of police work is the fact that the task of policing is filled with basic uncertainties. Typically, a police officer enters a situation uncertain of the nature of the problem. Split-second decisions must often be made on the basis of inadequate information. More important, Brown emphasizes, the police officer faces a basic choice about means and ends. The officer must decide how serious the problem is and what disposition is appropriate. These decisions are not simple matters of technical competence: there is no "right way" to handle all situations. The discretionary decision involves the exercise of power and the distribution of justice in society. This is a profoundly important moral and political decision.

Brown argues that administrative controls over police officers—primarily through SOP manuals—only increase the uncertainties of police work. Officers not only face an uncertain field situation but must also deal with uncertainty about how the department will respond to their actions. Coping with the police bureaucracy has become a major element of the police officer's work experience. Finally, Brown concludes that because of the inherent uncertainties of police work, there are no easy administrative solutions to the control of police discretion.

REVIEW

1 Discuss how police discretion creates problems related to the equal protection of the law.

2 What is meant by the "myth of full enforcement"?

3 Explain how the work environment of policing contributes to the exercise of police discretion.

4 What elements of the criminal law encourage the exercise of discretion?

5 Explain the differences between delegated and unauthorized discretion.

6 Describe the nature and function of an SOP manual.

7 Discuss the principal advantages and limitations of SOP manuals.

8 Describe the impact of a new policy statement of firearms discharges in the New York City Police Department.

9 Explain the concept of administrative rule making.

10 What are the basic limits on our ability to control police discretion?

REFERENCES

1 Roscoe Pound, cited in Wayne R. LaFave, *Arrest: The Decision to Take a Suspect into Custody* (Boston: Little, Brown, 1965), p. 63.

2 John A. Gardiner, *Traffic and the Police: Variations in Law-Enforcement Policy* (Cambridge: Harvard University Press, 1969).

3 Nathan Goldman, *The Differential Selection of Juvenile Offenders for Court Appearance* (New York: National Council on Crime and Delinquency, 1963).

4 Catherine H. Milton, et al., *Police Use of Deadly Force* (Washington, D.C.: Police Foundation, 1977), p. 30.

5 Kenneth C. Davis, *Police Discretion* (St. Paul: West Publishing, 1975), pp. 12–13.

6 O. W. Wilson, cited in LaFave, *Arrest*, p. 61.

7 Davis, *Police Discretion*, 71.

8 California, Attorney General, *The Police in the California Community* (Sacramento, Attorney General of California, 1973), p. 1–12.

9 Davis, *Police Discretion*, chap. 2.

10 Ibid., chap. 3.

11 Herman Goldstein, *Policing a Free Society* (Cambridge: Ballinger, 1977), pp. 119–120.

12 Ibid.; Davis, *Police Discretion*, chap 3.

13 LaFave, *Arrest*, p. 9.

14 Goldman, *The Differential Selection of Juvenile Offenders*.

15 Carl McGowan, "Rule-Making and the Police," *Michigan Law Review* 70 (March 1972): 653.

16 Joseph Goldstein, "Police Discretion Not to Invoke the Criminal Process: Low-Visibility Decisions in the Administration of Justice," *Yale Law Journal* 69, no. 4 (1960) 543–588.

17 Jerome Skolnick, *Justice without Trial* (New York: John Wiley, 1967), p. 14.

18 James Q. Wilson, *Varieties of Police Behavior* (New York: Atheneum, 1973), p. 7.

19 LaFave, *Arrest*, p. 70.

20 Wilson, *Varieties of Police Behavior*, p. 21.

21 National Commission on the Causes and Prevention of Violence, *Law and Order Reconsidered* (New York: Bantam Books, 1970), pp. 600–621.

22 Davis, *Police Discretion*, pp. 62–66.

23 LaFave, *Arrest*, chap. 5.

24 Albert J. Reiss, *The Police and the Public* (New Haven: Yale University Press, 1971), pp. 134–135.

25 LaFave, *Arrest*, chap. 21.

26 Reiss, *Police and the Public*, pp. 134–135.

27 Ibid., p. 147; Donald J. Black, *The Manners and Customs of the Police* (New York: Academic Press, 1980), pp. 105–108.

28 Wilson, *Varieties of Police Behavior*, p. 49.

29 Black, *Manners and Customs of the Police*.

30 Ibid., p. 103.

31 Ibid., p. 101.

32 Ibid., p. 104.

33 Sanford J. Ungar, *FBI* (Boston: Little, Brown, 1976).

34 Lawrence W. Sherman, *Scandal and Reform: Controlling Police Corruption* (Berkeley: University of California Press, 1978), pp. 141–144.

35 Wilson, *Varieties of Police Behavior,* pp. 95–99.

36 U.S., Bureau of Justice Statistics, *The Sourcebook of Criminal Justice Statistics, 1980* (Washington, D.C.: U.S. Government Printing Office, 1981), pp. 395–398.

37 James Q. Wilson, "The Changing FBI—The Road to Abscam," *Public Interest* 59 (Spring 1980); 3–14.

38 Joyce Sichel, et al., *Women on Patrol: A Pilot Study of Police Performance in New York City* (Washington, D.C.: LEAA, 1978), p. 35.

39 President's Commission on Law Enforcement and Administration of Justice, *The Challenge of Crime in a Free Society* (New York: Avon Books, 1968), pp. 265–272; U.S., National Advisory Commission on Criminal Justice Standards and Goals, *Police* (Washington, D.C.: U.S. Government Printing Office, 1973), pp. 21–28; American Bar Association, *Standards Relating to the Urban Police Function* (New York: ABA, 1973), pp. 144–147.

40 Goldstein, *Policing a Free Society,* p. 119.

41 National Advisory Commission, *Police,* p. 21.

42 Skolnick, *Justice without Trial,* pp. 71–73.

43 California, Attorney General, *The Police in the California Community,* pp. 8–11.

44 Omaha Police Division, *Standard Operating Procedure Manual* (Omaha: Author, n.d.).

45 Peter K. Manning, *Police Work* (Cambridge: MIT Press, 1977), p. 165.

46 James J. Fyfe, "Administrative Interventions on Police Shooting Discretion: An Empirical Examination," *Journal of Criminal Justice* 7 (Winter 1979): 309–323.

47 *Omaha World Herald,* June 12, 1981.

48 Kenneth C. Davis, *Discretionary Justice* (Urbana: University of Illinois, 1971).

49 Ibid., pp. 52–96.

50 Ibid., pp. 97–141.

51 Goldstein, *Policing a Free Society,* pp. 120–122.

52 Davis, *Discretionary Justice,* pp. 142–161.

53 Kenneth C. Davis, "An Approach to Legal Control of the Police," *Texas Law Review* 52 (April 1974): 703–725.

54 Texas, Criminal Justice Council, *Model Rules for Law Enforcement Officers: A Manual on Police Discretion* (Washington, D.C.: International Association of Chiefs of Police, 1974).

55 Carl McGowan, "Rule-Making and the Police," *Michigan Law Review* 70 (March 1972): 659–694.

56 Michael K. Brown, *Working the Street: Police Discretion and the Dilemmas of Reform* (New York: Russell Sage Foundation, 1981), p. 303.

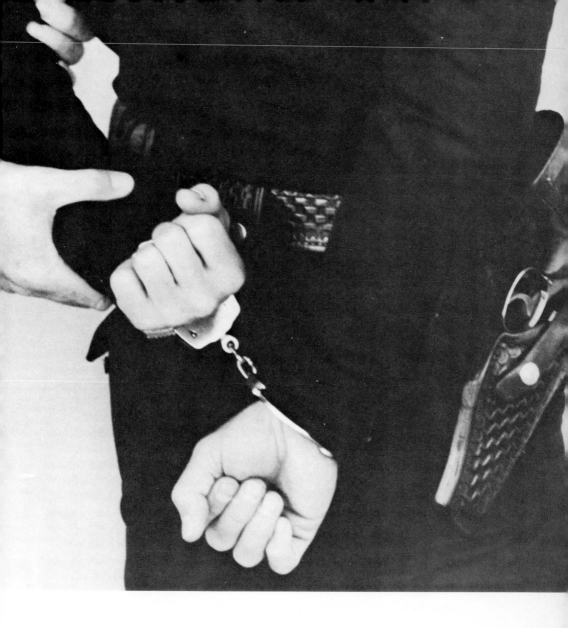

CHAPTER 8

POLICE CORRUPTION

THE PROBLEM

"For as long as there have been police," Lawrence Sherman observes, "there has been police corruption."[1] Corruption is the oldest and most persistent problem in American policing. The history of law enforcement agencies is the story of repeated scandals over corrupt practices. In his study of crime and law enforcement in colonial New York, Douglas Greenberg found numerous complaints about misconduct by law enforcement officials. Robert Ireland found that the office of sheriff was often auctioned off to the highest bidder in pre-Civil War Kentucky—individuals bought the job with the understanding that they could recoup their money through graft. In both New York City and Chicago major scandals involving the police are regular occurrences. In New York scandals have erupted once every twenty years with almost perfect regularity.[2]

Corruption is not a small problem. The Pennsylvania Crime Commission reported in 1974 that "police corruption in Philadelphia is ongoing, widespread, systematic, and occurring at all levels of the police department."[3] A year earlier the Knapp Commission reported that corruption in the New York City Police Department was also widespread. Corruption takes many forms—from the gratuity or occasional bribe to the regular payoff. The Knapp Commission investigation revealed that police officers engaged in extensive theft of narcotics and sold important information about criminal cases to defense attorneys. In the past, promotions and favored assignments could be obtained only by bribing superior officers in corrupt police departments.

The cost of police corruption is extremely high. Journalist David Burnham of *The New York Times* identified four "hidden social costs." First, corruption represents a "secret tax" on businesses that have to pay off the police to avoid harassment. Second, corruption undermines the enforcement of the law, allowing widespread illegal activity—some trivial, some serious—to flourish. Third, corruption destroys the department itself, robbing the police officer of self-respect, and respect for superior officers and the department as a whole. Effective discipline becomes impossible when corruption is systematic. Fourth, knowledge of the existence of corruption undermines the public's faith in the police and the entire criminal justice system.[4] Corruption impedes the drive for police professionalism by undermining public trust and confidence.[5] Self-policing is another hallmark of a profession, and corruption flourishes when officers fail to police their dishonest colleagues.

Police corruption is a problem of enormous magnitude. Dealing with it effectively requires a sophisticated understanding of what it is, how it occurs, why it exists, and how it might be controlled. Corruption has persisted for so long in part because public officials refused to deal with it realistically. The first stage in the process is admitting that it exists. The need for candor, Herman Goldstein argues, is paramount. Police officials have traditionally attempted to ignore the problem and deny that it exists.[6]

A Definition

Herman Goldstein defines police corruption as "acts involving the misuse of authority by a police officer in a manner designed to produce personal gain for himself or for others."[7] Police corruption is a complex and multidimensional phenomenon; it takes many forms and can exist at many different levels.

Not all illegal activity is police corruption. The two key elements are misuse of authority and personal gain. Police corruption includes illegal activity by a police officer *acting as a police officer*. When an individual who happens to be a police officer steals something from a neighbor, for example, this is not police corruption. The individual is committing an illegal act but not using his or her authority as an officer to do so. But when that individual enters a building as an officer and steals some property, then police corruption is occurring.

Not all illegal activity by the police results in personal gain. Excessive use of physical force, an illegal search and seizure, the systematic use of illegal wiretaps—to cite only a few examples—are illegal but do not benefit individual officers. Such acts do not fall within the category of police corruption.

TYPES OF CORRUPTION

Dealing effectively with corruption requires recognition of the many different types of corruption.[8] Different acts have different causes and, consequently, call for different strategies of control. Moreover, corrupt acts are not all equally serious. The free meal provided by a restaurant is far less serious than the regular payoff for protecting narcotics dealers. It is less serious in terms of the amount of money involved, the consequences to the community, and the cost in terms of the individual officer's self-respect.

Gratuities

The most common and most extensive form of corruption involves the receipt by police officers of small gratuities or tips. For example, officers may receive on their beat free meals at a restaurant, free service from a dry cleaner, or discounts on the purchase of merchandise at a store.

Gratuities are generally viewed as an extremely minor form of corruption. In many cities they are not considered corruption at all. The owners of commercial establishments offer free service or discounts for many different reasons, some of them admirable. A merchant may genuinely feel that officers are underpaid for the valuable service they render and, therefore, are entitled to a few "breaks." A restaurant owner may feel that having police cars parked out front while the officers are eating will deter robbers. The merchant may also hope that the police will return the favor by providing a little extra patrol coverage.

A moral distinction is often made between different types of gratuities. Discounts and free service are generally regarded as relatively unimportant. The payment of cash to an officer, however, is quite different. Here the act becomes less a friendly gratuity and more an outright bribe. Where the officer initiates the act, it becomes extortion or a "shakedown." The Knapp Commission defined this issue in terms of the distinction between "grass eaters" and "meat eaters": grass eaters are those officers who passively accepted gratuities or bribes offered to them; meat eaters, on the otherhand, were officers who aggressively solicited payments.[9]

Bribes

A second category of corruption includes acts which subvert the administration of criminal justice, with the result that a law violator avoids arrest or punishment. For example, an officer stops a vehicle for speeding and asks to see the driver's license. The driver hands the officer her license and a $10 bill. The officer keeps the money, returns the license, and lets the person go with only a warning. Chicago journalist Mike Royko described a more aggressive version of the traffic-stop bribe: The officer stops a vehicle for speeding. While inspecting the driver's license he indicates that he is selling pencils for the policemen's ball. The officer suggests that the driver might want to buy a ten dollar pencil. The driver buys the pencil and is allowed to go with only a warning.[10]

In crowded downtown business districts where parking is often difficult to find, many store owners count on their customers and suppliers being able to double-park in front of the store and routinely pay the officer on the beat a few dollars a week not to ticket them. In the construction industry, contractors often find it convenien to pay the police to ignore various city ordinances. In addition to avoiding traffic citations for trucks illegally parked by construction sites, journalist David Burnham discovered that contractors regularly pay the police $50 a week to avoid summonses for having piles of bricks or other construction materials blocking the sidewalk.[11]

The most systematic and well-organized corruption of the administration of justice involves a regular payoff for the protection of ongoing illegal activity—usually gambling or narcotics. New York City slang referred to this as "the pad." According to the Knapp Commission, officers "on the pad" in New York City received anywhere from $300 to $1500 per month to protect illegal gambling activities, while a bar owner in Philadelphia paid a total of $800 per month to members of six different units within the Philadelphia police department in order to operate an illegal after-hours operation.[12]

Not all regular payoffs are for the nonenforcement of the law. Individuals, especially businesspeople, can pay for *extra* enforcement. A major department store in New York City, according to David Burnham, paid a $5000 "finder's fee" to two detectives for locating a stolen truck. Another clothing store offers 50 percent discounts to police officers in return for extra patrol coverage in the immediate vicinity of the store. This illustrates the problem raised by seemingly harmless gratuities. It is often not clear where a "gratuity" ends and a "bribe" begins.

Information may also be sold before arrests are made. An Omaha detective was fired after being caught selling information to drug traffickers about investigations in progress and pending raids. Even after an arrest has been made, an officer may corrupt the administration of justice in many ways. Robert Daley reported in 1978 that New York City detectives regularly sold information to defense attorneys about pending cases.[13] An officer may take a bribe to alter important testimony against a defendant at the preliminary hearing or trial. In some instances the officer simply "forgets" or "can't remember" key points. In one instance narcotics dealers in New York City apparently paid $50,000 to have police officers destroy an incriminating tape recording.

Theft or Burglary

Officers commit corrupt acts when they appropriate goods or money that do not belong to them during the course of their work. One example is the organized burglary ring. In 1958–1960 major scandals erupted in Chicago, Denver, and Omaha when it was revealed that groups of officers were actively engaged in burglary. In some instances the officers committed the burglary themselves. In others, they provided protection while a citizen-burglar committed the act.[14]

Examples of isolated theft include an officer who picks up a drunk on the street, finds $100 in the person's wallet, and keeps half of it. The individual was unconscious at the time, and when he wakes up, he has a difficult time persuading anyone that he actually had $100 in his wallet when he was arrested. Or narcotics officers raid a motel where a drug transaction is taking place. They find several thousand dollars in cash and narcotics and keep half for themselves. According to Robert Daley's account in *The Prince of the City,* New York City detectives in the Special Investigations Unit (SIU) regularly divided these "scores" among all members of their team. Narcotics were used to supply their informants.[15]

A final example: weapons or other valuable goods "disappear" from the police department's property room. Officers appropriate them for their own personal use or for sale.

Illegal Administrative Actions

A police officer can take illegal administrative actions because of his or her access to valuable information. For example, a person engaged in a private lawsuit against someone else bribes a police officer for damaging information about the person contained in police files. Or the desk sergeant may receive a kickback for every arrested person he refers to a certain bail bondsman or private defense attorney.

Internal Corruption   Corrupt acts may also be confined within the police department itself with no direct involvement of the public. In some departments it is necessary to "buy" promotion to higher rank. Some departments even had set prices for each rank. Officers are sometimes assessed a fixed "voluntary" contribution for an important local politician. Officers who do not contribute cannot expect positive evaluations, good assignments, or promotion.

LEVELS OF CORRUPTION

Not only are there many different kinds of corrupt acts, but also different levels within a department. Some departments are more corrupt than others: in some, corruption is the exception; in others, it is pervasive.

Lawrence W. Sherman developed a typology to distinguish different levels in terms of "the *pervasiveness* of corruption, its *organization,* and the *sources* of bribes."[16] Sherman identified three different types.

"Type I: Rotten Apples and Rotten Pockets"

Corruption is least serious when it is confined to a few police officers acting on their own. The so-called rotten-apple theory is widely used to explain the existence of a few corrupt officers in a generally honest department. In this situation, the bad officers are operating on their own, without the cooperation or approval of other officers.

The rotten-apple theory is commonly used by police chiefs *after* corruption has been exposed in their departments. It is a convenient way of explaining what has happened without admitting that the problem might be more serious. If the rotten-apple theory is accepted, the solution is simply a matter of identifying and removing the bad officers. It denies the need for examining general procedures and practices within the department.

When several corrupt officers begin cooperating with each other, the situation can be described as a "rotten pocket." Examples of rotten pockets are numerous. Typically, officers within a unit will share the proceeds of graft: money accepted for protecting a gambling operation is divided equally among all patrol officers on the beat, with an extra share or shares for supervisors. Narcotics officers who "score" a large sum of cash in a drug raid will divide the money among their partners. The cases of organized burglary are examples of rotten pockets. The corrupt acts depended upon the active cooperation of several officers within one unit.[17]

The existence of a rotten pocket makes the elimination of corruption far more difficult. Because several officers are directly involved, they are reluctant to testify against each other. The corruption is protected through group solidarity. *The Prince of the City* dramatizes the extreme personal agony of Lieutenant Leuci in having to testify against his partners who were involved in corruption.[18]

The existence of a rotten pocket perpetuates corruption in two important ways. First, new officers are socialized into illegal activity. Often they are simply presented with the fruits of ongoing corruption. New officers are understandably reluctant to question veteran officers within the unit. Soon they too become accomplices and are tainted by their own participation. Second, members of rotten pockets ultimately earn promotion. Thus, the longer corruption flourishes, the more supervisory officers there will be who are actively corrupt themselves. This encourages the maintenance and spread of corruption.

"Type II: Pervasive Unorganized Corruption"

Corruption reaches a higher degree of existence when, according to Sherman, a department "has a majority of personnel who are corrupt, but who have little relationship to each other."[19] All of the officers in a department, for example, might be taking bribes for not issuing traffic tickets. Or a majority might be soliciting discounts from merchants in their area. Corrupt acts are *pervasive* in the sense that most of the officers are involved. But it is *unorganized* because officers are not actively cooperating with each other.

"Type III: Pervasive Organized Corruption"

The most serious problem exists when corruption involves virtually all members of the department acting in a systematic and organized fashion. The most obvious example is the systematic payoff for the protection of illegal activities. According to Sherman's typology, this situation usually involves ongoing relationships between the police and organized crime. In his study of "Rainfall West," William Chambliss described how this type of corruption affected one restaurant owner. In order to stay in business he had to pay $200 a month to the beat officers (which was divided up equally among them) and $250 a month for the higher-ranking officers (which was also divided among several officers). Failure to pay meant that the owner faced a steady stream of harassment "raids" over possible violations of the building and fire codes as well as ordinances regulating restaurants.[20]

The Knapp Commission found that in New York City a newly assigned plain-clothesman was not entitled to his share for about two months, while he was checked out for reliability. The earnings lost by this delay were made up to him in the form of two months' "severance pay" when he left the division.[21]

Indicators of Corruption

Not all departments are corrupt, and not all corrupt departments are equally corrupt. Nor does the degree of corruption remain the same in one department. The relevant question, according to Sherman, is: "Why are there different kinds and extents of police corruption in different communities, and in the same communities at different points in their history?"[22]

Sherman utilized certain *indicators* of corruption to answer this question. He makes an important distinction between "corruption *events* and corruption *arrangements*." An event is a one-time transaction. An example would be an officer taking a bribe for not issuing a speeding ticket. Similar events may occur many times, but they are unrelated to each other. A corrupt arrangement, however, involves "a continuing relationship among parties to the corruption." The best example is the regular payoff for protecting gambling activities.

Sherman identified the following four indicators of the degree of corruption.[23]

Active Cooperation Among Officers   This condition is indicated by corrupt events that involve two or more officers. While "the exact number of officers participating in each arrangement cannot always be ascertained . . . it is always possible to distinguish between those arrangements involving only one officer and those involving two or more."

Passive Cooperation Among Officers   Officers who do not themselves directly participate in or benefit from a corrupt act contribute to the maintenance of corruption within the department. First, they contribute by not reporting the corrupt acts of other officers to the proper authorities. Second, they contribute by failing to arrest individuals who have paid other officers for protection of illegal activities.

Citizen-Police Cooperation   Some forms of corruption require no cooperation by citizens (for example, burglary committed by officers in uniform). Other forms not only involve citizens but are often initiated by them.

Duration of Cooperation   The degree of corruption in a department "is measured by the relative numbers of corruption arrangements and events each year."

THEORIES OF CORRUPTION

Explaining the existence of police corruption is not easy. As we have already seen, corruption takes many different forms and can exist at many different levels. An adequate theory of corruption must be able to account for these variations.

Theories of police corruption fall into three different categories, depending upon whether they focus on the individual officer, the American social structure, or characteristics of law enforcement agencies.

Individual-Officer Explanation

The rotten-apple theory is one of the most popular explanations of police corruption. By focusing on the individual it explains corruption in terms of the moral failure of a few officers. According to this view, corruption spreads because the rotten apple spoils the rest of the barrel.

The rotten-apple theory serves the needs of both the public and the police department. By identifying corruption with a few individuals it provides a relatively simple explanation which avoids the necessity of examining more complex issues.

The police department itself finds the rotten-apple theory convenient Blame can be attached to a few guilty officers, thus allowing the department to avoid the question of whether corruption is pervasive and sustained by certain departmental procedures or policies. The department can also salvage its own public image by removing the guilty officers (that is, the ones who have been caught) and claiming that they were the exceptions and not the rule.

Despite its popularity, the rotten-apple theory is rejected by most experts. First, it fails to explain the pervasiveness and persistence of police corruption—otherwise one would have to assume that there are an enormous number of "bad" people recruited into police work. On the contrary, studies of police recruitment indicate that persons attracted to policing are relatively idealistic, perhaps more so than the population at large. The rotten-apple theory, then, fails to explain how individual officers become corrupt.

Second, the rotten-apple theory fails to explain the differences between departments and differences within a particular department over time. If corruption is to be explained in terms of a few "bad" people, then some departments must have attracted a disproportionately high number of rotten apples over long periods of time. Recruitment policies do make a difference, however. Procedures to screen out applicants with records of prior misconduct can be an effective means of controlling corruption.

Social-Structure Explanations

Most experts agree that police corruption is rooted in the American social structure. Important features of society, government, and politics actively encourage the corruption of law enforcement.[24] The most immediate cause of police corruption is the nature of U.S. law. Two aspects of the law in particular contribute to corruption: the criminal law and regulatory ordinances.

The *criminal law* in every state includes statutes that govern standards of morality. The most important are those dealing with gambling, drinking, drugs, and various sexual practices. These laws create what are often called "victimless" crimes. The activity is made criminal, but it is victimless in the sense that there is no complaining party who is forced to do something against his or her will. In short, people gamble because they want to; both prostitute and patron mutually agree to exchange sex for money.[25]

The so-called victimless crime statutes are also viewed as unenforceable: because they involve activities which many people regard as recreation or entertainment, there is widespread public resistance to vigorous law enforcement. Moreover, because they are victimless crimes, there is no complaining party to bring an act to the attention of the police.

Unenforceable laws governing moral standards promote corruption because they create large groups with an interest in subverting law enforcement. Interest groups include both consumers and suppliers. The consumers—people who gamble, or wish to drink after the legal closing hour, or patronize a prostitute—do not want to be deprived of their chosen form of recreation. Even though the consumers may not actively corrupt police officers (by offering bribes, for example), their existence creates a climate that tolerates active corruption by others.

The suppliers of illegal services are the heart of the police corruption problem. Vice is big business. In 1967 the President's Commission on Law Enforcement estimated that organized crime elements received gross revenues of $50 billion per year from gambling activities. Profits were estimated to be in the range of $6 to $7 billion. The people engaged in supplying vice activities have an obvious interest in maintaining their profitable business. And the profits are so large that they have no trouble paying the necessary expenses. From this perspective, police corruption is simply a routine business expense—in effect, an insurance policy that guarantees continuation of the business.[26]

Organized crime can be viewed as another causal factor in police corruption. William Chambliss emphasizes the intimate connection between the law, the political structure, the police, and criminal activity. "Organized crime," he argues, "becomes not something that exists outside law and government but is instead a creation of them."[27] Neither police corruption nor organized crime are isolated phenomena that can be explained in terms of a few bad people. They *can* be explained in terms of the nature of American society and the role of the law.

The most serious forms of police corruption, where the degree of corruption reaches Sherman's type III, are almost always related to systematic payoffs for the protection of vice. The Knapp Commission investigation into the New York City police department revealed the most systematic forms of payoffs involved the protection of gambling.[28] Corruption becomes a regular "arrangement" because of the high stakes involved and the fact that those people providing illegal services are well organized to make regular payoffs.

Political Influence   Organized crime and systematic police corruption generally flourish where they are supported by political influence. Chambliss argues that "the people who run the organizations which supply the vices in American cities are members of the business, political, and law enforcement communities—not simply members of a criminal society."[29] The corruption of the police by those with a need to avoid prosecution goes hand in hand with the corruption of other segments of the political system.

John A. Gardiner observes that "corruption is a persistent and practically ubiquitous aspect of political society."[30] Corruption is an exchange relationship involving the distribution of goods and services. Government exists to regulate the conduct of society. Corruption is an attempt to alter the rules and affect the distribution of goods and services. Corruption, or at least the desire to corrupt, Gardiner argues is an inevitable consequence of the basic regulatory function of government.

The degree of direct political influence and its effect on police corruption varies. In *Scandal and Reform,* Sherman cites the example of Oakland, California, where the police department successfully resisted external political influence and even succeeded in reducing corruption in other branches of local government.

Other factors affect the degree of political influence.[31] *Community characteristics* are an important variable. Sherman suggests that there will be less corruption in "communities with a more public-regarding ethos." In other words, some communities develop traditions of efficient and honest public service. Other communities develop traditions of self-serving, or "private-regarding" attitudes toward government. Corruption is more likely to flourish in the latter.[32]

The extent of *culture conflict* within a given community also affects the degree of police corruption. American society is a heterogeneous mixture of different races, religions, ethnic groups, and cultural lifestyles. In some communities, however, conflict is more pronounced than in others. Cultural conflict frequently expresses itself in the laws governing moral standards. Thus, there is greater likelihood of corruption in communities where there is severe conflict over gambling or prostitution than in communities where consensus prevails.

In his theory of corruption, McMullen argues that conflict over the goals of the legal system is a basic precondition for corruption. "A high level of corruption is the result of a wide divergence between the attitudes, aims, and methods of the government of a country and those of the society in which they operate."[33] In the United States there is great conflict over the goals of the legal system regarding gambling;

for example: one segment of the public expects the legal system to suppress gambling; another segment, as a consequence, finds it necessary to corrupt the agents of the legal system in order to allow gambling to exist.

Conflict over the goals of the legal system is also evident in the second aspect of the American legal system: *regulatory ordinances.* Many of the specific forms of corruption we have discussed involve the relatively minor regulatory functions of government: traffic, parking, the use of sidewalks and other public places. Corruption arises out of conflicting expectations about the legal system. An example is the store owner who bribes the police to not issue tickets for double-parking in front of his store. The legitimate functions of government include traffic regulation as a means of ensuring the orderly flow of daily life. Yet the store owner seeks to subvert that particular regulation in order to further his own immediate goals (allowing customers to stop their cars and shop at his store).

Corruption involving regulatory ordinances illustrates the important distinction between two different types of corruption. Some forms of corruption involve the use of deviant means to further deviant goals (bribery to protect illegal gambling). But other forms of corruption, Sherman points out, involve the use of deviant means to achieve socially legitimate ends. The store owner who bribes the police to not issue tickets for doubleparking is pursuing a socially legitimate goal—the operation of a successful business.[34] In either case, however, conflict over the goals of the legal system is the explanatory cause of police corruption.

Law Enforcement Organization Explanations

The existence of corruption can also be explained by factors related to law enforcement organizations. These factors fall into two categories: those which are *inherent* in the nature of police work and those which are *specific* to particular organizations. It is also important to distinguish between those factors which cause corruption in the first instance and those which sustain it once it already exists.

The Work Setting   The work setting of policing enhances the opportunities for corruption. It does not cause corruption but it creates an environment where other causal factors can operate.[35]

Police officers typically work alone or in pairs. In this respect, policing has been characterized as low-visibility work. Low-visibility has two dimensions: first, the officer is not directly observed by supervisors; and second, the officer is not observed by large segments of the public. An encounter typically involves an officer (and possibly a partner) and the citizen-suspect. Operating essentially alone, the officer routinely exercises enormous discretion in making important decisions.

The combination of low visibility and discretion creates an environment in which corruption can begin and then flourish. The absence of effective supervision, management experts agree, invites inefficiency and misconduct. Once misconduct has begun, the absence of supervision permits it to continue. The essential point is that the absence of *direct* supervision is an inherent feature of police work.

It is no accident that the most extensive forms of corruption typically occur in those units where low visibility and discretion are greatest. Virtually all investigations indicate that corruption reaches its greatest levels in plainclothes-detective units, especially those working in the area of vice. The officer in plainclothes, simply because of the lack of a uniform, has even *lower* visibility than the patrol officer. Detectives, moreover, are expected to exercise greater discretion and display greater initiative than other officers.[36]

The nature of police work contributes to corruption in other ways. As Goldstein points out, "The average officer—especially in large cities—sees the worst side of humanity. He is exposed to a steady diet of wrongdoing. He becomes intimately familiar with the ways people prey on one another." As a consequence, the officer easily develops an extremely cynical attitude toward people. Constant exposure to wrongdoing can lead to the belief that "everyone does it." Goldstein suggests that the officer easily comes to view corruption "as a game in which every person is out to get his share."[37]

In addition to the generally corrosive effect of routine police work, officers are exposed to immediate temptations. They are offered bribes or find money, drugs, or property that can easily be taken. The worst forms of corruption occur in those units where the temptations are greatest—detective work related to vice.

Corruptors and Corruptees The existence of factors in the social structure, external to the police department, raises the question of where responsibility lies for initiating corrupt acts. In the public mind, the corrupt officer is usually viewed as the guilty party. Journalist David Burnham observes that "there is considerable evidence, however, that the policeman is less the extortionist and more the victim." Police officers frequently find that the smaller gratuities, the free meals for example, are practically forced upon them.[38]

The distinction between grass eaters and meat eaters is useful in this context. The grass eaters are those officers who passively accept bribes offered to them. In the case of the meat eater, the initiative has passed from the citizen to the police officer. Officers tend to become meat eaters in departments where corruption is tolerated.

Department Characteristics Corruption, Sherman reminds us, varies from department to department, and within the same department over time. These variations can be explained in part by the internal characteristics of individual departments.

The *quality of management and supervision* has a major effect on the extent of corruption. Corruption tends to flourish in unprofessional departments with poor management practices and inadequate supervision. When officers learn that their conduct is not being closely monitored, that misconduct is not likely to be detected or punished, then they are less likely to be deterred from committing corrupt acts.

The impact of improved management upon corruption is illustrated by the examples of those departments which have successfully reduced or eliminated corruption. William Parker became chief of the Los Angeles Police Department in 1950, inheriting an organization with a long history of corruption. By instituting an extremely centralized and authoritarian style of management, Parker succeeded in eliminating corruption within a few years. Even Parker's worst critics conceded that the Los Angeles police were honest. In New York City, Commissioner Patrick Murphy (1970–1973) significantly reduced corruption by imposing improved management procedures, including primarily more effective supervision of officers.[39]

Closely associated with the quality of management and supervision is the *attitude of the top administrator.* Corruption is less likely to flourish in departments where the chief or commissioner has made it clear that it will not be tolerated.[40] Examples of the successful reduction or elimination of corruption have been almost entirely based on the role of a strong top administrator who took a firm, public stance against corruption: Parker in Los Angeles, Murphy in New York, Vernon in Oakland, and others. Conversely, corruption tends to flourish in those departments where the top administrator, through words and deeds, communicates to rank-and-file officers a lack of concern about corruption.

The *atmosphere within the department* is also a major contributor to police corruption. Corruption will flourish in those departments where it already exists and where, among the rank and file, prevailing attitudes tolerate misconduct. Conversely, it will not flourish where the peer pressure of rank-and-file officers discourages it. The atmosphere within the department is, in large part, a consequence of the factors previously cited: management practices and the attitude of the top leadership. Poor management and ineffective leadership allow corruption to begin and a corruption-tolerant atmosphere to prevail.

The significance of the atmosphere within the department lies not in explaining corruption in general but in explaining how individual officers become corrupt. Stoddard explains corruption in terms of the socialization of new police recruits into the code of conduct in which corruption is a normal part of the job. William A. Westley and others have stressed the importance of a distinct police "subculture" in shaping the attitudes and behavior of individual police officers. Where that subculture tolerates or encourages corruption, new recruits will learn to accept it as normal.[41]

Careers in Corruption

In "Becoming Bent: Moral Careers of Corrupt Policemen," Lawrence Sherman analyzes the process by which officers are socialized into the practice of corruption. Corrupt officers are not born; they are not inherently dishonest prior to joining the police force. They become corrupt by passing through "a painful process of choices."[42]

Sherman uses the concept of a moral career—as distinct from an occupational career—to describe the process of becoming corrupt. Irving Goffman defines a moral career as a "regular sequence of changes . . . in the person's self and in his framework of imagery for judging himself and others." In other words, the process of becoming corrupt involves significant changes in the way officers think about themselves and other police officers.

The moral career of a corrupt officer begins with relatively minor "perks." The officer accepts free meals and begins to think of them as a normal, if not expected, part of the job. Pressure from other officers and from the persons offering the perks is extremely important in this first step. The literature on police work is filled with stories of police officers being unable to pay for meals even though they want to. Sherman writes that the "moral experience about accepting these perks usually occurs in the recruit's first days on duty, and the peer pressure to accept them is great." Thus, the officer is initiated almost immediately into the first stage of becoming corrupt.

The second and third stages of becoming corrupt, according to Sherman, involve regulatory offenses: an officer accepts a free drink from a bar owner and allows the bar to remain open after the legal closing hour, or a bribe from a driver who has exceeded the speed limit. Peer pressure is important if the officer knows that other officers routinely do the same thing. At this point, the individual officer is still passively accepting such offers.

The remaining stages of the moral career gradually transform the officer into a meat eater. Corrupt acts involve more serious violation of the law, become more systematic, and involve larger amounts of money; the officer begins to *initiate* corrupt acts. The fourth, fifth, and sixth stages in Sherman's hypothetical model involve regular payoffs for the protection of gambling, prostitution, and narcotics trafficking. Sherman points out that "Accepting narcotics graft . . . is the most difficult moral experience of all." Officers must adjust their self-image to accept the fact that they are actively assisting the sale and distribution of what they know to be an illegal and destructive narcotic. At this point the moral career is complete. The officer has reached the final point of not just accepting but actively furthering illegal and harmful activities.

Entire organizations become corrupt by a similar process. Just as the individual officer moves through different stages, so a police department progresses from minor and limited acts of corruption to pervasive and extensive corruption. The "moral career" of a department can be viewed as moving through the three stages identified by Sherman. Initially, corruption involves isolated individuals or a few isolated groups. When virtually all officers are engaged in corrupt acts, the second stage has been reached. The final stage involves "pervasive organized corruption," in which virtually all officers are engaged in systematic arrangements with criminal elements.[43] A police department becomes progressively corrupt because corruption is not actively combated by the department's leadership.

Summary

An adequate sociological theory of police corruption takes into account the different variables involved. In summary, these factors include:

Law and Politics   The nature of the law in American society creates significant opportunities for corruption. The demand for illegal services gives rise to business groups who supply those services. These business groups have both an interest in and the resources to corrupt agencies of government.

Community Characteristics   The characteristics of a particular community affect the extent of corruption. Corruption is more prevalent where there is greater conflict over the goals of the legal system and where local traditions have established an atmosphere that tolerates corruption.

Department Characteristics   Corruption will develop and flourish where there is poor management, involving inadequate supervision and a failure to take a strong stance against corruption.

Peer Pressure   Where corruption already exists, the individual officer will be more likely to become socialized into a pattern of corruption.

THE COSTS OF CORRUPTION

The costs of police corruption are enormous. What is not generally appreciated, however, are the different *kinds* of costs involved. Corruption involves more than just the particular officers engaged in illegal activities. It involves virtually every aspect of policing.[44]

Law Enforcement

Corruption undermines the basic law enforcement function of the police. Whether the corrupt act involves a small bribe to ignore a traffic violation or a sizable and regular payoff to protect a gambling operation, illegal activity is being tolerated.

The cost to society, the police department, and the individual officer can be measured in different ways. In terms of the cost to society, corruption undermines the potential deterrent effect of the law. It communicates the message that criminal activity is permissible. In the case of gambling operations, corruption protects and supports organized crime. The enormous revenues generated by organized crime, in turn, support other illegal activities and the further corruption of government agencies.

Public Respect

Corruption does not remain a secret. Knowledge of corrupt acts spreads throughout society. The more pervasive the corruption, the more widespread the knowledge of it. The result is serious damage to the reputation of the police department in the community. The loss of public respect is felt in several different ways.

Police work depends heavily on citizen cooperation. The police depend upon citizens to report crimes and to provide information relevant to investigations. The dynamics of particular police-citizen encounters are in part the product of the attitudes toward the police that the citizen brings to the encounter. Where the police have a reputation for being corrupt, citizens are more likely to be indifferent, uncooperative, or even hostile.

The lack of public respect also damages recruitment efforts. Qualified persons are much less likely to seek employment with an organization that has a bad reputation. In a more general sense, corruption undermines the quest for professional status. One of the hallmarks of professionalism is an acceptance of an occupation as a profession by the public. A reputation for corruption is one of the main obstacles to attainment of professional status.

Corruption is also a contributing factor to poor police-community relations. Public opinion polls consistently show that minority groups hold the police in lower esteem than do members of the white majority. In large part, this is because vice-related corruption is most extensive in minority neighborhoods. Minority groups see more corruption and as a natural consequence develop a more critical attitude toward the police. Corruption is not the sole cause of poor police-community relations, but it aggravates an existing problem.

Management and Supervision

Corruption undermines efforts to establish professional management and supervision within a police department. Corruption makes a mockery of all departmental rules and regulations. The new officer, upon being initiated into the practice of corruption, learns to disregard the official department rhetoric about honesty and professionalism. The real rules governing police conduct are those of the informal code, tolerating corruption.

Effective supervision becomes difficult, if not impossible, when rank-and-file officers know that their supervisors are engaged in corrupt practices. The supervisor cannot discipline a subordinate when the latter can potentially expose a superior's misconduct. The undermining of supervision extends to all areas of police work, not just corrupt practices themselves. Thus the supervisor of a detective unit cannot effectively impose standards of efficiency related to criminal investigations after standards of conduct have already been undermined.

Corruption is a key ingredient in the so-called blue curtain between police and public. The knowledge that all officers are guilty of corruption reinforces the worst features of the police subculture. William A. Westley argues that the sense of isolation and alienation from the public encourages the belief that violence is justifiable, and that the police may lie to protect each other from charges of misconduct.[45] Corruption only reinforces the need to deny all charges of misconduct and to protect one's fellow officers at all costs.

In a reformed police department, the dynamics of the police subculture are reversed. Pride in the organization's reputation for honesty and professionalism become an important weapon against corruption. It reinforces the sense of personal honesty in the individual officer, encourages the reporting of corrupt acts by others, and provides support for supervisors who take action against corrupt officers. One of the aspects of professionalism is self-discipline: in the professionalized police department, the subculture becomes the mechanism for occupational self-governance.

CONTROLLING CORRUPTION

The history of the police in America does not inspire confidence about the prospects for eliminating corruption. It is as old as law enforcement itself. Reform efforts have been notably unsuccessful. Herman Goldstein observes that "The history of reform provides many illustrations of elaborate attempts to eliminate dishonesty followed by rapid reversion to prior practices."[46] Yet there are notable instances of cities that have successfully reduced or eliminated corruption. The reform of the Los Angeles police under Chief William Parker in the 1950s is a commonly cited example. Sherman calls the reform of the Oakland police department during the same period, "one of the most lasting of any American police agency."[47]

What are the conditions for the successful control of corruption? The first condition is a realistic set of objectives. Some of the most important causal factors in corruption are firmly rooted in the American social and political structure. These factors are not likely to change. As a consequence, John A. Gardiner suggests that "the relevant question becomes one of finding ways to *reduce,* not eliminate, the frequency of corruption."[48] The second condition involves a distinction between preventing and eliminating corruption; preventing corruption in a "clean" department is much easier than eliminating it in a corrupt department. Each situation calls for a different approach.

Corruption control strategies can be divided roughly into two categories. *External* strategies involve changing the environment in which a police department exists and/ or using corruption control agencies that are outside of the department. *Internal* strategies involve changing the policies and procedures of the department itself.[49]

External Corruption Control Strategies

Public Opinion   Mobilizing *public opinion* is a first step toward reform. Corruption cannot be eliminated when large segments of the public tolerate its existence. Public support for reform, meanwhile, provides the political backing needed by the reform-minded police administrator. It also encourages the honest police officer—or the corrupt officer who has experienced a change of heart—to come forward and provide information. The reform effort in New York City in the mid-1970s depended heavily on formerly corrupt officers who "turned" and provided information to investigators about corrupt practices.[50]

Scandal—the exposure of corruption—is an important device for mobilizing public opinion. The scandal is an established tradition in American politics. It typically involves a dramatic revelation about misconduct. As an event, scandal usually includes extensive coverage in the news media, followed by expression of outrage by prominent citizens, political figures, or the media itself. The immediate result is often a demand that the police chief be fired.

Scandals tend to be temporary events. (The Watergate scandal was unique in lasting for over two years.) After the initial headlines and outrage, interest often quickly fades. The news media move on to other events, and the public quickly forgets. Scandal can serve to initiate or at least create the conditions for reform, but it cannot sustain it.[51]

The *news media* can play an important role in both creating a scandal and mobilizing public opinion. The exposure of corruption in the New York City Police Department in the 1970s, for example, was largely the result of the efforts of one journalist, David Burnham of *The New York Times*. Burnham's front-page article on corruption published on April 25, 1970, set in motion the official investigation. Burnham himself has described his role as a journalist in terms of "trying to describe those practices and procedures that stop a particular agency from achieving its stated goals." That is, Burnham was primarily concerned about the fact that corruption undermined the law enforcement mission of the New York City police.[52]

Decriminalization Repeal of many of the laws dealing with vice is commonly cited as a potential remedy for police corruption. The protection of gambling in particular is the source of the most systematic and organized form of corruption. Legalizing gambling, it is commonly argued, would alter the environment in which the police operate, reducing the conflict over the goals of the legal system, and thereby removing one of the greatest temptations for corruption.[53]

Decriminalization is also proposed by many experts as an important criminal justice reform for reasons unrelated to police corruption. The laws dealing with gambling, many sexual practices, alcohol-related offenses, and certain soft drugs overload the system and in many respects invade the legitimate privacy of individuals.

Yet decriminalization is no panacea. Legalization of gambling and the establishment of legitimate, regulated, and taxed gambling enterprises have not eliminated illegal gambling activities. Numbers rackets, for example, continue to flourish. Moreover, while there is wide public support for the decriminalization of the possession of marijuana and other soft drugs, legalization of heroin and other addictive drugs is a very different matter. Finally, no one seriously proposes the elimination of the various regulative ordinances. Traffic laws are a necessary and proper function of government. Their existence maintains an environment in which corruption is a continuing temptation.

Decriminalization, then, represents an important possible solution to *part* of the police corruption problem. It could eliminate some of the major corruption-inducing factors in the external environment.

Altering the Political Environment Sherman argues that police departments are not necessarily at the complete mercy of their political environment. It is possible for the police to exert a positive influence and to alter that environment. He cites the case of the Oakland police department in the 1950s. The chief of police threatened to arrest politicians who were involved in gambling and other illegal activities. As a result, he succeeded in eliminating corruption within the police department and reducing the corrupting influences in the environment.[54]

Investigating Corruption: External Mechanisms   When corruption exists within a police department, the question becomes one of choosing the most effective strategy to investigate it. The media can play an important role in exposing corruption and mobilizing public opinion. Other external mechanisms are available.[55]

Corruption involves illegal acts. The act of corruption is itself a crime. State laws dealing with bribery, extortion, malfeasance in office, and others may be used to fight corruption. The local *prosecutor* or state *attorney general* has authority to investigate and bring indictments. There are limitations to this approach, however. Where corruption pervades local government, the prosecutor is often reluctant to take action against political associates. The prosecutor may also be directly involved in corrupt activities. Gathering information about corruption is extremely difficult. In some cases the use of a *grand jury* can ensure greater political independence for the prosecutorial effort and facilitate information gathering.

Police corruption may also involve violations of federal law. Thus the local U.S. attorney has authority to investigate and seek indictments. Herbert Biegel points out that the U.S. attorney has jurisdiction under the Hobbs Act of 1970 regarding gambling-related extortion. Federal perjury statutes may also be used. Two federal laws deal with false testimony under oath and can be effective weapons during the grand-jury stage of an investigation. Biegel himself was a special U.S. attorney investigating corruption in Chicago from 1970 to 1972.[56]

The use of the U.S. attorney has certain advantages. A federal prosecutor is less likely to be associated with local politicians who are involved in corrupt activities. In the case of extremely serious levels of corruption, special prosecutors, special grand juries, or "strike forces" may be used. U.S. attorneys are not widely used, however, because police corruption is essentially a local crime, subject to local jurisdiction.

Special investigating commissions have also been extremely effective in combating police corruption. The most famous example is the Knapp Commission, which investigated the New York City police in the early 1970s. The Pennsylvania Crime Commission investigated the Philadephia police and issued its report in 1974.[57]

Special commissions have the advantage of political independence. As an appointive body, a special commission can be completely free of connections with ongoing political corruption. The appointment of a special commission also generates considerable publicity, thereby helping to mobilize important public support for the campaign against corruption.

Special investigating commissions have serious limitations, however, limitations shared by all external mechanisms for investigating police corruption. The basic problem lies in the fact that they are indeed outsiders and lack intimate knowledge of the inner day-to-day workings of the department. Moreover, external investigations arouse the hostility of the rank and file. There is a natural tendency for the police to close ranks, deny the existence of corruption, and refuse to cooperate with investigators.[58]

All investigations of police corruption face the difficult problem of obtaining the kind of intimate information which only a working police officer can supply. The Knapp Commission investigation in New York City relied on a few key officers who "turned" and began to cooperate with investigators. Officers David Durk, Frank Serpico, and Robert Leuci provided the most important evidence for investigators. They did so, however, only at a tremendous personal cost: ostracism within the department and even potential threats against their lives. *The Prince of the City* portrays the great personal agony of Detective Leuci as he gradually provided information about officers who were close to him.[59]

The Knapp Commission also gathered information through questionable methods. The commission used concealed microphones and tape recorders and employed double agents. Moreover, evidence against allegedly corrupt police officers was presented in sensationalized public hearings where the accused had little opportunity to defend themselves. In short, many of the guarantees of due process were suspended. The American Civil Liberties Union called the Knapp Commission's tactics a civil liberties "disaster."[60] The controversy of the Knapp Commission tactics serves to dramatize the difficulty of investigating corruption and gathering solid evidence in the face of the group solidarity of the police. Because of the problems associated with external mechanisms, experts agree that internal methods can be far more effective.

Internal Corruption Control Strategies

The case of police departments that successfully eliminated or reduced corruption suggests that reform begins with and depends primarily on the *posture of the top administrator*.[61] The leader of the department must make it clear that corruption will not be tolerated and that action will be taken against corrupt acts. William Parker in Los Angeles, Wyman Vernon in Oakland, Clarence Kelley in Kansas City, and Patrick Murphy in New York City were successful in fighting corruption because of their strong public stand against it, backed up with concrete actions.

Drawing the Line   The greatest dilemma facing the police administrator in initiating a fight against corruption is the question of where to draw the line. Not all corrupt acts are equally serious. There is room for legitimate debate about whether certain gratuities, such as discounts on meals, should be considered corruption at all. Eliminating these minor perks, moreover, presents extremely difficult problems: they are often too numerous and too petty to be able to fight. Also, gratuities are often forced upon police officers.

Several police chiefs noted for their success in fighting corruption have taken the position that no gratuities, however small, are tolerable. Patrick Murphy told his officers, "Except for your paycheck there is no such thing as a clean buck."[62] William Parker in Los Angeles and O. W. Wilson believed that even a free cup of coffee compromised the integrity of the police. The argument against all gratuities is premised on the belief that this one small step creates a climate in which successively larger steps become possible. Sherman's analysis of the "moral career" of the corrupt officer lends support to this argument. The alternative view rests on the assumption that the anticorruption effort should focus on serious acts of corruption. The minor perks are too numerous and too petty to worry about.

Whatever position the top administrator takes, the evidence suggests the need for candor and the need to support policy statements with action. Part of the cynicism of police officers arises from the contradiction they see between public declarations of honesty and the daily practice of corruption.

The *morale* of the department is another dilemma faced by the reform-minded police executive. Corruption, whether alleged or proven, damages the morale of the entire department. Even the honest police officer suffers through guilt by association in the public mind. The administrator who launches an anticorruption campaign—in effect admitting that corruption exists—often encounters resentment and hostility from the rank and file. Patrick Murphy aroused deep hostility among New York City police officers because of his constant pronouncements against corruption. A hostile rank and file can easily sabotage other policies initiated by the chief.[63]

One technique for maintaining the morale of a department is to *reward the honest officer.* In a corrupt department, the honest officer leads an extremely lonely existence. Herman Goldstein, moreover, points out that "Many competent officers have found that to have reported corruption even once had the effect of permanently impairing their careers." Peer pressure and the evaluation process for promotions encourage officers to silently accept the corrupt acts of others. The lack of rewards for honesty, finally, encourages some honest officers to become corrupt, in the belief that everyone else is doing it and that there is no reward for honesty.[64]

Goldstein suggests that honest officers should be rewarded both for their corruption-free reputations *and* evidence of their willingness to report corrupt acts. The latter would include bribes offered by citizens as well as bribes accepted by police officers.

The most effective way to fight corruption on a continuing basis is through *improved administrative practices.* "Corruption thrives best," Goldstein observes, "in poorly run organizations where lines of authority are vague and supervision is minimal."[65] Administration can be improved in several ways. The traditional approach has been through greater centralization of decision making. William Parker kept corruption out of the Los Angeles Police Department in part by maintaining one of the most centralized administrative styles in all policing. Comparisons have also been made between the corruption-free FBI, with its centralized administrative style and the scandal-ridden Drug Enforcement Agency (and its predecessors), which was administered in an extremely decentralized fashion. In New York City, Patrick Murphy centralized control of vice and narcotics enforcement, the principal areas of corruption, even while he decentralized other parts of the department.

Modern management has traditionally emphasized increasing the number of supervisors relative to rank-and-file employees. This is particularly important in policing where officers work alone or in pairs for the most part. In New York City, for example, the number of sergeants increased by 40 percent as a result of the anticorruption crusade.

To fight corruption effectively, it is generally agreed, a police department needs a strong *internal investigative unit.* These internal-affairs units derive their strength from two factors. First, they must be fully supported by the top administrator. Here the administrator's attitude toward corruption is critical. If the leader of the department is serious about fighting corruption, an internal-affairs unit will pursue that objective. Department leaders must prove their committment by taking appropriate action against proven acts of corruption.

Second, an internal-affairs unit must have sufficient resources to carry out its mission. When Patrick Murphy took command of the New York City police there was one staff member of the Internal Affairs Division for every 533 line officers. He increased the size of the IAD and reduced the ratio to one IAD staff member for every 64 line officers. Sherman found that "Central City" and Oakland had equivalent ratios of 1:110 and 1:216.[66]

Administrative techniques for combating corruption, according to Sherman, can be divided into two categories: postmonitory and premonitory. *Postmonitory* techniques concentrate on investigating past corruption. *Premonitory* techniques concentrate on reducing the chances that corruption will occur. Sherman argues that premonitory techniques seem to be more effective in reducing the level of corruption.[67]

REVIEW

1 Give a definition of police corruption.
2 Provide examples of the five major types of police corruption.
3 What are useful indicators of the degree of corruption in a police department?
4 Why is the rotten-apple theory a poor explanation of police corruption?
5 How does the American social structure contribute to police corruption?
6 In what ways is corruption facilitated by the work setting of policing?
7 What are the major costs of police corruption?
8 Describe the major external strategies for controlling police corruption.
9 What are the most effective internal strategies for controlling corruption?
10 Explain the difference between premonitory and postmonitory control strategies.

REFERENCES

1 Lawrence W. Sherman, ed., *Police Corruption: A Sociological Perspective* (Garden City: Anchor Books, 1974), p. 1.
2 Samuel Walker, *Popular Justice* (New York: Oxford University Press, 1980), pp. 19, 45.
3 Pennsylvania Crime Commission, *1973–74 Report* (Harrisburg: Attorney General of Pennsylvania, 1974), p. 96.
4 David Burnham, "How Police Corruption Is Built into the System—And a Few Ideas for What to Do about It," *Police Corruption,* ed. Sherman, pp. 310–311.
5 Wilbert E. Moore, *The Professions: Roles and Rules* (New York: Russell Sage Foundation, 1970), chap. 13.
6 Herman Goldstein, *Police Corruption: A Perspective on Its Nature and Control* (Washington, D.C.: Police Foundation, 1975), pp. 6–8.
7 Ibid., p. 3.
8 Ibid., pp. 16–22.
9 Knapp Commission, *Report on Police Corruption* (New York: George Braziller, 1973), p. 4.

10 Mike Royko, *Boss* (New York: Dutton, 1971).

11 Burnham, "How Police Corruption Is Built into the System," p. 305.

12 Knapp Commission, *Report,* p. 1; Pennsylvania Crime Commission, *1973–74 Report,* p. 97.

13 Robert Daley, *Prince of the City: The True Story of a Cop Who Knew Too Much* (Boston: Houghton-Mifflin, 1978).

14 Ralph Lee Smith, *The Tarnished Badge* (New York: Thomas Y. Crowell, 1965).

15 Daley, *Prince of the City.*

16 Sherman, *Police Corruption,* p. 7.

17 Smith, *The Tarnished Badge.*

18 Daley, *Prince of the City.*

19 Sherman, *Police Corruption,* p. 9.

20 William Chambliss, "The Police and Organized Vice in a Western City," in *Police Corruption,* ed. Sherman, pp. 153–170.

21 Knapp Commission, *Report,* p. 74.

22 Sherman, *Police Corruption,* p. 3.

23 Lawrence W. Sherman, *Scandal and Reform: Controlling Police Corruption* (Berkeley: University of California Press, 1978), pp. 195–201.

24 Goldstein, *Police Corruption,* pp. 23–28.

25 Ibid., p. 23; Sherman, *Police Corruption,* pp. 22–23.

26 President's Commission on Law Enforcement and Administration of Justice, *The Challenge of Crime in a Free Society* (New York: Avon Books, 1968), p. 441.

27 Chambliss, "The Police and Organized Vice in a Western City," p. 154.

28 Knapp Commission, *Report,* pp. 71–90.

29 Chambliss, "The Police and Organized Vice in a Western City," pp. 169–170.

30 John A. Gardiner, "Law Enforcement Corruption: Explanations and Recommendations," in *Police Corruption,* ed. Sherman, p. 316.

31 Sherman, *Scandal and Reform.*

32 Sherman, *Police Corruption,* pp. 16–17.

33 M. McMullan, "A Theory of Corruption," *Sociological Review* 9 (June 1961): 184–185.

34 Sherman, *Scandal and Reform,* pp. 11–14.

35 Sherman, *Police Corruption,* p. 12.

36 Daley, *Prince of the City.*

37 Goldstein, *Police Corruption,* p. 25.

38 Burnham, "How Police Corruption Is Built into the System," p. 306.

39 Gerald E. Caiden, *Police Revitalization* (Lexington: Lexington Books, 1977), pp. 267–272; Sherman, *Scandal and Reform.*

40 Goldstein, *Police Corruption,* pp. 40–41.

41 Stoddard, "A Group Approach to Blue-Coat Crime," in *Violence and the Police,* ed. William A. Westley (Cambridge: MIT Press, 1970), pp. 110–118.

42 Sherman, *Police Corruption,* pp. 191–208.

43 Sherman, *Police Corruption,* pp. 7–12.

44 Goldstein, *Police Corruption,* pp. 9–12.

45 William A. Westley, *Violence and the Police* (Cambridge: MIT Press, 1970).

46 Goldstein, *Police Corruption,* p. 37.

47 Sherman, *Scandal and Reform,* p. xxxiv.

48 Gardiner, "Law Enforcement Corruption," p. 316.

49 Goldstein, *Police Corruption,* pp. 37–51.

50 Daley, *Prince of the City.*

51 Sherman, *Scandal and Reform.*

52 David Burnham, *The Role of the Media in Controlling Corruption* (New York: John Jay Press, 1977).

53 Goldstein, *Police Corruption,* pp. 38–39.

54 Sherman, *Scandal and Reform,* pp. 141–143.

55 Goldstein, *Police Corruption,* pp. 48–50.

56 Herbert Biegel, "The Investigation and Prosecution of Police Corruption," *Journal of Criminal Law and Criminology* 135 (1974): 135–156.

57 Knapp Commission, *Report;* Pennsylvania Crime Commission, *1973–74 Report.*

58 Goldstein, *Police Corruption,* pp. 32–34.

59 Daley, *Prince of the City.*

60 Sherman, *Scandal and Reform,* pp. 259–260.

61 Goldstein, *Police Corruption,* 28–30.

62 Ibid., p. 29.

63 Ibid., pp. 32–35.

64 Ibid., pp. 50–51.

65 Ibid., p. 42.

66 Lawrence W. Sherman, *Controlling Police Corruption: Summary Report* (Washington, D.C.: Department of Justice, 1978), p. 10.

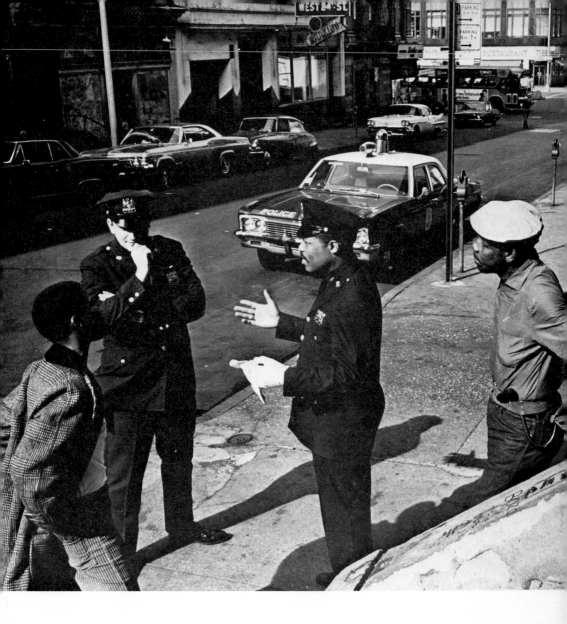

CHAPTER 9

POLICE-COMMUNITY RELATIONS

THE POLICE AND THE COMMUNITY

Police-community relations is one of the most complex and controversial areas of American policing. The problem is most serious in terms of relations between the police and minority groups. This chapter will review police-community relations, analyze the seemingly contradictory evidence, and arrive at a balanced understanding of this highly controversial subject.

An important distinction exists between statistical *evidence* of police misconduct—as a source of police-community tensions—and the *perception* of misconduct. The perception of misconduct is, in many respects, as serious a problem as actual misconduct. In contacts between police officers and citizens, the image of the police in the eyes of the citizen is extremely important. This chapter will seek to examine the sources of citizen perceptions of the police where these perceptions contribute to police-community tensions.

Most urban police departments today maintain special police-community relations units. This chapter will examine the activities of these units and review evaluations of their impact on police-community relations.

Evidence of the Problem

Evidence of a police-community relations problem is abundant. Some specific examples include:

1 A history of violent disorders between the police and the black community. Major episodes of violence occurred in 1917–1919, 1941–1943, and 1964–1968. Each episode was marked by allegations of serious police misconduct against black citizens.[1]

2 Continuing complaints about police abuse expressed by black community leaders. Lennox Hinds, former executive director of the National Conference of Black Lawyers, charges that "Police abuse is a fact of life in every black community—none of us is immune. Each day letters and petitions come to my desk describing in gross and horrifying detail the experience of blacks in every walk of life at the hands of the police."[2]

3 A 1978 report by the U.S. Civil Rights Commission found that in Memphis, Tennessee, "A significant number of Memphians, notably the poor and members of the black community, express not only a lack of confidence in the Memphis Police Department but also outright fear and distrust."[3]

4 Hearings by the California legislature in 1972 found that serious tensions existed between the police and the Mexican-American community in the state.[4]

5 A 1980 *Newsweek* poll found that 44 percent of black respondents believed there was police brutality in their community.[5]

Contrary Evidence

Police-community relations is an extremely complex subject. While there is abundant evidence of police-community tension and conflict, there is also contrary evidence. James Q. Wilson points out that "The single most striking fact about the attitudes of citizens, black and white, toward the police is that in general these attitudes are positive, not negative."[6] Public opinion polls consistently confirm Wilson's statement.

Day-to-day policing in American cities is not continual warfare or combat. Most contacts between police and citizens, including minority citizens, are characterized by civility and cooperation. Incidents of possible misconduct are statistically infrequent. The typical eight-hour tour of duty for the big-city cop is *not* marked by an arrest, the use of physical force, or a shooting incident.

Defining the Problem

Police-community relations may be defined broadly or narrowly. A *broad definition* includes all aspects of relationships between the police and the public. "Community," in this sense, refers to all persons living within the jurisdiction served by a particular law enforcement agency. "Relations" refers to the full range of police activities and police contacts with citizens. Adopting this view, a report on *The Police in the California Community* advised that

> community and police relationships can be neither understood nor enhanced by focusing solely on surface, symptomatic behavior as has been the tendency in the past. Such things as alleged police brutality, harassment of certain segments of the community, and differential provision of police services, to the extent they occur, reflect deeper and more pervasive problems which must be addressed.[7]

A more *limited definition* of police-community relations refers to relations between the police and specific segments of the community where there are recurring tensions and conflicts. It focuses on the nature of those conflicts and the specific incidents or alleged incidents that create them.

Areas of Conflict

Relations between the police and most citizens are positive. Conflict is mainly concentrated in relations between the police and specific segments of the community. The major areas of conflict include:

Minority Groups

1 *Black Americans.* Contemporary and historical evidence clearly suggests that the most serious police-community relations problems involve black Americans.

2 *Hispanic Americans.* In communities with large Hispanic American communities—particularly Los Angeles, Houston, and Denver—serious police-community relations problems have developed.[8]

3 *Native Americans.* In both urban and rural areas where there are significant numbers of Native Americans, police-community relations problems exist.

4 *Asian Americans.* Periodically, in cities with large Asian-American communities—New York, San Francisco, Los Angeles—conflicts between the police and the Asian-American community have emerged.

Alternate-Lifestyle Groups

1 *Homosexuals.* Violent confrontations between the police and gay people have occurred in San Francisco and New York City. Gay spokespersons have accused the police in these and other cities of harassment and entrapment.[9]

2 *Young people.* Conflict with the police is far more prevalent among young people than middle-aged or older people. The problem does not involve all young people but primarily those whose appearance (hair style, clothes), behavior (hanging out in public parks, cruising city streets, etc.), or suspected activity (possible drug usage) goes against conventional middle-class values.

Women

1 *Inadequate protection.* Women's groups in Oakland and New York City sued the local police departments for failing to protect women who were the victims of spouse abuse.[10]

2 *Harassment.* The Chicago police were sued after it was discovered that women were being strip-searched for such minor offenses as traffic violations.

PUBLIC OPINION AND THE POLICE

Public opinion about the police is a useful starting point for analyzing police-community relations. Major sources of data include private opinion polling organizations (the Gallup Poll, Louis Harris, etc.), the U.S. Justice Department, and individual scholars.

Table 9-1 represents data gathered by the 1975 National Crime Survey.

Police performance was rated as "good" or "average" by 84 percent of white respondents and 74 percent of black respondents. A major task in analyzing police-community relations involves explaining the apparent paradox between persistent allegations about police misconduct and racism on the one hand, and the generally favorable opinions expressed by blacks in opinion polls on the other hand.

Long-Term Trends

Public attitudes about the police are highly stable over time. The 1975 data presented in Table 9-1 show that 9 percent of whites and 19 percent of blacks rated the police performance as "poor." A 1966 survey conducted by the National Opinion Research Center found nearly identical attitudes: 7 percent of whites and 16 percent of blacks rated the police as "poor."[11]

Variables

Race or minority status, age, and income are the variables that explain differences in opinion about the police. Blacks are only half as likely to rate the police as "good" and twice as likely to rate them as "poor." This pattern is found consistently in all surveys of public opinion about the police.

TABLE 9-1
EVALUATION OF POLICE PERFORMANCE BY SELECTED RESPONDENT CHARACTERISTICS

Respondent characteristics	Evaluation of police performance (%)					Estimated number
	Good	Average	Poor	Don't know	No answer	
Age						
16–29	29	48	16	6	0	4,971,233
30–49	38	42	13	6	0	4,627,084
50 or older	50	33	8	9	0	5,788,018
Race						
White	47	37	9	7	0	10,872,109
Black / other	24	50	19	7	0	4,514,226
Sex						
Male	40	41	13	5	0	6,882,142
Female	40	40	11	8	0	8,504,193
Family income						
Less than $5,000	40	36	14	9	0	2,898,064
$5,000–11,999	38	42	13	6	0	5,173,635
$12,000 or more	42	42	10	5	0	5,654,310
Not ascertained	36	40	13	11	1	1,660,690

Source: U.S., Department of Justice, *The Police and Public Opinion* (Washington, D.C.: Author, 1977), p. 13.

Along with race, age is an important variable. Table 9-1 shows that people in the 16–29 age group are twice as likely to rate the police as "poor" than are people in the 50 and older group. Evaluation of police performance improves steadily with age. Family income has some impact on opinion about the police. Poor people are more likely to rate the police as "poor" than are people with higher incomes. But the data on "good" evaluations of police performance do not yield a clear trend. Sex appears to have no impact on evaluations of police performance. Men and women hold nearly identical opinions about the police.

Intercity Variations

Attitudes toward the police vary from city to city. Negative ratings of police performance by blacks range from a high of 29 percent in Cleveland to a low of 12 percent in Atlanta (see Table 9-2). Significantly the National Crime Survey data on thirteen major cities suggests that white and black attitudes are closely linked. In cities where white evaluations of police performance are relatively high, black evaluations are also relatively high; where white evaluations are relatively low, black evaluations are also relatively low.

Specific Criticisms of Police Performance

The National Crime Survey asked respondents what they perceived as needed improvement in police performance. The results are indicated in Table 9-3. Signifi-

TABLE 9-2
RATINGS OF POLICE PERFORMANCE BY RACE AND AGE IN ATLANTA AND CLEVELAND

Race and age	Rating of police in Atlanta (%)				Rating of police in Cleveland (%)			
	(Positive) 1	2	3	(Negative) 4	(Positive) 1	2	3	(Negative) 4
White:	7	33	46	13	10	31	44	15
16–29	6	28	53	13	5	23	53	19
30–49	7	31	48	14	8	30	46	16
50 or older	9	39	39	13	15	38	35	12
Black/other:	8	25	54	12	5	15	50	29
16–29	6	19	61	15	3	10	51	36
30–49	8	25	54	13	5	13	54	29
50 or older	14	36	41	8	9	23	47	22

Source: U.S., Department of Justice, *The Police and Public Opinion* (Washington, D.C.: Author, 1977), pp. 39, 40.

cantly, whites and blacks gave somewhat similar responses. Both perceived a need for greater police protection. The need for more police officers of a certain type, in certain areas, or at certain times was indicated most often by both whites and blacks. The need to "hire more policemen" was the second most frequent response by whites and third most frequent by blacks.

TABLE 9-3
PERCEIVED NEED FOR IMPROVEMENT OF LOCAL POLICE BY RACE

	% White	% Black
No improvement needed	17	9
Improvement needed	65	75
Don't know	16	14
No answer	2	2
Most important suggested improvement:		
Hire more policemen	27	18
Concentrate on more important duties, serious crime, etc.	11	11
Be more prompt, responsive, alert	12	20
Improve training, raise qualifications or pay; recruitment policies	4	4
Be more courteous, improve attitude, community relations	7	12
Don't discriminate	1	4
Need more traffic control	1	0
Need more policemen of certain type (foot, car) in certain areas or at certain times	28	25
Other	8	5

Source: U.S., Department of Justice, *The Police and Public Opinion* (Washington, D.C.: Author, 1977), pp. 39, 40.

Blacks were much more critical of the quality of police service. The need for greater promptness, responsiveness, and alertness ranked second among blacks. Blacks also perceived the need for improvements in courteousness and police officer attitude. Although blacks were more concerned about ending discrimination, this item was indicated by only 4 percent of the black respondents.

Race and Attitudes Toward the Police

The data on attitudes toward the police provide a useful perspective on the police-community relations question. Race is an important variable but attitudinal patterns are complex. Two aspects deserve comment.

First, as we have already noted, the majority of black Americans have a positive attitude toward the police. Only about one-quarter or less rate the police as "poor." The number rating the police as "poor," however, is consistently twice that of whites. The heart of the police-community relations problem involves one segment of the black community. Patterns of police interaction with the black community are complex and do not affect all segments of the community in the same way. These patterns of interaction are examined in detail in the following section.

Second, blacks are often critical of the police for the same reasons as whites. Both whites and blacks express a desire for more not less police protection. This contradicts the popular stereotype that blacks are critical of overly aggressive police activity (for example, large numbers of field interrogations, arrests, etc.). The lack of adequate police protection—*underpolicing*—is perceived by many blacks as a serious problem. The demand for more police protection should not be surprising. Victimization surveys indicate that blacks are more heavily victimized by crime than whites.[12] As a result, the demand for more police protection coexists with criticism of excessive police activity.

Police Perception of Citizen Attitudes

Police officers do not have an accurate perception of citizen attitudes. While survey data indicate that citizens are highly supportive of the police, officers are generally unaware of this. Westley argues that a perception of public hostility is a main ingredient in the police subculture. It fosters an us-versus-them attitude and a feeling that officers need to stick together, even to the point of lying about the misconduct of other officers.[13]

The gap between citizen attitudes and police perception of those attitudes affects police-community relations. Officers tend to overestimate the extent of hostility in the black community. In one survey, police officers consistently predicted that public attitudes toward the police were worse than they actually were. Groves and Rossi argue that "overperception" of black hostility affects police behavior: "There is considerable evidence that violent police overreaction to relatively slight hostile acts led what might have been minor incidents into major disorders with heavy tolls of life and property."[14]

THE POLICE AND THE BLACK COMMUNITY

The primary focus of the police-community relations problem involves relations between the police and the black community in the big cities. As we have already indicated, these patterns of interaction are complex. In this section we will examine these patterns in detail, looking at both the perception of police misconduct and the available evidence on actual misconduct.

Complaints About Police Practices

Complaints about police practices voiced by the black community fall into three general areas: police field practices, police administrative practices, and employment practices.

Police Field Practices Specific actions by police officers in the field that give rise to complaints include:

1 *"Harassment,"* usually in the form of overly aggressive field interrogations
2 *Selective enforcement,* in the form of discriminatory arrest patterns
3 *"Brutality,"* in the form of excessive use of physical force, verbal abuse, and discourtesy
4 *Deadly force,* in which blacks are shot and killed more often than whites
5 *Underenforcement,* in which the police fail to provide adequate police protection for law-abiding citizens

Police Administrative Practices Policies and procedures within the police department that give rise to complaints include:

1 *Disposition of citizen complaints,* in which the police department fails to discipline officers guilty of actual misconduct and dismisses most citizen complaints as "unfounded"
2 *Climate of racism,* in which racially prejudiced attitudes are allowed to flourish among police officers

Employment Practices Employment practices that give rise to complaints include:

1 *Recruitment,* the failure of police departments to recruit minority group police officers in proportions equal to their number in the community
2 *Promotion,* in which black officers are discriminated against in promotional opportunities
3 *Assignment,* in which black officers are denied preferred assignments and incompetent officers are assigned to minority neighborhoods

The preceding list of complaints represents the *perception* of police misconduct on the part of the black community. Each of these complaints has been identified in the various studies of police-community relations.

In the following section we will examine the *available evidence* on police practices as it relates to these perceptions.

POLICE FIELD PRACTICES

Police Presence

The police presence is much larger in minority neighborhoods than in other parts of the urban community. Bayley and Mendelsohn argue that "The police seem to play a role in the life of minority people out of all proportion to the role they play in the lives of the dominant [white] majority."[15] A larger proportion of police officers are assigned to low-income and minority-group neighborhoods, and police have more frequent contacts with minority-group individuals.

The heavy police presence exists because residents of those areas are heavy "consumers" of police services. Victimization surveys indicate that low-income people are more frequently victimized by crime than middle- and upper-income people. Low-income people also rely more often on the police for emergency services than middle- and upper-income groups. Poverty is associated with a higher incidence of family breakdown, alcoholism, mental illness, and drug abuse, which often result in problems requiring police intervention. James Q. Wilson argues that "the average patrolman in a big city is most frequently in contact, not with the 'average' citizen, but with a relatively small number of persons who are heavy users of police services (willingly or unwillingly)."[16]

Contact between police and low-income minority citizens is skewed even further because of lifestyle patterns. For low-income males, the street is a primary recreation area. Werthman and Piliavin found that juvenile gangs regard the street corner as a "private place" where they socialize with their friends.[17] These persons have the highest levels of contact with the police. They are the most visible to the police and the most aware of police presence. Street-corner groups are also frequent sources of complaints about "disorder." Finally, because low-income minority-group males are disproportionately involved in crimes of burglary and robbery, they are more frequently regarded as suspects. The San Diego Field Interrogation study found that two-thirds of all persons subject to field interrogations were minority-group males.[18]

The major source of police-community tensions, in short, is the special nature of contacts between police and low-income minority group males. As Table 9-1 indicates, race and age are the two most important variables in citizen evaluations of the police. Minority youths have the lowest opinion of the police.

The patrol car aggravates the problem of selective contact between the police and the community. The patrol car isolates the police officer and prevents regular, informal contacts. Police officers tend to have direct contact with people most often in "problem" situations (that is, where there is usually someone who does not welcome police intervention). The patrol car isolates the police from law-abiding, middle-class residents in minority neighborhoods, preventing the development of more positive attitudes on both sides.

Harassment

A frequent complaint voiced by minority spokespersons is that the police harass minority citizens, especially young males. *Harassment* is usually defined as a greater tendency to stop, question, and frisk. The President's Commission on Law Enforcement found that the practice of field interrogations was "universally resented" by minorities.[19] As we have already seen, the nature of the police presence in minority neighborhoods, together with the lifestyle of young, low-income males, results in a high level of contact between these two groups. The question, however, is whether or not active harassment exists.

Evidence indicates that the police do stop and question young, low-income males more frequently than any other group. The San Diego Field Interrogation study found that 100 percent of the subjects of field interrogations were male, that 66 percent of them were black and Mexican-American, and that almost two-thirds of them were juveniles.[20]

Jerome Skolnick argues that police disproportionately select young, low-income, minority-group males for field interrogations because "a disposition to stereotype is an integral part of the policeman's world."[21] Police officers are trained to be suspicious and develop a visual shorthand for "suspects."

> Suppose police are on the lookout for a robbery assailant and have nothing but a vague description of a Negro male. Under these circumstances innocent Negro males will easily be assimilated to the policeman's stereotype of the subject. Thus, in a high-crime area a disproportionate number of black men will be stopped, not necessarily out of racial prejudice, but rather because black men in a high-crime area will tend to fit the description of the suspect.[22]

This results in a form of stereotyping that, in turn, can produce de facto racial discrimination on the street.

The issue of harassment and field interrogations was examined by the San Diego study. Interviewing the subjects of field interrogations, it found little evidence of harassment. The report concluded that "The majority of all citizens who were subjects of FI contacts felt that the contact was justified and properly conducted."[23]

In short, the issue of harassment is extremely complex. On the one hand there is the appearance of harassment of young, black males by the police. This appearance is a product of several factors: the nature of the police presence in minority-group neighborhoods, the lifestyle of young low-income males, and the inherent tendency of police to stereotype. The only available statistical evidence, however, is ambiguous. The police do stop and question young minority males in disproportionate numbers, but the subjects of field interrogations do not necessarily feel that they were being harassed.

Police Brutality

Accusations of police brutality are among the most frequent issues in police-community relations. Many minority-group spokespersons charge that brutality is pervasive; they further charge that the police systematically cover up incidents of brutality and refuse to discipline guilty officers. The police deny these charges, arguing that most allegations of brutality are without foundation in fact.

Part of the controversy involves the definition of *brutality*. While there is general agreement that excessive physical force constitutes brutality, there is disagreement about other forms of conduct. Minority citizens adopt a much broader definition of brutality. According to a mail survey by the President's Commission on Law Enforcement (Table 9-4), black community leaders were much more willing to define verbal abuse and rudeness as brutality.

How extensive is police brutality? Available evidence on this question is subject to differing interpretations. In studies conducted for the President's Commission on Law Enforcement in 1966 Reiss found that police officers used "undue force" in 37 out of 3826 observed encounters.[24] Whether or not this is an unacceptably large percentage or a surprisingly low percentage depend upon one's values. Some people argue that any instance of "undue force" is unacceptable. Others argue that the use of force is legitimated by law and that, inevitably, a certain number of questionable incidents will occur.

The *perception* of excessive use of force is at least as important as, and perhaps more important than, its actual incidence. A single incident can affect people's perceptions of police conduct out of all proportion to its statistical significance. Single incidents also have a cumulative effect. Reiss observes that "in the course of time, police misconduct cumulates over a population of citizens so that a sizable minority of citizens experience police misconduct at one time or another."[25] The perception of misconduct is further aggravated by the belief that police departments fail to discipline guilty officers.

With respect to verbal abuse, regarded by many minorities as a form of brutality,

TABLE 9-4
POLICE ACTION PERCEIVED BY COMMUNITY LEADERS AS
POLICE BRUTALITY

Police action	% White (N = 130)	% Black (N = 54)
Unnecessary use of force to point of injury, bloodshed, etc.	96.9	96.2
Rough handling	73.0	75.9
Verbal abuse (name calling, profane language, etc.)	65.3	85.1
Rudeness (sarcasm, ridicule, curtness, disrespect)	54.6	70.3
Other*	9.2	12.9
No answer	3.0	0

*Primarily constitutional rights violations and discrimination mentioned.
Source: President's Commission on Law Enforcement and Administration of Justice, *Field Surveys*, vol. 5, *A National Survey of Police and Community Relations* (Washington, D.C.: U.S. Government Printing Office, 1967), p. 151.

Reiss found that police officers "openly ridiculed or belittled" citizens in 5 percent of all encounters.[26] The day-to-day working language of police officers has been characterized as "profane, loud and good-humored."[27] Part of that profanity includes the casual use of racial and ethnic labels, many of them derogatory. To the insider, the working police officer, these labels are a normal part of the working environment. To the outsider, however, an ethnic or racial slur can be highly offensive. As with the use of excessive force, verbal disrespect cumulates over time. A number of isolated episodes can appear as a pattern of racial prejudice.

Officer Attitudes and Behavior

The relationship between police officer attitudes and behavior is extremely complex. Attitudes can be measured in terms of observed verbal statements or responses to survey questionnaires. Behavior can be measured in terms of official acts such as arrest or the use of force.

Reiss found that three-fourths of the officers observed expressed some form of racial prejudice. Yet his data failed to identify a pattern of racial discrimination in official acts. Using the same data set, Robert Friedrich concluded that "In general, a policeman's attitude toward blacks seems to exert only a limited influence on his behavior toward blacks." Part of the explanation lies in the fact that an officer is not completely free to act out his or her feelings. Attitudes are constrained by the presence of other officers (who may not be prejudiced) or by the expectations of the organization. The officer who knows that the department will investigate and possibly discipline misconduct will be less likely to act out prejudicial attitudes. According to Friedrich, "the expression of personal feelings is muted or deflected into different channels."[28]

White Cops–Black Cops

The issue of racial discrimination becomes more complex when the race of the police officer is introduced as a variable. Critics allege that the police are the servants of a "white power structure," systematically oppressing the black community. Whatever the institution role of the police, the behavior of individual officers is more complex. A number of studies indicate that black police officers are more punitive than white officers.

Reiss found that black police officers used undue force at a slightly higher rate than white officers (9.8 per 100 black officers, compared with 8.7 per 100 white officers). Donald Black, using data from the same field studies, found that black officers were more likely to arrest black suspects than were white officers. Finally, James Fyfe found that black officers were just as likely to use deadly force as white officers (the fact that black officers appeared to use deadly force more often disappeared when he controlled for the officers' place of assignment).[29]

The behavior of police officers is more readily explained by factors associated with the police role than with the officer's race (see Chapter 11). White officers are not all sinners and black officers are not all saints. Particular incidents of misconduct are more readily explained by situational factors.

Arrest

Contradictory evidence exists concerning possible racial discrimination in arrest practices. In an early study, Nathan Goldman found that police were more likely to arrest black juveniles than white juveniles. Piliavin and Briar reached a similar conclusion. Black and Reiss, however, did not find evidence of racial discrimination. While black juveniles were more often arrested, they attributed this to the fact that officers more willingly complied with the request of a black citizen that the black juvenile be arrested. Lundman, Sykes, and Clark reached a similar conclusion, arguing that "it would appear that the higher arrest rate for black juveniles is attributable to black complainants who lobby for formal police action."[30]

Underenforcement

The issue of arrest patterns is two-sided. The systematic failure to arrest can be as discriminatory as a pattern of excessive arrests. Failure to arrest denies the victim or victims the protection of the law. In the case of an assault, failure to arrest the assailant leaves the victim vulnerable to repeated and possibly more serious assault. Where the failure to arrest is more systematic, it leaves an entire neighborhood or community vulnerable to criminal victimization.

Historically, the police in the United States took a tolerant attitude toward crime among blacks: crimes by blacks against blacks were often ignored. This denial of justice to the black victim represents a form of official racism. This practice was historically most evident in Southern states, but it also existed, and to some extent still exists, in Northern states.[31]

Underenforcement of the laws is especially evident with respect to crimes of vice. In most urban communities a certain level of vice is allowed to flourish in the form of prostitution, drug trafficking, gambling, and after-hours bars. Traditionally, vice activities have been segregated, through selective enforcement, in certain areas of the community. Usually, these are the low-income, minority-group areas.

Vice is usually accompanied by corruption to a greater degree in minority neighborhoods.[32] Tolerance of vice discriminates against the residents of minority areas in several ways. It allows crime to flourish in the neighborhood, exposing law-abiding citizens and their families to crime. The corruption associated with vice undermines respect for law enforcement and damages police-community relations. The greater existence of vice and corruption in minority group neighborhoods may explain the fact that in the 1966 National Opinion Research Center public opinion poll, ten times as many nonwhites as whites indicated that the police were "almost all corrupt."[33]

Equality of Police Services

Some critics of the police have alleged that the police provide a higher level of service to white neighborhoods than black neighborhoods. In the case of *Burner v. Washington, D.C.,* black citizens sued the Washington, D.C., police department, alleging inferior service. Peter Bloch examined the issue of equality of police services in Washington by comparing one area that was about 90 percent black with an area that was over 90 percent white. He defined police "inputs" in terms of service calls per officer, the total number of police per 100 reported robberies, and the number of officers per 100 index crimes. He found that "police inputs are distributed equally and that both neighborhoods were receiving levels of police service equal to their apparent needs."[34]

Professionalism and Police Tactics

Ironically, police professionalism may in some respects contribute to police-community relations problems. Professionalism has often been associated with an aggressive approach to law enforcement, as reflected in more systematic field interrogations. The result is a higher rate of contact between police and young black males and a greater sense of police harassment. Both the President's Commission on Law Enforcement (1967) and the Kerner Commission (1968) noted that police-community relations problems existed in some of the best police departments. Ostrom and Whitaker agree, noting that "Two of the departments most frequently characterized as 'professional,' Oakland and Los Angeles, have also been observed to take strong punitive actions against blacks."[35]

To deal with this problem, many police experts in the 1970s proposed an alternative approach to police professionalism. They recommended that less emphasis be placed on attempting to achieve efficiency by means of a highly centralized administrative structure. A number of police departments, responding to these suggestions, experimented with team policing, a more decentralized approach to police administration. Improved police-community relations was one of the major goals of team policing.

Other departments attempted to improve police-community relations through greater use of foot patrol. This was based on the belief that the greater "efficiency" of motor patrol produced negative side effects in terms of police-community relations.

Deadly Force

The bitterest complaint of minorities about police conduct involves the use of deadly force. Many minority group spokespersons charge that the police maintain an "open season" on shooting black citizens.

The analysis of the police use of deadly force raises difficult questions of interpretation. All available data indicates that minorities are shot and killed by the police out of all proportion to their representation in the population. James Fyfe concludes that "blacks and Hispanics are everywhere over-represented among those on the other side of police guns." Paul Takagi argues that "In proportion to population, black youngsters and old men have been killed by police at a rate 15 to 30 times greater than that for whites."[36]

Other studies, however, have reached different conclusions. The Chicago Law Enforcement Study Group analyzed police shootings in Chicago between 1974 and 1978. As Table 9-5 indicates, it found that when police shootings were controlled for felony arrests, blacks were shot less frequently than whites. Felony arrests represents

TABLE 9-5

AVERAGE ANNUAL RATES AT WHICH POLICE SHOT CIVILIANS IN CHICAGO, 1974–1978, BY VICTIM'S RACE

Race of civilians shot	Average annual number of civilians shot			
	Per 100,000 population-1970 census	Per 100,000 population-updated[a]	Per 1,000 forcible felony arrests[b]	Per 10,000 arrests for "all offenses"[c]
White	1.0	1.4	5.6	2.9
Black	6.6	5.3	4.5	3.8
Hispanic[d]	4.1	2.6	4.3	3.6
Total	3.2	[e]	4.7[f]	3.6

[a] Based on population estimates reported in *Chicago Tribune,* May 18, 1980.

[b] Forcible felony arrests include arrests for murder, rape, armed and strong arm robbery, aggravated battery, aggravated assault, and burglary.

[c] All arrests by the Chicago Police Department are included, from murder through petty larceny. Only arrests for traffic violations are excluded. Source: Chicago Police Department annual statistical summaries.

[d] Population and arrest figures for Hispanics are estimated since neither the 1970 Census nor Chicago Police Department statistical reports adequately specify a "Hispanic" category. Census Bureau staff and staff from the U.S. Commission on Civil Rights aided in estimating Hispanic population figures. Chicago Police Department reports have categories for White, Black, Indian, Chinese, Japanese, and "other" races. After consultation with Police Department statisticians, we determined that the "other" category could be used as a rough surrogate measure for Hispanic arrestees. Some Hispanics may be included in the White category and some non-Hispanics may be included in the "other" category of arrestees. The race of the shooting victims was not estimated, however. Police records specified whether the individuals were White, Black, Puerto Rican, Mexican or otherwise.

[e] No revised estimate of the total population was indicated in the source used for updated population figures—*Chicago Tribune,* May 18, 1980.

[f] Using a standard "Z" test for equality of proportions, none of the differences between the rates in this column are statistically significant at the .05 level.

Source: William A. Geller and Kevin J. Karales, *Split-Second Decisions: Shootings of and by Chicago Police* (Chicago: Chicago Law Enforcement Study Group, 1981), p. 119.

a better estimate of the persons "at risk," that is, in situations where there is high potential for a violent encounter with the police. The Chicago study concluded that "a definitive conclusion on the possible role of racism as a motivating factor in police shootings of civilians is impossible without far more extensive and intensive data and statistical analysis techniques than we have been able to use."[37]

In sum, there is no question that minorities are shot more often than whites by the police. The important question is the extent to which shootings of minorities are unjustified.

POLICE ADMINISTRATIVE PRACTICES

Administrative practices within police departments are a major source of police-community mistrust. The most serious problems involve the disposition of citizen complaints about police misconduct.

Disposition of Citizen Complaints

The U.S. Civil Rights Commission report of police-community relations in Memphis concluded that "the single most aggravating factor . . . is the failure of the existing internal and external mechanisms which purportedly exist to prevent and combat" police misconduct. The report cited two disciplinary actions taken against Memphis police officers in 1976. In February two officers who shot and killed a 16-year-old boy fleeing from the scene of a burglary were temporarily suspended for two days and then reinstated. In April two officers were fired for killing a dog.[38]

The two Memphis incidents contribute to the feeling among many minorities that a double standard of justice exists. Minor violations of department regulations are punished severely, while serious misuse of force against citizens, especially minority citizens, is overlooked. Paul Jacobs reported that traditionally the Los Angeles Police Department rarely disciplined officers for shooting and killing a citizen but would severely punish them for damaging a patrol car.[39]

Among minorities there is widespread feeling that civilian complaint procedures and internal disciplinary mechanisms exist only for the protection of the department. Art Garcia, of the East Los Angeles Legal Services office, argues that "dealing with the Los Angeles Police Department is very difficult. You find that their primary interest . . . is trying to protect the police officer."[40]

The vast majority of formal complaints filed against police officers are not sustained. Table 9-6 shows the disposition of complaints filed with the St. Louis Police Department in 1975. Four dispositions are possible: unfounded, exonerated, not sustained, and sustained. Slightly fewer than 10 percent (58 out of 594) of the complaints were sustained. Significantly, only 3 percent of the complaints involving physical abuse were sustained, while 29 percent of the complaints involving improper handling of assignment were sustained.

Table 9-7 indicates the disciplinary action taken by the St. Louis Police Department in 1975 as a result of a citizen complaint. In the 85 cases where the complaint was sustained, officers generally received only a written or oral reprimand. Only six officers were suspended and two were demoted (for periods of six months). No officers were fired, although three chose to resign voluntarily while under investigation.

The perception that officers who are found to be guilty of misconduct are not punished contributes to police-community conflict. Citizens believe that the internal-review procedures exist only for the purpose of whitewashing complaints. As a result, many people argue that procedures for *external* review of police conduct are needed. (The major forms of external review are discussed in Chapter 10.)

Trends in Citizen Complaints

Citizen complaints of police misconduct are difficult to sustain. The St. Louis data are typical of dispositions in other police departments. In part this is because such complaints are inherently difficult to prove. While the standards of proof that prevail in a court of law do not apply to an internal disciplinary procedure, the allegation still must meet some minimal standards of proof. Generally, however, there are no third-party witnesses to the incident. The allegation then becomes a "swearing contest" between the officer and the complaining citizen. In the absence of third-party verification of the complaint, the investigating officers are inclined to believe the testimony of the officer.

TABLE 9-6
COMPLAINTS AGAINST POLICE OFFICERS, ST. LOUIS POLICE DEPARTMENT, 1975*

Types of complaints	Unfounded	Exonerated	Sustained	Not sustained	Withdrawn	Pending	Appealed	Total
Total	79	40	58	352	36	29	7†	594
Physical abuse	23	11	8	140	12	15	2	209
Verbal abuse	7	2	2	59	5	0	0	75
Improper attitude or manner	11	4	12	45	5	2	0	79
Lack of police action	4	3	5	10	1	2	1	25
Improper handling of assignment	12	9	25	30	2	6	1	84
Unjust arrest, summons, etc.	6	7	2	18	2	1	1	36
Money and/or property missing	9	2	1	21	4	2	0	39
Harassment	6	1	2	21	4	1	2	35
Bribery or attempted bribery	0	0	1	0	0	0	0	1
Property damaged by police	1	1	0	8	1	0	0	11

*Explanation of complaint dispositions: Unfounded—the complaint was not based on facts, as shown by the investigation, or the incident complained of did not occur; exonerated—the action complained of did occur, but the investigation disclosed that the actions were reasonable, lawful and proper; not sustained—insufficient evidence available to either prove or disprove the allegations in the complaint; sustained—investigation disclosed sufficient evidence to support the allegations in the complaint.

†Not sustained findings upheld in seven Citizen Appeal Hearings

Source: St. Louis Police Department, *Annual Report,* 1975, p. 21.

TABLE 9-7
DISCIPLINARY ACTIONS RESULTING FROM CITIZEN COMPLAINTS
AND PROCEDURAL VIOLATIONS, ST. LOUIS POLICE
DEPARTMENT, 1975

Citizen complaint total	85
Board Hearing—six day suspension	1
Board Hearing—three day suspension	1
Resigned—under investigation	3
Demoted—six months	2
Probationary period extended 90 days and Written Reprimand	1
Probationary period extended six months	1
Four week suspension	1
5 day suspension	2
4 day suspension	1
2 day suspension and complainant reimbursed	1
2 day suspension	1
1 day suspension	1
24 hours court and/or overtime	4
16 hours court and/or overtime	1
Written Reprimand and complainant reimbursed	1
Written Reprimand	25
Oral Reprimand and counseled	1
Oral Reprimand	13
Cautioned and reinstructed	3
Reinstructed	18
Discussion	1
No action taken	2
Procedural violation total	75
5 day suspension	3
2 day suspension	3
40 hours court and/or overtime	1
24 hours court and/or overtime	1
Written Reprimand	8
Oral Reprimand	16
Cautioned	1
Reinstructed	39
Counseled	3

Source: St. Louis Police Department, *Annual Report,* 1975, p. 21.

A citizen complaint reflects the *perception* of police misconduct. Whether or not a formal violation of the law or of departmental rules occurred, the citizen believes something wrong happened. Long-term trend data on citizen complaints indicate that citizens are increasingly willing to file formal complaints. This trend can be viewed as a consumer revolution. As consumers of police services, citizens have increasingly higher expectations about the quality of the services they receive. And they are more willing to complain about practices that they were willing to tolerate in the past.[41]

In New York City the number of civilian complaints increased dramatically over a twenty-year period. In the mid-1950s the number of complaints filed with the Civilian Complaint Review Board (CCRB) averaged about 150 per year. By the 1970s the annual average was more than 3000 complaints (see Chapter 10, Table 10-1). It is unlikely that police conduct in New York City deteriorated by a factor of 20 during this period. In fact, one could argue that police conduct may have improved as a result of higher recruitment standards, better training, and more effective supervision. The twentyfold increase in civilian complaints probably reflects a change in citizen attitudes. Citizens are less willing to tolerate what they believe to be police misconduct and more willing to take formal action against it.

Changes in the administration of civilian complaints by the New York City Police Department also encouraged greater citizen complaints. The existence of the CCRB became more well-known, and the department actively encouraged citizens to make use of it. In its early years, police officials engaged in practices that tended to discourage citizens from filing formal complaints.[42]

The civil rights movement in the United States is an important component of the consumer revolution. It represents the demand for equal treatment of minorities in all areas of American life. This has affected employment, education, and housing as well as the administration of criminal justice. Thus, black citizens have been more willing to bring complaints about police conduct. With this in mind, however, it should also be noted that half the complaints processed by the New York CCRB were brought by white citizens. The demand for higher quality of services has affected all Americans.

POLICE EMPLOYMENT PRACTICES

Racial discrimination in police employment is a source of police-community relations tensions. In no jurisdiction of the United States does the percentage of minority-group officers in the law enforcement agency equal the percentage of minorities in the population.

Equal employment opportunity is required by law. Discrimination in employment is unconstitutional under the equal protection clause of the Fourteenth Amendment and is prohibited by the Civil Rights Act of 1964 and other federal laws. Equal employment opportunity is also viewed as an important factor in police-community relations. The report on *The Police and the California Community* argued that:

> The basis of support for policing our society must come from all citizens. Given this basic tenet, it follows that police agencies should be representative of the populations they serve. To be otherwise diminishes their ability to respond empathetically to many community concerns and reinforces the perception held by some segments of the minority public that law enforcement agencies represent the force of the dominant society and are institutionally designed to preserve the status quo.[43]

The National Advisory Commission on Civil Disorders, appointed to investigate the riots of the 1960s, argued that discriminatory police employment practices contributed to the riots. In every city, the percentage of minority-group officers was substantially lower than the percentage of minorities in the community. In Cleveland minorities represented 34 percent of the population but only 7 percent of the sworn officers. In Detroit minorities represented 39 percent of the population but only 5 percent of the sworn officers.[44]

Since the mid-1960s, police departments have made some progress in the recruitment of minorities. The most notable progress occurred in Washington, D.C., and Detroit. By 1977, 45 percent of the officers in Washington and 31.7 percent of the officers in Detroit were racial minorities. Table 9-8 indicates the number and percentage of minorities in selected police departments in 1977.

Promotion

Minorities are even more seriously underrepresented in supervisory ranks. In 1968 the National Advisory Commission on Civil Disorders found that minorities represented only 4 percent of the sergeants in twenty-eight selected big cities. Meanwhile, only 2.2 percent of lieutenants and 1.9 percent of captains were minorities.[45]

Some improvement has occurred since 1968. The most significant progress has occurred in Washington, D.C., and Detroit. The Metropolitan Police Department in Washington had thirteen minority officers at the rank of captain or higher in 1978, compared with three (all captains, none at higher ranks) in 1968. Detroit had a total of twenty-eight minority officers at the rank of captain or higher in 1978, compared with only one in 1968.[46]

The presence of minorities in supervisory ranks has a special impact on police-community relations. Command personnel are highly visible to the public, frequently appearing in the media as spokespersons for the department. The presence of minorities in high-level positions creates, if nothing else, the image that the department is responsive to minority concerns.

Assignment

The final personnel practice that contributes to police-community relations problems involves the assignment of individual officers. While no hard data are available, some

TABLE 9-8
MINORITY-GROUP POLICE OFFICERS BY SELECTED CITIES

City	Total officers	Black	Spanish surname	Native American	Total minority	% minority
Boston	2102	83	0	0	83	3.9
Cleveland	1906	213	7	0	220	11.5
Dallas	1997	99	71	3	173	8.6
Detroit	5688	1786	17	4	1807	31.7
Houston	2988	120	140	1	261	4.3
Kansas City	1192	146	16	1	163	13.6
Oakland	642	101	39	x	140	21.8
Miami	698	73	103	0	176	25.2

Source: Adapted from FBI, *Uniform Crime Reports, 1978* (Washington, D.C.: Author, 1979); Police Executive Research Forum, *Police Practices: The General Administrative Survey* (Washington, D.C.: Police Foundation, 1978).

critics charge that police departments deliberately assign incompetent officers to minority-group precincts. The President's Commission on Law Enforcement reported that in Philadelphia officers known as "goof-offs" were assigned to the ghetto areas of north Philadelphia as a form of discipline. Albert Reiss commented that "slum police precinct stations, not unlike slum schools, collect the 'rejects' of the system."[47]

The assignment of incompetent officers to one section of town is a form of discrimination in the sense that the police department willfully provides a lower quality of service to that area. This practice could have serious consequences. The incompetent officer is presumably more likely to use deadly force without justification or commit some other form of misconduct.

Whether or not this practice is widespread is not known. It is possible however, that the practice has been curtailed by union contracts. (The crime commission studies cited above were conducted before police unionism became widespread.) Contracts typically specify that assignment is based on seniority, a policy that restricts the ability of the chief to engage in arbitrary or discriminatory assignment.

Summary

The evidence suggests that police departments engage in discriminatory employment practices. Racial minorities are underrepresented at all ranks. Employment discrimination damages police-community relations in two important ways. First, it creates an *image* that the department is unresponsive to the concerns of minorities. Second, it *substantively* damages police-community relations by excluding different perspectives from police decision making. Minority-group officers are more likely to have closer ties with minority neighborhoods and, as a result, communicate their concerns to the police department.

THE POLICE ROLE

A major source of the police-community relations problem involves the basic role of the police. James Q. Wilson argues that it is the *function* of the police rather than their manner of operating that creates tensions with the community.[48]

As a social-control agency the police have the responsibility of maintaining the status quo. The criminal law expresses the norms of society, and the police have the task of apprehending those who violate these norms. The police and the entire criminal justice system are the most coercive agency of social control in modern society. Peter Manning argues that the police "are inextricably linked to the political status quo and are, in effect, duty bound to sustain and uphold it."[49]

The power-maintenance function of the police inevitably creates conflict with individuals or groups that are out of power. In American society, racism and economic inequality produce sizable numbers of such people. The most powerless groups are low-income, minority youths. The police play an important *symbolic* role. The report on *The Police in the California Community* comments that "Lacking influence in government power circles, minority citizens have come to regard police actions as manifestations of the conscious intent of the majority society, through government, to exclude them from participation."[50]

Many features of contemporary policing enhance the symbolic role of the police. The uniform and the marked patrol car are designed to increase the visibility of the police. Patrol itself is designed to create the impression of police omnipresence. The police officer's handgun, meanwhile, is a constant reminder of the ultimate coercive nature of police power. The sheer visibility of the police creates a lightning-rod effect: the officer on the beat attracts the accumulated resentment and anger of powerless citizens.

Research confirms the symbolic role of the police. McCaghy and Thiessen argue that citizen attitudes toward the police reflect not specific police practices but more general beliefs about the community. They comment that "some of our findings suggest that 'attitude toward the police' is not a self-contained concept but part of a more global concept of satisfaction with community leaders, the community itself, and even general satisfaction with life."[51]

Implications

The idea that police-community relations problems are the result of the police role helps to explain much of the ambiguous data on police field practices. Research on arrest practices, field interrogations, and the use of deadly force has not consistently produced evidence of racial discrimination: while some research has found evidence of discrimination, other research has not. More important than the empirically verifiable evidence of racist practices, however, is the *perception* of injustice. The perception of injustice, in turn, is a product of the symbolic power-maintenance function, which is inherent in the police role.[52]

IMPROVING POLICE-COMMUNITY RELATIONS

The report on *The Police in the California Community* warned that "The complexity of community and police relationships . . . precludes any simple explanations and/or answers."[53] Resolving conflict and improving police-community relations is not an easy task. In this section we examine the steps taken by police departments themselves to improve relations with the community.

Police-Community Relations Units

Police departments have responded to the police-community relations problem by creating specialized units designed to carry out formal activities to improve relations with the community. This approach rests on the assumption that the police department itself has a major responsibility for seeking solutions to the problem. In his influential *Police Administration* text, O. W. Wilson recommended that all large police departments establish a formal community relations unit.[54]

Such units are today found in most medium-sized and large departments. One recent survey found them to be an established part of American police administration. All eighty-five of the departments (300 officers or more) responding to the survey maintained a PCR unit.[55]

Origins   An LEAA study concluded that "The typical community relations program was born in an atmosphere of crisis."[56] The history of PCR programs supports the argument that PCR programs have usually been hastily designed reponses to a major crisis, usually a riot or civil disturbance (see Chapter 1).

The idea that the police had some responsibility for attempting to improve police-community relations first appeared in the 1940s. In the wake of a series of riots in 1943, some departments began to undertake police-community relations activities. These efforts emphasized race-relations training for police officers. The first formal PCR unit did not appear until 1957. The St. Louis Metropolitan Police Department is credited with establishing the first permanent unit.[57]

The riots of the 1960s gave great emphasis to formal PCR units. Most of the existing units were established in the late 1960s, according to two national surveys. Given the crisis atmosphere that leads to the creation of PCR units, it is not surprising that many fade in importance when the crisis passes. A 1975 *New York Times* survey found that many if not most of the units had faded. Even where programs continued to exist, the scope of their activities had been reduced, often for budgetary reasons.[58]

PCR Unit Programs   PCR units engage in a wide variety of different programs. No uniformity exists from department to department. Lee Brown developed a typology of PCR programs. The four types are (1) "externally oriented" units that emphasize "joint police-community cooperation"; (2) "youth-oriented" programs that focus specifically on juvenile problems; (3) "service-oriented" programs that attempt to alleviate basic social problems; and (4) "internally oriented" programs based on the "premise that every officer is a police-community relations officer."[59]

The most common type is the externally oriented PCR unit. O. W. Wilson recommends that the major responsibilities of these units include:

Acting as liaison with formal community organizations, such as the police-citizen council or other neighborhood groups

Establishing a working relationship with other community relations organizations in the region

Participating in the development of community relations programs for the department as a whole

Publicizing police objectives, problems, and successes

Acting as the communications link for information transmitted from citizens' organizations to the police department

Suggesting improvements in practices by police officers which have a bearing on police-community relations

Identifying training needs through interviews with citizen representatives, consultation with the internal investigations unit, and conferences with supervisors[60]

Klyman and Kruckenberg found that PCR units spent "the greatest amount of time . . . doing police-school liaison or teaching . . . and on crime prevention programs." In the units surveyed, an average of 17.9 percent of officers' time was devoted to police-school liaison or teaching, 16.8 percent was devoted to crime prevention programs (for example, teaching citizens about physical security for their homes), and 12.1 percent to public information and press relations.[61]

"Ride-along" programs and "storefront" offices were popular approaches to the police-community relations problem in the late 1960s. The 1973 survey of PCR units by Reasons and Wirth found that 54 percent conducted ride-along programs and 42 percent maintained storefront offices. A ride-along program is intended to increase public understanding of police work by allowing citizens to spend several hours in a patrol car. Normally, the ride-along car is driven by a PCR unit officer, not a patrol officer, and the car does not respond to calls for service.[62]

Storefront offices are designed to make the police department more accessible to the public. Typically, the department maintains one or more storefront offices in neighborhoods where relations with the community are tense. The offices are usually staffed by officers assigned to the PCR unit, not by regular patrol officers. These officers are responsible for answering questions about police activities, taking complaints about misconduct, and providing other services requested by citizens. Storefront offices are designed not only to be more accessible (saving citizens a time-consuming trip to headquarters) but also to provide a more informal atmosphere which would enhance communication between police and citizens.

Effectiveness   Despite their popularity, PCR units have not been able to demonstrate effectiveness in improving police-community relations. The President's Commission on Law Enforcement found that minorities regarded PCR programs as "public relations puff," and a "deliberate 'con game'."[63]

PCR units suffer from several problems. An LEAA report argued that by virtue of being separate units, they "tended to be marginal to the operations of the police department," with little or no relationship to patrol or criminal investigation activities. Furthermore, units often had weak commitment from the chief administrator. Programs were created in response to a crisis, and the department lost interest when the crisis passed.[64]

The LEAA report also found that PCR units often had unclear objectives. "Improving police-community relations" is an extremely broad and vague goal. Consequently, most units primarily engage in *public relations* activities. Public relations may be defined as an effort to improve the image of the department, not necessarily to make any changes in police operations. Renault Robinson, a prominent black Chicago police officer, argued that

> As police/community relations programs began to take shape, they focused on press relationships, speakers bureaus, a publication of monthly magazines and other periodicals praising police services and other activities. . . . Many departments thought it wasn't necessary that their practices be changed in order to improve the relationships between the police and the community, but merely that their approach to selling themselves to the public be revised.[65]

Specific police-community relations activities failed to address the part of the community that had complaints about police services. The largest amounts of time were spent in police-school liaison and crime prevention activities. Yet young school-children are not usually a serious police-community relations problem. Crime prevention programs, meanwhile, reach home residents or businesspeople who do not have complaints about police misconduct. Similarly, ride-along programs tend to attract people who already have a favorable attitude toward the police.

The sources of police-community relations problems lie in basic elements of routine police work, in the handling of citizen complaints, in employment practices, and in the fundamental nature of the police role. PCR unit programs fail to address these sources of the problem.

Why then do PCR units continue to exist? The maintenance of PCR units is related to the reasons that brought them into existence. As a form of crisis management PCR units were often intended to be little more than a visible manifestation of an attempt to address the problem. The *image* projected by the establishment of the unit was more important than the *substance* of the units programs. PCR units continue to exist for reasons of image rather than substance. A PCR unit permits a department to say that it is doing something about the problem. Conversely, abolishing a PCR unit opens the department to criticism that it is abandoning its commitment to improving police-community relations.

The weakness of PCR units is the fact that they are peripheral to basic police operations. PCR unit activities do not directly affect day-to-day operations. Also, community representatives perceive that they are not central to the police mission. Real improvement in police-community relations depends upon improvement in basic police operations. The sources of the police-community relations lie in police field practices, internal administrative practices, police employment policies, and the police role.

REVIEW

1 What evidence indicates the existence of a police-community relations problem in the United States?

2 Compare the evaluation of police performance by white and black citizens.

3 Compare the need for improvement in policing as seen by whites and blacks.

4 What aspects of policing are the major sources of police-community tensions?

5 Describe the police practices that are perceived by some people as "harassment."

6 What is meant by "police brutality"?

7 How does the underenforcement of the laws affect minority communities?

8 How are the most complaints about police misconduct disposed of by police internal-investigation units?

9 Discuss the symbolic aspects of the police role and its impact on police-community relations.

10 How effective are police-community relations units in resolving tension and conflict?

REFERENCES

1 Samuel Walker, *Popular Justice: A History of American Criminal Justice* (New York: Oxford University Press, 1980), pp. 164–166, 195–199, 222–227.

2 U.S., Department of Justice, *A Community Concern: Police Use of Deadly Force* (Washington, D.C.: U.S. Government Printing Office, 1979), p. 8.

3 Tennessee Advisory Committee to the U.S. Civil Rights Commission, *Civic Crisis—Civic Challenge: Police-Community Relations in Memphis* (Washington, D.C.: U.S. Government Printing Office, 1978), p. 3.

4 California Assembly, Select Committee on the Administration of Justice, *Hearings,* "Relations Between the Police and Mexican-Americans," 3 vols., 1972.

5 *Newsweek,* June 2, 1980.

6 James Q. Wilson, "The Police in the Ghetto," in *The Police and the Community,* ed. Robert F. Steadman (Baltimore: Johns Hopkins University Press, 1972), p. 53.

7 California, Attorney General, *The Police in the California Community* (Sacramento: Attorney General of California, 1973), pp. 1–8.

8 U.S. Commission on Civil Rights, *Police Practices and the Preservation of Civil Rights* (Washington, D.C.: U.S. Government Printing Office, 1979), pp. 12–15, 19–24.

9 Ibid., pp. 7–12.

10 Nancy Loving, *Responding to Spouse Abuse and Wife Beating: A Guide for Police* (Washington, D.C.: Police Executive Research Forum, 1980), pp. 36–37.

11 President's Commission on Law Enforcement and Administration of Justice, *The Challenge of Crime in a Free Society* (New York: Avon Books, 1968), p. 256.

12 U.S., Department of Justice, *Criminal Victimization in the United States, 1978* (Washington, D.C.: U.S. Government Printing Office, 1980).

13 William A. Westley, *Violence and the Police* (Cambridge: MIT Press, 1970).

14 Thomas J. Crawford, "Police Overperception of Ghetto Hostility," *Journal of Police Science and Administration* 1, no. 2 (1973): 168–174; Eugene Groves and Peter Rossi, "Police Perceptions of a Hostile Ghetto: Realism or Projection," *American Behavioral Scientist* 13 (May–August, 1970): 727–743.

15 David H. Bayley and Harold Mendelsohn, *Minorities and the Police* (New York: Free Press, 1969). p. 109.

16 Wilson, "The Police in the Ghetto," p. 61.

17 Carl Werthman and Irving Piliavin, "Gang Members and the Police," in *The Police: Six Sociological Essays,* ed. David J. Bordua (New York: John Wiley, 1967), p. 58.

18 John E. Boydstun, *San Diego Field Interrogation: Final Report* (Washington, D.C.: Police Foundation, 1975), p. 61.

19 President's Commission on Law Enforcement and Administration of Justice, *Field Studies,* IV, *The Police and the Community,* vol. I (Washington, D.C.: U.S. Government Printing Office, 1967), pp. 66, 85.

20 Boydstun, *San Diego Field Interrogation,* p. 61.

21 Jerome Skolnick, *The Police and the Urban Ghetto* (Chicago: American Bar Foundation, 1968).

22 Ibid.

23 Boydstun, *San Diego Field Interrogation,* p. 55.

24 Albert Reiss, "Police Brutality—Answers to Key Questions," *Trans-Action* 5 (1968): 10–19.

25 Albert Reiss, *The Police and the Public* (New Haven: Yale University Press, 1971), p. 151.

26 Ibid., p. 142.

27 Skolnick, *The Police and the Urban Ghetto.*

28 Robert Friedrich, "Racial Prejudice and Police Treatment of Blacks," in *Evaluating Alternative Law-Enforcement Policies,* eds., Ralph Baker and Fred A. Meyer, Jr. (Lexington: Lexington Books, 1979), pp. 160–161.

29 Reiss, "Police Brutality"; Donald Black, *The Manners and Customs of the Police* (New York: Academic Press, 1980), pp. 105–108; James J. Fyfe, "Who Shoots? A Look at Officer Race and Police Shooting," *Journal of Police Science and Administration* 9 (December, 1981): 367–382.

30 Nathan Goldman, *The Differential Selection of Juvenile Offenders for Court Appearance* (New York: National Council on Crime and Delinquency, 1963); Irving Piliavin and Scott Briar, "Police Encounters with Juveniles," *American Journal of Sociology* (September 1964): 206–214; Donald Black and Albert J. Reiss, "Police Control of Juveniles," *American Sociological Review* 35 (February 1970): 63–77; Richard J. Lundman, Richard E. Sykes, John P. Clark, "Police Control of Juveniles: A Replication," *Journal of Research in Crime and Delinquency* 15 (January 1978): 84.

31 Wayne R. LaFave, *Arrest: The Decision to Take a Suspect into Custody* (Boston: Little, Brown, 1965), pp. 110–114.

32 *The Knapp Commission Report on Police Corruption* (New York: George Braziller, 1973), p. 75.

33 President's Commission on Law Enforcement and Administration of Justice, *The Challenge of Crime,* p. 256.

34 Peter B. Bloch, *Equality of Distribution of Police Services—A Case Study of Washington, D.C.* (Washington, D.C.: Urban Institute, 1974).

35 Elinor Ostrom and Gordon Whitaker, "Community Control and Government Responsiveness," report presented at the Workshop in Political Theory, Indiana University, n.d., p. 309.

36 James J. Fyfe, "Reducing the Use of Deadly Force: The New York Experience," in U.S. Department of Justice, *Police Use of Deadly Force* (Washington, D.C.: U.S. Government Printing Office, 1978), p. 29; Paul Takagi, "A Garrison State in a 'Democratic' Society," *Crime and Social Justice* (Spring and Summer, 1974): 30.

37 William A. Geller and Kevin J. Karales, *Split-Second Decisions: Shootings of and by Chicago Police* (Chicago: Chicago Law Enforcement Study Group, 1981), p. 140.

38 Tennessee Advisory Committee, *Civic Crisis–Civic Challenge,* pp. 1, 88.

39 Paul Jacobs, *Prelude to Riot* (New York: Vintage Books, 1968), pp. 13–60.

40 California, "Relations Between the Police and Mexican-Americans," p. 5.

41 Walker, *Popular Justice,* pp. 231–232.

42 Ronald Kahn, "Urban Reform and Police Accountability in New York City: 1950–1974," in *Urban Problems and Public Policy,* eds. Robert L. Lineberry and Louis H. Masotti (Lexington: Lexington Books, 1975), pp. 107–127.

43 California, *Police in the California Community,* pp. 1–19.

44 National Advisory Commission on Civil Disorders, *Report* (New York: Bantam Books, 1968), chap. 11.

45 Ibid., p. 322.

46 Police Executive Research Forum, *Police Practices: The General Administrative Survey* (Washington, D.C.: Police Foundation, 1978), n.p.

47 President's Commission on Law Enforcement, *Task Force Report: The Police,* pp. 165–166; Reiss, *Police and the Public,* p. 168.

48 Wilson, "The Police in the Ghetto," p. 66.

49 Peter K. Manning, *Police Work* (Cambridge: MIT Press, 1977), p. 361.

50 California, *The Police in the California Community,* p. 7–4.

51 Charles H. McGahy and Victor Thiessen, "The Nature and Correlates of Criticism of Police," NCJ no. 16577 (Washington, D.C.: NCJRS Library, n.d.).

52 Jack L. Kuykendall, "Police and Minority Groups: Toward a Theory of Negative Contacts," *Police* 15 (September–October, 1970):47–56.

53 California, *The Police in the California Community,* pp. 1–7.

54 O. W. Wilson and Roy C. McLaren, *Police Administration,* 4th ed. (New York: McGraw-Hill, 1977), p. 240.

55 Fred A. Klyman and Joanna Kruckenberg, "A National Survey of Police-Community Relations Units," *Journal of Police Science and Administration* 7 (March 1979):74.

56 U.S., Department of Justice, *Improving Police/Community Relations* (Washington, D.C.: 1973), p. 4.

57 Lee P. Brown, "A Typology of Police-Community Relations Programs," *The Police Chief* (March 1971):16–21.

58 *The New York Times,* February 10, 1975, p. 1.

59 Brown, "A Typology," 16–21.

60 Wilson and McLaren, *Police Administration,* p. 240.

61 Klyman and Kruckenberg, "A National Survey of Police-Community Relations Units," 74.

62 Charles E. Reasons and Bernard A. Wirth, "Police-Community Relations Units: A National Survey," *Journal of Social Issues* 31 (Winter 1975):27–34.

63 President's Commission on Law Enforcement, *Field Studies,* IV, vol. I, p. 58.

64 U.S., Department of Justice, *Improving Police/Community Relations,* pp. 3–4.

65 Renault E. Robinson, "The Chicago Police Department: An Agenda for Change," NCJ no. 28044 (Washington, D.C.: NCJRS Library, n.d.).

CHAPTER **10**

ACCOUNTABILITY OF THE POLICE

THE ACCOUNTABILITY ISSUE,

Making the police accountable for their actions is one of the major tasks of a democratic society, since democracy requires that public officials be answerable for their conduct. The issues discussed in previous chapters—discretion, corruption, community relations—have to do with the question of accountability: How can we define proper police conduct, and how can we ensure that the police conform to that standard? The answer to this question is not easy. The most heated controversies surrounding the police, such issues as the "exclusionary rule" or civilian review boards, are essentially debates about the best method of achieving accountability.[1]

Dimensions of Accountability

Accountability has two dimensions: being accountable *for* something and being accountable *to* someone.

The police are a public service agency and are therefore accountable for the service they render. Police service can be evaluated in terms of both product and process. We are concerned both with what they do and how they do it. The police are expected to prevent crime and apprehend criminals. They are accountable, therefore, for how effectively and efficiently they perform these services. The police role includes many other tasks—providing emergency assistance, maintaining order, and so forth—and they are accountable for these activities as well.

The police are also accountable for the manner in which they operate. In a democratic society, the police are expected to conduct themselves in a legal manner. As they enforce the law, they must not themselves break the law. Lawlessness on the part of law enforcement officials is one of the hallmarks of totalitarian societies.

A basic dilemma facing the police is the tension between the demands for both a product and a process. The demand for a "product"—arrests, confessions, etc.—puts pressure on the police to bend and sometimes break the law.[2] The controversy over *Miranda v. Arizona,* for example, is basically a debate over priorities. Should we emphasize obtaining confessions, as critics of the *Miranda* warning argue, or should we emphasize strict conformity to the rule of law, as *Miranda* mandates? Herbert Packer defined this issue as the tension between the "crime control" and "due process" models of criminal justice.[3]

The second dimension involves being accountable *to* someone. In a democratic society the police are accountable to both the public and the law. The power of the people to control public agencies is one of the primary ingredients of a democracy. Public control is exercised through the legislature, which defines the role and power of police agencies, and through the authority of elected officials to appoint the leaders of law enforcement agencies. Agencies can also be controlled through legislative control over their budgets.

Public control of law enforcement agencies, while an essential element of a free society, can be carried to excess. The corruption and inefficiency of the American police through much of their history is a direct consequence of political interference. Balancing public control with professional standards is an inherent dilemma of the police in a free society.

The police are also accountable to the law. In this sense, the police are accountable to the courts and to the judges who apply the law. Through such landmark decisions as *Mapp, Escobedo,* and *Miranda,* the courts emerged in the 1960s as one of the most important mechanisms for achieving accountability.

DEPARTMENTAL PERFORMANCE

The police are accountable for their performance on a departmental level. The public has the right to ask, How well is this department functioning? Is it carrying out its mission effectively and efficiently?

What to Measure?

Evaluating the performance of a police department poses serious problems. As the National Commission on Productivity commented, "it is often difficult to know what to measure."[4] Police service involves intangible human services that cannot always be reduced to quantifiable units.

The police role includes three basic elements: law enforcement, order maintenance, and service. The latter category, as we have seen, involves a vast array of different tasks. Existing measures of police department performance only relate to the law enforcement aspect of the police role. No meaningful indicators have been developed to measure police performance in the areas of order maintenance and service. Since law enforcement activities account for only 20 percent of police officers' time, the bulk of police work is essentially unevaluated.[5]

Existing Measures

The existing measures of police performance are seriously inadequate and do not provide a reliable basis for evaluating the law enforcement activities of the police. Traditionally, two measures have been used, the crime rate and the clearance rate.

Crime Rate   The official crime rate is constructed on the basis of data compiled in the *Uniform Crime Reports* (UCR). The UCR involves "crimes reported to police" which are compiled by local law enforcement agencies and then forwarded to the FBI, which publishes them in the annual *Uniform Crime Reports* (UCR). The crime rate is determined by computing the number of Part I Offenses (the eight "index crimes (murder, assault, rape, robbery, burglary, theft, auto theft, arson) per 100,000 people.[6] Traditionally, a police department has been considered successful if the crime rate in its jurisdiction goes down, or is significantly lower than comparable areas.

The UCR system does not provide a reliable measure of police performance. The limitations of UCR data are well known to criminologists. Because it does not account for crimes *not* reported to the police it is not a true indicator of actual level of criminal activity: fluctuations in the crime rate may only reflect changes in the reporting of crime. UCR figures are also not audited. Some departments are more sophisticated in their record keeping than others. UCR figures may be affected by sloppy record keeping or deliberate manipulation.[7] In one well-known case, the Washington, D.C., police were caught manipulating crime reports by deliberately lowering the estimated value of stolen goods. The result was a smaller number of thefts and a consequent "reduction" in the crime rate.[8] This incident also illustrates the problems with UCR definitions. Despite improvements in the system, similar crimes may not necessarily be defined and recorded in the same manner. This undermines meaningful comparisons between jurisdictions and over time.

Recently, the UCR system has been supplemented by the use of victimization surveys in police experiments.[9] The Kansas City Preventive Patrol Experiment and the Cincinnati Team Policing Project, for example, utilized such surveys in their evaluations. This technique corrects for the problem of unreported crime and is therefore regarded as more reliable than the UCR. Victimization surveys are expensive, however, and subject to limitations of their own.

Clearance Rate   The second traditional measure of police success is the clearance rate. A crime is "cleared" when the police have identified a suspect and taken that person into custody. The rate is simply the percentage of crimes that are cleared or solved. Nationally, about 21 percent of all index crimes are cleared. The rates for individual crimes range from a high of 76 percent for murder to a low of 20 percent for larceny.

The clearance rate suffers from serious limitations as a measure of police success. As a base it uses UCR data on the number of crimes committed. Yet we know that only about half of all crimes are reported. Since only one-fourth of all thefts are reported (24.6 percent in 1978) the actual clearance rate is only 5 percent instead of the 20 percent rate indicated by the FBI.[10]

A second problem with the clearance rate is the fact that it does not take into account the ultimate disposition of the case. It measures arrests, not convictions. A crime is cleared even if the case is dismissed the next morning. To overcome this problem there is now some effort to recognize "quality" arrests. A study by the Institute for Law and Society found that in Washington, D.C., a very small number of officers were making the bulk of the arrests that resulted in felony convictions. Identification of "quality" arrests permits meaningful distinctions between the performance of individual officers.[11]

A final problem with the clearance rate is the fact that different departments use various methods for "clearing" crimes. Often a suspect is arrested and charged with one or more crimes (for example, a series of burglaries). The detectives believe he committed several others but do not have sufficient evidence for prosecution. In some cases the department will officially clear all the crimes that detectives believe the suspect committed. Other departments use stricter standards and clear only those crimes for which a suspect is arrested and charged. In short, there are no uniform standards to control the process of clearing crimes.

Police-Population Ratio

Attempts have been made to compare the relative efficiency of different police departments. Traditionally the issue has been defined in terms of the ratio of police officers to population in the community. In theory there is some optimum level of police strength. Figure 10-1 indicates the police-population data for selected cities in 1978. The average for all cities is 2.5 employees per 1000 inhabitants. Clearly, however, there are wide ranges in police-population ratios for cities of all sizes.

The police-population ratio is an inadequate measure of police efficiency for several reasons. First, the figures fail to take into account the characteristics of the community. Because of the crime rate, other workload factors, or community preference, one community may need a larger police force than another of the same size.[12]

FIGURE 10.1
Full-time police protection employees, selected cities, 1974. *(U.S. Department of Commerce, Social Indicators III, Washington, D.C., 1980, p. 214.)*

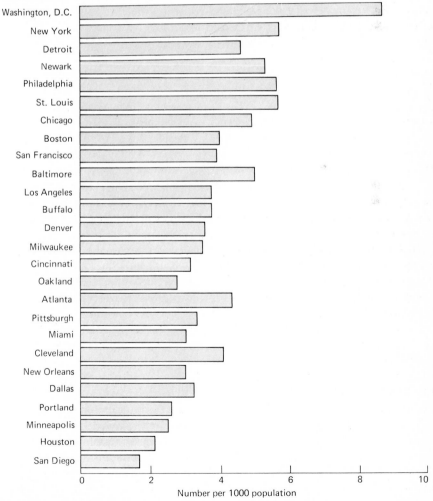

Number per 1000 population

A more serious problem is the fact that figures on the number of employees bear little relationship to actual police work. The efficiency of a department depends a great deal on the percentage of sworn officers and how those officers are assigned. Some departments are far more likely than others to assign a high proportion of officers to patrol duty. Finally, such data do not indicate what officers actually do on the street. If they are slow to respond to calls and undertake little self-initiated activity, the department is relatively inefficient no matter what the police-population ratio, while a relatively small number of active and well-supervised officers can be highly efficient.[13]

Measuring Due Process

There are no systems currently in use for measuring the extent to which police conform to standards of due process. John R. Hepburn has proposed one such system. Due process compliance would be indicated by the "ratio of warrants sought for each warrant issued." Denial of a large percentage of warrant requests would suggest that police officers were not complying with legal standards.[14]

INDIVIDUAL OFFICER PERFORMANCE

More attention has been given to the performance of individual officers. This has primarily involved responses to allegations of misconduct by particular officers. The search for accountability, in this respect, has been a process of crisis management: an attempt to find a solution after a problem has developed.

Police officials, officers on the street, lawyers, elected officials, minority-group spokespersons—all agree on the need for police accountability. They disagree, however, about how to achieve it. The various mechanisms for achieving accountability fall into two basic groups: external and internal. *External* mechanisms of review control involve some person or agency outside the police department. *Internal* mechanisms involve some person or persons within the department itself.

Current practice in the United States today involves a mixture of different mechanisms of accountability operating simultaneously. The relative strength of different mechanisms change over time (the courts became extremely important in the 1960s, for example). Meanwhile, some departments, for example, have stronger and more effective internal affairs units.

THE COURTS

The Warren Court and the Due Process Revolution

Through the power of judicial review, the courts have the right to examine the activities of police officers and departments. Beginning in the mid-1950s the courts emerged as one of the most important mechanisms of police accountability. A few landmark Supreme Court decisions—*Mapp, Escobedo, Miranda*—generated enormous political controversy. The impact of these and other decisions on the police is still being felt.

The *Mapp, Escobedo,* and *Miranda* decisions were part of a broader historical development, often called the *due process revolution.* The author of this revolution was the U.S. Supreme Court under Chief Justice Earl Warren. The Warren court included other judges who were important figures in their own right: William O. Douglas, Hugo Black, Felix Frankfurter, and William Brennan.[15]

The due process revolution which spanned the period from the mid-1950s to the mid-1970s, involved a body of Supreme Court decisions that emphasized the rights of the individual. The Court greatly expanded the scope and meaning of the concept of due process. Virtually every aspect of American society was affected by the Court's decisions. The most important area was civil rights. The Warren court issued the landmark *Brown v. Board of Education of Topeka* in 1954, declaring segregated schools unconstitutional. The Supreme Court also made important decisions regarding free speech, voting rights, and legislative reapportionment.

The entire criminal justice system was affected by the due process revolution. Although we are primarily concerned here with decisions involving the police, the Court also made historic decisions regarding the right to counsel, juvenile court, and prisoners' rights. In each case, the Court challenged traditional practices and ruled in favor of the rights of the individual.

Mapp v. Ohio   The *Mapp* case[16] originated in Cleveland, Ohio, in 1957. Three police officers sought entrance into Dolree Mapp's home in search of a man wanted for questioning about a recent bombing. After she refused to admit them, the officers forced their way in. Mapp demanded to see a search warrant. "A paper, claimed to be a warrant, was held up by one of the officers. She grabbed the 'warrant' and placed it in her bosom. A struggle ensued in which the officers recovered the piece of paper and as a result of which they handcuffed [Mapp] because she had been 'belligerent'." The police did not find the man they sought. But they arrested Mapp for possession of pornographic materials, which they found on her premises. She was eventually convicted for possession of pornographic material.

Mapp appealed her conviction on the grounds that her rights under the Fourth and Fourteenth Amendments had been violated. The forced entry by the police and the questionable search warrant (no warrant was produced by the prosecution at her trial) violated the Fourth Amendment protection against "unreasonable searches and seizures." The Supreme Court agreed and overturned her conviction.

The Exclusionary Rule   In its 1961 decision, the Court invoked the exclusionary rule: "all evidence obtained by searches and seizures in violation of the Constitution is, by that same authority, inadmissible in a state court." The exclusionary rule is essentially a sanction against illegal searches and seizures.[17]

The exclusionary rule should be seen as a mechanism of accountability. On appeal, the courts examine police conduct and, upon finding misconduct or illegal activity, impose a sanction. The exclusionary rule was not something new in 1961. The U.S. Supreme Court had invoked it in federal court proceedings in 1914 in the case of *Weeks v. United States.* The California Supreme Court applied it to California proceedings in 1955 *(People v. Cahan).* By the time of the *Mapp* decision the exclusionary rule was in effect in about half the states.

The Fourteenth Amendment   The *Mapp* decision was important not just because of the exclusionary rule but because the case involved a proceeding in a state court. At the heart of the due process revolution was the application of guarantees in the Bill of Rights to the states by means of the Fourteenth Amendment.

The Fourteenth Amendment declares: "nor shall any State deprive any person of life, liberty, or property, without due process of law; nor deny to any person within its jurisdiction the equal protection of the laws." Whether or not the due process clause incorporated the Bill of Rights and applied them to the states was a matter of disagreement and controversy for many years. In 1937, the U.S. Supreme Court ruled that it did not incorporate the Bill of Rights in their totality *(Palko v. Connecticut)*. On a case-by-case basis over the next two decades, the Court ruled that the Fourteenth Amendment incorporated selected parts of the Bill of Rights and applied them to the states. In *Mapp,* the Court applied the Fourth Amendment to state proceedings.[18]

By linking the Fourth Amendment to the Fourteenth Amendment, the Court assumed the power to examine the constitutionality of searches and seizures conducted by state and local police officers. Whenever it found misconduct, it imposed the penalty of overturning convictions. It is important to note that the Court justified its imposition of the exclusionary rule on the grounds that other methods of examining police conduct had failed. It cited a similar decision by the California Supreme Court which argued that "other remedies have completely failed to secure compliance with the Constitutional provisions."

Escobedo v. Illinois   With the 1964 *Escobedo* case,[19] the Supreme Court examined another aspect of police procedure: interrogation of suspects in custody. Danny Escobedo was held, although not formally charged, and questioned by the police about the death of his brother-in-law. His attorney arrived at the police station and asked to see his client. The police told him he could not. Escobedo, meanwhile, made several requests to see his attorney but was told that his lawyer "didn't want to see" him. At one point, while Escobedo was being moved from one room to another, he and his lawyer came within sight of each other.

Ultimately, Escobedo was convicted. Statements he made while interrogated without the assistance of his attorney provided part of the basis for the conviction. In 1964 the Supreme Court overturned the conviction on appeal on the grounds that Escobedo's rights had been violated. The Court used the Fourteenth Amendment to link the Sixth Amendment guarantee of assistance of counsel to a state proceeding. The right to counsel at trial had been established the year before in the landmark *Gideon v. Wainwright* decision. The question then became, at what point in a criminal proceeding does a person have the right to counsel. In *Escobedo,* the Court ruled that a person had the right to counsel when "the investigation is no longer a general inquiry into an unsolved crime but has begun to focus on a particular suspect."

The *Escobedo* decision ignited a storm of protest from the police, but two years later the Court went even further in examining police practices with the more controversial *Miranda* decision.

Miranda v. Arizona   In *Miranda,*[20] the Court examined the problem of confessions made by persons in police custody. The Fifth Amendment to the Constitution guarantees protection against self-incrimination. Voluntary confessions are not prohibited by the Fifth Amendment. Under what circumstances, however, are confessions by people in custody truly "voluntary"?[21]

To answer this question the Court examined the details of in-custody interrogation. As it had in *Escobedo,* the Court relied upon current police manuals and textbooks on criminal investigation. It found that these books advised subtle and often not-so-subtle techniques to get people to confess. The Court found these techniques to be coercive and likely to induce people to waive their protection against self-incrimination. In fact, the Court found the atmosphere inside the police station inherently coercive.

To guarantee protection against self-incrimination, the Court ruled that a suspect had to be advised of certain rights. The famous *Miranda* warning derives from the Court's opinion in this case. Chief Justice Warren ruled that "when an individual is taken into custody or otherwise deprived of his freedom by the authorities in any significant way and is subjected to questioning, the privilege against self-incrimination is jeopardized." Consequently certain procedural safeguards are necessary. The suspect

> must be warned prior to any questioning that he has the right to remain silent, that anything he says can be used against him in a court of law, that he has the right to the presence of an attorney, and that if he cannot afford an attorney one will be appointed for him prior to any questioning if he so desires.

The Impact of Supreme Court Decisions

What impact did the Supreme Court decisions have on police practices? The *Mapp, Escobedo,* and *Miranda* decisions generated immediate controversy. Liberals hailed the decisions as important steps forward in the continuing pursuit of individual liberty. The police and political conservatives savagely attacked the decisions and the Supreme Court itself. The Court had "handcuffed" the police, critics charged. In a time of rising crime rates and civil disorder, the Court had made it more difficult to apprehend suspects, obtain evidence, and secure confessions.[22]

Despite the heated opinion on both sides, the impact of the Court's decisions was not great in either direction. Police infringement upon individual liberties did not end overnight, nor were the police greatly hampered in their effort to combat crime.

The Impact of Mapp   At the time of the *Mapp* decision, the exclusionary rule already prevailed in twenty-six states and at the federal level. It was not, therefore, an entirely new innovation.

In a study of the impact of the exclusionary rule in Boston, Sheldon Krantz and associates found that the impact was negligible: "Very few motions to suppress [evidence] are raised, and very few of these are granted." In a sample of 512 cases in District Court, motions to suppress were raised in only 48, or 9.4 percent of the total. Of these 48 motions, only 10 were granted, representing 20.8 percent of the motions and 1.9 percent of all cases. Motions to suppress were related to the seriousness of the charge. The more serious the charge, the greater the likelihood of a motion to suppress.[23]

Krantz also found that the individual officer and individual judge played an important role in motions to suppress. Certain officers were more likely than others to conduct illegal searches, therefore giving rise to a motion to suppress. Certain judges, meanwhile, were much more likely than others to grant motions to suppress.

In a study of the exclusionary rule in Chicago, Dallin Oaks found that motions to suppress evidence were heavily concentrated in cases involving three types of offenses. Of 649 motions raised in one twelve-day period, 24 percent involved narcotics cases, 28 percent involved possession of concealed weapons, and 26 percent involved gambling offenses.[24]

Finally, a General Accounting Office study found the exclusionary rule to have little effect on the prosecution of federal criminal cases. The GAO studied 2804 cases handled by U.S. attorneys during July and August of 1978. Of those cases that were closed, less than 11 percent of the defendants filed motions to have evidence suppressed under the Fourth Amendment. Moreover, between 80 and 90 percent of the motions were denied. The GAO also examined 9400 potential felony violations that were screened by U.S. attorneys. Only 15 percent involved search-and-seizure issues. Of all the cases where prosecution was declined, only 0.4 percent were declined because of search-and-seizure problems.[25]

The Impact of Miranda   A study of police interrogations in New Haven, Connecticut, concluded that "not much has changed after *Miranda*," and "the impact on law enforcement has been small."[26] There were several reasons for this. Interrogations play only a small role in the investigative process, the study found. Because of limited resources, the police tended to arrest suspects only when they already had a substantial amount of evidence.

The New Haven study also concluded that the police adapted to the new guidelines specified by *Miranda*. They continued to question suspects and often succeeded in obtaining statements. The study pointed out that despite the *Miranda* warnings, the atmosphere in the police station and in the interrogation room was inherently coercive: despite being advised of their right to remain silent, suspects were induced to talk.

A study of the impact of *Miranda* in Washington, D.C., reached similar conclusions. It found that the police did not always comply fully with the *Miranda* requirement (in about two-thirds of the cases, the police gave either part or none of the warning). Only 7 percent of those arrested (1262 out of 15,430) requested an attorney, even though volunteer attorneys were readily available. Finally, 40 percent of those arrested gave statements to the police, despite their right to remain silent.[27]

In short, Supreme Court decisions have apparently had little direct impact on police crime-fighting activities, although they have had a significant impact in other areas.

Police Reform   Supreme Court decisions have been a major stimulus to reform. In effect, the Court defined new standards of conduct, and police departments were forced to improve their procedures to meet these new standards. Since the mid-1960s, when the most important decisions occurred, American police departments have made significant improvements in personnel standards. Recruitment and training standards are generally higher. Departments have also improved their systems of supervision and discipline. Walker argues that Supreme Court cases were the most important forces for change in the entire criminal justice system since the 1960s.[28]

Public Awareness   The Court decisions increased public awareness of the details of the criminal process. The *Escobedo* and *Miranda* decisions, for example, enhanced public understanding of that phase of the criminal process between arrest and trial. The public is more knowledgeable about both police procedures and the rights of the individual.

One consequence of increased awareness is higher public expectations about police performance. The Court decisions defined an ideal against which actual performance is measured. By raising public expectations, the decisions generated pressure for continued police reform.

Political Backlash   The *Mapp, Escobedo,* and *Miranda* decisions generated a strong political backlash. A great segment of the public, as well as the police, believed that the Court was "coddling" criminals. The decisions coincided with a substantial rise in the crime rate and with extensive civil disorder. The result was a demand for "tougher" law enforcement.

In 1968 both Richard Nixon and George Wallace ran for president on platforms that promised to "get tough" with criminals and to change the Supreme Court. President Nixon fulfilled part of that promise by appointing to the Supreme Court judges who disagreed with the main thrust of the due process revolution.[29]

The Courts as a Mechanism of Accountability

As a mechanism of accountability, the courts have both strengths and weaknesses. The major strength has been the ability of the courts, through judicial review, to set new standards of police conduct. The Supreme Court acted, in large part, because existing mechanisms had failed. In this respect, the Court stimulated police reform.

The major weakness of the courts lies in the fact that they are an *external* agency. The courts cannot supervise day-to-day police operations. Moreover, they cannot guarantee compliance with their decisions. They can only review cases after the fact, and problems come to their attention only when a case is prosecuted.[30] The *Mapp* decision, for example, is relatively useless when a suspect is not prosecuted. Finally, court decisions encourage the police to develop strategies of evasion—notably, lying. Oaks's study of the impact of the exclusionary rule, for example, found a significant increase in the number of cases where the officer claimed that the suspect had "dropped" the narcotics.[31]

Other Legal Remedies

Four other legal remedies are available to persons who believe themselves to be victims of police misconduct. Because these remedies involve the examination of police practices and the potential imposition of penalties, they should be considered alternative external mechanisms for police accountability.

Damages under State Law   A person or persons who feel victimized by police misconduct can sue for damages under state law by bringing a civil suit against the individual officer. Typically, damages are sought when a person has been physically abused or killed.[32]

The number of successful damage suits against the police has risen dramatically. The total damages paid by the city of Los Angeles for police-related cases increased from $7000 in 1965 to $275,000 in 1970 and almost $1.5 million in 1975. The city of Detroit paid a total of $14 million in damages for police brutality cases between 1970 and 1980.[33]

Damage suits directly benefit the individual who brings and wins the suit. They can also indirectly benefit the entire community by forcing the department to make improvements. The Omaha police, for example, revised their regulations on deadly force in response to a decision by the Eighth Circuit Court of Appeals. In this case the police department sought to prevent situations that might give rise to suits in the future. Partly as a result of revising its firearms guidelines, firearms incidents by Omaha police officers declined by more than half and almost disappeared completely by 1980.[34]

Damages under Federal Law   A person who feels victimized by police misconduct can also bring suit under federal law. An 1871 law, now 42 U.S.C. 1983, provides that a person can sue for damages if he or she has been deprived of any rights by an official acting "under color of law" (that is, in an official capacity). Damage suits of this kind are often referred to as "1983 actions." The principal benefit of this remedy is that a person can bring suit against local officials in federal court. In many localities, the federal courts are more sympathetic to the rights of individuals than local courts (especially in cases involving the local police).[35]

The Limits of Damage Suits   As a mechanism of police accountability, damage suits have only limited utility. Lawsuits are expensive and time-consuming. Often attorneys do not consider the potential damages worth their time. Damage suits are relevant only in cases where there has been substantial harm. They are not relevant in cases involving minor harassment or mild abuse. Finally and most important, like judicial review, damage suits operate on a case-by-case basis. They do not provide a mechanism for monitoring the day-to-day conduct of the police.

Injunction   A third legal remedy involves an injunction. Where police misconduct is systematic (for example, harassment of black males, of gays, etc.) the victims can petition the court to issue an injunction halting the practice. Injunctions are not an effective remedy, however. It is difficult to prove in court that systematic harassment exists or that it is the result of official policy.[36]

Criminal Sanction   The fourth and final remedy is the criminal sanction. The person who feels victimized charges the police officer with criminal conduct. This is not an effective remedy and has been used rarely, if at all. It is difficult to prove that in some misconduct the police officer had criminal intent. In the use of deadly force or physical force, the officer can rely on a probable-cause defense.[37]

CIVILIAN REVIEW

Civilian review of the police is a popular idea with many critics of the police; it is equally unpopular with police officers. The concept arouses strong passions on both sides. Police officers have been generally successful in preventing the establishment of civilian review boards and, in at least two important cases, have succeeded in having existing review boards abolished.

The Concept

The concept of civilian review involves the creation of an independent (that is, outside the police department) body to review instances of alleged police misconduct. In theory, the members of the review board are to be citizens (that is, not employees of the police department) representing a broad segment of the community. Under most civilian review proposals, members are appointed by the mayor.

In theory the civilian review board functions as an appellate court. Citizens who feel they are the victims of police misconduct and who are not satisfied with how the police department handled their complaint can bring their case before the board. Generally, civilian review boards have only had the power to recommend disciplinary action to the head of the police department. Boards have not had the power to impose sanctions themselves. However, the Philadelphia Police Advisory Board (1958–1967) had the power to examine general police practices and to recommend changes in policy.[38]

The primary justification for civilian review boards is the argument that police departments fail to discipline their own officers. Critics of the police regard internal review procedures as a "whitewash."[39] William A. Westley argued that intense group solidarity is one of the main aspects of the police officer subculture. The high value placed on solidarity justified secrecy and even lying to protect other officers who were guilty of some misconduct.[40]

Mechanisms to provide an independent review of police conduct exist in several cities today. There are significant differences, however, in terms of their scope, authority, and staffing. The term *civilian review* is often misleading.

The New York CCRB

The most famous civilian review board was the New York City Civilian Complaint Review Board (CCRB). The tumultuous history of the CCRB merits attention because it illuminates many of the problems with the civilian review concept.[41]

The New York CCRB originated in the mid-1950s under pressure from the U.S.

Justice Department, which threatened to conduct its own investigation of misconduct by New York City police officers. In its original form, the CCRB was not a true "citizen" review. Complaints about police misconduct were simply forwarded to deputy police commissioners, who reviewed the case and made recommendations to the police commissioner. In its first two years the CCRB handled an average of 80.5 cases per year. It recommended charges against the officer in about 20 percent of the cases (see Table 10-1).

Between 1955 and 1966 the powers of the CCRB were gradually expanded by Mayor Robert Wagner. At the same time, the number of complaints filed increased,

TABLE 10-1
NEW YORK CITY CIVILIAN COMPLAINT REVIEW BOARD DISPOSITIONS RESULTING IN A RECOMMENDATION OF CHARGES

Mayoral administration	Year	Total number of dispositions	Total number of cases in which charges are recommended	Percent of dispositions resulting in the recommendation of charges Per year	Per process
Impellitteri					20.50
	1953	74	12	16.22	
	1954	87	21	24.24	
Wagner					8.63
	1955	196	21	10.71	
	1956	166	22	13.25	
	1957	142	6	4.23	
	1958	126	9	7.14	
	1959	106	8	7.55	
	1960	186	20	10.75	
	1961	198	12	6.06	
	1962	209	13	6.22	
	1963	171	9	5.26	
	1964	N.A.	N.A.	N.A.	
	1965	N.A.	N.A.	N.A.	
	1966	123 (1/1–6/29)	20	16.22	
Lindsay					3.51
	1966	146 (6/30–11/8)	4	2.74	
	1966	123	5	4.07	
	1967	1,099	39	3.55	
	1968	1,291	37	2.87	
	1969	1,976	88	4.45	
	1970	2,161	125	5.78	
	1971	3,407	114	3.35	
	1972	3,718	132	3.55	
	1973	3,082	83	2.69	
	1974	3,239	83	2.56	

Source: Ronald Kahn, "Urban Reform and Police Accountability in New York City: 1950–1974," in *Urban Problems and Public Policy,* eds. Robert L. Lineberry and Louis H. Masotti (Lexington: Lexington Books, 1975), p. 113.

Note: Three figures are given for 1966. The first represents the original CCRB; the second, Mayor Lindsay's civilian-dominated CCRB; and the third, the police-dominated CCRB following the November referendum (see text).

reaching a high of 209 in 1962. As the civil rights movement gained momentum, the issue of police conduct became an increasingly explosive one. A riot erupted in New York in the summer of 1964 following the fatal shooting of a black youth by an off-duty police officer.

Mayor John Lindsay transformed the CCRB in 1966. He expanded the board to seven members: four civilians appointed by the mayor and three police officials appointed by the commissioner. The four-to-three majority transformed the board into a genuine "civilian" review mechanism. The new CCRB began operations on June 30, 1966. During its brief four-month existence it handled a total of 146 cases and recommended charges against the officer involved in only 4 of those cases.

The idea of a civilian majority on the CCRB enraged police officers. The Patrolmen's Benevolent Association (PBA), their fraternal group and later their union, succeeded in having the question of the CCRB placed on the ballot in the November elections. In the referendum, the voters of New York voted to abolish the citizen-dominated CCRB by a two-to-one margin. It was then replaced by a police-dominated CCRB which continues to exist.

Philadelphia

A similar fate befell the Philadelphia Police Advisory Board (PAB). The PAB was established in 1958 and functioned with little publicity for several years. When police conduct became a heated issue in the 1960s, however, the police applied political pressure to the mayor who abolished the PAB in 1967.[42]

Kansas City

The Office of Citizen Complaints (OCC) was created by the Kansas City Board of Police Commissioners in 1970.[43] The OCC has a five-person staff and its office is physically separate from police headquarters. Complaints are received by the OCC staff and then forwarded to the police department where they are investigated by the department's Internal Affairs Division. Based on the Internal Affairs report, the OCC staff makes a determination and forwards its recommendation (if any) to the Board of Police Commissioners and to the police chief.

Because the OCC relies upon the Internal Affairs report, it is not a truly independent review mechanism. An evaluation of the OCC noted the lack of independent investigatory power and found that the community is not generally aware of the OCC's existence. The OCC's office director is a former police officer, and this undoubtedly allayed the fears of police officers that it would be too "independent."

Detroit

In 1974 the city of Detroit established a Board of Police Commissioners to "oversee the policies and procedures of the Detroit Police Department.[44] The board consists of five civilians appointed by the mayor. To handle complaints about police misconduct, the board created the Office of the Chief Investigator (OCI). The OCI staff receives complaints, investigates them, and then submits its reports to the Citizen Complaint Subcommittee of the board. The board recommends disciplinary action, if needed, to the chief of police.

The formal disciplinary process is governed by the collective-bargaining contract between the city and the police union. The contract provides that an officer's guilt or innocence be established through procedures that guarantee due process for the individual officer.

On the one hand, the Detroit OCI appears to be a truly independent civilian review mechanism. One board member called it "the best civilian review board model in the nation." On the other hand, its powers are severely limited. It can only recommend disciplinary action. The actual imposition of discipline can only come after a separate fact-finding process, as outlined in the collective-bargaining agreement.

Civilian Review: Pro and Con

Pro   The advocates of civilian review emphasize the seriousness of the police-community relations problem (see Chapter 9). A large part of the problem is the lack of communication and trust between the police and minority-group communities. That lack of trust is accentuated by the belief that police departments fail to discipline their own officers who are guilty of misconduct. In fact, most citizen complaints are dismissed as unfounded by police internal review procedures.

Civilian review, its advocates argue, would theoretically provide an independent evaluation of citizen complaints. This would accomplish two things. First, it would ensure that justice is done and that actual misconduct is punished. Second, it would improve public trust in the police. Even where complaints were not sustained, the public would have a greater sense that the review was truly independent and impartial.

Finally, civilian review would provide for better representation of the entire community. One of the major problems of the police today, civilian review advocates argue, is the isolation of the police from the community. Civilian review, with members representing all segments of the community, would break down that isolation.

Con   Opponents of civilian review object to the fact that the police are singled out for special treatment. Why civilian review of the police and not of other social agencies? The police argue that they are professionals and, like other professional groups, are capable of disciplining their own members. Most complaints about police misconduct are without merit. They point out that during the four-month existence of the New York CCRB, only 2 percent of the complaints resulted in a recommendation of charges against the officer involved.

Critics also point out the procedural problems involved in civilian review. Too often, they argue, it is a case of "trial by publicity," with the officer presumed guilty at the start. Civilian review proceedings too often lack sufficient procedural safeguards to ensure a fair review of the fact and to allow officers involved an opportunity to challenge the allegations and present their version of the events.

Critics also point out that civilian review boards are so controversial that they become divisive issues themselves. A review board cannot function effectively while in the midst of controversy. Finally, critics argue that there is no way to guarantee that the membership of the board is truly representative of the community.

COMMUNITY CONTROL

The radical solution to the problem of police accountability is community control. Under this proposal the public would exercise direct control over police operations through elected officials. The demand for community control arises from the feeling that the police are isolated from the public and that police policies do not reflect either the needs or the desires of particular communities. Community control involves a *decentralized* approach to police policy making. In theory, different communities would be able to develop policies to suit their particular needs. As a strategy, community control is designed to make the police more responsive to the needs of the people and of particular communities.[45]

The Berkeley Proposal   Community control has been a concept rather than a reality. No community has adopted anything resembling it. In Berkeley, California, a community control proposal was placed on the ballot in 1971. The city would be divided into three major areas: the "black area," the "campus area," and the "white area." These would be subdivided into five neighborhoods: two in the black area, two in the white area, and one in the campus area. Each neighborhood would have its own police force, governed by an elected council of fifteen members. The council would choose a police commissioner and develop general policy for the department.[46]

The proposal originated with the Black Panther party in Berkeley and was then supported by white radicals in the campus area. In the referendum, the proposal was defeated by a two-to-one margin. Significantly, precincts in the black neighborhoods voted against the proposal.

Community Control Evaluated

While attractive in theory, the community control concept involves a number of serious practical problems. Neighborhoods are neither well-defined nor homogenous. In any city it is difficult if not impossible to draw a line that completely separates white neighborhoods from black neighborhoods. In reality, there are many mixed neighborhoods and transition areas, where the population is shifting from predominantly white to predominantly black or vice versa.[47]

The fact that neighborhoods are not homogenous is an equally difficult problem. The community control concept rests on the assumption that all black residents of one area want the same kind of police service and that all white residents of another area want another kind of police service. In fact, there are many different points of view within each area. It is an offensive racial stereotype to assume that all black people want the same kind of police service. There are many different points of view about police service in any community.[48] Coping with these differences is one of the major problems facing the police. It is doubtful that community control would alleviate this problem.

The financing of a community-based police force is also problematic. If each neighborhood is to finance its own department, then the low-income neighborhoods will suffer the most: they have the greatest demand for police service but the lowest tax base to support it. If tax revenues are distributed by some other formula (population, workload, etc.) it is not clear who would have the power to make the allocations.

In the final analysis, community control appears to resemble American police administration in the nineteenth century. Then police departments were extremely decentralized and subject to a high degree of direct public control. Yet the price for this was an equally high level of corruption and inefficiency.

People's Representative

A final external mechanism of accountability is the Swedish concept of *ombudsman* or people's representative, a concept that has been adopted by several other European countries. A people's representative is an official critic of government agencies. Employed by the government itself, the representative has the responsibility of receiving complaints about official misconduct, investigating agency performance, and serving as an advocate for the citizen-client.

This concept has been adopted by a variety of agencies at different levels of government. Some universities, for example, have a representative to handle complaints by students. Depending upon the agency, the power of the representative varies. In some cases, they may initiate an investigation without a citizen complaint. Generally, they have the power to recommend changes but not to enforce them. One of the advantages of using a people's representative, according to its advocates, is that it can effect changes in administrative policy and procedures and thereby avert future complaints. Representatives can also serve to conciliate particular grievances on an informal basis. The major disadvantages of the concept lie in the fact that, as a government employee, the representative is to a certain extent an insider rather than an outsider. There is often a reluctance on the part of one government employee to criticize too harshly another government employee whom he or she will have to work with again in the future.

To date, the concept has not been widely applied to the police One advantage of having a city government representative is that it does not single out the police department.

INTERNAL MECHANISMS OF ACCOUNTABILITY

Internal mechanisms of accountability rely upon procedures within the police department. They are preferred by law enforcement personnel. The police argue that they can best handle matters of discipline themselves, since outsiders do not and cannot understand the realities of police work. Police also argue that other professions, such as law, medicine, and teaching, are allowed to handle disciplinary matters internally.

There are two models of internal mechanisms of accountability. The *professional model* resembles the system of professionalism used by other occupations. It relies upon extensive training of individual practitioners, the development of a code of professional ethics, with discipline handled by members of the professional group. The *bureaucratic model* relies upon an elaborate system of formal procedures designed to provide guidance for the individual practitioner. Discipline is handled within the agency through an equally elaborate system of formal procedures.

The professional model and the bureaucratic model are two different approaches to the problem of controlling the conduct of police officers. The professional model relies upon an internalized sense of professional ethics. The bureaucratic model relies upon a set of written procedures.

The Professional Model

The question of police professionalism is a matter of much debate and controversy. Are the police *professionals* in the true sense of the word? The police themselves answer affirmatively. They argue that police officers routinely handle critical life-and-death matters and are called upon to exercise broad discretion. Others argue that the police are not and cannot hope to be professionals in the true sense of the word. James Q. Wilson argues that police officers are "subprofessionals," and members of a "craft."[49]

Professionalism Defined The debate over police professionalism is often confusing because different definitions are used. For many people, a profession refers simply to an important job. Professionalization often refers to improvement, such as raising the entrance requirements for a particular job.

To understand the nature of police professionalism it is necessary to define precisely the meaning of a profession. Sociologists have identified the key elements that define an occupation as a profession.

Key Elements of a Profession Professionalism consists of three key elements: professional knowledge, professional autonomy, and the service ideal.[50] *Professional knowledge* consists of mastery of a body knowledge about a complex and esoteric subject. Mastery of this subject is gained through intensive study over a long period of time. The doctor, for example, spends several years in medical school and as an intern. At the end of this long training, the professional possesses expertise about a subject that few other people possess.

Professional autonomy refers to the manner in which members of a profession conduct their affairs. As masters of a complex body of knowledge, the professionals have a monopoly. Members of the profession control entrance into the profession (through their control over entrance to professional schools and licensing) and define the content of the body of professional knowledge (through control over curricula, professional journals, etc.). Finally, members of the profession are responsible for disciplining members of the profession. The professional-ethics committee of the bar, for example, can investigate alleged misconduct and recommend disbarment of a guilty attorney.

The autonomy of a profession is authorized by the power of the state. State law forbids the practice of medicine by someone who has not been properly trained and licensed. The bar association has the power to license attorneys. In effect, the professions are legalized monopolies.

In return for this monopoly power, members of a profession subscribe to the *service ideal*. The professional has an obligation to serve the best interests of the client. Both the legal and medical professions have formal codes of ethics. The service ideal also involves a commitment to serve the larger community. Both the legal and medical professions, for example, encourage giving free assistance to people who cannot afford to pay.

The Police Occupation Evaluated   Given this abstract definition of a profession, to what extent do the police approximate it? Clearly, the police fail to meet some of the basic elements of a profession. The body of knowledge about policing is extremely limited. Even in the best police departments, officers receive a rather brief period of training (400 hours is the standard recommended by several commissions). The most important parts of that body of knowledge (the relevant local criminal law, criminal procedure, departmental procedures) could be mastered by a reasonably intelligent person in a relatively short period of time.

With respect to professional autonomy, the police are clearly not a true profession. The police themselves do not control entry into the profession, nor do they define the content of professional knowledge. These decisions are made in the political arena and are determined by elected officials. Finally, and perhaps most important, the police do not control discipline of members of the occupation. In fact, many would argue that the inadequacy of internal self-discipline is the greatest single shortcoming of the police occupation.

With respect to the service ideal, the police approximate some aspects of a true profession. There has been some progress in the direction of the police thinking of themselves as public servants with an obligation to serve all citizens equally and fairly. The law enforcement code of ethics (Exhibit 10.1) represents an attempt to develop an internal code of professional conduct.

The Development of Police Professionalism   Despite the fact that the police lack many of the key elements of a true profession, they continue to insist that they are professionals. For most reform-oriented police officials, progress is defined in terms of professionalization. To understand the nature of the professional self-concept of the police it is necessary to analyze the nature and direction of police professionalization.

Police professionalization emerged at the beginning of the twentieth century (see Chapter 1). According to Walker, the reform agenda included eliminating political interference, attracting qualified police officials, upgrading personnel standards, and developing improved techniques of management control. As Skolnick points out, police professionalization has been based on a "narrow view of managerial efficiency and organizational interest."[51]

EXHIBIT 10.1

Law Enforcement Code of Ethics

As a Law Enforcement Officer, my fundamental duty is to serve mankind; to safeguard lives and property; to protect the innocent against deception, the weak against oppression or intimidation, and the peaceful against violence or disorder; and to respect the Constitutional rights of all men to liberty, equality and justice.

I will keep my private life unsullied as an example to all; maintain courageous calm in the face of danger, scorn, or ridicule; develop self-restraint; and be constantly mindful of the welfare of others. Honest in thought and deed in both my personal and official life, I will be exemplary in obeying the laws of the land and the regulations of my department. Whatever I see or hear of a confidential nature or that is confided to me in my official capacity will be kept ever secret unless revelation is necessary in the performance of my duty.

I will never act officiously or permit personal feelings, prejudices, animosities or friendships to influence my decisions. With no compromise for crime and with relentless prosecution of criminals, I will enforce the law courteously and appropriately without fear or favor, malice or ill will, never employing unnecessary force or violence and never accepting gratuities.

I recognize the badge of my office as a symbol of public faith, and I accept it as a public trust to be held so long as I am true to the ethics of the police service. I will constantly strive to achieve these objectives and ideals, dedicating myself before God to my chosen profession . . . law enforcement.

Source: Federal Bureau of Investigation, *Uniform Crime Reports, 1978* (Washington, D.C.: U.S. Government Printing Office, 1979), p. 229.

The Rhetoric of Professionalism   Why do the police continue to call themselves professionals? The rhetoric of professionalism among the police exists for two reasons. First, there has been considerable progress in policing. The continued upgrading of personnel standards and the development of technical specialties (for example, criminalistics) appear to be similar to the development of training according to the professional model.

Second, and more importantly, the rhetoric of professionalism serves other purposes. Peter Manning argues that the police use this rhetoric in presenting themselves to the public.[52] Viewing oneself as a professional builds self-esteem and cohesiveness. Calling oneself a professional allows one to stake out and defend an area of expertise. The police can present themselves as the experts on the subject of crime. And by presenting themselves as professionals the police can gain and maintain a certain amount of autonomy. They can reject proposals for change made by outsiders on the grounds that the outsiders lack professional expertise. In this way they are better able to maintain control over their own affairs.

Summary   The police are not true professionals. Certain aspects of police work do resemble other professions (police routinely deal with critical life-and-death, life-

and-liberty matters; they routinely exercise discretion, etc.). But the police lack many of the key elements of a true profession.

As a mechanism of accountability, professionalism has some limited utility. Professionalization has raised personnel standards, eliminating many of the worst abuses. The professional self-concept reminds the individual officer of his or her duty to serve society and to handle all citizens equally and fairly. Police professionalism has failed, however, to develop an effective system of group self-discipline. Police officers tend toward group solidarity and to deny allegations of misconduct by individual officers. The most effective systems of discipline in American policing are essentially bureaucratic in nature.

The Bureaucratic Model

The bureaucratic model functions by means of developing written procedures for various police actions. The procedures are collected and codified in standard-operating-procedure (SOP) manuals. A detailed SOP manual is one of the hallmarks of a modern, well-managed police department. Although departments with good SOP manuals are usually referred to as professional, it is more accurate to see this approach as the bureaucratic model.

Functions of the SOP　The SOP manual has several different functions. Its primary purpose is to limit and *control discretion* on the part of police officers (see Chapter 7). The written procedures do not and cannot eliminate discretion but can limit it by specifying actions that are definitely prohibited.

The second function of the SOP manual is to provide *guidance for police officers.* Policing involves an infinite range of situations, including unpredictable behavior by citizens. The SOP manual makes the job somewhat easier for the officer by defining certain categories of situations and behavior and indicating the proper response. Departments without good SOP manuals impose an unfair burden on their officers by asking them to make decisions in each case.

A third function of the SOP manual is to serve as the basis for *supervision and discipline.* By defining proper police procedures, the SOP manual provides a standard against which individual officers can be evaluated. Officers who correctly follow procedures can be rewarded, and officers who fail to follow procedures can be disciplined.

A fourth function of the SOP manual is the *implementation of police policy.* The manual can describe the procedures for handling, for example, domestic disputes or minors in possession of alcohol. By establishing departmentwide procedures it not only controls the discretion of individual police officers but also reflects departmental decisions about basic objectives and the allocation of resources.

Personnel Supervision　The bureaucratic model of accountability depends upon effective personnel supervision. An SOP manual sets forth a department's intended policy. The quality of personnel supervision determines the extent to which policy is translated into actual practice.

Effective supervision consists of several different elements, including training, inspections, and records. Recruit training provides all new officers with a basic orientation to the policies and procedures of an agency. In-service training for experienced officers is intended to accomplish two things. First, it provides a refresher in existing policies and procedures. Second, it can be used to instruct officers in new concepts and techniques. Regular inspection of individual officers and particular units within an agency is designed to ensure that existing policies and procedures are being followed.

Records are an important element of the bureaucratic model of accountability. Written records should be seen as a management strategy to monitor and control the behavior of police officers. This is part of the reason why officers frequently complain about paperwork.

The importance of written records is, in part, inherent in all bureaucratic agencies. Records provide evidence of who did what and when. Records assume additional importance in police agencies. Officers generally work alone or in pairs, free from direct supervision. Records become a substitute for direct supervision. By requiring that officers fill out a report on all contacts with citizens, a department forces officers to account for their time. An increasing number of departments require officers to file reports on all firearms discharges This requirement discourages officers from firing their weapons in a manner not consistent with department policy.

Records are only one supervisory strategy. Other strategies can be used to enhance accountability. Sergeants, for example, can adopt an aggressive or a passive supervisory strategy. An aggressive strategy involves frequent contact with the officers under the sergeants' command. A passive strategy involves little or no contact. According to traditional management thinking, an aggressive strategy, or close supervision, ensures greater compliance with department policies and procedures. Unfortunately, little research has been done on police supervisory strategies at the sergeant level.

Internal Affairs Units

An internal affairs unit is the primary means by which a police department monitors itself. Experts on police administration agree that an effective internal affairs unit is an essential feature of a well-run department.

The role of an internal affairs unit can include (1) investigation of citizen complaints, (2) review of incident reports filed by police officers (for example, firearms discharge), and (3) self-initiated investigation of possible officer misconduct. Not all internal affairs units have the same role. Some departments have special committees, for example, to investigate firearms incidents.[53]

In terms of organizational structure, the head of an internal affairs unit usually reports directly to the chief executive. The Internal Affairs Bureau (IAB) in the Memphis Police Department consists of eleven sworn officers and three civilian clerks. The results of investigations are sent directly to the director of police, the top executive.[54]

Internal affairs units may be characterized as strong or weak. The key variable is the attitude of the chief executive. As Herman Goldstein argues, internal affairs units are effective mechanisms of accountability where they have the full support of the police chief.[55] Full support means that the chief indicates publicly that he or she is serious about investigating misconduct and acts on recommendations for disciplinary action. The effectiveness of internal affairs units is undermined where the chief does not impose discipline where misconduct has been found.

The resources of an internal affairs unit are also an important variable. It has to have sufficient personnel if it is to conduct meaningful investigations.

Internal affairs units serve several functions. The basic function is internal accountability. It is an essential ingredient of good management that an organization monitor the performance of its employees and impose a proper amount of discipline where misconduct is found. An internal affairs unit is the investigatory arm of an organization's self-policing effort.

An internal affairs unit plays an important function with respect to police-community relations. One of the bitterest complaints voiced by police critics is the allegation that departments cover up or whitewash incidents of misconduct. In fact, most citizen complaints are dismissed as unfounded. This contributes to the popular belief that the police refuse to discipline themselves. An effective internal affairs unit, one that recommends discipline and has its recommendations acted on, can play a vital role in improving police-community relations.

Finally, internal affairs units function as an alternative to external mechanisms of accountability. Many departments have been forced to strengthen their internal affairs units under the threat of external investigation or review. O. W. Wilson stated that "It is clearly apparent that if the police do not take a vigorous stand on the matter of internal investigation, outside groups—such as review boards consisting of laymen or other persons outside the police service—will step into the void."[56]

Internal affairs units encounter two serious problems. Internally, officers assigned to the unit are regarded with suspicion by other officers. Their role involves policing the other officers. Some officers regard them as spies or finks. Externally, internal affairs units are accused of covering up incidents of misconduct. Many people, especially those who file complaints, refuse to believe that complaints are seriously investigated. In short, internal affairs units face a difficult, two-sided problem of trust and credibility. On the one hand there are pressures to maintain good relations with other officers. On the other hand there is the need to maintain credibility in the eyes of the public.

INTERACTION OF EXTERNAL AND INTERNAL MECHANISMS

The quest for meaningful accountability of the police involves many different approaches. No single method is completely effective. In actual practice the accountability of the police has been enhanced by a mix of different approaches. External and internal mechanisms of accountability interact in a dynamic fashion. The failure of internal mechanisms created a demand for external mechanisms. Successful litigation and the continued demand for civilian review boards forced departments to improve their internal review mechanisms.

REVIEW

1 What are the two dimensions of accountability?

2 Discuss the limitations of existing measures of police department performance.

3 What is the basic difference between internal and external mechanisms of accountability?

4 Discuss how the due process revolution affected police procedures.

5 How has the *Miranda* decision affected the ability of the police to interrogate suspects and obtain confessions?

6 What are the basic objectives of the concept of civilian review?

7 Discuss the major problems with the concept of community control of the police.

8 Discuss the basic differences between the professional and bureaucratic models of accountability.

9 To what extent are the American police a true profession?

10 Explain how a standard-operating-procedure manual increases the accountability of the police.

REFERENCES

1 Monrad G. Paulsen, et al., "Securing Compliance with Constitutional Limitations: The Exclusionary Rule and Other Devices," in National Commission on the Causes and Prevention of Violence, *Law and Order Reconsidered* (New York: Bantam Books, 1970), chap. 17.

2 Jerome Skolnick, *Justice without Trial* (New York: John Wiley, 1966).

3 Herbert Packer, *The Limits of the Criminal Sanction* (Stanford: Stanford University Press, 1968), chap. 8.

4 National Commission on Productivity, *Opportunities for Improving Productivity in Police Services* (Washington, D.C.: U.S. Government Printing Office, 1973), p. 9.

5 Ibid., pp. 7–9.

6 Federal Bureau of Investigation, *Uniform Crime Reports, 1978* (Washington, D.C.: U.S. Government Printing Office, 1979).

7 For a summary of criticisms of the UCR, see Gwynn Nettler, *Explaining Crime,* 2d ed. (New York: McGraw-Hill, 1978), chap. 4.

8 David Seidman and Michael Couzens, "Getting the Crime Rate Down: Political Pressure and Crime Reporting," *Law and Society Review* 8 (September 1974): 457–493.

9 U.S., Department of Justice, *An Introduction to the National Crime Survey* (Washington, D.C.: U.S. Government Printing Office, 1977).

10 U.S., Department of Justice, *Criminal Victimization in the United States: 1978* (Washington, D.C.: U.S. Government Printing Office, 1980).

11 Brian Forst, et al., *What Happens after Arrest?* (Washington, D.C.: Institute for Law and Social Research, 1977), pp. 47–60.

12 George Barbour, "Measuring Local Government Productivity," in *The Municipal Yearbook, 1973* (Washington, D.C.: International City Management Association, 1973).

13 James Q. Wilson and Barbara Boland, *The Effect of the Police on Crime* (Washington, D.C.: U.S. Department of Justice, 1979), pp. 3–4.

14 John R. Hepburn, "Crime Control, Due Process, and the Measurement of Police Performance," *Journal of Police Science and Administration* 9 (March 1981): 88–98.

15 Archibald Cox, *The Warren Court* (Cambridge: Harvard University Press, 1968).

16 *Mapp v. Ohio* 367 U.S. 643 (1961).

17 Paulsen, "Securing Police Compliance," pp. 391–396.

18 Henry J. Abraham, *Freedom and the Court,* 3d ed. (New York: Oxford University Press, 1977), pp. 36–56.

19 *Escobedo v. Illinois,* 378 U.S. 478 (1964).

20 *Miranda v. Arizona,* 384 U.S. 436 (1966).

21 Yale Kamisar, *Police Interrogation and Confessions* (Ann Arbor: University of Michigan Press, 1980), pp. 1–25.

22 Ibid., pp. 95–112

23 Sheldon Krantz, et al., *Police Policymaking* (Lexington: Lexington Books, 1979), p. 190.

24 Dallin H. Oaks, "Studying the Exclusionary Rule in Search and Seizure," *University of Chicago Law Review* 37 (Summer 1970): 665–757.

25 Cited in Bureau of National Affairs, *Criminal Law Reporter,* May 23, 1979, pp. 2185–2186.

26 M. Wald, et al., "Interrogations in New Haven: The Impact of Miranda," *Yale Law Journal* 76 (July 1967): 1519–1648.

27 R. J. Medalie, et al., "Custodial Police Interrogation in Our Nation's Capital: The Attempt to Implement Miranda," *Michigan Law Review* 66 (May 1968): 1347–1422.

28 Samuel Walker, *Popular Justice* (New York: Oxford University Press, 1980), pp. 229–232.

29 Ibid., p. 236.

30 Packer, *Limits of the Criminal Sanction,* pp. 240–241.

31 Oaks, "Studying the Exclusionary Rule"; "Police Perjury in Narcotics 'Dropsy' Cases: A New Credibility Gap," *Georgetown Law Review* 60 (November 1971): 507–523.

32 Paulsen, "Securing Police Compliance," pp. 396–399.

33 Gerald E. Caiden, *Police Revitalization* (Lexington: Lexington Books, 1977), p. 179; *Law Enforcement News,* May 12, 1980.

34 *Omaha World-Herald,* June 12, 1981.

35 Paulsen, "Securing Police Compliance," pp. 399–402.

36 Ibid., pp. 402–405.

37 Ibid., pp. 405–407.

38 President's Commission on Law Enforcement and Administration of Justice, *Task Force Report: The Police* (Washington, D.C.: U.S. Government Printing Office, 1967), pp. 200–202.

39 Tennessee Advisory Committee to the U.S. Civil Rights Commission, *Civic Crisis—Civic Challenge: Police Community Relations in Memphis* (Washington, D.C.: U.S. Government Printing Office, 1978), p. 88.

40 William A. Westley, *Violence and the Police* (Cambridge: MIT Press, 1970).

41 Ronald Kahn, "Urban Reform and Police Accountability in New York City: 1950–1974," in *Urban Problems and Public Policy,* eds. Robert L. Lineberry and Louis H. Masotti (Lexington: Lexington Books, 1975), pp. 107–127.

42 Paulsen, "Securing Police Compliance," pp. 412–414.

43 Hartford Institute of Criminal and Social Justice, *Civilian Review of the Police—The Experiences of American Cities* (Hartford: Hartford Institute of Criminal and Social Justice, 1980), pp. 14–19.

44 Ibid., pp. 9–13.

45 Arthur Waskow, "Community Control," *Trans-Action* (December 1969).

46 Jerome Skolnick, "Neighborhood Police," in *Police in America*, eds. Jerome Skolnick and Thomas Gray (Boston: Little, Brown, 1975), pp. 288–291.

47 Albert Reiss, *The Police and the Public* (New Haven: Yale University Press, 1971), pp. 208–212.

48 Robert Wintersmith, *Police and the Black Community* (Lexington: Lexington Books, 1974).

49 James Q. Wilson, *Varieties of Police Behavior* (New York: Atheneum, 1973), p. 283.

50 Wilbert E. Moore, *The Professions: Rules and Roles* (New York: Russell Sage, 1970), pp. 3–22.

51 Samuel Walker, *A Critical History of Police Reform* (Lexington: Lexington Books, 1977); Skolnick, *Justice without Trial*, p. 238.

52 Peter K. Manning, *Police Work* (Cambridge: MIT Press, 1977), pp. 127—128.

53 O. W. Wilson and Roy C. McLaren, *Police Administration*, 4th ed. (New York McGraw-Hill, 1977), pp. 211–218.

54 Tennessee Advisory Committee, *Civic Crisis—Civic Challenge*, pp. 59–61.

55 Herman Goldstein, *Police Corruption* (Washington, D.C.: Police Foundation, 1975), pp. 40–41.

56 Wilson and McLaren, *Police Administration*, p. 212.

CHAPTER 11

POLICE OFFICERS

POLICE CAREERS

The quality of law enforcement personnel is a key issue in American policing. Routine police work involves the exercise of individual judgment in critical decisions affecting the life and liberty of citizens. The quality of police services a community receives depends to a great extent on the competence of individual officers.

From Recruitment to Retirement

Many factors influence the quality of law enforcement personnel. Public attention focuses on recruitment standards. There is much debate over the question of what qualifications are necessary and proper. Recruitment, however, is only one stage in a longer process of personnel management. In this chapter we shall examine police personnel from a *career* perspective, looking at all of the stages from recruitment to retirement.

Each stage in the process is important in determining the quality of law enforcement personnel. A department may succeed in recruiting highly qualified officers but fail to provide them with adequate training. Or, it might lose many of its best young officers because of poor management practices. The failure of departments to provide meaningful career opportunities for its younger, educated officers is today a serious problem for the American police.

Beyond the Stereotypes

Understanding of police officers is hindered by popular stereotypes about police and policing. There exist two principal stereotypes—one anticop and one procop, both of which are highly distorted images of the police. The anticop stereotype views police officers as uneducated, untrained, bigoted, violence-prone, and corrupt. The procop stereotype views them as saints, heroic individuals, risking their lives in the face of hostility from the public, the media, and the courts.

Neither stereotype accurately portrays the police. In this chapter we approach the subject from the perspective of occupational sociology: What kinds of people are attracted to police work? Why? What kind of training do they receive? How are they socialized into certain attitudinal and behavior patterns? It is important to keep in mind that police officers are individual human beings. Different individuals respond to the same influences in different ways. In their strengths and weaknesses police officers are no different than persons employed in other occupations.

RECRUITMENT

The recruitment of police officers involves the interaction of two factors: the decision of certain individuals to seek law enforcement as a career, and the selection process used by law enforcement agencies.

Who Seeks Law Enforcement as a Career?

Bayley and Mendelsohn argue that "one does not need a special theory to explain why men go into police work—as many police detractors would suggest. One explains recruitment to the police force as one explains recruitment to any occupation, namely in terms of its status, rewards, minimal educational requirements, and conditions of service."[1] In short, people seek law enforcment as a career for rational reasons related to their own circumstances and rewards and opportunities offered by the job.

Sex and Race   Policing in the United States today is overwhelmingly a white male occupation. In 1975 only 6.5 percent of all police officers were black, despite the fact that blacks represented 11 percent of the total population.[2] The gap between black officers and black citizens is even wider in cities with large black communities. Meanwhile only 2 percent of all police officers are female, despite the fact that women represent slightly more than half of the population.

The underrepresentation of minorities and women can be attributed in part to the traditional image of the police. In the eyes of many black Americans the police represent the white power structure. Young black males give the police lower evaluations than any other group. For this reason, many potentially qualified black males are reluctant to apply for jobs with the police. Nicholas Alex points out that the black officer faces the problem of a dual identity—part police officer, part member of the black community.[3]

Women are underrepresented because of the traditional masculine image of the police. Traditionally, police officers have portrayed their occupation as dangerous and physically demanding. The subculture among police officers perpetuates this image. Female police officers are not welcomed by veteran police officers. Susan Ehrlich Martin characterizes the process of taking a job as a police officer as "breaking and entering" for a woman. As with other male-dominated occupations, then, many qualified women choose not to apply.[4]

Employment discrimination reinforces and perpetuates the image of policing as a white male occupation. Discrimination against racial minorities contributes to the image that the police are part of the white power structure. Discrimination against female applicants reduces the number of female officers who could serve as role models for other potential applicants.

Social and Economic Status   Considerable research has been devoted to the question of the social and economic background of police officers. The consensus of opinion confirms John H. McNamara's finding that police officers come "primarily from the lower-middle-class segments of society." Table 11-1 indicates the backgrounds of recruits in the New York City Police Academy. Background is defined in terms of the occupations of recruits' fathers. Westley's study of Gary, Indiana, and Bayley and Mendelsohn's study of Denver police officers yielded similar findings.[5]

McNamara's data show that over two-thirds (69.7 percent) of the recruits came from families where the father was a manual worker, either skilled or unskilled. Po-

TABLE 11-1
OCCUPATIONAL LEVELS OF POLICE RECRUITS' FATHERS

Occupational level	Percent of recruits' fathers	Percent, work force, New York S.M.S.A.
Professional, technical, managers, officials, proprietors	10.8	22.2
Clerical, sales	9,4	27.2
Craftsmen, foremen	19.3	11.3
Operatives	16.6	17.3
Service, household workers	28.1*	11.8
Laborers	5.7	3.4
Not reported	10.1	6.7

*One-third of the recruits' fathers in this category were recorded as having the occupation of police officer or an occupation involving police-type duties, for example, private detective or watchman.
Source: John H. McNamara, "Uncertainties in Police Work: The Relevance of Police Recruits' Backgrounds and Training," in The Police: Six Sociological Essays, ed. David J. Bordua (New York: John Wiley, 1967), p. 193.

licing was relatively unattractive to persons whose fathers held white-collar or professional-level jobs. Bayley and Mendelsohn conclude that police officers are "upwardly mobile" and that the choice of police work as a career "represents an advance over what their parents were able to obtain."[6]

Career Aspirations   Surveys of police officers consistently indicate two main reasons why they chose law enforcement as a career. Officers are about equally divided between those who were attracted by the prospect of job security or other material benefits of the job and those who were attracted by the nature of police work. Table 11-2 indicates the main reason for the decision to become a police officer as expressed by white and black officers in Chicago, Boston, and Washington, D.C. One-third (36 percent) of all officers were attracted by job security or other economic attraction. Another third (30 percent) indicated that they were "always interested in being a policeman," while another 14 percent said that they were attracted by the prospect of working with people or the variety in the work.

Because of civil service, police officers enjoy a high degree of job security. They are relatively well protected against arbitrary dismissal and periodic unemployment. The appeal of job security is especially strong for people from lower-middle-class and blue-collar backgrounds, where unemployment is a constant threat. James Q. Wilson found that "security" was the primary motivation for 76.2 percent of the Chicago officers who joined the department during the depression of the 1930s. It was the primary motivation for 48.5 percent of the officers who joined during the prosperous 1950s.[7]

The recent financial problems of American cities has undermined some of the traditional job security of police employmen The New York City Police Department laid off several thousand officers in the late 1970s, while Philadelphia, Detroit, and other cities laid off several hundred officers each.

The nature of police work itself is an important attraction. Officers indicate that

TABLE 11-2
REASONS GIVEN BY BLACK AND WHITE MALES FOR BECOMING POLICE OFFICERS

Ethnicity of Officer	Main reason for decision to become police officer							
	Friends or family in police work	Always interested in being a policeman	Prestige and/or respect of job	Likes working with people	Variety in the work	Security in job	Economic attraction in job	Other or hard to say
Total	11	30	4	7	7	29	7	5
White officers	15	30	1	6	7	29	5	7
Black officers	1	25	—	11	6	28	17	12

Source: President's Commission on Law Enforcement and Administration of Justice, *Field Surveys III, Studies in Crime and Law Enforcement in Major Metropolitan Areas,* vol. 2, sec. 2, "Career Orientations, Job Satisfaction, and the Assessment of Law Enforcement Problems by Police Officers." (Washington, D.C.: U.S. Government Printing Office, n.d.), p. 18.

they were attracted by what they perceived to be an exciting, nonroutine, outdoor activity affording an opportunity to work with people. Contrary to popular stereotypes, police officers appear to be relatively idealistic, perhaps even slightly more so than the average person.[8]

Experience on the job does not always support a police recruit's original expectations. While many officers begin their careers with a high degree of idealism, they often become very cynical about the public, the police department, the criminal justice system, and their own career prospects. Research indicates that officers undergo considerable change in attitude, particularly during their first year on the street.[9]

Blacks and whites appear to seek out law enforcement careers for roughly the same reasons. Nicholas Alex concluded that "the motives of the white policeman for choosing policework seem little different from those of the black policeman."[10] Other studies, however, suggest that blacks are relatively more attracted by the economic benefits of the job. Table 11-2 shows that 17 percent of black officers were drawn by economic attractions, compared with only 5 percent of the white officers. The underrepresenation of blacks on the police departments is reflected in the fact that only 1 percent of black officers were attracted by family or friends, compared with 15 percent of white officers. Employment discrimination in certain respects is a self-perpetuating phenomenon.

Women also appear to be attracted to police work for the same reasons as men. Virginia Ermer concluded that "a comparison of the responses of males and females suggests that they do not differ dramatically in their reasons for becoming police officers."[11] Table 11-3 shows the primary reason for joining the police department as expressed by 42 female officers in New York City. Ermer's study confirms the findings of other research that relatively few people are attracted to police work because of a "law enforcement orientation." The anticop stereotype views police officers as persons who were essentially attracted by the opportunity to use coercive force: to

TABLE 11-3
PRIMARY MOTIVATION FOR BECOMING A POLICE OFFICER AMONG BLACK AND WHITE FEMALE OFFICERS IN NEW YORK CITY

	% Black (N = 16)	% White (N = 26)	Total (N = 42)
Salary	44	50	48
Security	6	8	7
Interesting Work	0	19	12
Family Influence	6	8	7
Don't Know	0	4	2
Total Nonpolice Oriented	56	88.5	76
Opportunity to Help Others	31	4	14
Law Enforcement Orientation	13	8	10
Total Police Oriented	44	11.5	24

Source: Virginia B. Ermer, "Recruitment of Female Police Officers in New York City," *Journal of Criminal Justice* 6 (Fall 1978):241.

stop and frisk, to use physical force, to make arrests, and to use firearms. The available evidence indicates that there is no support for this view. Indeed, the evidence suggests that police officers are surprisingly uninterested in the purely law enforcement aspects of police work.

Selection

Given a certain pool of applicants, what criteria do police agencies use to select new officers? Selection criteria are a matter of great controversy and considerable litigation. Two questions are involved: What criteria will result in the selection of the best-qualified officers? Do certain criteria or procedures discriminate against any group of applicants?

Education   Most police departments require only a high school diploma as the minimum level of educational attainment. According to the National Manpower Survey of the Criminal Justice System, 81.3 percent of all departments require a high school diploma or the equivalent. Only 5.5 percent require some college education, while 13.3 percent either require less than a high school diploma or have no requirement at all.[12]

Many experts argue in favor of higher educational requirements. The President's Commission on Law Enforcement recommended that "The ultimate aim of all police departments should be that all personnel with general enforcement powers have baccalaureate degrees." Five years later the National Advisory Commission on Criminal Justice Standards and Goals endorsed this goal.[13]

Requiring a college degree for entry into police work is based on several arguments. First, the complexity of police work demands "an understanding of human behavior and a knowledge of the social, political, and economic environment."[14] Second, good police work demands an ability to understand the increasingly complex legal requirements governing such issues as search and seizure, interrogation, and the use of force. Finally, it is argued that police agencies need to raise their requirements to keep pace with the generally rising levels of educational attainment in society. Between 1960 and 1970 the percentage of adults completing high school rose from 43 percent to 60 percent.

The college degree requirement is opposed primarily on the grounds that it would unduly restrict the available pool of potential applicants. In particular, there is concern that it would exclude many potential minority-group applicants who do not enjoy the same educational opportunities as whites. Finally, there is no conclusive evidence that higher education leads to better police performance. In *The Quality of Police Education,* Lawrence Sherman argued that the available research on the subject was inconclusive, largely because of faulty methodology.[15]

Despite the fact that few police departments have raised their *minimum* requirements, the level of educational attainment among American police officers has been rising. Before 1959 an estimated 19.3 percent of all sworn officers had less than a high school diploma. By 1970–1974 that figure had dropped to 7.8 percent. The National Manpower Survey estimated that the percentage of officers with one year or more of college would rise from 46.4 percent in 1974 to 75.2 percent by 1985. According to the survey, the "remarkable rate of growth in the levels of educational attainment" had produced an "educational generation gap" between older and younger officers.[16]

The rising levels of educational attainment are the result of several factors. First, the educational levels of all Americans have been rising, so departments could expect more highly educated groups of applicants. Second, the federal Law Enforcement Education Program scholarship program in the 1970s stimulated college work among people interested in law enforcement. Third, the LEEP program facilitated college work by people who were already sworn officers. Finally, with the passage of time, officers recruited when standards were lower retire, thereby raising the average of the profession as a whole.

Increasing numbers of better-educated officers create problems for police departments. Often, the more educated officer is critical of traditional police practices and more willing to voice those criticisms. They are also often interested in broader career opportunities. Existing personnel systems are extremely inflexible and do not provide adequate opportunities for the talented and ambitious officer. David Farmer concludes that "police departments have made no effective provisions for the educated officer."[17] Research on personnel turnover suggests that officers with more education are more likely to resign and seek other employment.[18]

Residency Requirements   About half of all police departments require their officers to live within the city. Some of these require the individual to be living within the city at the time of application, while others require relocation sometime after appointment.[19]

Residency requirements are intended to ensure that officers are familiar with the community they police. Also, it is argued that residency enhances an officer's commitment to the community, decreasing the possibility that the officer will regard the community as a foreign or hostile territory. Residency requirements are opposed on the grounds that they restrict the pool of potential applicants, excluding many potentially qualified persons, and that they are an unacceptable restriction on a person's freedom to choose a place of residence.

Testing and Screening Procedures   A variety of procedures are used to examine applicants, screen out the unqualified, and select new recruits. The most common are the written examination, a background investigation, and an oral interview. More than 90 percent of all agencies use all three. Slightly more than one-third use some form of clinical appraisal, usually a psychological test, to screen applicants. And 31 percent of the agencies examine applicants with a polygraph or lie detector.[20]

Physical Requirements   Virtually all departments have minimum requirements for age, height, weight, and visual acuity. Standards vary for each of these items, however. Most departments require recruits to be 21 years old, although some accept recruits as young as 18. Most departments will accept no one over the age of 34, although some accept recruits as old as 50. Height and weight requirements have been changing in the past fifteen years, primarily because of legal challenges. The minimimum height requirement of 5 feet 9 inches has been successfully challenged as discriminating against both female and minority group (particularly Hispanic) applicants. Agencies are now required to demonstrate that a particular requirement is job-related, that is, necessary for the performance of the job. Many traditional requirements served only to reinforce the "macho" image of the police and were not necessary for actual police work.[21]

Criminal Record   A criminal record does not automatically bar an individual from police work. According to a survey by the Police Foundation, 96 percent of the agencies would reject an applicant with an adult felony conviction, and 90 percent would reject an applicant with a juvenile felony conviction. But only 51 percent would reject an applicant because of an adult misdemeanor conviction, and only 45 percent would reject the person with a juvenile misdemeanor conviction.[22]

Responsibility for Recruitment

Most police departments do not have complete responsibility for recruiting new officers. Under existing civil service systems responsibility is shared with an outside agency. Typically, the outside agency—usually called a personnel department or civil service department—has the primary responsibility for recruitment. These duties include developing job descriptions, establishing pay scales, advertising existing openings, developing and administering examinations, and certifying a list of qualified candidates. The police department typically has responsibility for administering certain examinations (background investigations, oral interviews, polygraph examinations) and, in some cases, selecting the final list of recruits.[23]

The concept of civil service was designed to eliminate favoritism and political influence in the recruitment of police officers and to ensure that recruits are selected on the basis of impersonal, objective criteria. Typically, the personnel or civil service department handles all personnel matters for all agencies for that unit of government.

EQUAL EMPLOYMENT OPPORTUNITY

Under the laws of the United States all persons are guaranteed equal opportunity in seeking employment. Discrimination on the basis of race, color, religion, sex, or national origin is prohibited by federal law and various state and local laws. Despite these legal guarantees, employment discrimination does exist in American law enforcement. The two major areas of discrimination are race or ethnic background and sex.[24]

Evidence of Discrimination

Minorities and women are underrepresented in American law enforcement agencies. That is, the proportion of minorities or women as sworn officers does not equal their representation in the community served. How serious must the underrepresentation be to constitute evidence of discrimination? LEAA guidelines state that a significant disparity exists where the percentage of a minority group in an agency is less that 70 percent of percentage of that group in the community.[25]

Minority Status   Minorities constitute approximately 14 percent of the total U.S. population. Yet in 1970 less than 7 percent of all sworn police officers in the country were of minority background. The problem is particularly serious in the big cities that have sizable minority communities. In some cities, minorities are now a majority of the population. Table 11-4 shows the representation of minorities on selected police departments, compared with the ethnic composition of the city. Particularly significant disparities exist in Cleveland and St. Louis. Even in those cities that have the highest number of minority officers, the percentage still trails their representation in the community.

Sex   Women are even more seriously underrepresented than minorities in American law enforcement agencies. Table 11-4 indicates the percentage of female officers in selected cities. The underrepresentation of women is a legacy of traditional male orientation of American policing. The first woman to become a sworn police officer was Lola Baldwin in 1910. Until the late 1960s women were largely confined to specialized duties (juvenile, vice, etc.) and in many cities barred from promotion to higher rank.[26]

Need for Corrective Action

Employment discrimination needs to be eliminated for two principal reasons. The first is the simple fact that discrimination is illegal. Law enforcement agencies are required to afford equal employment opportunity to all persons by the U.S. Constitution and various federal, state, and local laws.

The second reason is a practical one. Employment discrimination prevents law enforcement agencies from effectively carrying out their duties. This is particularly

TABLE 11-4
MINORITY AND FEMALE POLICE OFFICERS IN SELECTED CITIES

City	Total officers	Black	Spanish surname	American Indian	Total minority	% Minority	Female officers	% Female
Boston	2102	83	0	0	83	3.9%	27	1.2%
Cleveland	1906	213	7	0	220	11.5	68	3.5
Dallas	1997	99	71	3	173	8.6	78	3.9
Detroit	5688	1786	17	4	1807	31.7	676	11.8
Houston	2988	120	140	1	261	4.3	140	4.6
Kansas City	1192	146	16	1	163	13.6	29	2.4
Oakland	642	101	39	0	140	21.8	14	2.1
Miami	698	73	103	0	176	25.2	47	6.7

Source: Adapted from FBI, *Uniform Crime Reports, 1978* (Washington, D.C.: U.S. Government Printing Office, 1979); Police Executive Research Forum, *Police Practices: The General Administrative Survey* (Washington, D.C.: Police Foundation, 1978.).

true with regard to racial discrimination. Law enforcement agencies that do not adequately reflect the composition of the communities they police have difficulty winning the confidence and trust of the people. The President's Commission on Law Enforcement argued that "if police departments, through their hiring or promotion policies, indicate that they have little interest in hiring minority group officers, the minority community is not likely to be sympathetic to the community."[27]

The presence of a proper proportion of minority officers serves several functions. First, it enhances the image of the department, dispelling the idea that it is an all-white occupying army in the ghetto. Second, minority officers serve to sensitize white officers to important aspects of minority culture. Finally, minority officers are more likely to live in the neighborhood and, as a result, to have better contacts with people in the community.

Legal Basis for Equal Employment Opportunity

Equal employment opportunity is based on several aspects of American law.[28] *The Fourteenth Amendment* to the Constitution guarantees "equal protection of the laws" to the citizens of all states. The most important statutory guarantee is *Title VII of the 1964 Civil Rights Act,* which prohibits discrimination because of race, color, religion, sex, or national origin. The law covers all employment practices: hiring, promotion, compensation, dismissal, and all other terms or conditions of employment.

Title VII of the 1964 Civil Rights Act was amended by the *Equal Employment Opportunity Act of 1972.* This law expanded the jurisdiction and strengthened the powers of the federal Equal Employment Opportunity Commission (EEOC). It allowed the employees of state and local governments to file employment discrimination suits with the EEOC, strengthened the investigatory powers of the EEOC (allowing it to better document allegations of discrimination), and permitted the U.S. Justice Department to sue state and local governments for violations of Title VII.

Other federal statutes also prohibit employment discrimination. Title VI of the 1964 Civil Rights Act prohibits discrimination in any program receiving federal funds. The 1972 State and Local Fiscal Assistance Act, which provides revenue-sharing funds to state and local governments, also prohibits discrimination. In 1973, LEAA developed equal employment opportunity guidelines for criminal justice agencies receiving LEAA funds. Finally, other executive orders and statutes directly or indirectly prohibit discrimination.

Federal laws are paralleled in most states by employment discrimination statutes. The Utah Advisory Commission to the U.S. Commission on Civil Rights, for example, noted that discrimination was prohibited by the Utah Anti-Discriminatory Act. The law allowed individuals to file discrimination complaints with the Utah Industrial Commission, and the Commission itself adopted rules calling for the cancellation of contracts with agencies guilty of discrimination.[29]

Remedies for Discrimination

For an individual who feels victimized by employment discrimination, the basic remedy is a formal complaint or lawsuit. Existing laws provide for complaints with the federal Equal Opportunity Employment Commission or equivalent state agency. An alternative is a lawsuit in state or federal court. The complaint or suit may be on behalf of the individual or, as a *class action,* on behalf of all persons similarly affected.

If the agency or court finds that discrimination exists, it can order one or more corrective actions. The plaintiffs can be awarded back pay or, in the case of discriminatory dismissal, reinstatement. Changes in employment practices can also be ordered. Courts, for example, have invalidated certain tests, required agencies to develop validated tests and/or examination procedures, and ordered agencies to set specific goals for the recruitment of minorities and women. Frequently, these settlements are agreed to before trial in a negotiated *consent decree.* In 1980, for example, the Los Angeles Police Department signed a consent decree with the Justice Department awarding $2 million in back pay and agreeing that 45 percent of all new recruits would be black or Hispanic and that 20 percent of all new recruits would be women.[30]

Termination of federal funds is another action that can be taken where discrimination exists. The city of Chicago, for example, lost over $100 million in federal revenue-sharing funds in 1976 because of employment discrimination in the police department.[31]

De Facto Discrimination

Discrimination may take several forms. The most obvious is where there is a clear and explicit policy of discrimination. Until recently, for example, most police departments had separate procedures for female officers. Women were employed with a different job title, subject to different recruitment standards, with different pay, and often barred from promotion to certain jobs.

More prevalent and yet more difficult to identify is *de facto* discrimination. This is discrimination that is the indirect result of policies or practices that are not intended to discriminate. Courts have consistently ruled in favor of plaintiffs where the evidence indicates that the effect of a certain policy or practice results in discrimination, regardless of the intent.

To eliminate the discriminatory effect of recruitment practices, the EEOC requires that all tests and examinations be job-related. An agency must provide evidence that "the test is predictive of or significantly correlated with important elements of work behavior which comprise or are relevant to the job or jobs for which candidates are being evaluated."[32] Height requirements have frequently been invalidated, for example, because agencies could not prove that a person less than 5 feet 9 inches could not perform effectively as a police officer.

Affirmative Action

Executive Order 11246, issued by President Lyndon Johnson in 1965, requires all federal contractors and subcontractors to develop *affirmative action* programs. Subsequent executive orders have amended and expanded the original executive order.[33]

In essence, the concept of affirmative action means that employers must take active steps to ensure equal employment opportunity. Affirmative action is result-oriented in the sense that it focuses on the results of employment practices. It is not sufficient for an agency to simply stop discriminating; it must take steps to correct past discrimination.

Affirmative action programs consist of several elements. With respect to the recruitment process, agencies must make every effort to advertise job openings and actively seek out and encourage applicants. All tests and screening procedures must be validated as job-related, with potentially discriminatory procedures eliminated.

The most controversial element of affirmative action involves goals and timetables. The Office of Federal Contract Compliance (OFCC) regulations for affirmative action programs require agencies to develop plans to correct employment discrimination. These plans must include specific goals and timetables. OFCC regulations state that "(c) Goals should be significant, measurable and attainable;" and that "(d) Goals should be specific for planned results, with timetables for completion." In short, an agency should determine a proper level of minority and female representation and, if it does not currently meet that level, develop a recruitment and promotional plan that would correct the problem.

Reverse Discrimination   The main question is whether goals and timetables necessarily entail quotas. Under a quota arrangement, a certain percentage of openings are reserved for particular groups. In 1974, for example, the Detroit police department adopted a policy of promoting one black officer to sergeant for each white officer promoted. Largely as a result of its policy, Detroit has one of the best records for minority employment.

On behalf of white officers, the Detroit Police Officers Association sued the department, claiming that the affirmative action plan discriminated against whites because of their race. Federal District Court ruled in favor of the white officers and struck down the department's minority quota system for promotions. As of this writing, the question of affirmative action plans, and quotas in particular, has not been settled by a definitive ruling from the Supreme Court.[34]

CAREER OPPORTUNITIES

Policing is not just a job but a long-term commitment. As with other occupations, the job becomes a way of life, and the police officer's identity merges with the job. An officer's career is not a static phenomenon; it changes over time. The job expectations, attitudes, and behavior of the officer can also change over time.

Police career paths, however, are extremely limited. Three basic choices are open to American police officers. First, they can *seek promotion to higher rank* and enter supervisory and managerial work. Second, they can *seek assignment to a desired unit* (criminal investigation, juvenile, etc.). Third, they can simply *remain patrol officers.*[35]

Virtually all police agencies promote from within the department. Officers do not have the option of transferring to another department at the same or higher rank; rather, they enter the new agency at the bottom and lose all seniority. The ability to seek career advancement by changing employers, which is an important aspect of careers in the private sector, does not exist for the American police.

Movement from one agency to another usually involves a transfer from a small agency to a large metropolitan police department (typically for better pay) or from a state or local agency to a federal law enforcement agency (typically for better pay and career opportunities). In both of these two cases, however, the individual sacrifices previous seniority.

Lateral Entry

Lateral entry refers to the recruitment of supervisory personnel from other police agencies and the transfer of officers from one agency to another without loss of seniority. It is seen as a means of enhancing police professionalism by creating expanded career opportunities and by permitting departments to bring in fresh blood and new ideas. The President's Commission on Law Enforcement endorsed the concept of lateral entry in 1967.[36] Despite similar recommendations by other experts, lateral entry is practiced by only a few police departments.

It is opposed for several reasons. First, officers in a given department jealously guard the few promotional opportunities that do arise. Vacancies are regarded as theirs, and they resent the idea that outsiders would get these jobs. Second, police pension systems are local in nature and cannot be transferred to other cities or states. For this reason, the President's Commission recommended the development of a national police retirement system, which would permit the transfer of personnel without the loss of benefits. A few initial experiments with portable police pensions have been tried.[37]

TRAINING

The new recruit is initiated into the world of policing and into the department during the training period. Large departments generally maintain their own police academy; small departments now generally send their recruits to state-run training academies. Formal training for all sworn officers is now required in all but a few states.

The police academy experience is an extremely important phase of an officer's career. Westley, Harris, Van Maanen, and Niederhoffer describe the experience as a formative rite of passage, an experience that shapes an officer's attitudes about the job, the department, and the public. The recruit is usually extremely anxious: concerned about doing well but uncertain about what is expected. The recruit adopts the insignia of the new job—the uniform, the badge, the weapon, the nightstick—and, more importantly, learns the military system of discipline—to take orders and not question authority.[38]

The formal training curriculum is heavily weighted toward the technical aspects of police work: the details of criminal law and procedure; internal departmental regulations and procedures; the care and use of firearms. The total number of hours of training range from a high of 560 and 545 hours in Arizona and California, respectively, to a low of 120 and 150 in Nevada and Wyoming, respectively. Table 11-5

TABLE 11-5
HOURS SPENT IN BASIC TRAINING BY SUBJECT AREA AND STATE, 1976

State	Introduction to criminal justice system	Agency policies and procedures	Legal subjects	Juvenile	Patrol procedures	Criminal evidence investigative procedures	Community and human values/problems	Traffic	Physical training	Emergency medical training (first aid)	Weapons	Detention	Other
						Basic curriculum hours							
Alabama	6	22	28	6	19	46	14	48	4	8	24	3	12
Alaska	29	17	35	—	16	54	—	13	17	10	8	—	71
Arizona	10	8	74	4	39	39	14	39	—	14	25	—	14
Arkansas	NA	NA	NA	NA	NA	NA	NA	NA	NA	NA	NA	NA	NA
California	10	0	28	8	40	34	20	20	14	10	12	0	4
Colorado	5	2	47	8	15	34	12	15	18	24	20	4	60
Connecticut	21	—	86	8	85	43	26	62	10	28	32	—	—
Delaware	9	4	57	4	18	103	16	56	27	21	35	—	—
Florida	13	12	51	6	18	79	22	32	28	20	39	—	—
Georgia	10	3	45	2	45	33	14	28	18	14	20	0	10
Hawaii	—	—	—	—	—	—	—	—	—	—	—	—	—
Idaho	7	—	30	4	62	36	19	20	35	18	22	—	27
Illinois	20	21	58	8	2	19	49	20	15	8	10	18	0
Indiana	13	18	85	8	5	98	16	20	30	16	49	2	40
Iowa	23	24	31	4	6	36	25	31	18	20	16	0	16
Kansas	6	5	19	3	43	39	6	14	25	10	30	0	0
Kentucky	15	27	80	7	32	55	32	35	44	24	35	6	8
Louisiana	—	—	—	—	—	—	—	—	—	—	—	—	—
Maine	17	20	59	—	35	71	19	24	34	40	24	43	7
Maryland	12	18	58	9	32	55	18	55	27	40	28	—	7

State													
Massachusetts	NA	NA	NA	NA	NA	NA	NA	NA	NA	NA	NA	NA	NA
Michigan	7	11	52	6	40	30	12	28	28	14	24	3	—
Minnesota	NA	NA	NA	NA	NA	NA	NA	NA	NA	NA	NA	NA	NA
Mississippi	—	—	—	—	—	—	—	—	—	—	—	—	—
Missouri	—	—	—	—	—	—	—	—	—	—	—	—	—
Montana	3	8	37	8	58	56	16	8	22	16	45	3	—
Nebraska	15	20	55	5	27	69	17	31	20	10	22	2	9
Nevada	1	4	38	4	8	32	6	8	0	0	14	0	5
New Hampshire	4	37	44	4	6	68	16	36	40	12	22	—	6
New Jersey	7	—	50	6	30	19	30	22	32	10	25	3	41
New Mexico	6	—	13	—	12	6	10	13	10	8	20	3	—
New York	8	8	50	4	27	36	16	25	14	10	23	—	64
North Carolina	12	—	66	6	12	21	8	8	9	10	3	2	5
North Dakota	6	10	51	2	20	28	7	60	0	10	4	—	4
Ohio	9	3	5	6	67	97	16	21	16	14	26	—	—
Oklahoma	18	6	24	6	16	8	16	24	0	14	24	4	—
Oregon	11	18	47	6	24	50	31	39	28	8	26	0	50
Pennsylvania	NA	NA	NA	NA	NA	NA	NA	NA	NA	NA	NA	NA	NA
Rhode Island	9	35	125	5	90	52	10	65	60	20	25	4	—
South Carolina	10	12	52	5	70	30	28	40	50	8	30	—	—
South Dakota	NA	NA	NA	NA	NA	NA	NA	NA	NA	NA	NA	NA	NA
Tennessee	5	8	32	8	25	32	7	22	41	20	40	—	—
Texas	11	12	42	4	38	38	12	34	10	10	19	2	8
Utah	3	12	26	40	25	38	23	44	32	20	24	—	33
Vermont	5	12	25	8	15	40	—	40	35	40	30	—	—
Virginia	2	9	29	4	5	48	5	15	9	14	24	—	40
Washington	31	11	73	6	43	85	51	54	28	30	24	4	—
West Virginia	—	—	—	—	—	—	—	—	—	—	—	—	—
Wisconsin	6	19	16	8	35	36	22	34	8	14	22	0	20
Wyoming	4	4	20	4	28	36	6	18	8	10	12	0	—

Source: U.S., Department of Justice, *Sourcebook of Criminal Justice Statistics—1979* (Washington, D.C.: U.S. Government Printing Office, 1979), p. 211.

outlines the amount of hours devoted to various aspects of the basic training programs in different states.

The trend toward mandatory training and the upward trend of the average hours of training are important positive developments. They are part of the general upgrading of police personnel standards in the past two decades. Nonetheless, the police academy experience still has important deficiencies. The curricula in many police academies fail to give recruits guidance on common, critical situations that officers encounter. The issue of discretion is often ignored. While officers may receive several hours of training in the use of firearms, they are offered no guidance on when to use them. The handling of domestic disturbances (which require judicious exercise of discretion) is also frequently ignored.

As a result, the new officer receives his or her most important training on the street under the supervision of a field training officer (FTO). The FTO plays an important role in shaping the behavior of the new recruit. Often recruits are told to "forget all that crap" they were told in the academy. Under the supervision of the FTO, recruits learn "the ins and outs of the police role," and "what kinds of behavior are appropriate and expected of a patrolman." Van Maanen argues that "This traditional feature of police work—patrolmen training patrolmen—ensures continuity from class to class of police officers regardless of the content of the academy instruction. In large measure, the flow of influence from one generation to another accounts for the remarkable stability of the pattern of police behavior."[39]

Reality Shock

The initial experience of actual police work is often a rude awakening for the new officer.[40] The reality shock involves the discovery that many of the officer's preconceptions about police work are not valid. Most recruits tend to be somewhat idealistic and are attracted to police work by the opportunity to work with and help people. The new officer soon discovers that citizens can be hostile and belligerent. As a result, officers' attitudes undergo considerable change during the first year on the job. McNamara found a significant increase over time in the percentage of officers who agreed with the statement that "Patrolmen almost never receive the cooperation from the public that is needed to handle police work properly." Only 32 percent of new recruits agreed with the statement, compared with 50 percent of the officers who had completed two years of police work. There was a similar increase in the percentage of officers believing that it was necessary to use force to gain respect in "tough" neighborhoods. Regoli and Poole, meanwhile, found a "precipitous drop" in the level of professional commitment among police recruits after only six months on the job.[41]

THE POLICE PERSONALITY

Considerable research has been devoted to the question of whether there is a distinct police personality. The police personality is said to consist of certain pathological traits: secrecy, violence, authoritarianism, and so forth. This stereotype is usually advanced by people who are critical of the police. Unfortunately, a large amount of social science research has failed to examine critically the assumptions behind this stereotype.

Westley's Police Subculture

The idea of a police subculture was first advanced by William A. Westley in his study of the Gary, Indiana, police in 1950. Eventually published as *Violence and the Police*, his study was a landmark in research on the American police. Using the perspective of the sociology of occupations, Westley sought "To isolate and identify the major social norms governing police conduct, and to describe the way in which they influence police action in specific situations."[42] In short, he wanted to find out why police act the way they do.

Westley argued that a distinct subculture existed among the police which stressed the values of secrecy and violence. Certain basic aspects of the police role allowed police officers to justify lying (even under oath) and the unwarranted use of force.

The police officer, Westley argued, views the public as an enemy: "He seldom meets it at its best and it seldom welcomes him." Most police contacts are with persons who do not want contact with the police; they represent "an unpleasant job, a threat, the bad ones, unpleasant and whining, self-concerned, uncooperative, and unjust." Other professionals whom the police has regular contact with—lawyers, the media, social workers, etc.—also tend to have negative attitudes about the police. Fully 73 percent of the officers Westley interviewed believed that the public was hostile to the police.[43]

As a result of this perceived public hostility, officers believe that they can only rely on fellow officers: "They lean on one another for moral support. . . . The public must be repudiated and the group affirmed." To guard against public intrusion, the police become a closed and secretive group: "Secrecy among the police stands as a shield against the attacks of the outside world." Westley devised a questionnaire that asked officers if they would report a fellow officer whom they knew took money from a citizen (a person arrested for drunkenness). He found that 73 percent said they would not report their fellow officer. Thus, group solidarity was more important than honesty: "illegal action is preferable to breaking the secrecy of the group."[44]

Westley then argued that the police subculture justifies violence. Feeling isolated and disliked, police are especially concerned about maintaining public respect in encounters with citizens. When respect is not freely granted by the citizen, officers feel justified in gaining respect through physical force. More than a third (39 percent) of the officers Westley interviewed felt that disrespect justified the use of force. Two-thirds of the officers (66 percent) rationalized the use of force on some illegal basis.

Skolnick's "Working Personality"

Jerome Skolnick built upon Westley's original insights and described what he called the "working personality" of the police officer. The police role contains two principal variables: *danger* and *authority*. The potential for danger is a constant feature of police work. According to Skolnick, "danger typically yields self-defensive conduct"; officers learn to be continually concerned about their own safety. They become suspicious of the public and rely primarily on the support of fellow officers. In dealing with potential danger, officers develop "a perceptual shorthand to identify certain kinds of people" as potential danger. A list of certain cues and signals, with special emphasis on a person's physical appearance, alert the officer to potential danger.[45]

Authority further isolates the officer from the public. As Bittner argues, the authority to use force distinguishes the police officer from other people and is the key element of the police role. Not only do officers react in response to threats to authority, but, Skolnick argues, "authority . . . becomes a resource to reduce perceived threats."[46] The officer learns to use arrest, the threat of arrest, physical force, or the threat of deadly force to assert authority and maintain control of people and situations.

Niederhoffer: Cynicism and Authoritarianism

In *Behind the Shield,* former New York police officer Arthur Niederhoffer argued that *cynicism* and *authoritarianism* were also parts of the police personality.

Police officers are cynical about both the outside world and the inside world of the police system. They see humanity at its worst; dealing day in and day out with crime, violence, and disorder, they learn that people are capable of the worst kinds of behavior. Their view of humanity is distorted because they have few encounters with positive human behavior. At the same time, police officers become cynical about the criminal justice system and the department itself. They see instances of the miscarriage of justice (plea bargaining, perjury, etc.) and soon learn that the police themselves do not honor their own code of professionalism. They see corruption and illegal conduct firsthand.[47]

Niederhoffer also argues that police officers are authoritarian: "The police system transforms a man into the special type of authoritarian personality required by the police role." He emphasized the fact that officers do not enter policing with this trait but are transformed once on the job through "strenuous socialization." According to the F scale developed by psychologists, the authoritarian personality is characterized by "conventionalism, cynicism, aggression, superstition and stereotypy, projectivity, and good versus bad people." Authoritarian people, in other words, divide the world into good and bad people, project their own fears onto others, stereotype people, and label as deviant those who do not conform to conventional standards of behavior.[48]

The Police Personality Assessed

The concept of a police personality achieved wide popularity in the late 1960s. In the midst of the police-community relations crisis, critics of the police were receptive to the idea that all police were secretive, violent, cynical, and authoritarian. The concept of a police personality became a stereotype and a cliché.

More recently, this concept has been subjected to criticism. Reviewing the literature, Joel Lefkowitz argued that "A significant portion of the relevant literature is primarily mere opinion." Moreover, "Almost all of the research studies reviewed are methodologically inadequate to the task of supporting reasonable inferences" about existence or origins of a police personality. He concluded that the personalities of police officers "do differ in systematic ways from the rest of the population, but differ in an evaluatively neutral sense." In short, police officers are somewhat different, but the personality traits are not pathological.[49]

Bayley and Mendelsohn reached similar conclusions in their study of Denver police. They found that "on all personality scales the data show that policemen are absolutely average people." Moreover, they found that police recruits were somewhat more idealistic than people in the community. Police officers were somewhat more conservative than the population at large (regardless of whether they were Republican or Democratic) but not authoritarian.[50] John McNamara, using the same F scale employed by Niederhoffer, found evidence that police recruits were less authoritarian than the general public and less punitive in their attitudes than community leaders.[51]

Robert M. Regoli has challenged Niederhoffer's analysis of police cynicism. He found that the scale Niederhoffer used to measure cynicism has low validity. He also found that cynicism is a multidimensional phenomenon: cynicism toward relations with the public; cynicism toward organizational functions; cynicism about police dedication to duty; cynicism about police social solidarity; and cynicism about training and education. Regoli concludes that "it is possible that police can be cynical toward one aspect of the occupation and not others, or toward any combination of aspects simultaneously."[52]

Cynicism also has certain positive features. It functions very much like a callus, in that it hardens the individual's feelings. A certain amount of callousness is necessary for a police officer. An officer encounters many unpleasant and even repulsive situations. Cynicism provides a protective covering that allows the officer to perform the job. Also, the officer often has to do unpleasant things, such as take a person into custody. A degree of detachment allows the officer to handle the situation in an impersonal manner.[53]

ATTITUDES AND BEHAVIOR

The relationship between attitudes and behavior is a key issue. Do certain attitudes exist among the police, and do those attitudes translate into on-the-job behavior? Can we explain patterns of arrest or the use of deadly force in terms of police attitudes?

Attitudes toward Minorities

Police attitudes toward minorities has received particular attention. Are police officers prejudiced? If so, does this prejudice translate into discriminatory police practices?

Evidence of prejudicial attitudes exists, but the signficance of those attitudes is complex. Bayley and Mendelsohn concluded that police prejudices exist "only slightly more so that the community as a whole." In other words, the police were not that different from the general population. The relationship between attitudes and behavior, however, is even more complex.[54] In their field studies for the President's Crime Commission, Black and Reiss found that 75 percent of the officers made racist comments. However, they found little evidence of discriminatory behavior. The relationship between attitudes and behavior was extremely weak. Other situational factors explained behavior.[55]

White and Black Officers

The black police officer occupies a unique position within the big-city police department. Nicholas Alex argues that the black officer is "an unclassifiable hybrid agent," who is "placed in a special category by the department, his white colleagues, white civilians, and the lower-class Negro community."[56] Many white officers regard the black officer with suspicion, as not being one of them. Many members of the black community, meanwhile, regard the black officer as a traitor to the community, as a servant of the white power structure. The black officer, in short, has a dual identity: part police officer, part member of the black community.

There appear to be important differences between the attitudes and behavior of white and black officers. In a survey of 522 police officers assigned to minority-group neighborhoods in thirteen large cities, Peter Rossi found that black officers had more positive attitudes toward their assigned districts. They were less likely to rate the assignment more difficult than other assignments, three times more likely than white officers to live in the precinct where they worked, and more likely to have friends there. The black officers were also more likely to believe that the residents of the area where they were assigned were "honest" and "industrious."[57]

The evidence on police officer behavior, however, suggests that black officers are more punitive toward black citizens than white officers. They are more likely to arrest black citizens than white officers and more likely to use physical force. Donald Black suggests that the arrest patterns reflect the fact that black officers are more willing to comply with the request of black complainants that an arrest be made. Also, in domestic disputes, it is possible that black officers are better able to identify with the plight of the abused female and, consequently, more likely to arrest the abusing male.[58]

Fyfe found that black officers used deadly force more often than white officers in New York City. This could be explained by other variables. Black officers were more likely to be assigned to high-crime neighborhoods where violent encounters were more frequent. Also, black officers were more likely to live in high-crime neighborhoods and, as a result, encounter situations where they would use deadly force while off duty.[59]

Male and Female Officers

Several studies indicate that there is no significant difference in the attitudes and behavior of male and female police officers. Ermer found that women were attracted to police work for the same reasons as men. The question of behavior as police officers has been the subject of much controversy. Male officers have tended to oppose the use of female officers on patrol, arguing that women lack the size and strength to assert the necessary authority in confrontations with hostile citizens. Studies comparing the performance of male and female officers refute this allegation.

Bloch and Anderson compared eighty-six new female recruits with eighty-six new male recruits in Washington, D.C. They concluded that males and females

> performed patrol work in a generally similar manner. They responded to similar types of calls for police service while on patrol and encountered similar proportions of citizens who were dangerous, angry, upset, drunk or violent. Both men and women officers were observed to obtain similar results in handling angry or violent citizens. There were no reported incidents which cast serious doubt on the ability of women to perform patrol work satisfactorily.[60]

Slight differences between the men and women were found, but they were not significant. Female officers made slightly fewer arrests and issued fewer traffic citations. On the other hand, female officers were less likely to engage in conduct unbecoming an officer.

A study of women patrol officers in New York City reached similar conclusions. Sichel et al. compared forty-one male and forty-one female officers over a seven-month period in 1975–1976. They found that "the women's 'style' of patrol was almost indistinguishable from the men's." Table 11-6 analyzes techniques used by male and female officers to control citizens. They used the various verbal and non-

TABLE 11-6
FREQUENCY OF OFFICERS' CONTROL ATTEMPTS BY TECHNIQUE OF CONTROL

Technique of control	Frequency of technique of control (%) by sex of subject officer	
	Female	Male
Verbal techniques	78	76
Ordering	27	29
Requesting	19	20
Recommending	22	19
Reasoning	6	4
Verbal manipulating	3	2
Threatening	1	2
Nonverbal techniques	22	24
Official acts	7	9
Use of body without touch	3	4
Physical contact	11	10
Gentle	2	3
Rough	9	7
Display of weapon	1	1
Use of weapon	<1	<1
Total	100(N = 1094)	100(N = 1014)

Note: All observations of subject officer control attempts are counted and distributed in this table. Thus, a single control attempt will appear twice here if both the civilian and the police observer reported it. The table excludes 386 observations of control attempts performed jointly by a subject officer and his or her partner.
Source: Joyce L. Sichel, et al., *Women on Patrol: A Pilot Study of Police Performance in New York City* (Washington, D.C.: U.S. Department of Justice, 1978), p. 35.

verbal techniques at nearly identical rates. The New York study also found that female officers were "slightly less active" than male officers, but that "civilians rated the female officers more competent, pleasant and respectful."[61]

Assignment

Police officer attitudes are affected by the type of assignment. Patrol duty assignments vary considerably in terms of the volume of work, the nature of the work, and the degree of stress placed upon the officer. Evening shift (4:00 P.M. to midnight) is the most demanding of the three shifts. It involves a higher volume of work and the most difficult kinds of conflicts (domestic disturbances, crimes in progress, etc.). With respect to location, low-income precincts have a higher volume of stressful situations. Finally, officers are more likely to encounter citizen hostility in minority-group neighborhoods.

The President's Commission on Law Enforcement found that officers assigned to predominantly minority-group, low-income neighborhoods had lower job satisfaction than officers assigned to predominantly white neighborhoods. Officers in these precincts were more likely to say that there was "nothing good" about the job, and that they would not advise a young man to go into police work. Job satisfaction in these precincts was lower for both black and white officers.[62]

Changing Attitudes

Police officer attitudes change over time. Two factors influence these changes. First, as recruitment patterns change, the profile of American police officers change. Today there are more minority and female officers and more officers with college educations than there were fifteen years ago. Second, the social environment changes. The riots of the 1960s may have skewed the responses on attitude surveys taken at that time. The emergence of unions has eliminated some of the serious morale problems that existed in the 1960s.

Attitudes toward the Supreme Court provide an example of long-term change. When they first appeared, the *Mapp, Escobedo* and *Miranda* decisions aroused the anger of many if not most police officers. Stephen Wasby, however, found that officers gradually adjusted to these decisions: "a generational effect seemed to exist, as younger officers were learning to live with the new criminal procedure rules."[63]

The attitudes of black officers has also changed over time. Eva Buzawa argues that a "new" black officer appeared in the 1970s. This officer was more militant and more likely to initiate legal action to end racial discrimination than was the "old" black officer.[64]

STYLES OF POLICE WORK

Individual police officers carry out police work with different styles. A basic distinction exists between officers who are relatively aggressive and those who are relatively passive. Aggressive police work involves a high number of field interrogations, traffic citations, arrests, or other officer-initiated activities. The passive officer initiates little activity and responds only to calls radioed by the dispatcher.

Officers may be more aggressive for one of several reasons. The young officer who is ambitious for promotion or assignment to the detective bureau initiates activity in the hope of impressing the superior officers. Other officers may be aggressive simply because of temperament: they enjoy contact with people and the excitement of unpredictable encounters. Aggressive patrol behavior may also be stimulated by the management style of a supervisor. One sergeant may demand more activity of his or her officers than another sergeant. Some departments demand greater activity as a matter of departmentwide policy. This is accomplished through formal or informal quotas on traffic citations or field interrogations.[65]

Career Styles

James Leo Walsh identified three distinct career styles: The "street cops" were officers attracted to policing by the prospects of a secure work environment (good pay, good job security, etc.). The "action seekers" were attracted to policing by the potential for exciting work, particularly crime-fighting tasks. The "middle-class mobiles" were attracted by the professional status of policing and the opportunities for career advancement and upward social mobility. The street cops are likely to be much less aggressive than the other two, who would seek out activity either for the immediate excitement (action seekers) or for eventual reward (middle-class mobiles).[66]

Styles of policing are also subject to change over time. The officer who started out as a middle-class mobile may change into a street cop after several years when it becomes evident that promotion will not be possible. Maintaining an officer's commitment to the job and to high standards of performance is a critical problem for American police agencies. Because promotional opportunities are limited, many officers become resigned to low achievement. Performance then suffers, and in some cases the temptations of corruption become more attractive.

To deal with this problem experts have proposed different kinds of career development. One proposal calls for the creation of career specialization. A person could remain at the rank of police officer and yet specialize in a particular area (criminal investigation, juvenile work, etc.). The officer would be eligible for additional pay increases based on increasing mastery of the specialty and demonstrated meritorious performance.[67]

The Use of Power

William K. Muir began his study of the police by asking, What makes a good police officer? Muir's approach is unique because most studies have begun by asking why police officers are bad. The key to being a good police officer, Muir argues, is how that individual handles the exercise of coercive power. "Coercion is a means of controlling the conduct of others through threats to harm." Muir's analysis resembles Egon Bittner's in that he sees the threat of force as the principal element in the police role.[68]

The professional police officer, Muir concludes, is one who develops two virtues: passion and perspective. "Intellectually, he has to grasp the nature of human suffering. Morally, he has to resolve the contradiction of achieving just ends with coercive means." Officers who fail to achieve this balance fall into one of three categories. The "enforcers" have passion but no perspective. They act, often in anger, but they have little understanding of the nature of their acts. The "reciprocators" have perspective but no passion. They tend to be too objective, too detached from situations they encounter, and fail to act. Finally, the "avoiders" have neither passion nor perspective.

Muir's approach has the virtue of approaching police behavior from the standpoint of the inherent elements of the police role, namely the exercise of power. Most other studies begin by exploring different personality types (authoritarianism, etc.) or social characteristics (education, etc.).

The moral dilemmas inherent in the exercise of power raise what Carl Klockars calls the "Dirty Harry problem." Police officers often confront situations where they believe a legitimate end can only be achieved by an illegal means. An officer may feel certain that a person is engaged in criminal activity yet lack probable cause for an arrest. The illegal alternatives "range from falsifying probable cause for a stop, to manufacturing a false arrest to legitimate an illegal search, to simply searching without the fraudulent covering devices of either."[69] Perjury in court is also a way of illegally facilitating the conviction of a criminal defendant.

In some instances, the officer resorts to illegal action in the genuine belief that the end (arrest and conviction of a criminal) justifies the means. Police cynicism about the administration of criminal justice, especially the belief that the rules of criminal procedure benefit criminals, encourages the choice of this option. In these cases there is a clear moral dilemma. In other cases of illegal activity, however, there is no moral dilemma. Illegitimate ends do not justify illegal means. Such situations would include the arrest of a citizen for reasons of racial prejudice or simply personal dislike.

Predicting Police Performance

The demand for better police performance has stimulated research into the question of what factors might successfully predict good or bad performance on the job. Existing selection procedures are based on the assumption that certain characteristics automatically *dis*qualify an applicant. Written examinations are used in the belief that a certain minimal level of intelligence is necessary for adequate police performance. Psychological tests are used to screen out applicants with obvious psychological problems. Background investigations are used to identify persons whose past behavior (criminal conduct, difficulty in adjusting to jobs, etc.) suggests they might not make good police officers.

The proposal to raise minimum educational requirements for police recruits is based on the assumption that education is correlated with performance. The President's Crime Commission recommended that eventually all police officers be required to have a four-year college degree. It is assumed that the college-educated officer will be better prepared to handle the complexity of the job than the officer with only a high school education. Lawrence Sherman, however, argues that there is no conclusive evidence that higher education correlates with better police performance.

Cohen and Chaiken undertook the most systematic attempt to identify the background characteristics that would predict successful police performance. They studied 1608 New York City police officers who were among 2002 officers appointed in 1957. They correlated background characteristic variables with eighteen performance variables.

One of the major problems encountered in this and other studies is the fact that "no entirely satisfactory method has been developed to measure objectively the performance of policemen once appointed." Existing performance measures are self-fulfilling, they "tend to reflect the internal standards of police departments rather than the requirements of the community being served."[70] The lack of adequate performance measures is one of the greatest weaknesses of existing police personnel systems. Departments do not have adequate means of identifying and rewarding officers who perform well. Personnel systems are punishment oriented: officers are punished when they are caught doing something wrong.[71]

Cohen and Chaiken concluded that few of the background characteristics studied predicted successful police performance. The major exception was the recruit's training score, which was "one of the most powerful and consistent predictors of later police performance." This conclusion was true for white officers but not black officers. Indicators of the performance of black officers were complicated by a variety of factors.[72]

JOB STRESS

The problem of job stress in policing has recently begun to receive considerable attention. It is now recognized that police work is an extremely stressful occupation. William Kroes points out that job stress can seriously affect an officer's health, personality, family relations, and job performance.[73]

Much of the writing on the subject has been alarmist, using exaggerated estimates of suicides, divorces, and alcoholism among police officers. One article in *New York* magazine described police officers as "Time Bombs in Blue." A balanced understanding of the phenomenon of job stress begins with the recognition that stress is common to all occupations.

Stressors

Factors which produce job stress are called stressors. Many stressors that affect police officers are common to other occupations. The more important of these include excessive red tape, lack of participation in decision making, inadequate resources to accomplish one's job, job overload, and inequalities in pay or job status within the organization. Police work has its own unique stressors. The most important is the combination of long periods of inactivity and sudden, unpredictable danger. The boredom that results from prolonged periods of uneventful patrol takes its psychological toll. Yet at all times the officer is aware of the potential for sudden, unpredictable, and often malicious danger. Hostile relations with the public are another important stressor. The police role automatically includes conflict with many segments of the public. The police car accentuated the problem by removing the officer from the street and eliminating informal and often cordial contact with members of the public. The patrol car creates many health problems as well. Back trouble is the most common physical ailment among police officers. Finally, officers suffer the frustration of seeing many of their arrests result in dismissal in court.

Evidence of Stress

While there is much discussion of job stress in policing, the available evidence does not provide a reliable measure of the dimensions of the problem. Attention generally focuses on three problems: suicide, heart attack, and alcoholism. Reviewing the data on suicide, Arthur Niederhoffer concluded that it was too old and had too great an emphasis on New York City to provide a reliable index of the size of the problem. Heiman studied suicides in New York City from 1964 to 1973. The suicide rate among police officers was 17.2 per 100,000 compared with an overall rate for the city of 8.3 and a rate of 11 per 100,000 for males in the city. In short, the suicide rate appears to be high but not outrageously high.[74]

Turning to the problem of divorce, Niederhoffer found inconsistent evidence. Some studies claimed to find divorce rates as high as 30 percent of an entire police department. Other evidence put the rate much lower. Niederhoffer concluded that there was little support for the alarmist view of soaring divorce rates. The divorce rate among police officers appears to be higher than the national average, but not spectacularly higher.

Job Stress and the Family

A police officer's family life is affected by the stressful features of the job. The work schedule is an important stressor. Police officers, especially young officers, generally work irregular hours. Some departments determine shift assignments according to seniority. In these cases, a young officer will work the 4:00 P.M. to midnight or midnight to 8:00 A.M. shifts for many years. Other departments rotate shift assignments frequently. In these cases, an officer is continually adjusting his or her work, sleeping, and family life habits. Working irregular hours under either system disrupts relations with the officer's spouse, the children, and one's social life.

A second stressful feature of the job is the nature of the work itself. A police officer encounters many unpleasant things in the course of his or her job. The officer sees humanity, and in many cases the criminal justice system, at its worst, including many unsavory things within the police department. In addition, the danger of the job is a constant preoccupation. Many police officers prefer to not talk about these things at home. The result is often an isolation from family members that the others do not understand.

The folklore of policing includes the widespread belief that officers develop closer relations with their partners than with their own spouses. In part this is because the partner is someone who shares and understands the unpleasant aspects of the job.

Children

The discussion of job stress, suicide, divorce, and other problems shifts our attention away from the fact that most police officers are normal people who lead normal lives. Like other people, police officers maintain families and have aspirations for their children's success in life.

Niederhoffer surveyed police officers and police officers' wives (he apparently did not survey the husbands of female officers) about their aspirations for their children. Only 9 of 182 officers and 6 of 184 officers' wives indicated they wanted their son to choose law enforcemen as a career. Both officers and wives indicated a strong preference for law or medicine as a career for their son. These preferences suggest that officers and their wives are upwardly mobile. As we have seen, many officers choose to enter law enforcement because it was a step upward on the social scale. They maintain similar aspirations for their own children.[75]

THE RIGHTS OF POLICE OFFICERS

It is often forgotten that police officers have all the civil and constitutional rights as other citizens. This was not always the case. In the past the law held that all public employees, including police officers, gave up certain rights when they took public employmen This policy was based on the view that public employment was a privilege and the employee accepted it on the employer's terms. In the past twenty years this view has been challenged, and public employees now enjoy the rights of other citizens.

Police officers enjoy the First Amendment rights of freedom of speech, assembly, and religion. Officers may not be barred from employment or suffer discipline for political or religious activities. This right is not absolute, however, and departments may place restrictions on an officer's participation in partisan political activity, such as running for political office. Political or religious activity *on the job* is not permitted. The right of freedom of speech includes, to a limited extent, the right of an officer to criticize his or her own department. Generally, a department may discipline an officer if the public criticism harms the effectiveness of the department.

The private lives of police officers are also protected by the Constitution. An individual may not be barred from employment or disciplined because of marital status or sexual preference. Homosexuality, for example, is not a job-related disqualification. A few departments have even begun to actively recruit homosexuals. An officer's financial status is also protected, despite the fact that police departments traditionally disciplined officers for failure to pay private debts.

Officers also enjoy procedural due process protections on the job. They may not be fired or disciplined without adequate cause. Due process in personnel decisions is guaranteed in part by existing civil service regulations and, in some departments, by union contract. Florida and other states have enacted a "police officers' bill of rights" (see Chapter 12).

The American Civil Liberties Union recently published a short handbook entitled *The Rights of Police Officers,* summarizing the current state of the law.[76]

PERSONNEL TURNOVER

Police officers leave their jobs in one of three ways: retirement (or death), dismissal, and voluntary resignation. The rate at which officers voluntarily resign is extremely important. Because of the high cost of recruiting and training a new officer, a high rate of turnover can impose a serious burden on a department. Even more important is the question of *which* officers choose to resign. If a department is losing its worst officers, it would suggest that the management of the department is working well.

Unfortunately, little is known about personnel turnover in law enforcement. The National Manpower Survey estimated that turnover rates are much higher for small departments than for large departments. The national average for all sworn officers is 8 percent per year. Large departments (400 or more officers) have a turnover rate of only 4 percent per year, while deputy sheriffs have a turnover rate of 16 percent per year. Little research has been done regarding the reasons why officers choose to leave, however.[77]

REVIEW

1 What are the main reasons why individuals seek careers as law enforcement officers?

2 Discuss the reasons for and against requiring college educations for all police recruits.

3 Approximately what percentage of all police officers are minorities? What percentage are women?

4 Explain what provisions of the 1964 Civil Rights Act apply to police recruitment.

5 Define the concept of affirmative action and explain how it is applied in practice.

6 Describe the basic career paths open to a police officer.

7 What is the "reality shock" experienced by police officers?

8 Discuss the main elements of the police subculture.

9 Are there any major differences between the performance of male and female police officers?

10 Describe the different styles of work adopted by police officers.

REFERENCES

1 David Bayley and Harold Mendelsohn, *Minorities and the Police* (New York: Free Press, 1969), p. 32.

2 U.S., Department of Justice, *The National Manpower Survey of the Criminal Justice*

System, vol. 2, *Law Enforcement* (Washington, D.C.: U.S. Government Printing Office, 1978), p. 13.

3 Nicholas Alex, *Black in Blue* (Englewood Cliffs, N.J.: Prentice-Hall, 1969), pp. 133–170.

4 Susan Ehrlich Martin, *Breaking and Entering: Policewomen on Patrol* (Berkeley: University of California, 1980).

5 William A. Westley, *Violence and the Police* (Cambridge: MIT Press, 1970), p. 205; Bayley and Mendelsohn, *Minorities and the Police,* p. 6.

6 Bayley and Mendelsohn, *Minorities and the Police,* p. 6.

7 James Q. Wilson, "Generational and Ethnic Differences among Career Police Officers," *American Journal of Sociology* 69 (March 1964): 522–528.

8 Bayley and Mendelsohn, *Minorities and the Police,* p. 15.

9 John H. McNamara, "Uncertainties in Police Work: The Relevance of Police Recruits' Backgrounds and Training," in *The Police: Six Sociological Essays,* ed. David J. Bordua, (New York: John Wiley, 1967), pp. 207–215.

10 Nicholas Alex, *New York Cops Talk Back* (New York: John Wiley, 1976), p. 9.

11 Virginia B. Ermer, "Recruitment of Female Police Officers in New York City," *Journal of Criminal Justice* 6 (Fall 1978): 233–246.

12 U.S., Department of Justice, *National Manpower Survey,* p. 17.

13 President's Commission on Law Enforcement and Administration of Justice, *The Challenge of Crime in a Free Society* (New York: Avon Books, 1968), p. 279; U.S., National Advisory Commission on Criminal Justice Standards and Goals, *Police* (Washington, D.C.: U.S. Government Printing Office, 1973), p. 369.

14 National Advisory Commission, *Police,* p. 372.

15 Lawrence W. Sherman, et al., *The Quality of Police Education* (San Francisco: Jossey-Bass, 1978).

16 U.S., Department of Justice, *National Manpower Survey,* p. 3.

17 David Farmer, "The Future of Local Law Enforcement: The Federal Role," in *Crime and Justice in America: Critical Issues for the Future,* eds. John T. O'Brien and Marvin Marcus (New York: Pergamon Press, 1979), p. 93.

18 Bernard Cohen and Jan M. Chaiken, *Police Background Characteristics and Performance* (Lexington: Lexington Books, 1973), p. 37.

19 Terry Eisenberg, et al., *Police Personnel Practices in State and Local Governments* (Washington, D.C.: Police Foundation, 1973), p. 22.

20 Ibid., p. 20.

21 Ibid., pp. 18–19.

22 Ibid., p. 23.

23 U.S., Department of Justice, *Civil Service Systems: Their Impact on Police Administration* (Washington, D.C.: U.S. Government Printing Office, 1979).

24 U.S., Equal Employment Opportunity Commission, *Affirmative Action and Equal Employment: A Guidebook for Employers,* vol. 1 (Washington, D.C.: U.S. Government Printing Office, 1974).

25 Published in 28 *Code of Federal Regulations* 42.306.

26 Samuel Walker, *A Critical History of Police Reform* (Lexington: Lexington Books, 1977), pp. 84–94.

27 President's Commission on Law Enforcement and Administration of Justice, *Task Force Report: The Police* (Washington, D.C.: U.S. Government Printing Office, 1967), p. 163.

28 U.S. Equal Employment Opportunity Commission, *Affirmative Action and Equal Employment.*

29 Utah Advisory Committee to the U.S. Civil Rights Commission, *Affirmative Action in Salt Lake's Criminal Justice Agencies* (Washington, D.C.: Government Printing Office, 1978), p. 6.

30 *Criminal Justice Newsletter,* December 8, 1980, p. 6.

31 James B. Jacobs and Jay Cohen, "The Impact of Racial Integration on the Police," *Journal of Police Science and Administration* 6, no. 2 (1978): 182.

32 U.S., Equal Employment Opportunity Commission, *Affirmative Action and Equal Employment,* vol. 2 (Washington, D.C.: U.S. Government Printing Office, 1974), p. D2.

33 Ibid., D15–D25.

34 Lawrence W. Sherman, "Enforcement Workshop: Minority Quotas for Promotions," *Criminal Law Bulletin* 15 (January–February, 1979): 79–84.

35 McNamara, "Uncertainties in Police Work," p. 186.

36 President's Commission, *The Challenge of Crime in A Free Society,* pp. 283–284.

37 William Hewitt, *New Directions in Police Personnel Administration* (Lexington: Lexington Books, 1975).

38 Westley, *Violence and the Police,* pp. 153–159; Richard N. Harris, *Police Academy: An Inside View* (New York: John Wiley, 1973); John Van Maanen, "Observations on the Making of Policemen," *Human Organization* 32 (1973): 407–418.

39 Van Maanen, "Observations on the Making of Policemen."

40 Westley, *Violence and the Police,* pp. 159–160.

41 McNamara, "Uncertainties in Police Work," pp. 221–222; Eric D. Poole and Robert M. Regoli, "Changes in the Professional Commitment of Police Recruits: An Exploratory Case Study," *Journal of Criminal Justice* (Fall 1979): 243–247.

42 Westley, *Violence and the Police,* p. 11.

43 Ibid., pp. 49, 107.

44 Ibid., pp. 109–152.

45 Jerome Skolnick, *Justice without Trial* (New York: John Wiley, 1966), pp. 42–70.

46 Ibid., p. 67.

47 Arthur Niederhoffer, *Behind the Shield* (Garden City: Anchor Books, 1969), pp. 95–108.

48 Ibid., pp. 109–160.

49 Joel Lefkowitz, "Psychological Attributes of Policemen: A Review of Research and Opinion," *Journal of Social Issues* 31, no. 1 (1975): 3–26.

50 Bayley and Mendelsohn, *Minorities and the Police,* pp. 15–18.

51 McNamara, "Uncertainties in Police Work," p. 195.

52 Robert M. Regoli, "An Empirical Assessment of Niederhoffer's Police Cynicism Scale," *Journal of Criminal Justice* 4 (Fall 1976): 237.

53 Jonathan Rubinstein, *City Police* (New York: Ballantine Books, 1973), p. 200.

54 Bayley and Mendelsohn, *Minorities and the Police,* p. 144.

55 Albert Reiss, *The Police and the Public* (New Haven: Yale University Press, 1971), p. 147.

56 Alex, *Black in Blue,* p. 210.

57 Peter H. Rossi, et al., *The Roots of Urban Discontent: Public Policy, Municipal Institutions, and the Ghetto* (New York: John Wiley, 1974).

58 Donald J. Black, *The Manners and Customs of the Police* (New York: Academic Press, 1980), pp. 107–108.

59 James J. Fyfe, "Who Shoots? A Look at Officer Race and Police Shooting," *Journal of Police Science and Administration* 9 (December, 1981):367–382.

60 Peter B. Bloch and Deborah Anderson, *Policewomen on Patrol: Final Report* (Washington, D.C.: Police Foundation, 1974), p. 2.

61 Joyce L. Sichel, *Women on Patrol: A Pilot Study of Police Performance in New York City* (Washington, D.C.: Department of Justice, 1978).

62 President's Commission on Law Enforcement and Administration of Justice, *Field Surveys* III, *Studies in Crime and Law Enforcement in Major Metropolitan Areas,* vol. 2, Section 2, "Career Orientations, Job Satisfaction, and the Assessment of Law Enforcement Problems by Police Officers."

63 Stephen Wasby, *Small Town Police and the Supreme Court: Hearing the Word* (Lexington: Lexington Books, 1976). p. 218.

64 Eva S. Buzawa, "The Role of Race in Predicting Job Attitudes of Patrol Officers," *Journal of Criminal Justice* 9, no. 1 (1981):65–66.

65 James Q. Wilson, *Varieties of Police Behavior* (New York: Atheneum, 1973), pp. 95–99.

66 James Leo Walsh, "Career Styles and Police Behavior," in *Police and Society,* ed. David Bayley (Beverly Hills: Sage Publications, 1977), pp. 149–167.

67 National Advisory Commission, *Police,* pp. 362–366.

68 William K. Muir, *Streetcorner Politicians* (Chicago: University of Chicago Press, 1977), p. 37.

69 Carl B. Klockars, "The Dirty Harry Problem," *Annals* 452 (November 1980):33–47.

70 Cohen and Chaiken, *Police Background Characteristics and Performance,* p. 4.

71 McNamara, "Uncertainties in Police Work," pp. 177–178.

72 Cohen and Chaiken, *Police Background Characteristics and Performance,* pp. 87, 90–91.

73 William H. Kroes, *Society's Victim, The Policeman: An Analysis of Job Stress in Policing* (Springfield: Charles C. Thomas, 1976); Clinton W. Terry, "Police Stress: The Empirical Evidence," *Journal of Police Science and Administration* 9 (March 1981):61–75.

74 Arthur Niederhoffer, *The Police Family* (Lexington: Lexington Books, 1978), p. 53.

75 Ibid., p. 105.

76 Gilda Brancato and Eliot E. Polebaum, *The Rights of Police Officers* (New York: Avon Books, 1981).

77 *National Manpower Survey,* 2, p. 2.

CHAPTER **12**

POLICE UNIONS

THE HIDDEN REVOLUTION

Nearly three-fourths of all American police officers are members of unions. The unions are powerful economic and political institutions; not only do they represent the interests of their members with regard to salaries and fringe benefits but they have a strong voice in many areas of law enforcement policy. Also, police unions are important factors in local politics, supporting or opposing candidates for office and other political issues.[1]

Police unions represent the hidden revolution in American police administration. The emergence of police unions may be the most significant development in policing in the last fifteen years. Previously, police chiefs had almost unlimited power in managing their departments. Many chiefs were virtual dictators. Today, however, chiefs find their power severely limited by union contracts. In many cases, decisions can only be made through collective-bargaining negotiations. In other cases, the chief finds it necessary to informally contact the union and gain its approval before making a decision. This transfer of power, from the chief to the union, has been unnoticed by many police management experts.

The impact of police unions has been felt in several different areas.[2]

1 *Salaries and fringe benefits.* Unions are largely responsible for the significant improvements in police salaries and fringe benefits since the mid-1960s.

2 *Personnel management.* The unions now have a significant voice in crucial personnel management decisions. Union contracts usually specify formal grievance procedures which protect individual officers from arbitrary punishment. Some contracts spell out promotion criteria.

3 *Law enforcement policy.* Unions now exercise a strong voice in shaping general law enforcement policies. The New York City police union, for example, fought the development of a fourth shift designed to provide extra personnel during busy hours.

4 *Police-community relations.* Police unions are especially active in the area of police-community relations. They have successfully defeated citizen review board proposals in several cities. They have also brought suit against affirmative action programs designed to recruit more minority group officers.

5 *Professionalization.* The impact of police unions on the professionalization of the police is a matter of great controversy. In 1958 the IACP labelled unions the "death knell of professionalization."[3] More recently, experts have found that unions have opposed many reforms traditionally identified with professionalism (for example, educational incentive pay). On the other hand, the National Symposium on Police Labor Relations in 1974 declared that unions were "a positive force for effective labor relations, which is a key to good police administration."[4]

The purpose of this chapter is to examine the nature of American police unionism. It will examine what unions are, how and why they are formed, how the collective-bargaining process works, and what issues are covered in collective bargaining.

Definition of Terms

What is a police union? The term is often used interchangeably with the term employee organization. Yet, there are fundamental differences between unions and other kinds of employee organizations.[5]

The term *employee organization* refers to any group which police officers join as police officers. This includes social and fraternal groups whose main activities may be recreation or community service. Employee organizations are voluntary associations in the sense that individuals may choose to join or not join.

A *police union* is a particular kind of employee organization. Unions are organizations which have a legally binding contract or other formal agreement with the employer. The legal status of unions is specified by state law or local ordinance. Unlike other employee organizations, the employer is not free to ignore the union; the law requires collective-bargaining negotiations.

The relationship of the individual officer to the union varies according to local law. A *union shop* exists where all employees are required to join the union. An *agency shop* exists where employees who do not join the union are required to contribute the equivalent of union dues. In so-called right-to-work states an *open shop* exists where employees are not required either to join the union or to contribute to it.[6]

Collective bargaining is the process by which unions negotiate with their employers. The U.S. Department of Labor defines collective bargaining as "The method of determining conditions of employment through bilateral negotiations between representatives of the employer and employee organizations. An agreement is set forth in a mutually binding *contract.*"[7] The actual mechanics of collective bargaining are defined by statute and vary from state to state. Contacts between the union and the employer are sometimes described by other terms such as meet-and-discuss or meet-and-confer sessions. The final agreement may be referred to as a contract, an agreement, or a memorandum of understanding. Exhibit 12.1 contains the first paragraph of the memorandum of understanding between the City of Oakland, California, and the Oakland police union.

EXHIBIT 12.1

MEMORANDUM OF UNDERSTANDING, CITY OF OAKLAND, CALIFORNIA, AND OAKLAND POLICE OFFICERS ASSOCIATION, 1976

We, the undersigned, duly appointed representatives of the City of Oakland and of the Oakland Police Officers Association, a recognized employee organization, hereinafter referred to as "City" and "Association," having met and conferred in good faith in accordance with the Meyers-Milias-Brown Act, and having agreed on certain recommendations to be submitted to the City Council of the City of Oakland, do hereby jointly prepare and execute on the 15th day of July , 1976, the following written Memorandum of Understanding. It is understood that the provisions herein set forth supersede previous Memoranda of Understanding between the City and Association.

THE ORIGINS OF POLICE UNIONISM

American police officers attempted to organize police unions on three different occasions (see Chapter 1). The first two efforts, 1917–1919 and 1943–1946, were defeated by the combined opposition of police chiefs, elected officials, the courts, and public opinion. The third attempt, beginning in the 1960s, was successful and established police unionism on a permanent basis.[8]

Why did police officers seek to organize unions? The first two efforts were prompted primarily by economic factors. Both occurred during wartime when inflation caused a serious decline in the purchasing power of police salaries. The successful effort in the 1960s was prompted by a more complex mixture of economic, social, and political factors. These factors continue to shape the nature of American police unionism. The most important include:[9]

1 *Lagging salaries and benefits.* By the mid-1960s salaries and benefits earned by police officers had fallen behind those in other professional or semiprofessional occupations. Police work was not an attractive career, and departments had difficulty attracting qualified recruits. The President's Commission on Law Enforcement reported in 1967 that 65 percent of the police departments were under their authorized strength. In 1960 police officers had a median annual salary of $5321, while professional and technical employees enjoyed a median salary of $7124. Skilled workers and supervisors had a median salary of $5699. Additionally, police officers enjoyed limited fringe benefits and few opportunities for career advancement.[10]

2 *Poor police management.* Rank-and-file officers were angry not only about their salaries but also about management practices in most police departments. Problems existed in both professional and unprofessional departments. In professional departments, the chief often ruled with an iron hand, and police officers had little protection against arbitrary discipline. In unprofessional departments, personnel decisions involving transfer or promotion were often based on favoritism, reflecting the power of different cliques.

3 *Social and political alienation.* The social and political alienation of police officers was perhaps the most important factor behind police unionism. Officers were angry about several different developments. First, they were upset with Supreme Court decisions that favored criminal suspects. They were also angry about allegations of police brutality, and other criticisms that seemed to make them the scapegoats for the nation's civil rights problem. In several important cities, unions organized to fight proposals designed to improve police-community relations. Stephen Halpern concluded that "opposition to civilian review boards has been one of the major rallying points in organizing policemen."[11] Finally, the police were angry over what they perceived as a general lack of support by the public.

4 *A new generation of police officers.* The police union movement was lead by a new generation of police officers. They were younger and less willing to accept the traditional arguments that unions were a threat to professionalism. This new generation saw other groups using militant tactics to achieve their goals, and they simply borrowed the same style and tactics.

5 *The law-and-order mood.* Although police officers perceived a lack of public support, in fact public opinion was highly supportive of the police. Political protests and demonstrations, together with the riots, created a law-and-order mood among a majority of the public. This mood created an opportunity for police unionism to succeed. According to the National Symposium on Police Labor Relations, "Police unions have achieved relatively easy gains because of broad public concern about safety on the streets and the need to back law enforcement."[12]

6 *A new legal climate.* By the late 1960s public employee unionism had greater legal support. The courts were willing to accept the right of public employees to form their own unions. A 1965 Public Employees Law in Michigan, for example, helped the Detroit police union establish itself. This situation contrasted sharply with the 1940s when unfavorable court decisions were one of the major causes of the defeat of police unionism.[13]

The Process of Unionization

Police unions were formed in an atmosphere of conflict and controversy. Police officers themelves were angry, and the struggle to form unions often embittered public officials and other groups in the community. In particular, the police union movement was created by and was a contributor to the police-community relations crisis. In Boston, New York City, Cleveland, and elsewhere, unionism was stimulated by police officer opposition to liberal mayors who proposed police-community relations programs.

Case Study: Detroit   The Detroit Police Officers Association (DPOA) evolved out of an existing social club. A 1965 law gave Michigan public employees the right to form unions and bargain collectively. In 1965 patrol officers in Detroit could earn a maximum salary of $7335 per year. After receiving a $1000 raise in 1966 the officers demanded another substantial raise in 1967. City officials strongly opposed this demand.[14]

Angry and alienated, Detroit police officers responded with a series of job actions. First, they began a ticket-writing slowdown. The number of traffic tickets issued during May and June dropped by 71 percent. The city not only refused to negotiate with the police officers but retaliated against the leaders of the slowdown. Many patrol officers were transferred to new precincts, and some traffic unit officers were reassigned to foot patrol. Officers then responded with a blue-flu epidemic, as large numbers of officers called in sick. In one precinct, only two officers reported for duty. The city went to court and obtained an injunction halting the blue flu.

The blue flu forced the city to negotiate with the union. City officials recognized the DPOA, agreed to rescind all punitive transfers and suspensions arising from the slowdown, and met most of the officers' salary demands. By 1974 maximum salaries for patrol officers had risen to $15,000 a year.

Case Study: Boston   The Boston Police Patrolmen's Association (BPPA) was founded in 1965 by officers who were angry over both low pay and criticism of the police by the black community. Younger officers were also alienated by the favoritism that dominated personnel decisions in the department. It was run by an establishment of senior officers who gave promotions and favored assignments to their friends.[15]

Dick MacEachern, president of the BPPA, was transferred four times in one year—an attempt to punish him for his union activity. He also claimed that his supervisors watched him constantly, looking for possible violations of departmental regulations. The BPPA was also opposed by a rival organization, the Collective Bargaining Federation (CBF), dominated by senior officers. Finally, in September 1967 the BPPA won an election to be recognized as the bargaining agent for police officers in Boston.

The BPPA was very active and quite successful in local politics. In 1966 it successfully lobbied for legislation granting collective-bargaining rights to the police. Between 1968 and 1970 it defeated several proposals by Mayor Kevin White designed to improve police-community relations. These included a civilian review board, a requirement that officers have name tags sown on to their uniforms (to prevent them from being removed), and that civil service requirements be modified to facilitate the recruitment of minority-group applicants. The BPPA also opposed many of Commissioner Robert DiGrazia's proposals to reorganize the department. By the 1970s, the BPPA was one of the most militant and aggressive police unions in the country. In 1980 it succeeded in forcing a halt to another plan to reorganize the department.

CONTEMPORARY POLICE UNIONISM

The Extent of Union Membership

The majority of sworn police officers in the United States today belong to or are represented by unions. An October 1975 survey by the U.S. Department of Labor estimated that 54 percent of all officers employed by state and local governments were members of unions. A different survey put the figure at 73 percent.[16]

The police are not the most heavily unionized group of public employees; firefighters (72.4 percent) and public school teachers (68.8 percent) are more unionized. Public welfare workers, by contrast, have a low rate (39 percent) of union membership. The figure for all full-time employees in state and local government is 49.9 percent (see Table 12-1).

Membership in unions is not evenly distributed among police departments; the big-city departments are the most heavily unionized, and the small departments the least unionized. According to the International City Management Association, 82 percent of the police in cities with populations between 250,000 and 500,000 people are unionized. In cities with populations between 10,000 and 25,000 people, only 37 percent of the police are unionized. Union membership is extremely high in some states (New York, 84.2 percent, California 72.4 percent) and extremely low in others (Mississippi, 5.2 percent, Arkansas, 10.6 percent). These figures parallel the extent of union membership in the private sector. Police unionism is strongly influenced by the political environment, including the degree of unionism in the community.

TABLE 12-1

PERCENT OF FULL-TIME EMPLOYEES ORGANIZED BY FUNCTION AND LEVEL OF GOVERNMENT

Function	State and local governments	State governments	Local governments
Total	49.9	39.6	53.9
Education	58.0	28.6	64.7
Teachers	68.6	33.4	72.5
Other	37.2	26.2	43.3
Highways	46.3	59.0	34.4
Public welfare	39.0	37.5	40.2
Hospitals	42.1	50.2	33.1
Police protection	54.0	47.4	55.0
Local fire protection	72.4	—	72.4
Sanitation other than sewerage	48.1	—	48.1
All other functions	36.9	37.5	36.6

Source: U.S. Department of Labor, *Labor-Management Relations in State and Local Governments: 1975,* (Washington, D.C.: U.S. Government Printing Office, 1977), p. 1.

The Fragmentation of Police Unionism

Police unionism is highly fragmented. There is no single national police union. This contrasts sharply with the private sector, where employees in one industry usually belong to one national union (the United Auto Workers, the United Steel Workers, etc.). Most police unions are local independent organizations, or members of national federations that exert little control over their affiliated chapters.[17]

As a consequence of this fragmentation, there is no single spokesperson for rank-and-file police officers, nor a common set of political objectives. Police union political strength is greatest at the local rather than the national level.

The fragmentation of police unionism is a product of what economists call the "market" for police work. Wages in private industry are influenced by competition at the national level. Therefore, it is in the interests of employees to organize all employees in that industry. Police salaries, on the other hand, are determined in a local market. Salaries in one department do not directly influence salaries in another. Economically, there is little incentive to organize a single union. Police officers have been reluctant to pay dues to a national organization for what appears to be minimal return.

National Federations

A majority of local police unions are affiliated with national federations. The national leadership, however, exercises little direct control over the locals. Many local unions, moreover, belong to no federation at all. Competition between the national federations has been bitter, as each group seeks more local unions as affiliates.

The major national federations include:

1 *The Fraternal Order of Police (FOP)*. First organized in Pittsburg in 1915, the FOP is the oldest and largest national organization of police officers. The FOP survived the disaster of the 1919 Boston police strike and continued as a social and fraternal organization. By the late 1970s it had 150,000 members in 1000 local lodges.

Membership in the FOP is open to all sworn police officers. Civilians are eligible for associate-membership status. Officers join as individuals, while local groups are chartered as lodges. FOP membership is strongest in Pennsylvania, Ohio, Illinois, Indiana, and Florida.

Originally, the FOP opposed unionism and collective bargaining. In response to the changing attitudes of its members, it reversed its position in the late 1960s and now endorses unionism. Some but not all FOP lodges are unions with collective-bargaining contracts.

2 *The International Conference of Police Associations (ICPA)*. For many years the chief rival of the FOP was the International Conference of Police Associations (not to be confused with the IACP). Founded in 1953, by the late 1970s it represented over 200,000 police officers in 175 local groups. Like the FOP, the ICPA originally opposed unionism but changed its position in response to the changing attitudes of police officers.

In 1978 the ICPA split over the question of affiliation with the AFL-CIO. Ed Kiernan, president of the ICPA, cast the deciding vote in favor of affiliation. The future of the ICPA remains in doubt. Kiernan and his supporters reorganized as:

3 *The International Union of Police Associations (IUPA)*. The IUPA was founded in 1979 as an affiliate of the AFL-CIO. Connection with the principal labor federation in the country was intended to give the IUPA greater political and organizational support. Estimates place the IUPA membership at between 30,000 and 50,000, representing between 110 and 150 locals.[18]

4 *The American Federation of State, County and Municipal Employees (AFSCME)*. As its name suggests, AFSCME represents employees of state, county, and city goverments engaged in a variety of occupations. Only an estimated 9000 of its members are police officers. Police membership is strongest in Connecticut, Maryland, and Michigan. In some cities (Baltimore, for example), the police officers belong to a separate local; in other cities they belong to a mixed local with other employees.

5 *International Brotherhood of Teamsters*. The Teamsters are the largest and most controversial union in the country. Although primarily truck drivers, the membership now includes workers in many other occupations. No precise figures are available, but an estimated 20,000 police officers are members of the Teamsters. Most of these are police officers in small departments in the Midwest.[19]

6 *International Brotherhood of Police Officers (IBPO)*. Established in 1964, the IBPO was one of the first attempts to form a single national union modeled after other unions. Today it claims 38,000 members in 280 locals. Most of these locals are small police departments. The IBPO is strongest in New England.

7 *The National Union of Police Officers (NUPO)*. The NUPO was founded in

1969 and initially claimed a membership of 10,000. Today it is estimated that its membership has fallen to 3000 and its future is uncertain.

A National Police Union? The issue of whether or not to form a national union of police officers is one of the most controversial questions in police unionism. Critics of police unions argue that a national police union would have too much power and create the possibility of a police state. Related to this issue is the question of whether or not police unions should affiliate with the AFL-CIO. Opponents of affiliation argue that it would compromise the independence of the police, particularly during labor disputes. The police need to be completely impartial in any conflict in order to enforce the law fairly. In the case of a labor dispute there would be a tendency to be loyal to the union side.

Supporters of a single police union argue that it would provide many benefits. Size means strength, and a single union would be one of the largest unions in the country. Size allows a union to support a full-time staff that can provide direct benefit. It can provide local unions with assistance in legal problems or negotiating tactics. Large size would also greatly increase the political power of police officers at the national level.[20]

Several attempts have been made to form a single national union of police officers. The IBPO and the NUPO have not succeeded. It is still too early to predict the success of the IUPA.

COLLECTIVE BARGAINING

Police represent the interests of their members primarily through collective bargaining. *Collective bargaining* is defined as "the method of determining conditions of employment through bilateral negotiations." The National Labor Relations Act of 1935 (also known as the Wagner Act) established collective bargaining as the basic method for settling labor-management problems in this country.

The *basic principles* of collective bargaining are that (1) employees have a right to form organizations of their own choosing; (2) employers must recognize the existence of such organizations; and (3) employees have a right, through negotiations, to participate in determining the conditions of their employment.

Several *assumptions* underlie these principles. First, it is assumed that conflict between employers and employees is, to a certain extent, inevitable. The interests of society as a whole are best served by creating a mechanism for resolving these conflicts peacefully. Second, collective bargaining is viewed as promoting democracy. Unions allow individual employees to have a voice in matters involving their employment and provide their members with effective political representation in the community. Finally, it is assumed that the individual employee has little if any power with respect to the employer and cannot negotiate terms of employment on an equal basis. Collective bargaining provides a more equal power relationship.[21]

Public-Sector Collective Bargaining

Economists divide the economy into the private sector and the public sector. The private sector exists where the employer is a private individual or corporation; the public sector involves government agencies as employers. The police are part of the public sector.

Collective bargaining in the public sector is different from the private sector in important respects. The 1935 National Labor Relations Act established collective bargaining for most of the private sector, but with several exemptions. It exempted agricultural workers, employees of certain small businesses, and public employees. As a result, public employees are covered by different legislation, and public sector unions operate in a very different legal context.[22]

State labor laws vary considerably. Fourteen states have no laws at all governing public-employee unions. Ohio has no law, but unions are covered by municipal ordinances in some cities. Of the thirty-six states that do have laws, twenty-nine specifically refer to police. The Michigan law is extremely comprehensive and is closely modeled after the federal National Labor Relations Act.

Labor laws generally address three key issues: (1) the right of public employees to form unions; (2) strikes; (3) procedures to resolve deadlocked negotiations.

The right of public employees to form unions was generally not recognized until the late 1950s and early 1960s. Legal doctrine maintained that a job as a public employee was more a privilege than a right. The individual took the job on the terms offered. The law now recognizes the right of public employees to form unions. State laws generally affirm this right and, more important, require employers to negotiate with unions.

In most states, strikes by public employees are forbidden by law. Some state laws single out the police as not having the right to strike. This approach rests on the assumption that the police (and other public employees) provide a necessary and critical service, without which the public health and safety would be endangered. Attempts to outlaw strikes have not been successful, however. New York has a very punitive law banning public employee strikes, but there have been repeated strikes anyway. Only two states, Montana and Vermont, permit police to strike under certain circumstances.

Procedures to resolve deadlocked negotiations are often provided by law as an alternative to strikes. A common approach is compulsory binding arbitration. When the two sides cannot reach an agreement the dispute is submitted to a neutral third party, who determines a fair settlement. This settlement is binding on both sides.

Labor laws not only vary but are continually changing. It is necessary to check the statutes of a particular state to determine the current legal status of police unions. The Bureau of National Affairs publishes the *Government Employee Relations Report*, which provides information on recent developments.[23]

The Scope of Collective Bargaining

What does collective bargaining cover? What issues may and may not be negotiated? Who is covered by collective bargaining? These questions involve the *scope* of collective bargaining.[24]

The 1935 National Labor Relations Act defined the scope of collective bargaining as "wages, hours, and other terms and conditions of employment." With some variation, state labor laws contain similar language. The phrase is extremely ambiguous, however. It is not always clear what "other terms and conditions of employment" refers to. With respect to the police, for example, does it include such issues as standards for promotion or two-officer patrol cars?

The scope of collective bargaining involves three distinct categories. First, there are subjects which *must* be settled by collective bargaining. These include salaries, fringe benefits, and number of hours per week. Second, there are subjects which *may* be negotiated. The union and the employer may negotiate a grievance procedure but are not required to. Third, there are subjects which *may not* be negotiated. The union and the employer may not agree to something which is illegal. They may not, for example, agree to some practice that clearly discriminates against women or minorities.

Collective Bargaining and Civil Service Many personnel procedures are governed by civil service laws and regulations. About half of all existing police union contracts preserve the authority of civil service laws and regulations. The other half involve some mixture of the authority of union contracts and civil service.[25]

Key Issues in Collective Bargaining[26]

Union Recognition The first issue in collective bargaining is official recognition of the union by the employer. The bitterest police strikes in the 1960s were the result of the employer's refusal to recognize and negotiate with the union. Today the issue is largely settled, and unions are generally accepted as a fact of life. The National Symposium of Police Labor Relations recommended that "the right to recognition should no longer be an issue in police labor relations. . . . Employees have a right to form and be represented by responsible labor organizations of their choice."[27]

Unit Determination Determining the bargaining unit is the second key issue. Generally, labor law rests on the principle of "commonality of interest." A union should represent all employees whose jobs are essentially the same or who have the same interests.

This concept has been implemented differently in different cities. In Pittsburg the union represents all officers up to the rank of captain. In Detroit and Boston the union represents only employees at the rank of police officer. In Boston a separate union, the Superior Officers Federation (SOF) represents sergeants, lieutenants, and captains. Civilian employees are often represented by a separate union of their own. In other words, officials in some cities must deal with three or four separate unions representing employees of the police department.

Management Rights Both the union and the employer seek to negotiate a contract that gives it the greatest amount of control over decision making. The goal of management, according to the Police Executive Research Forum, is to obtain "contract language that allows maximum discretion and flexibility in running the department."[28]

The power that management retains is usually spelled out in a management rights clause. These clauses may be characterized as strong or weak. A strong clause gives management a great deal of control. A weak clause gives the union a larger voice in management affairs. Exhibit 12.2 contains excerpts from the management rights section of the 1973 contract between the City of Detroit and the Detroit Police Officers' Association.

EXHIBIT 12.2

**MANAGEMENT RIGHTS AND
RESPONSIBILITIES, SECTION IX**

A.   The union recognizes the prerogatives of the department to operate and manage its affairs in all respects in accordance with its responsibilities and powers of authority. . . .

D.   The department reserves the right to discipline and discharge for just cause. The department reserves the right to lay off personel for lack of work or funds; or for the occurrence of conditions beyond the control of the department; or when such continuation of work would be wasteful and unproductive. The department shall have the right to determine reasonable schedules of work and to establish the methods and processes by which such work is performed

E.   No policies or procedures covered in this agreement shall be construed as delegating to others or as reducing or abridging any of the following authority conferred on city officials: . . .

4 The responsibility of department heads governed by charter provisions, ordinances, and departmental rules and as limited by the provisions of this agreement
   (a) To recruit, assign, transfer, or promote employees to positions within the department;
   (b) To suspend, demote, discharge, or take other disciplinary action against employees for just cause;
   (c) To relieve employees from duties because of lack of work, lack of funds, or disciplinary reasons;
   (d) To determine methods, means, and employees necessary for departmental operations;
   (e) To control the departmental budget; and
   (f) To take whatever actions are necessary in emergencies in order to assure the proper functioning of the department.

Source: Contract between the City of Detroit
and Detroit Police Officers Association, 1973.

Union Responsibilities   Management rights clauses are usually balanced by a clause specifying the union's responsibilities. Basically, the union agrees to honor the contract, cooperate in administering it, and refrain from striking. Exhibit 12.3 contains excerpts from the union responsibilities clause of the Detroit contract.

EXHIBIT 12.3

UNION RESPONSIBILITIES, SECTION VIII

A.   Recognizing the crucial role of law enforcement in the preservation of the public health, safety, and welfare of a free society, the union agrees that it will take all reasonable steps to cause the employees covered by this agreement, individually and collectively, to perform all police duties, rendering loyal and efficient service to the very best of their abilities.

B.   The union, therefore, agrees that there shall be no interruption of these services for any cause whatsoever by the employees it represents; nor shall there be any concerted failure by them to report for duty; nor shall they absent themselves from their work or abstain, in whole or in part, from the full, faithful, and proper performance of all the duties of their employment.

C.   The union further agrees that it shall not encourage any strikes, sit-downs, stay-ins, slow-downs, stoppages of work, malingering, or any acts that interfere in any manner or to any degree with the continuity of the police services.

Source: Contract Between City of Detroit and Detroit Police Officers Association, 1973.

Salaries and Benefits   The basic bread-and-butter issues of union negotiations involve salaries and fringe benefits. The cost to the employer and actual benefit to the employee of fringe benefits is often hidden by complex procedures. Today, fringe benefits often equal as much as 30 percent of basic salaries. Exhibit 12.4 indicates a brief checklist of the various items related to salaries and benefits.[29]

EXHIBIT 12.4

**ECONOMIC ISSUES SUBJECT TO
COLLECTIVE BARGAINING**

- base rates of pay and cost of living provisions;
- shift differential pay;
- longevity pay;

- overtime pay;
- call-in or call-back pay;
- pay for work performed out of job classification;
- paid meal periods;
- court time pay;
- uniform replacement and cleaning allowances;
- allowances for equipment and hardware;
- creation of new or increased coverage of existing insurance programs;
- education bonus pay and cost reimbursement;
- increased pension benefits and severance pay;
- reimbursement for unused sick leave;
- vacation time off;
- holiday time off (or pay, if worked);
- sick leave accrual;
- funeral leave;
- personal or business time off;
- time off to attend school;
- time off for union business;
- leaves of absence for political reasons;
- time off to negotiate with management;
- shortening of work day/work week;
- disability time off with full pay;
- minimum manning requirements; and
- restrictions on duties performed or assigned.

Source: "Police Unions," *Public Management*
59 (April 1977), 2–3.

Grievance Procedures   One of the major sources of police unionism involved police officer complaints about arbitrary disciplinary actions by police chiefs and other supervisors. Consequently, the achievement of a formal grievance procedure has been one of the main objectives of union negotiators. Grievance procedures normally specify what subjects are covered, the steps involved (where to file the grievance, time limits, etc.), the method for resolving the grievance, and the disciplinary actions that can be taken. Civil service regulations often contain a similar set of procedures.

Grievance procedures often appear to be extremely complex. Essentially, however, they provide *due process* for the individual police officer. The officer is granted an opportunity to present his or her complaints and to appeal unfavorable decisions.

Police Officers' Bill of Rights   The most extensive guarantees of the rights of individual police officers are found in a police officers "bill of rights." In some cases these provisions have been included in the union contract.[30] In other cases they have been enacted into law. Exhibit 12.5 represents excerpts from the Florida Law Enforcement Officers' Rights law.

EXHIBIT 12.5

FLORIDA LAW ENFORCEMENT OFFICERS' BILL OF RIGHTS

112.532 Law enforcement officers' rights.—All law enforcement officers employed by any employing agency shall have the following rights and privileges:

(1) RIGHTS OF LAW ENFORCEMENT OFFICERS WHILE UNDER INVESTIGATION—Whenever a law enforcement officer is under investigation and subject to interrogation by members of his agency for any reason which could lead to disciplinary action, demotion, or dismissal, such interrogation shall be conducted under the following conditions:

(a) The interrogation shall be conducted at a reasonable hour, preferably at a time when the law enforcement officer is on duty, unless the seriousness of the investigation is of such a degree that immediate action is required.

(b) The interrogation shall take place either at the office of the command of the investigating officer or at the office of the local precinct or police unit in which the incident allegedly occurred, as designated by the investigating officer or agency.

(c) The law enforcement officer under investigation shall be informed of the rank, name, and command of the officer in charge of the investigation, the interrogating officer, and all persons present during the interrogation. All questions directed to the officer under interrogation shall be asked by and through one interrogator at any one time.

(d) The law enforcement officer under investigation shall be informed of the nature of the investigation prior to any interrogation, and he shall be informed of the names of all complainants.

(e) Interrogating sessions shall be for reasonable periods and shall be timed to allow for such personal necessitites and rest periods as are reasonably necessary.

(f) The law enforcement officer under interrogation shall not be subjected to offensive language or be threatened with transfer, dismissal, or disciplinary action. No promise or reward shall be made as an inducement to answer any questions.

(g) The formal interrogation of a law enforcement officer, including all recess periods, shall be recorded, and there shall be no unrecorded questions or statements.

(h) If the law enforcement officer under interrogation is under arrest, or is likely to be placed under arrest as a result of the interrogation, he shall be completely informed of all his rights prior to the commencement of the interrogation.

(i) At the request of any law enforcement officer under investigation, he shall have the right to be represented by counsel or any other representative of his choice, who shall be present at all times during such interrogation whenever the interrogation relates to the officer's continued fitness for law enforcement service.

Management Policies   In an occupation such as policing it is difficult to specify precisely what issues involve "terms and conditions of employment." Both sides seek to gain as much control over the day-to-day running of the department as possible. Some of the specific issues involved include the selection of work assignments, the staffing of patrol cars, educational requirements, and standards for promotion.[31]

In many cities the procedures for assigning officers to different shifts are spelled out in the union contract. Such procedures limit the flexibility of the police chief in running the department. Some contracts contain provisions requiring two-officer patrol cars in certain situations. The Oakland contract contains a generous educational-incentive pay section, while other contracts have abolished existing incentives. In Michigan, a court has ruled that the standards for promotion are part of the "terms and conditions of employment" and therefore are subject to negotiations. As a result, the city cannot arbitrarily change the promotional standards.[32]

THE PROCESS OF COLLECTIVE BARGAINING

Collective bargaining is a complex process, involving many different participants and many different stages. In practice it is a continuous process. The National Symposium argued that "in a labor-management situation there is really bargaining taking place 365 days a year." Collective bargaining has been described as a "continuing dialogue" involving "shared management."[33]

Participants

One of the special characteristics of public-sector bargaining is that it is *multilateral*.[34] This means that more than two sides are involved in the bargaining. Private-sector bargaining is *bilateral*, involving only the union and the employer. Responsibility for a city police department is divided among the police chief (or commissioner and/or public safety director), the mayor (or city manager), the city council, and in some cases the state legislature. The mayor can agree to a contract, but the ability to pay for it rests with the city council, and in some cases the state legislature, which controls the relevant tax rates.

The divided authority of management is a critical problem in all public-sector unionism. Division of authority invites division of responsibility. An aggressive union can play one side off against the other. It becomes easier for the police chief or the mayor or the city council to pass the buck. Some critics attribute the near-bankruptcy of New York City in the mid-1970s to the overgenerous settlements with the different public-employee unions.

Bargaining Teams

In contract negotiations, each side is represented by a bargaining team. For the union, the chief negotiator is often the union's business agent (its paid staff member), a few police officers, and in some cases the union's attorney. For the employer, the team is usually composed of a representative of the mayor, an expert on financial matters, a representative of the city legal department, and in some cases a representative of the police chief.

The Role of the Chief The diminished role of the police chief in contract negotiations is the most obvious illustration of the impact of police unions. Whereas police chiefs were once all-powerful, they are now greatly reduced in power. Juris and Feuille found that in twenty-two of thirty-nine departments the chief played no role in contract negotiations. The National Symposium felt compelled to urge that the chief not be excluded: "to leave this person out of preparation for negotiations can be fatal."[35]

Stages of Collective Bargaining

Collective bargaining is an extended process involving many stages. The major stages include:

1 *Preparation for negotiations.* Each side develops its proposal, sets negotiating priorities, researches its proposals, and selects a bargaining team.

2 *Formal negotiations.* The two teams meet and try to agree to a mutually satisfactory contract. Negotiations can extend over several weeks, months, or even years.

3 *Impasse settlement.* When negotiations are deadlocked and the two sides cannot reach an agreement, an impasse exists. Several different mechanisms for reaching a settlement exist (see below).

4 *Contract administration.* Once a contract is signed it has to be administered. This is a continuous, 365-days-a-year process. Each side usually has a chief contract administrator. Each side seeks to make sure that the other side is complying with the contract. Also, the provisions of a contract are not always clear, and often disagreements about its meaning need to be settled.

Bargaining Tactics

Each side can use conventional or unconventional tactics during bargaining. Conventional tactics involve using the established procedures of formal negotiations. Unconventional tactics involve going outside the established procedures. Each side, for example, can use the *media* to win public support for its side and thereby put pressure on the other side. Frequently, the union engages in *lobbying* to win the support of elected officials. Finally, unions can use *militant tactics* such as picketing or job actions. Picketing in this context is for informational purposes. The object is to influence public opinion. So-called job actions are disguised strikes and include such things as writing extreme numbers of traffic tickers (or no tickets at all) or having large numbers of officers call in sick.[36]

Impasse Settlement

When contract negotiations are completely deadlocked, other means of settling the impasse must be used. In extreme cases, unions have gone on strike in an effort to force a settlement. Because there is widespread opposition to strikes by police officers and other public employees, alternative methods for reaching settlements exist.[37]

The three basic alternatives include mediation, fact-finding, and arbitration. *Mediation* is a voluntary approach in which the two sides agree to use a neutral third party to help achieve a settlement. The Federal Mediation Service of the U.S. Department of Labor offers this service. The recommendations of a mediator are not compulsory. *Fact-finding* is similar to mediation in that a neutral third party gathers relevant data (often on how salaries compare with other agencies) and recommends a settlement. Fact-finding is also a voluntary, noncompulsory approach.

Arbitration also involves a third party and may be voluntary or compulsory. Procedures for compulsory arbitration are found in many state labor laws. In Michigan disputes are settled by the Michigan Employment Relations Commission. In Nebraska they are settled by the Commission on Industrial Relations. State laws vary considerably with respect to the procedures of the arbitration process. Compulsory arbitration is one of the main objectives of the new International Union of Police Associations. IUPA leaders regard strikes as damaging to the police as well as the community. Legislation requiring arbitration is seen as an alternative to strikes.[38]

STRIKES AND JOB ACTIONS

Strikes are the most controversial aspect of police unionism. The memory of the 1919 Boston police strike continues to hang over the head of police unionism. Opponents of strikes argue that it is irresponsible and unprofessional for police officers to withhold their services for any reason. Police protection, in this view, is absolutely essential to the well-being of the community. A strike, or potential strike, poses a major ethical dilemma for the individual police officer. Is the withholding of services a violation of professional ethics? Or is it a legitimate part of any job?[39]

Opposition to strikes leads some people to oppose police unions altogether. Unionism is incompatible with professionalism, in this view. The boundary lines between professions and nonprofessions is becoming blurred, however. Other professions, includings doctors, are forming unions. Some doctors have even considered striking.

Proponents of strikes argue that they are a necessary part of collective bargaining. Without the threat to withhold services, the union has no way to pressure the employer to make concessions in negotiations.

Union leaders tend to oppose strikes. They recognize that a strike breeds public hostility which harms the union in the long run. In many cases, however, union leaders are not able to control their members. Some are wildcat strikes, spontaneous actions by union members without the approval of the leadership.

The police are forbidden to strike by law in many states. Such laws, however, have not been successful. The most notable case is New York: a very punitive state law forbidding strikes has not prevented long and bitter strikes by police and other public employees.

Despite the publicity they receive, police strikes are relatively infrequent events. Police strike much less often, for example, than public school teachers. Table 12-2 shows strikes by public employees in 1978 and 1979. The fifty-two police strikes in 1979 represented only 8.8 percent of the total.

TABLE 12-2
WORK STOPPAGES IN GOVERNMENT BY FUNCTION, 1978–1979
(WORKERS AND DAYS IDLE, IN THOUSANDS)

Function	Stoppages		Workers involved		Days idle	
	Number	Percent	Number	Percent	Number	Percent
1978						
Total	*481	100.0	193.7	100.0	1,706.7	100.0
Administrative services	9	1.9	.9	.5	10.2	.6
Welfare services	7	1.5	.6	.3	4.5	.3
Law enforcement and correction	28	5.8	4.8	2.5	12.6	.7
Fire protection	18	3.7	4.6	2.4	22.4	1.3
Sanitation services	34	7.1	4.4	2.3	20.4	1.2
Education	264	54.9	119.5	61.7	1,165.1	68.3
Streets and highways	13	2.7	.4	.2	2.1	.1
Parks and recreation	1	.2	†	‡	.1	‡
Libraries	—	—	—	—	—	—
Museums	—	—	—	—	—	—
Hospitals and health services	18	3.7	2.6	1.3	25.6	1.5
Transportation and allied facilities	20	4.2	16.2	8.4	133.5	7.8
Other utilities	8	1.7	1.1	.6	6.7	.4
Other	10	2.1	5.9	3.0	38.7	2.3
Combinations	57	11.8	32.7	16.9	264.7	15.5
1979						
Total	593	100.0	254.1	100.0	2,982.5	100.0
Administrative services	28	4.7	12.1	4.8	50.7	1.7
Welfare services	6	1.0	2.3	.9	14.6	.5
Law enforcement and correction	52	8.8	17.6	6.9	156.3	5.2
Fire protection	6	1.0	1.1	.4	6.5	.2
Sanitation services	28	4.7	2.3	.9	12.5	.4
Education	314	53.0	123.7	48.7	1,866.4	62.6
Streets and highways	28	4.7	5.5	2.2	28.1	.9
Parks and recreation	1	.2	†	‡	†	‡
Libraries	—	—	—	—	—	—
Museums	—	—	—	—	—	—
Hospitals and health services	33	5.6	14.5	5.7	114.0	3.8
Transportation and allied facilities	19	3.2	30.9	12.2	294.8	9.9
Other utilities	11	1.9	3.3	1.3	59.5	2.0
Other	14	2.4	4.0	1.6	32.7	1.1
Combinations	54	9.1	36.8	14.5	346.1	11.6

*Totals do not equal the sum of the components because individual stoppages occurring in 2 groups of more have been counted in each. Workers involved and days of idleness have been allocated among the respective functions.
†Fewer than 50.
‡Less than 0.05 percent.
Note: Because of rounding, sums of individual items may not equal totals. Dashes indicate no data.
Source: U.S., Department of Labor, Work Stoppages in Government, 1979, (Washington, D.C.: U.S. Government Printing Office, 1981), p. 6.

Job Actions

A *job action* may be defined as any deliberate disruption of normally assigned duties. The term is used to describe actions taken by employees that have the same effect as a strike but are not strikes per se. Policing offers many possibilities for imaginative job actions. The most common has been the "blue flu," where large numbers of officers claim to be sick and refuse to report for duty. Detroit police officers used this tactic in 1967. Earlier, they had conducted a slowdown in the writing of traffic tickets. San Francisco police officers used the opposite tactic in 1975, writing massive numbers of tickets to protest a referendum which affected their pensions.[40]

Strikes

An actual police strike is a major crisis for any community. Strikes by officers in Baltimore (1974), San Francisco (1975), and New Orleans (1979) led to violence and disorder. Strikes also polarize the community, leaving both sides embittered. The actual impact of a strike on the public safety of a community is a matter of some debate. In most strikes, some officers have chosen to remain on duty, giving the city at least some minimal protection. Massive crime waves have not erupted during police strikes. A report by the International City Management Association concluded that "cities have realized that they can survive a police strike. . . . Crime does not increase, and the public adjusts to a reduction in service, often requesting only emergency service."[41]

It is easy to exaggerate the significance of strikes. As the figures in Table 12-2 suggest, strikes are rather rare events. Relations between the union and management tend to be peaceful. Stephen Halpern found a trend toward cooperative working relationships in Baltimore, Buffalo, and Philadelphia. Margaret Levi identifies a pattern of what she calls "collusive bargaining." Union and management leaders begin to identify with each other and reach informal agreements. Each side permits the other to make seemingly hostile public statements as part of the charade of collective bargaining. Under collusive bargaining, leaders do not necessarily represent the best interests of either the employee or the employer.[42]

IMPACT OF POLICE UNIONS

What is the long-term impact of unionism? Have the unions been the death knell of professionalization, as the IACP once feared? Or have they become a positive force in the improvement of policing? What will be the role of the unions in the foreseeable future? Will they play a larger role or will their importance diminish?

The impact of the unions has been felt in three substantive areas: finances, management, and law enforcement policy.

The Financial Impact

Police unions have had a dramatic impact on the stictly financial aspects of policing. Police salaries and fringe benefits increased substantially between the mid-1960s and the late 1970s. The unions were not solely responsible for these increases, but they were a major factor.[43]

The improvements in salaries and benefits have had a number of side effects. First, policing is a relatively more attractive career than it was in the mid-1960s. This enhances the ability of police agencies to recruit qualified officers. Second, improved salaries and benefits have also improved the morale of police officers and reduced frustration and alienation. Third, the gains made by police officers have strained the resources of city budgets. To a certain extent, union demands have generated a public backlash, which is a part of the national tax revolt. Whether or not police unions will be able to win continued gains in the 1980s is uncertain.

Police Management

The unions have also had a tremendous impact on police management. According to Juris and Feuille, "The 'traditional' autocratic authority of the chief in personnel matters has been undermined."[44] The new style of police administration involves "shared decision making." Specific issues are the subject of collective bargaining negotiations. Moreover, the chief regularly consults with union representatives during the contract administration phase. Finally, the police chief is often not even directly involved in the formal negotiations over the contract. In short, police chiefs have lost a great deal of power as a result of police unionism. Rank-and-file officers, through their unions, have gained power.

The Future of Professionalization

The impact of the unions on police professionalization remains unclear. The traditional argument against unions was that they would retard professionalization. In part this was due to the fact that police reform in the United States was usually achieved through the efforts of an autocratic chief.

Several studies of police unionism suggest that the unions have had a negative impact on professionalization. Juris and Feuille found that "many of the unions in our sample have systematically frustrated management's quest for professional status."[45] Albert argues that the Boston Police Patrolmen's Association succeeded in blocking many of the reforms proposed by Mayor Kevin White and Police Commissioner Robert DiGrazia.[46]

Unions affect professionalization in several ways. In some cities, for example, the union has opposed meritocratic personnel standards, such as incentive pay for educational achievement, additional points on promotional examinations for higher education, and higher entry-level requirements. Raising personnel standards by encouraging higher education has been one of the main items on the agenda of police professionalization.

By reducing the flexibility of management in running the department, unions can also affect professionalization. Reform-minded chiefs may have their innovations blocked by a tradition-oriented union. In New York City, the Patrolmen's Benevolent Association fought for ten years against the establishment of a fourth shift, to be deployed during the peak crime periods.[47]

A Role for the Unions?   Not all experts feel that the unions necessarily mean the end of professionalization. Kelling and Kliesmet argue that the unions may provide the basis for a more genuine form of professionalism.[48] Professionalization has traditionally been a top-down process, never involving the rank and file. Moreover, Kelling and Kliesmet point out that the police have always had to piggyback because they lacked the institutional capacity to develop their own expertise.

Unions could become the vehicle for rank-and-file officers developing a professional-style capability. Large organizations have the capacity to generate sufficient money to hire full-time staff. Unions could use dues money to employ a professional staff to conduct research and generate data on salaries, working conditions, and all other aspects of policing. Whether or not American police unionism will develop in this direction is an important question for the future.

The National Symposium on Police Labor Relations proposed a way to involve police unions in the professionalization process. The quest for professionalism should be a "joint effort" involving both union and management. The symposium *Guidelines* recommended that "each local unit of government establish a Committee on Professional Services (COPS) which will be charged with the responsibility of facilitating the process of professionalization." Each COPS would "define and make recommendations for the accomplishment of goals and objectives leading to the improvement of police services." The COPS would be independent of the formal collective bargaining process and deal with issues not subject to formal negotiations.[49]

Law Enforcement Policy

Many elected officials and concerned citizens express fears over the impact of police unions on the determination of law enforcement policy. This concern centered on two specific issues.[50]

First, there was concern that unions would subvert public control of the police. In a democratic society the control of all public agencies is exercised by the public through their elected representatives. The ability of an aggressive union to resist changes proposed by mayors and city council members raises the possibility of the police being independent of public control. In Boston, New York City, Cleveland, and other cities the police unions succeeded in defeating the recommendations of elected officials.

The second issue involves police-community relations. In Boston, New York, and other cities unionism was spurred by hostile relations between the police and the black community. Police officers turned to unions as a means of defense against criticism about racism and police brutality. In Boston the BPPA successfully defeated several proposals by Mayor White to improve police-community relations. In New York City the PBA led the fight to abolish Mayor Lindsay's Civilian Complaint Review Board. In other cities police unions have sponsored lawsuits to fight preferential hiring of minorities.

As spokespersons for the predominatly white rank and file, the police unions have fallen into the role of the chief opponents of efforts to improve police-community relations. The future of the police and race relations depends to a great deal on the role the unions take in the future.

REVIEW

    1 What is the difference between an employee organization and a police union?
    2 Define collective bargaining.
    3 What factors contributed to the rise of police unions in the 1960s?
    4 What percentage of American police officers are members of unions?
    5 What are the major national federations of police unions?
    6 Outline the management rights retained by the employer in most collective bargaining agreements.
    7 List the major kinds of issues covered by collective bargaining.
    8 Describe the different stages in the collective bargaining process.
    9 How common are strikes by police officers?
    10 Discuss the most unionism consequences of unionism for American policing.

REFERENCES

    1 Hervey A. Juris and Peter Feuille, *Police Unionism* (Lexington: Lexington Books, 1973).
    2 Hervey A. Juris and Peter Feuille, *The Impact of Police Unions: Summary Report* (Washington, D.C.: LEAA, 1973).
    3 International Association of Chiefs of Police, *Police Unions* (Washington, D.C.: Author, 1958).
    4 International Association of Chief of Police, *Guidelines and Papers from the National Symposium on Police Labor Relations* (Washington, D.C.: Author, 1974), pp. 3, 10.
    5 O. Glenn Stahl and Richard A. Staufenberger, *Police Personnel Administration* (North Scituate, R.I.: Duxbury Press, 1974), chap. 11.
    6 Marvin J. Levine and Eugene Hagburg, *Public Sector Labor Relations* (St. Paul: West Publishing, 1979), chap. 5.
    7 U.S., Department of Labor, *Labor-Management Relations in State and Local Governments: 1975,* (Washington, D.C.: U.S. Government Printing Office, 1977), p. 160.
    8 Sterling Spero, *Government as Employer* (Carbondale: Southern Illinois University Press, 1972), pp. 245–294; Samuel Walker, *A Critical History of Police Reform* (Lexington: Lexington Books, 1977), pp. 110–120, 171.
    9 Juris and Feuille, *Police Unionism,* pp. 18–24.
    10 President's Commission on Law Enforcement and Administration of Justice, *Task Force Report: The Police* (Washington, D.C.: U.S. Government Printing Office, 1967), p. 133.
    11 Stephen C. Halpern, *Police-Association and Department Leaders* (Lexington: Lexington Books, 1974), p. 87.
    12 IACP, *Guidelines and Papers from the National Symposium,* p. 25.
    13 Levine and Hagburg, *Public Sector Labor Relations,* chap. 5.
    14 John F. Nichols, "An Overview of the Police Labor Movement in Detroit," in *Guidelines and Papers from the National Symposium,* ed. IACP, pp. 26–32.
    15 Rory Judd Albert, *A Time For Reform: A Case Study of the Interaction Between the Commissioner of the Boston Police Department and the Boston Police Patrolmen's Association* (Cambridge: Operations Research Center, MIT, 1975).
    16 U.S., Department of Labor, *Labor-Management Relations in State and Local Governments: 1975;* International City Management Association, *Management Information Service Report,* vol. 8, no. 3 (March, 1976), *Police Unions,* p. 3.
    17 Juris and Feuille, *Police Unionism,* pp. 26–32, 44–52.

18 Bureau of National Affairs, *Government Employee Relations Report,* August 6, 1979, pp. 16–18.

19 *Law Enforcement News,* January 12, 1981.

20 George L. Kelling and Robert B. Kliesmet, "Resistance to the Professionalization of the Police," *Law Officer* 5 (September 1972): 16–22.

21 Harry Wellington and Ralph K. Winter, *The Unions and the Cities* (Washington, D.C.: Brookings Institution, 1972), pp. 51–75.

22 Bureau of National Affairs, *Government Employee Relations Report,* "Summary of State Labor Laws," August 20, 1979, pp. 501–523.

23 *Ibid.* See also regular issues, published weekly.

24 Walter Gershenfeld, et al., *The Scope of Public Sector Bargaining* (Lexington: Lexington Books, 1977).

25 John H. Burpo, *Police Unions in the Civil Service Setting* (Washington, D.C.: LEAA, 1979).

26 U.S., Department of Labor, *Collective Bargaining Agreements for Police and Firefighters,* Bulletin 1885 (1976).

27 IACP, *Guidelines and Papers from the National Symposium,* p. 3.

28 Steven A. Rynecki, et al., *Police Collective Bargaining Agreements: A National Management Survey* (Washington, D.C.: Police Executive Research Forum, 1978).

29 *Public Management* (April 1977), pp. 2–3.

30 Rynecki, *Police Collective Bargaining Agreements,* chap. 3.

31 U.S., Department of Labor, *Collective Bargaining Agreements,* chap. 8.

32 International City Management Association, *Police Unions,* 1976, p. 12.

33 IACP, *Guidelines and Papers from the National Symposium.*

34 Juris and Feuille, *Police Unionism,* pp. 41–52.

35 IACP, *Guidelines and Papers from the National Symposium,* p. 20; Juris and Feuille, *Police Unionism,* chap. 7.

36 Halpern, *Police-Association and Department Leaders,* pp. 96–97.

37 U.S. Department of Labor, *Collective Bargaining Agreements,* chap. 10.

38 *Government Employee Relations Report,* August 6, 1979, pp. 16–18.

39 IACP, *Guidelines and Papers from the National Symposium,* pp. 41–50.

40 William J. Bopp, et al., "The San Francisco Police Strike of 1975: A Case Study," *Journal of Police Science and Administration,* 5, no. 1 (1977) 32–42.

41 International City Management Association, *Police Unions,* 1976, p. 14.

42 Halpern, *Police-Association and Department Leaders,* pp. 101–104; Margaret Levi, *Bureaucratic Insurgency* (Lexington: Lexington Books, 1977), chap. 4.

43 Amedeo R. Odoni, "Recent Employment and Expenditure Trends in U.S. City Police Departments," in *Police Accountability,* ed. Richard C. Larson, (Lexington: Lexington Books, 1978), pp. 33–64.

44 Juris and Feuille, *The Impact of Police Unions: Summary Report* (Washington, D.C.: U.S. Department of Justice, 1973), p. 15.

45 *Ibid,* chap. 6.

46 Albert, *A Time for Reform.*

47 Levi, *Bureaucratic Insurgency,* chap. 4.

48 George L. Kelling and Robert B. Kliesmet, "Resistance to the Professionalization of the Police," *Law Officer* 5 (September 1972): 16–22.

49 IACP, *Guidelines and Papers from the National Symposium,* pp. 6–7.

50 Juris and Feuille, *Police Unionism,* chap. 8.

CHAPTER **13**

THE FUTURE OF THE
AMERICAN POLICE

In the previous twelve chapters we have examined the main elements of policing in the United States. It is appropriate to end with a consideration of the future. Any such discussion is necessarily speculative, since predicting the future is more art than science. At best we can make educated guesses, extrapolating from recent trends. This was the approach taken by *Project STAR,* the most ambitious attempt to anticipate changes in the criminal justice field.[1]

UNDERSTANDING CHANGE

Change is constant. While this statement might seem self-evident, it bears repeating. We need to be reminded that policing is in a constant state of change, as is every other element or our society. Many people believe that the American police are unchanging and that police departments are resistant to change. Such statements obscure the real changes that have occurred in American policing and hinder our ability to anticipate and to effect change in the future.

Types of Change

To understand social change we must first recognize that there are several different types, three of which were identified by James Q. Wilson in "The Future Policeman."[2]

Unplanned Near-Term Changes   Many important changes are the result of unplanned and unforeseen events. The riots of the 1960s, which had an enormous impact on the police, and the economic crisis of the late 1970s and early 1980s were neither planned nor anticipated.

Planned Near-Term Changes   Many changes in the short-run are the result of consciously planned change. The educational levels of police recruits, for example, rose dramatically from the early 1960s to the mid-1970s. This was the result of a conscious, planned effort to raise personnel standards. Several police departments successfully reduced or eliminated corruption within their ranks. This too was the result of planned effort.

Fundamental Long-Term Changes   The police are highly dependent upon the social and political environment in which they exist. The future of the police, consequently, will be shaped by fundamental long-term changes in the social structure and in the American political system. Changing levels of crime and violence are factors we cannot predict but which will inevitably have an enormous impact on the police. As we have seen, the long-term upsurge of violent crime beginning in the mid-1960s has had a significant effect on the police. Changing attitudes toward crime and law enforcement are an equally important factor. Social and political pressure to decriminalize or criminalize certain behaviors would have a profound effect on the working environment of the police.

The Police Response

Recognizing the different types of change helps us to understand how the police respond. For the most part the police *react* to change. Police administration is often a process of crisis management, attempting to devise hasty responses to unforeseen events. The police are reactive to the first and third types of change identified by Wilson: unplanned near-term changes and fundamental long-term changes. Only with respect to the second type, planned near-term changes, are the police playing an active, anticipatory role.

The Issues

Understanding change with respect to the police is facilitated when we separate the various issues. Three basic issues are involved.

Areas of Change   Change is a multidimensional phenomenon. It can and does occur in many different areas. It can occur simultaneously in one or more areas, or it can occur more rapidly in one area than other areas. Moreover, change in two areas may have contradictory or conflicting results. Inflation, for example, creates a simultaneous demand for higher police salaries and a reduction in government spending. The result is a serious conflict over taxation and public spending.

The principal areas of change include the external social and political environment, police organization and management, police operations, police personnel, and the knowledge base concerning police and policing.

Change Agents   The factors that bring about change are termed *change agents.* Some important change agents are impersonal and difficult to indentify precisely—inflation, for example. Other long-term changes in crime, violence, and disorder are important agents of change. Meanwhile, some change agents are personal and more readily identifiable. Professional associations such as the IACP, presidential commissions, and police unions are important change agents.

Evaluating Change   Once we have identified a particular form of change and analyzed how it occurred we face the question of evaluating its impact. Is this change for better or for worse? Has it improved or detracted from effective policing? The emergence of police unions, for example, poses these questions in a dramatic light. Have unions enhanced the status of policing, or have they damaged the progress of professionalization? Did the Supreme Court decisions in the *Mapp, Escobedo,* and *Miranda* cases hinder or improve the quality of law enforcement?

Evaluating change requires a clarification of goals. By what standards should we evalute police unions or controversial court decisions? One of the primary aspects of policing in the United States, and the source of much controversy, is the disagreement over the goals of law enforcement. The police mission includes the goals of law, order, and justice. Different people give different priority to these goals. Persons and groups with a crime-control perspective give top priority to the goals of law and order. Persons and groups with a due process perspective give top priority to the goal of justice.[3]

A LOOK AT THE RECENT PAST

The recent past provides the best available framework for predicting the future. Using time frames of ten, twenty-five, or fifty years, it is possible to identify important long-term and short-term trends. By analyzing the factors that produced these trends, together with estimates of new developments, we can make educated guesses about which of those trends are likely to continue and at what pace.

The Wickersham Commission reports and the report of the President's Crime Commission serve as useful benchmarks in measuring trends in policing.[4]

The Wickersham Commission

In 1931 the Wickersham Commission published two reports concerning the police.[5] The first report, *Police,* identified serious problems in the areas of personnel standards and management practices. Since then, most police departments have substantially raised personnel standards—by imposing minimum recruitment standards, developing training programs, and introducing more effective techniques of supervision and internal discipline. At the same time police departments have adopted the principles of modern management, as espoused by O. W. Wilson, for example, and improved both the structure and process of management.

The Wickersham report on *Lawlessness in Law Enforcement* found police brutality to be a routine and pervasive feature of policing. Police officials expressed open contempt for the U.S. Constitution. Today, police brutality has been substantially reduced. While it is still a problem, it is the exception and not the rule. Considering the totally unprofessional quality of police work that prevailed throughout the nineteenth century and most of the twentieth century, this is a significant accomplishment.

Equally important, from today's vantage point, are the issues that were not addressed by the Wickersham Commission, issues that are regarded as critical problems today: police-community relations, the control of discretion, alternatives to the quasi-military organizational form. These issues were addressed by the President's Crime Commission in 1967.

The President's Crime Commission

The Challenge of Crime in a Free Society, the report of the President's Commission on Law Enforcement and Administration of Justice, was a far more comprehensive survey of American criminal justice than the Wickersham reports. In particular, it surveyed a broader range of issues in policing.[6]

The most useful way to view the commission's report as a benchmark of change is to distinguish between areas of major change, areas of moderate change, and areas of little or no change.

Areas of Major Change

The Information Explosion   In all areas of criminal justice, including the police, there has been an information explosion since the mid-1960s. One former LEAA administrator termed this phenomenon the *research revolution.* Students of the police and criminal justice face an enormous task in simply keeping up with the publication of new research findings.[7]

Reading *The Challenge of Crime in a Free Society* today, it is evident that the report served to identify major gaps in our knowledge about police and policing. To cite only one example, the report noted that "There have been few scientifically controlled experiments concerning the deterrent effects of various patrol techniques."[8] In fact we knew very little about police patrol work prior to the President's Crime Commission. There was only the sketchiest information about what patrol officers did, how they spent their time, what situations they encountered, how they handled common situations.

The commission itself helped to correct this problem. It supported field research by Albert Reiss and others to investigate basic police operations. Funding from OLEA and LEAA supported wide-ranging research on all aspects of policing. James Q. Wilson observed that the result has been "an outpouring of research about police work of such volume as to dwarf anything that came before."[9]

As a result, there now exists a substantial knowledge base about the American police. The principal highlights include:

1 *Expenditure and employment data.* Each year the Justice Department publishes a report on *Expenditure and Employment Data for the Criminal Justice System,* which provides reliable, systematic data. A companion report on *Trends in Expenditure and Employment Data* helps to identify patterns of change.[10]

2 *Routine police work.* The President's Crime Commission supported field research by Albert Reiss, Donald Black, and others on routine police patrol work. Reiss's work was published as *Police and the Public.*[11] Other research has confirmed these initial findings. It is now possible to draw a general picture of routine police work: officers spend most of their time on non-law enforcement activities; most contacts with the public are in response to a citizen request for service; officers routinely exercise great discretion in handling specific situations. This knowledge base about routine police work provides a starting point for attempts to measure and improve the efficiency of policing.

3 *Effectiveness of police operations.* The effectiveness of police operations in two critical areas has been examined in pioneering studies. The Kansas City Preventive Patrol Experiment attempted to measure the effectiveness of routine patrol on criminal activity and citizen attitudes. Investigators concluded that patrol has no significant effect on either. The conclusions of the report must be regarded as tentative, due to methodological problems, but the experiment itself was a landmark event in opening up a new approach to thinking about police patrol.[12] Meanwhile, the Rand Corporation study on the *Criminal Investigation Process* questioned the effectiveness